Adolescents with Behavior Problems

Adolescents with Behavior Problems:
Strategies for Teaching, Counseling, and Parent Involvement

Vernon F. Jones
Lewis and Clark College

ALLYN AND BACON, INC.

Boston   **London**   **Sydney**   **Toronto**

Library of Congress Cataloging in Publication Data

Jones, Vernon F 1945-
    Adolescents with behavior problems.

    Bibliography: p.
    Includes index.
    1. Adolescent psychiatry. 2. Behavior
modification. 3. Exceptional children—Education.
4. Parent and child. I. Title.
RJ503.J66   616.8'9   79-19964
ISBN 0-205-06801-4

To my talented and loving wife, Louise, whose patience, support, and love provided the atmosphere that fostered and sustained the efforts necessary to write this book.

Contents

Preface

Professionals working with adolescents frequently state that they become frustrated in their attempts to serve as useful resources to adolescents. The purpose of this book is to assist professionals in understanding the factors that elicit adolescents' unproductive behaviors and to offer a variety of strategies for preventing behavior problems as well as for assisting adolescents in modifying their behavior.

A strong emphasis has been placed on providing concrete teaching and counseling strategies. However, the book also provides a theoretical analysis of adolescent development, the causes of unproductive behavior, and the rationale for employing the various strategies presented throughout the book. The book does not focus on one particular theoretical approach or one counseling paradigm, but rather offers a broad sociobehavioral approach to examining causes, preventions, and modification of behavior.

The book is based upon the belief that unproductive behavior is caused by the interaction of an environment that fails to meet adolescents' legitimate needs and the adolescents' skill deficits that prevent them from responding in productive ways to their environment. Behavior-problem adolescents are too often dealt with from the perspective that they must learn to alter their behavior in order to adjust to whatever environment adults choose to provide. A basic concept presented throughout this book states that professionals should examine both their style of interacting with adolescents and the extent to which their demands and expectations respond productively to adolescents' developmental needs.

The book's organization reflects this multidimensional approach to examining and modifying unproductive behavior. Part One provides an overview of adolescents' psychological and developmental needs and examines the relationship between these needs and unproductive adolescent behavior.

Part Two explores the impact various patterns of interpersonal communication have on adolescent behavior. The initial chapter focuses on important decisions adults must make in determining how they will interact with adolescents. This is followed by a presentation of communication skills which facilitate positive, therapeutic interactions. The final chapter focuses on methods for assisting adolescents in developing productive communication skills.

Part III examines the ways in which school environments can be altered so as to more effectively meet legitimate adolescent needs and thereby significantly reduce acting-out and avoidance behavior. An emphasis is placed on practical teaching strategies that can be employed by regular classroom teachers.

While Parts I, II, and III emphasize ways in which the environment can be altered in order to modify unproductive behavior, Part IV presents a wide range of practical strategies for assisting adolescents in altering their behavior. The strategies discussed in Part IV are organized under the general headings of self observation, behavioral counseling, and behavior contracting.

Part V acknowledges the important role that the family plays in influencing adolescents' behaviors. The section begins by examining the feelings and needs experienced by parents whose adolescents are having difficulty adjusting to society and its institutions. This is followed by a discussion of strategies professionals can employ in responding to these parents and involving them in working cooperatively with school personnel. Finally, several models are presented for providing parents with individual and group instruction in skills which will enable them to interact more effectively with their adolescent children.

The book is written for professionals who work with adolescents or who are training to teach or counsel adolescents. The book does not assume any prior knowledge of behavioral or developmental psychology.

The terms teacher and student are used extensively throughout the book. This choice was partially a matter of convenience and partially a response to the fact that most adolescents spend a significant portion of their waking hours in a school setting. However, the book is written for counselors, social workers, residential treatment staff, and psychologists as well as for teachers. While professionals from different fields will perhaps find specific sections of the book particularly applicable, the book provides a holistic approach to working with adolescents and most professionals will find that each chapter includes ideas and techniques that they can apply in their work with adolescents.

Whenever possible, an attempt has been made to avoid the use of pronouns referring to gender. Since the frequent use of "he or she" and similar wording is cumbersome, the word "he" has been used in most cases in which a singular pronoun was necessary. The reader should keep in mind that whenever he or she is used, the intent is to refer to both male and female adults or adolescents.

Grateful acknowledgment is given to several individuals whose contributions have helped to make this book possible. I wish to express my appreciation to Dr. Hill Walker for initially suggesting that a book like this was needed and for offering his encouragement. I wish to thank Gene McCann of the Allyn and Bacon staff for his assistance in clarifying the book's organization and Elydia Siegel for her fine copy-editing. I would also like to thank Louise Evans for typing the manuscript.

I would like to acknowledge my graduate students and colleagues whose application of the various intervention plans contributed in an important way to the ideas and examples presented throughout the book. Specifically, I would like to thank Carl Solomon for allowing me to report his data on a systematic desensitization program with a high school student, and Kathy Laird and Bobby Heagerty for allowing me to report their work with the PASS Program.

My deepest appreciation goes to my colleagues Heather Sheets and Dan Koretz who worked with me during some of my early experiences in teaching and counseling behavior-problem adolescents. Their insight, skill, and dedication were major factors in providing a foundation for my later work with adolescents.

Finally, no acknowledgment would be complete without my sincere appreciation to the many young people with whom I have been privileged to work. Their desire to survive and grow and their willingness to give me candid feedback concerning my interventions has been a satisfying and growing experience. My sincere hope is that this book will help provide struggling youngsters like them with more effective instruction and guidance.

Adolescents with Behavior Problems

Understanding Adolescent Behavior

Part I presents a brief summary of the major needs and developmental tasks of adolescence and discusses how the failure to meet these needs is a major cause of adolescents' acting-out behavior. Chapter 1 provides an overview of theoretical conceptualizations regarding the major developmental concerns of adolescence. Chapter 2 begins with an examination of developmental and social factors that tend to elicit behaviors that are often described as inappropriate. The Chapter concludes with a discussion of ways that schools fail to respond productively to adolescent needs and thereby intensify the conflicts adolescents experience.

Part I has been included because of the value associated with understanding adolescents and developing insights into why they respond as they do. The task for adults is to create environments that adolescents view as stimulating, safe, and conducive to personal growth and learning. An understanding of adolescent needs and the ways that environments frustrate these needs is crucial to developing growth-producing environments.

Part I provides the foundation for developing a philosophy of teaching and counseling that puts a major emphasis on creating healthy environments. The label "behavior-problem adolescent" is all too often placed upon young people who are responding in an understandable and even appropriate manner to an environment that does not support their legitimate developmental needs. Thoughtful interventions should always begin with a careful consideration of adolescents' needs and an examination into whether the environment fosters or hinders these needs.

In addition to assisting adults in creating positive environments, an understanding of adolescent behavior can also broaden their perspective in working with adolescents. When adults are concerned and committed, it is easy for them to become confused, frustrated, and hurt when their interactions with adolescents fail to have the desired effects. Developing an understanding of reasons why adolescents behave as they do helps to place their behavior in a more productive perspective. Understanding adolescents' behavior can help to decrease adults' self doubts and free them from narrow, personalized interpretations of adolescents' behaviors. This in turn can enable adults to view situations in a more relaxed manner and to examine a wider range of a alternative responses.

Indeed, it is in this factor of how a person sees himself that we are likely to find the most outstanding differences between high and low self-image people. It is not the people who feel that they are liked and wanted and acceptable and able who fill our prisons and mental hospitals. Rather it is those who feel deeply inadequate, unliked, unwanted, unacceptable, and unable.

Donald E. Hamachek
Encounter With The Self

CHAPTER
1

Understanding Adolescents: A Theoretical Perspective

When attempting to understand adolescents' behavior, it is important to realize that adolescents' needs are in many ways similar to those experienced by adults. While adolescents respond more intensely to certain issues and are subjected to a somewhat different set of societal expectations and variables, their needs and responses are similar to adults: Adolescents need to be accepted, liked, trusted, and treated with respect; they need to understand their environment and need to be involved in making decisions that affect them.

There are numerous models for categorizing needs that must be met in order for individuals to function effectively. A model that proves particularly useful in clarifying the developmental needs of adolescents was suggested by Coopersmith (1967) in his study on self-esteem. While self-esteem is influenced by a wide range of variables, most, if not all of the variables can be seen as influencing the degree to which people experience a sense of (1) significance, (2) competence, and (3) power or potency. Significance refers to the belief that people are liked by, and important to, someone who is important to them. Competence is defined as being successful at some task that has value and is reinforced within the environment. Power or potency refers to peoples' ability to control important parts of their environment. This Chapter will examine a variety of theoretical conceptualizations that describe the developmental and social factors that influence adolescents' attempt to develop a sense of significance, competence, and power.

3

THE NEED TO EXPERIENCE A SENSE OF SIGNIFICANCE

Before examining specific theories that emphasize the importance of developing a sense of significance, pause for a moment to consider the impact that feelings of significance have on your own life. Most people feel a real sense of emptiness, loneliness, or sadness during those times when they seriously question whether they are involved in a positive two-way relationship with at least one other person. Similarly, consider the feelings that were elicited the last time you met someone with whom you experienced a mutual attraction and with whom you could share a very real part of yourself. It is likely that this experience elicited feelings of excitement, exhilaration, and warmth.

Since adolescence is often characterized by an intense self-examination as well as an intense interest in interpersonal relationships, it is not surprising that the degree to which adolescents experience a sense of significance will affect both their self-concept and their behavior. It is therefore imperative when working with adolescents to understand and effectively respond to their need to be involved in meaningful, positive relationships with adults and peers.

In developing a theory of human behavior and motivation, Maslow (1968) stated that there are several basic needs that must be met before an individual can function effectively within an environment. Maslow postulated that until these needs are met, an individual will not be able to consistently move in the direction of growth and learning. Instead, varying amounts of energy will be expended attempting to meet one or more of the basic needs. Two of the needs that Maslow defines as basic relate directly to the adolescents' need to experience a sense of significance. Maslow notes that individuals have a need to experience a feeling of love and belonging and that they need to receive respect from significant others.

The need to experience a positive relationship in which the individual is understood and unconditionally accepted has also been postulated by Carl Rogers (1961). Other writers including Sydney Jourard (1971) have suggested that personal growth and learning are enhanced by relationships which include open two-way communication and a significant degree of self-disclosure from both parties. William Glasser's (1969) statements concerning ways to prevent school failure and increase youngsters' positive feelings and motivation also included a major emphasis on the quality of the adult-adolescent relationship and the degree to which youngsters perceive themselves as valued by adults.

Humanistic psychologists interested in psychotherapy are not alone in suggesting the importance of providing individuals with a sense of significance. Erik Erikson's conceptualizations concerning the developmental stages through which all individuals progress speak to the necessity of experiencing a sense of significance. Erikson (1968) lists the task of establishing a basic sense of trust in relationships with others as the first stage in human development. Erikson's theory also directs itself to the fact that adolescence is a time when emphasis is placed upon developing a sense of significance. While Erikson stated that the central theme associated with any given stage is not isolated to a specific period of development, he also stated that specific developmental concerns tend to emerge most powerfully at certain times in the life cycle and that these concerns must be successfully resolved if the individual is to deal effectively with later concerns. When outlining the central developmental tasks of adolescence, Erikson included the importance of developing an integrated, acceptable personal identity and the task of establishing mutually satisfying long-term relationships. Since their sense of identity is strongly influenced by the feedback they receive from others, it is obvious that a sense of being important to and cared for by others strongly influences adolescents' identity formation. The question, "Who am I?" must be answered within the context of the adolescent's system of personal interactions.

In addition to the importance of personal relationships in developing a satisfactory identity, Erikson stated that the major developmental task of late adolescence centers around establishing mutually satisfying personal relationships. The importance of this task is reinforced by Havighurst (1952) who lists the accomplishment of "achieving new and more mature relations with agemates of both sexes" (Havighurst, 1952, p.33) as a major adolescent developmental task.

The concern over an issue such as perceiving oneself as significant is not unique to any particular age group. All people experience a need to be seen as valued and liked by others. However, there are several characteristics of adolescent development that intensify this concern. A major factor contributing to the intensification of concerns regarding the quality of personal relationships is the fact that adolescents are moving into a stage of cognitive development where they begin to develop an ability to comprehend abstract, conceptual issues and to focus on the ideal and possible as well as the concrete and real. These new cognitive skills enable adolescents to analyze their own thoughts and feelings and therefore increase their self-consciousness and level of introspection. Similarly, adolescents become increasingly adept at hypothesizing about the thoughts and motives of others. For example, adolescents begin to ask themselves such questions as, "I wonder if he knows what I am feeling; if he thinks he knows, but I am fooling him; or if he really doesn't care?" Since adolescents' ability to hypothesize about others' thoughts and feelings is a new, and therefore rather unsophisticated, tool, it is not surprising that it is frequently employed with a fervor that creates exaggeration and diverts energy from such other tasks as schoolwork and household chores. Most parents of adolescents have observed this phenomenon in adolescents' long telephone conversations that inevitably preempt household chores. The effects of adolescents' intense concerns regarding their peers' thoughts are also experienced by teachers who are faced with the often arduous task of terminating numerous socially oriented student conversations in order to focus the classes' attention on the day's academic lesson.

In addition to their increasingly sophisticated cognitive skills, adolescents must learn to adjust to rapid physical changes. Since these physical changes occur simultaneously with adolescents' increased ability to hypothesize about their peers' thoughts and feelings, it is not surprising that adolescents experience an intense self-consciousness and a strong concern about being liked and accepted. Adolescents experience this increased self-consciousness in several ways. The first, often termed the "imaginary audience," refers to the fact that adolescents frequently feel "on stage." Adolescents often believe that others are observing those very qualities about which they are themselves most concerned. The second component of self-consciousness that is experienced more intensely during adolescence is referred to as the "personal fable"—adolescents tend to perceive themselves and their feelings as special and unique. It is difficult for them to realize that their concerns are shared by many of their peers and to a lesser degree by many adults.

Associated with their intensified self-consciousness is the fact that adolescents have a less stable sense of who they are. Whether people are in a classroom or at a party, they are an important part of that environment. When individuals are unsure of who they are or how they will react, they must consistently function in an environment characterized by a fairly high degree of instability. Adults are likely to have a higher degree of personal stability than adolescents. While adults may put on or take off a few pounds or develop a few gray hairs, their bodies are not going through dramatic and constant change. Also, most adults have developed a sense of who they are and are consequently fairly certain how they will act in a variety of situations. Therefore, as adults move from setting to setting, a major part of the setting—themselves—remains fairly consistent. This situation is much less likely to exist for adolescents. The changes occurring in their bodies and their cognitive skills create a situation in which they themselves are a rather unpredictable part of their environment. This instability tends to increase adolescents' self-consciousness and need for approval. This in turn increases adolescents' need for positive, supportive interactions with peers and adults.

A final factor that intensifies adolescents' need to experience a sense of significance is that adolescents are in what Kurt Lewin (1948) calls a marginal position. Depending upon their age, adolescents are at various stages of seeking independence from their parents. In addition, especially for younger adolescents, this desire to reduce dependence upon parents occurs at a time when peer relationships are fairly superficial and nonsupportive. Adolescence is therefore a period in which both home and peer relationships are frequently characterized by conflict and anxiety. Consequently, adolescents need relationships that provide a sense of significance and belonging. Adolescents' tendency to become involved in numerous male-female relationships is at least partially a response to the need for a sense of significance and support.

When interacting with adolescents, it is important to consider their intensified need for a sense of significance. It is also helpful to realize that this need is a healthy, normal factor associated with their developmental stage. Adults should take this need into consideration not only when examining their own interactions with adolescents, but also when determining the environmental factors that will facilitate adolescents' personal growth and learning.

Unless adults provide adolescents with opportunities to experience significance in their interactions with adults and peers who support accepted norms of behavior, they will quite understandably seek significance through less desirable relationships. When interactions within the family, school, and social institutions fail to respond adequately to this important need, adults should not be surprised when adolescents seek attention through acting-out behavior or from individuals who support and reinforce what may be considered undesirable behavior.

THE NEED TO EXPERIENCE A SENSE OF COMPETENCE

Prior to exploring the theoretical conceptualizations that support and explain the importance of experiencing a sense of competence, it may be helpful to consider the influence this factor has upon your own feelings and behavior. Take a moment to consider how you feel when you realize that you have achieved success at something that you define as important. Regardless of whether this sense of accomplishment is based upon your own evaluation or upon feedback from others, it is likely that you feel exhilarated and happy. Likewise, try to recall the feelings you experienced the last time you failed at an important task. How did this realization influence your attitudes and behavior? How long did your feelings last? Consider for a moment how it might feel to be an adolescent who is consistently confronted with feelings of failure.

Erikson (1968) states that the major developmental issue of early adolescence (industry versus inferiority) is centered around establishing a feeling of success or competence related to tasks that society defines as valuable. Within the school setting this usually includes such middle-class values as the importance of academic achievement, an ability to relate effectively to peers, and some degree of success in extracurricular activities. As Erikson suggests, failure to successfully resolve this developmental issue creates a sense of inferiority that will have a lasting impact upon the adolescent. Erikson's fifth stage of development (identity versus role diffusion) also speaks directly to adolescents' need to establish a sense of competence. During the past decade society has increasingly reinforced the concept that fulfillment and competence as an adult are related to peoples' ability to understand themselves and their relationship to the environment. Competence in the areas of self-awareness and interpersonal interactions have been added to vocational competence as indices of success.

Further theoretical support for the importance of developing a sense of competence comes from the theoretical conceptualizations offered by Piaget (1958), Kohlberg (1970), Lewin (1948), and Anna Freud (1946). All of these theorists have pointed to the fact that adolescents are confronted with the task of creating a sense of order out of a life space made increasingly complex by the development of new cognitive skills and hormonal changes. The difficulty of this task has been compounded during the past several generations by the increasing complexity of society and the breakdown of the traditional family structure.

Otto Rank (1945) has stated that the most all-encompassing developmental task of adolescence is the gradual attainment of independence from parents. During the years generally defined as adolescence, the individual must move from a position of being extremely dependent upon parental support to a position of psychological and financial independence. Ruth Benedict (1954) added an important perspective to the issue of adolescents' increasing independence and competence. Benedict noted that human development is most productive and healthy when it is experienced as a gradual, continuous process. Benedict stated that there are three major areas of development in which it is particularly important that individuals experience a gradual and continuous growth—(1) responsibility versus lack of responsibility, (2) dominance versus submission, and (3) the expression of one's sexuality. Since adolescence is a period during which each of these issues becomes paramount, it is particularly important that adolescents experience a gradual yet continuous growth in these areas.

While these theorists refer in general terms to adolescents' need to develop increased competence, Havighurst (1952) suggested that adolescents are faced with 10 developmental tasks. Havighurst defined developmental tasks as being midway between an individual need and a social demand. Developmental tasks refer to knowledge and skills that individuals must obtain at a certain stage in life in order to successfully cope with societal demands and expectations associated with later stages. Havighurst listed the 10 developmental tasks of adolescence as:

1. Achieving new and more mature relations with agemates of both sexes
2. Achieving a masculine or feminine social role
3. Accepting one's physique and using the body effectively
4. Achieving emotional independence of parents and other adults
5. Achieving assurance of economic independence
6. Selecting and preparing for an occupation
7. Preparing for marriage and family life
8. Developing intellectual skills and concepts necessary for civic competence
9. Desiring and achieving socially responsible behavior
10. Acquiring a set of values and an ethical system as a guide to behavior (Havighurst, 1952, pp. 33-71)

As in the case of adolescents' need to experience a sense of significance, several factors differentiate adolescents' striving to develop a sense of competence from that experienced by adults. Perhaps the major difference is that adults' need to experience a sense of competence is primarily a response to either social pressures and expectations or the individual's motivation for personal fulfillment. In contrast, adolescents' striving to achieve competence is, at least during early adolescence, partially a response to developmental factors. Adolescents' changing physical and cognitive characteristics create a situation in which adolescents are forced to develop competence in coping with these new factors.

The fact that adolescents are grappling with the task of coping with new cognitive and physical skills demands that adults respond sensitively to their need to experience a sense of competence. Especially during early adolescence, adults must be careful to provide thoughtful assistance in supporting adolescents in adjusting to their new skills. The key for adults is to develop a sensitivity that enables them to provide structure and support for adolescents when it is needed and to decrease it when it begins to stifle growth. Too much structure does not allow adolescents to explore various alternatives and thereby reduces the amount of productive disequilibrium they experience. However, too little structure may create a situation in which adolescents experience so much dissonance that a feeling of confusion and impotence blocks productive and necessary integration and synthesis.

Similarly, adults' expectations should not exceed adolescents' abilities in dealing with abstract concepts. When presenting new abstract concepts, adults should initially include concrete examples that assist adolescents in making the transition from concrete to abstract thinking. When adults fail to respond sensitively and effectively to adolescents' changing abilities, they contribute to creating situations in which adolescents fail to achieve a sense of competence.

It is important to realize that adolescents desperately need to feel competent at something. If adults fail to create situations in which adolescents can experience a sense of competence while coping with socially acceptable tasks, it is understandable that they will seek to obtain competence in less desirable ways. For example, the youngster who cannot find success through academic or athletic achievement may become adept at driving teachers to distraction. This seemingly inexcusable behavior may simply be the youngster's response to the legitimate need to be successful at some task that is recognized by his peers.

THE NEED TO EXPERIENCE A SENSE OF POWER

The final factor that influences adolescents' feelings and behavior concerns the degree to which they experience a sense of control over their lives. The importance of this variable can be appreciated by considering your own response to situations in which you have had little or no control in influencing decisions that you viewed as important. For example, recall how you felt the last time your superiors or colleagues made an important decision and either failed to consult you or did not listen to your views. If this decision affected you in an important way, it is likely that you were angry, hurt, and frustrated. Imagine how it might feel to have decisions consistently made in such a manner.

Adolescents are rapidly approaching adulthood in terms of their physical and cognitive abilities. While adults are obviously superior to elementary age children in cognitive skills and physical strength, this power differential quickly diminishes during adolescence. The change in adult-child relationships that occurs as a result of adolescents' increased size and skills is further intensified by adolescents' desire to experience greater independence and responsibility. As a result of these factors, head-on confrontations that strengthened authority and respect during the preadolescent period quickly begin to undermine authority and respect during adolescence.

As Piaget noted, adolescence is characterized by a major change in cognitive functioning. While major differences exist in the rate at which individuals develop formal operational thinking, most adolescents begin to develop an ability to understand and manipulate abstract, conceptual issues. This new skill significantly enhances adolescents' potential for understanding and gaining control over significant portions of their environment. This change in cognitive skills significantly closes the gap between adolescents and adults. Therefore, it is understandable that adolescents begin to expect and even demand to be treated as adults. As mentioned earlier, Benedict stated that adolescent development is facilitated by providing adolescents with an increasing amount of responsibility and increasing opportunities to experience an equalitarian, nonsubmissive role. Similarly, Rank emphasized the fact that the central developmental task of adolescence is the striving for a sense of independence. If adults

are to assist adolescents in making the transition from the dependency of preadoles-
cence to the independence desired in late adolescence, they must provide them with
opportunities to express and experiment with their new tools for controlling their own
lives.

Adolescents' increase in power is also reflected in their gradual development of a
more abstract, personalized value system. As outlined by Kohlberg (1970), moral
development progresses from a concrete, hedonistic stage to stages characterized by
individual principles regarding what is right and wrong. According to Kohlberg's
theoretical conceptualization and related research (Kohlberg and Gilligan, 1971), the
majority of young adolescents behave as they do in order to maintain good social
relations (Stage 3) or because they believe that it is right and necessary to follow rules
and show respect for authority (Stage 4). However, as adolescents develop increasing
cognitive skills and are exposed to a wider range of experiences, they begin to
experiment with the acceptability of changing rules that do not seem necessary or
effective (Stage 5) and even consider the possibility of judging actions on the basis of
how they themselves feel about the behavior (Stage 6). While these new values are
indicative of a higher level of morality, they may conflict with the need for stability,
consistency, and security expressed by adults. It is important that adults respond to
adolescents' growth and challenge by helping them to clarify their values. Furthermore, whenever possible, adults should assist adolescents in integrating their new values
into existing standards that support these values. When adults fail to provide such
assistance and instead demand that adolescents accept adults' predetermined values,
they deny adolescents' legitimate and healthy growth and increase the likelihood that
their need to express their power will be displayed in less productive ways.

The theoretical constructs discussed in the preceding paragraphs indicate that
adolescents do in fact experience a natural increase in their ability and desire to
control their environment. However, adolescents also experience considerable anxiety
and confusion, which adults often misinterpret as a power struggle. Since adolescents
are confronted with a life space that is often confusing, they will experience greater
uncertainty and greater fluctuation in moods, and they will exhibit what might appear
to adults as more irrational behavior. But this confusion and anxiety should not be
misinterpreted as hostility and defiance since such an interpretation frequently evokes
defensiveness, counteraggression, and overly rigid rules. Instead, adults should attempt
to provide adolescents with support, guidance, and reasonable amounts of structure as
they pass through what is often a difficult stage. It is helpful to realize that as they
become more familiar with their new physical characteristics and cognitive skills, their
behavior and people's responses to it will become more predictable and consequently
less anxiety producing. As this occurs, adolescents begin to behave more calmly and
consistently and can move on to a new set of development tasks.

It is extremely important to provide adolescents with gradually increasing amounts
of responsibility. As they move through adolescence, young people have an increasing
ability and associated need to understand and control their environment. When adults
block this need by failing to involve adolescents in the decision-making process, they
create a situation in which adolescents' need to experience a sense of potency may be
channeled into less socially accepted behaviors.

SUMMARY

In working with adolescents who are experiencing behavior problems, I have consistently found that within their school or home environments these adolescents fail to experience one or more of the essential ingredients of significance, competence, and power. Since individuals must possess a sense of significance, competence, and power in order to feel good about themselves, it is understandable that when adolescents are unable to meet these needs in socially acceptable ways, they become involved in unacceptable behaviors that fulfill these needs. For example, adolescents who are successful at stealing or disrupting classes soon discover that this behavior is reinforced by attention from a certain segment of their peer group. This peer reinforcement frequently provides adolescents with a sense of significance or social acceptance that they have not experienced at home or in school. At the same time, these behaviors may provide adolescents with a real sense of competence. Being the best at opening a locked car door, slipping the big bills from underneath the cash register, or disrupting a classroom requires real skill. Finally, these behaviors can provide adolescents with a sense of power. By stealing, adolescents may gain control or influence in the form of money. Similarly, disruptive behavior can provide adolescents with a sense of setting their own limits and standards or the feeling of control that comes from knowing that their behavior can predictably frustrate adults.

What appears to adults as unproductive behavior may in fact appear to adolescents as necessary and productive behavior in that it earns them much needed significance, competence, and power. Therefore, if behavior-problem adolescents are expected to act in ways that adults define as appropriate, adults must provide them with realistic opportunities for obtaining significance, competence, and power in ways that adults consider acceptable.

CHAPTER 2

Why Do Adolescents Act Out?

Almost all adolescent boys and an increasing number of adolescent girls commit some offense that would, by strict legal definition, be considered a delinquent act (Pepinsky, 1976). While a vast number of these offenses go unreported, the fact remains that reported delinquency has increased dramatically since 1960, and recent estimates suggest that approximately 12 percent of all adolescents will have some form of juvenile court record (Conger, 1977).

Although not all acting-out behavior is personally or socially destructive, the extent of such behavior is appalling. For example, in 1975 vandalism, theft, and assault in schools alone amounted to over $500 million in damages and caused nearly 70,000 serious injuries to teachers (DeCecco and Richards, 1975).

A more recent study conducted by the National Institute of Education (The ABC's of School Violence, 1978) reported that in an average month one out of every nine secondary school students will have something stolen, one in eighty will be attacked, (one-fifth of them seriously), and approximately 6000 will be robbed. Finally, the study indicates that vandalism to the schools will cost nearly $600 a year.

Youth violence is, however, not confined to the schools. More than one-half of all serious crimes are now committed by young people between the ages of 10 and 17 (Swift, 1977).

While such outwardly violent behavior is of great concern, the extent to which adolescents are involved in self-destructive behaviors must not be overlooked. For example, alcohol use among adolescents is rising, and alcohol is increasingly being used by younger adolescents (Johnson and Bachman, 1975). Even more frightening is the fact that the suicide rate among older adolescents nearly tripled between 1954 and 1974.

12

Resolution of the much publicized student rebellions of the late sixties and early seventies apparently did not eliminate basic factors that cause anger, helplessness, and a need for escapism among at least a significant portion of the adolescent population. This chapter will examine some of the factors that cause acting-out behavior among adolescents. This information will serve as a foundation for understanding and applying the preventative and curative strategies discussed throughout the remainder of the book.

As suggested in Chapter 1, adolescents' acting-out behavior is to some extent a response to the turmoil associated with obtaining and practicing the new skills that accompany the cognitive and physical changes that occur during adolescence. However, adolescents' acting-out behavior is also influenced by a variety of societal factors that intensify the difficulties associated with adjusting to the natural changes that take place during adolescence. The label "behavior-problem adolescent" is all too often placed upon young people who respond in understandable and often appropriate ways to environments that fail to meet their legitimate needs. This Chapter will examine developmental, social, and institutional factors that influence the degree to which adolescents behave in ways that are defined as unproductive or unacceptable.

A NATURAL RESPONSE TO DEVELOPMENTAL TASKS

Adolescence is a period characterized by major changes in physical characteristics and cognitive skills. In addition, it is a time when young people are seeking to develop a self-identity and to clarify their personal relationships and responsibilities. Therefore, it is only natural that adolescents will be actively and intensely involved in questioning and confronting those around them. When viewed from a more stable and sedate adult viewpoint, this intensity is often perceived as unproductive or annoying. Nevertheless, to a certain degree, adolescents' "acting-out" behavior is merely a natural part of dealing with the developmental tasks outlined below.

Practicing New Cognitive Skills

Piaget (Inhelder and Piaget, 1958) states that as adolescents enter the stage of formal operations, they develop an ability to understand abstract, conceptual issues and begin to focus on the possible and ideal as much as on the real. Therefore, adolescents are somewhat like children who, as they develop an ability to order and group objects, have an interest in practicing these new-found skills through such hobbies as collecting shells, coins, or stamps. However, since adolescents' new cognitive skills enable them to understand abstract concepts, their practice is more social, intense, and complex. Anyone who works with young adolescents is aware of the fact that in practicing their new skills, students frequently question such things as why they must study certain material, why students cannot smoke in school when teachers can, or why teachers can evaluate students while students do not have an opportunity to evaluate teachers.

A number of years ago I observed a good example of the type of acting-out behavior that can accompany an increase in cognitive skills. Approximately fifty eighth-grade students decided that many of their teachers were not treating them as adults and were refusing to listen to their legitimate concerns. In order to alter this situation, the students decided to have a sit-down strike during their lunch period and to subsequently refuse to talk to their teachers. This behavior provides an excellent example of young adolescents' need to respond to abstract, value-oriented issues. Since the event occurred during a time of student riots and sit-ins, it also demonstrates their tendency to model currently popular behavior.

This situation also indicates the benefits that can be derived from educators understanding adolescent development. If the administration and faculty had perceived this situation as student insubordination that needed to be squelched immediately in order to assure order, their behavior would have gone counter to the students' needs. Fortunately, the teachers were able to view the behavior as an understandable outcome of cognitive development and used the situation to assist the students in developing skills for productively channeling their resentment. This incident provides an excellent example of the concept that an understanding of student development, when accompanied by productive strategies for helping students to clarify and cope with their feelings and needs, can enable adults to view student confrontation as a "teachable moment" rather than an annoying or frightening experience.

As adolescents acquire more sophisticated cognitive skills, they also begin to conceptualize morality differently. Adolescents begin to question a law-and-order morality and instead consider the possibility of changing rules that do not appear to be in their best interests. In addition, some adolescents begin to consider the concept that justice should be based upon respect for individual rights and that individuals should judge their actions according to whether they have acted in the best interests of those concerned. As adolescents begin to develop higher levels of moral thought, they often come into conflict with those adults who operate at somewhat lower levels. Rather than involving students in dialogue designed to develop higher levels of moral thought, schools all too often tend to operate on a combination of fear of punishment (Stage 1) and law-and-order authoritarianism (Stage 4). If, as Piaget and Kohlberg state, adolescents are at a developmental stage where they are developing more mature cognitive and moral concepts, it is not surprising that conflict arises among adolescents and individuals and institutions that function at lower levels of moral development. Educators, counselors, and parents should constantly examine their interactions with adolescents to determine whether they are providing adolescents with opportunities and responsibilities commensurate with their developmental needs and skills.

Developing A Personal Identity

As discussed in Chapter 1, the development of a personal identity and the simultaneous movement away from dependence upon parents and other adults is a major developmental task for adolescents. It is only natural that both adults and adolescents will experience some confusion and conflict during the transition from a rather dependent adult-child relationship to an adult-adolescent relationship in which the adolescent seeks increasing amounts of equality. It is frequently difficult for parents to adjust to the role changes that are generated as their children become more able to make their own decisions and safely cope with extended amounts of freedom.

Similarly, teachers often find it difficult to accept the fact that adolescents' confrontative behavior is much less a response to adults' behavior than to the adolescents' need to discover their own limitations and abilities.

Teachers who find their profession exciting and rewarding have one common characteristic. Each seems to perceive the interchange with adolescents as a growth-producing, challenging, enjoyable experience. This appears to be based on these teachers' belief that adolescents' struggles and searching are not unlike their own. Rather than viewing adolescence as a temporary mutation or an awkward stage, these teachers view it as a period in which young people are beginning to struggle with important issues. Therefore, although these teachers do not need to identify with or seek constant approval from their students, they express a deep sense of respect and empathy for adolescents. Consequently, these adults are more able to view adolescents' challenges, not as personal attacks, but as responses to the process of growing up in a complex society. These teachers accept the fact that adolescents' attempts to develop a sense of who they are, what they value, and how much responsibility they can handle, will of necessity create confrontation. This perspective enables these adults to see their role not as controllers of adolescent behavior, but as that of helping adolescents learn productive ways to express their needs and wants.

Establishing Mutually Satisfying Peer Relationships

A number of theorists point to the fact that establishing healthy, mutually satisfying peer relationships is a major developmental task for adolescents. Therefore, it is to be expected that adolescents will devote a significant amount of time and energy to involvement in and examination of peer interactions. Indeed, many adolescents find their peers to be the single most interesting component of the school environment. This situation is probably even more true for students with behavior problems. Since these students frequently experience considerable academic failure, peer interactions are likely to replace school achievement as an area in which these students can gain attention and experience success. The frequency and intensity of peer interactions among young adolescents highlights the important role peer interactions play in the developmental process. The poking, fighting, talking, and put-downs common among junior high school students are to a large degree a response to the difficulties of establishing peer relationships when their own world is characterized by rapid change and intensified self-consciousness.

Unfortunately, rather than employ this interest as a motivating force, schools all too often create situations in which students are not encouraged to work together. Indeed, peer interaction is often discouraged and students are asked to compete with their peers. This situation is a definite factor contributing to the unproductive behaviors that are indicators of behavior disturbance in students.

It is not surprising that teachers often fail to accurately diagnose this problem and therefore place the blame on students, rather than on the instructional techniques being employed. As Brown (1975) notes, teachers receive little training in the techniques of group or peer instruction. In addition, most teachers were themselves students in classrooms that failed to employ social interaction as a key component in the learning process. Educators must both increase their awareness of the interaction patterns existing within learning environments and develop skills for employing student interaction as an integral part of the learning process. Adults must realize that there will be times when adolescents' concerns about their peer relationships will overshadow their interest in academic material. While adults should not consistently allow these concerns to supersede academic instruction, they should employ teaching strategies and develop classroom environments that acknowledge and respond to adolescents' need to interact with their peers.

FACTORS THAT INTENSIFY AND COMPOUND NORMAL DEVELOPMENTAL TASKS

While a certain amount of adolescents' active and confrontative behavior is a natural response to major developmental issues, the problems associated with growing up are increased significantly by a variety of social factors. The factors outlined below include several of the major social variables that serve to intensify the task of moving from childhood to adulthood.

Adjusting to a Complex Society

A major perspective offered by Margaret Mead is that the turmoil experienced by many American adolescents is not a universal, biological phenomenon, but is rather a response to the social/environmental factors impinging upon adolescents. Specifically, Mead noted that in societies characterized by relatively stable customs and values, the adolescent years are often less tumultuous than in rapidly changing societies in which young people are bombarded with vast amounts of information and many alternatives. In isolated, less technically advanced societies where values and norms are relatively stable, adolescents will be confronted with fewer ideas and situations that threaten their existing equilibrium. This situation may also exist in societies that place restrictions on the type of information available to young people. However, in societies such as the United States, adolescents are inundated with information and decisions. They are confronted with an almost unlimited number of practical and philosophical conflicts. Practical day-to-day conflicts include the pressure to achieve at any cost versus moral teachings regarding the value of honesty; physical, peer, and psychological pressures to experiment with their sexuality versus family, peer, or moral constraints; the need for a self-identity and personal congruence versus peer, school, or family pressures to conform; a need for independence versus a need to feel safe and dependent; a need to express their thoughts and feelings versus their skill deficits and societal norms that discourage or punish such expression; and a basic struggle with the issue of immediate personal gratification versus the necessity of responding in a manner that is both socially acceptable and likely to produce long-range personal benefits. In addition to these daily struggles, adolescents are faced with increasingly difficult decisions related to larger issues, such as the need for ecologically sound decisions versus the value of technology and consumerism; a compassion for those less fortunate versus the desire to advance themselves socially and financially; the need to protect their own and others' individual freedoms versus a dislike for violence and war; the personal and social benefits of an advanced educational experience versus the cost of such an education and its inability to guarantee either a personally or financially satisfying position; and the purported value of democracy versus the impotence associated with the myriad of issues and the size and complexity of the political system. Because they are faced with a myriad of value-laden issues, adolescents at times find themselves literally overloaded with new ideas, feelings, and choices. Since they cannot pinpoint the confusion and anxiety stemming from these value conflicts, adolescents often experience the sense of impotence and frustration which accompanies a diffuse existential anxiety. It is understandable that adolescents would respond to this overload by searching for ways to escape or by creating their own order in a world that appears complex and unpredictable.

While this view of adolescent behavior may seem rather negative, it has inherent within it the potential for constructive change. If adolescent conflict is to some degree a response to environmental pressures, ways can be found to reduce these pressures. Reducing these pressures and helping adolescents to perceive their life space as more ordered, controllable, and safe may take a sizeable step toward reducing those adolescent behaviors that are frequently labeled as emotionally disturbed, delinquent, or simply annoying.

Unfortunately, adults do very little to assist adolescents in their struggle to develop some order out of the confusion and uncertainty created by their confrontation with these conflicts. Rather, adults all too often provide adolescents with canned answers, moral platitudes, and educational experiences that require only that they respond correctly. If adults are to do more than attempt to shape adolescents' immediate behavior so as to increase adults' comfort, they must assist young people in pinpointing their concerns. They must then help adolescents to develop clear, well-thought-out values and goals. Finally, adults must aid adolescents in developing skills that can be employed to reach these goals.

Treatment as "Marginal People"

Lewin's term "marginal man" refers to the fact that while it is not acceptable for adolescents to act like children, neither are they given the responsibilities or social/interpersonal privileges normally associated with adulthood. More specifically, adolescents are expected not to display such outward signs of childlike behavior as open and spontaneous expression of feelings, extensive dependency, or inappropriate social behavior. On the other hand, adolescents are expected not to display uncomfortable amounts of such productive adult behavior as independent decision making, thoughtful but firm confrontation and criticism, and a demand for open, equalitarian relationships.

Compounding the difficulties associated with being marginal people is the fact that adults too often provide adolescents with varying and contradictory messages regarding which role they should play. Adults frequently interpret adolescents' level of maturity and social status according to their own needs. Therefore, when discussing a research paper that is due or a job that could earn money to purchase clothes, adults are likely to remind adolescents of their maturity and nearly adult status. However, when discussing student evaluation of teachers' work or debating the use of the family car, adults may focus on the adolescent's immaturity and lack of responsibility. It is understandable that adolescents find such situations both confusing and annoying.

When interacting with adolescents, adults must provide them with opportunities to demonstrate their ability to act responsibly. In addition to providing them with necessary practice in responsible behavior, adults will often find that their trust in adolescents becomes a self-fulfilling prophecy. Adolescents are striving to prove to themselves and others that they are competent. Consequently, they often respond with surprising maturity to adult trust, while responding with anger and resentment to adult lack of trust.

Lack of Preparation for Responsible, Self-Initiated Behavior

It is not uncommon to hear adults discuss the fact that adolescents cannot act in an adult manner and fail to respond appropriately when given responsibility. A thoughtful examination of adolescents' past experiences and some reflection on Benedict's (1954) statement regarding the value of gradual change should provide a much needed perspective on this situation. Like any skill, responsibility takes practice and will be acquired gradually. A young soccer player cannot maneuver a ball as deftly as Pelé. Neither does a coach, by choice, give a rookie quarterback his first starting assignment in a championship game. Responsibility must be given gradually and, as in the development of any skill, must be accompanied by continual feedback and guidance. An athlete attempting a move for the first time is not expected to execute it perfectly. Adults should expect adolescents to make mistakes when they take increased responsibility for their own learning and behavior. However, if obtaining the skills of self-direction, self-motivation, and self-evaluation is valuable, then adults must be willing to commit time and energy to assist adolescents in developing these skills.

For example, adolescents often fail to effectively cope with responsibilities found in schools that provide students with considerable unstructured time or in classrooms that place an emphasis on student-initiated learning. As is frequently the case when working with adolescents, this behavior is understandable. In many cases the students involved have not been exposed to school environments where they were allowed to decide how to use their time. Therefore, when suddenly confronted by this situation, students lack the skills and knowledge necessary to successfully cope. Furthermore, it is likely that when confronted with such an immediate change, some students will seriously question the schools' sincerity and motives. This skepticism might be particularly pronounced among students whose out-of-school environments are characterized by structure and authoritarianism. For these students the freedom might well be so unlike their existing world that it cannot be immediately integrated into an existing schema. Therefore, in addition to being confusing and anxiety provoking, this lack of structure could understandably be misinterpreted as softness, lack of concern, or incompetence.

Several years ago I spent some time talking to students at John Adams High School in Portland, Oregon. At the time, the school placed considerable responsibility on the students, and the learning environment was flexible and casual in comparison to more traditional school environments. Conversations with many of the alienated behavior-problem students indicated how frequently the students interpreted the casual atmosphere and lack of firm attendance policies as a lack of teacher concern. During a conversation with a group of students who were smoking outside the school, a student said, "If the teachers really cared or thought that what they were teaching was worthwhile, they'd be out here trying to get us into class." While educators might disagree with the student's logic, it is important to note that based on the student's past experience and beliefs, this interpretation was accurate. These students simply had not been previously involved in situations where the granting of personal freedom and an emphasis on individual responsibilty were associated with concern and caring. On the contrary, it is likely that much of their experience both in school and at home reinforced the association between lack of demands and lack of concern.

In addition to their skepticism, many of these students lacked the skills and attitudes necessary for them to function effectively in an environment that emphasized self-motivation. It is therefore not surprising that the school's program was less successful than anticipated and that the school has moved in the direction of increased structure. If adults expect students to function effectively in unstructured environments that demand skills in organizing time and supplying self-motivation, they must provide students with prior opportunities to gradually develop these skills.

The frequent failure of school programs that require students to demonstrate initiative and responsibility is not the only indication of adults' failure to provide adolescents with opportunities to develop skills in self-direction and responsibility. It is an interesting yet sad fact that businesses and institutions (including schools) find it necessary to expend considerable sums of money to assist their personnel in developing skills in such areas as effective use of time, assertiveness, and interpersonal communication. In many cases adolescents' unproductive behavior is based either on a lack of such skills or the use of these skills at a time and place that have not been approved by adults.

Ineffective Adult Modeling

The degree to which young adolescents model current media stars or popular peers reveals the importance role modeling plays in shaping adolescent behavior. Unfortunately, many (perhaps most) behavior-problem adolescents have not been consistently exposed to adults who have modeled warmth, excitement about life, competence in interpersonal skills, or concern. Adolescents who are involved in behavior problems at school or in the community are more likely than their better-behaved peers to have family relationships characterized by parental rejection or indifference, reciprocal hostility, and a lack of family unity.

Parents of delinquents are more likely to have minimal parental aspirations for their children, to be hostile or indifferent toward school, to have a variety of personal problems of their own, and to have police records (Ahlstrom and Havighurst, 1971; Cressey and Ward, 1969).

More specifically, fathers of delinquents are more likely to be rated by independent observers as cruel, neglecting, and inclined to ridicule their children (particularly sons); and less likely to be rated as warm, affectionate, or passive (Bandura and Walters, 1959; Glueck and Glueck, 1950; McCord, McCord, and Zola, 1959; and Powers and Witmer, 1951). In turn, their delinquent young, especially sons, are likely to have few close ties to their fathers, and to consider them wholly unacceptable as models for conduct (Glueck and Glueck, 1950) (Conger, 1977, pp. 583-584).

Given the poor parental modeling frequently available to adolescents who are experiencing behavior problems, it becomes especially important that adults who work with behavior-problem youngsters model consistent concern, warmth, and competence. This does not mean that behavior-problem adolescents should not be confronted with consistent structure and discipline. Indeed, as suggested earlier, low expectations and a lack of discipline often indicate a real lack of concern and respect for the individual. However, it is important that expectations be realistic and that discipline is handled in a manner that focuses on skill development, actively involves the adolescent, and maintains the adolescent's integrity.

Finally, it is important that adults model excitement, interest, and commitment. If adults accept responsibility for assisting adolescents in their struggle to understand, become a part of, and contribute to the adult community, adults must remain aware of and committed to the excitement and responsibility inherent within that position. To the extent that adults lose touch with their own struggles, questions, and potential for growth, they proportionately diminish their ability to assist adolescents in clarifying their struggles and their roles. This does not mean that adults must value what adolescents do, view life from their perspective, or accept all of their behavior. Rather, it means that adults must present models that indicate that the struggle to define an individual's values and role in society is meaningful, feasible, and worthy of effort.

A RESPONSE TO SCHOOLS' FAILURE TO MEET ADOLESCENTS' NEEDS

The public schools have been the focus of considerable criticism during the past decade. Books such as *The Underachieving School, Crisis in the Classroom,* and *Schools Without Failure* have focused attention on the possibility that schools may be contributing to students' behavior problems. Schools often fail to meet student needs that must be met before learning can take place. While some educators view this belief as an attack on the teaching profession or their own competency, a more productive and positive approach to this challenge is to realize that inherent within this criticism is an extremely optimistic and exciting concept. The central theme in this concept is that by creating school environments that meet students' psychological and developmental needs, educators can vastly reduce unproductive student behavior while simultaneously increasing student learning.

This section will focus on a variety of adolescent needs that are frequently not met within school environments. When schools fail to meet these needs, it is understandable that adolescents will respond by becoming frustrated and acting out. The goal of this section is to enhance the reader's awareness of ways in which school environments contribute to student anxiety and acting out. Parts II and III will present practical strategies for alleviating these problems.

Failure to Meet Basic Human Needs

Abraham Maslow's (1968) view of human nature and his hierarchy of human needs presents a useful backdrop against which to examine adolescent behavior. His theoretical position states that people are basically good and that they have an innate need to be competent and accepted. Destructive behavior is therefore not seen as intrinsic, but rather as a reaction to the frustration incurred when an individual's basic needs are not met. Maslow postulates that there is a hierarchy of basic human needs. He also suggests that lower level needs must be met before an individual can respond to higher order needs. While his hierarchy of needs has been broken down in a variety of ways, it includes the following components.

Self-Actualization
Self-Respect
Respect of Others
Belongingness and Affection
Safety and Security
Physiological

Maslow's model has inherent within it considerable potential for practical problem solving. Consider, for instance, the fact that the educational system has as its major goal assisting students to acquire demonstrable skills. Students are asked to change behavior so that they demonstrate new understandings and new ways of perceiving and relating to their environment. In essence, educators are attempting to assist students in the process that Maslow terms self-actualization. However, as Maslow points out, individuals will have extreme difficulty functioning at this level if lower level needs are not met first. Therefore, if educators expect students to perform meaningful academic tasks, they must first create environments that meet the more basic needs. The remainder of the chapter will examine ways in which schools often fail to meet adolescents' basic needs. This awareness, when combined with the practical strategies listed in Chapters 3 through 10, should enable the reader to sensitively examine and alter learning environments in order to insure that acting-out behavior is not primarily a response to a poor environment.

Physiological Needs It is often taken for granted that students' physical needs are met within the school environment. Schools normally provide students with adequate food and a thermostatically controlled environment. There are, however, many instances in which student acting-out behavior is intensified, if not touched off, by unmet physical needs.

I observed an excellent example of this concept several years ago while working with a boy whom I will call Ted. Ted was a rather physically mature fifth grade boy whose behavior was characterized by excessive movement about the room and a general unwillingness or inability to stay on task. Examination of the data indicated that Ted's undesirable behavior was much more intense prior to lunch. Consequently, the teacher began to examine classroom variables that might create more tension or distractability for Ted during the morning. Fortunately, Ted inadvertently provided some interesting and valuable information. One day as Ted gulped down the remains of a coke prior to climbing on the school bus, the driver commented that the coke must taste terrible on top of cereal. Ted calmly replied that the coke was his entire breakfast. Upon further investigation it was discovered that Ted's family ate dinner at 5:30 every evening and that Ted was not allowed to snack after dinner. Furthermore, Ted's breakfast frequently consisted of only a coke. It appeared obvious that such an eating schedule would tend to make Ted rather unsettled during the morning hours. Consequently, the teacher met with Ted's parents and asked them if they would be willing to provide him with a more adequate breakfast. Although this intervention did not change Ted into a model student, it was accompanied by a significant reduction in his morning out-of-seat behavior and a significant increase in his on-task behavior.

An interesting sidelight associated with Ted's intervention is that prior to instigating the program, I decided to discover how it would affect my behavior to exist on only one coke from 5:45 p.m. until 11:45 a.m. the next day. In maintaining this schedule for three consecutive school days, I discovered that I also became overly active, quite tense, and generally more irritable.

This finding has an interesting implication regarding the importance of meeting students' basic needs. When adults examine a student's environment from an adult perspective, it may appear that the environment is meeting the student's basic needs. However, if adults could exist within that environment for a period of time, they might discover that the environment is much less supportive or comfortable than they had expected. When working with behavior-problem adolescents, I have on several occasions spent a school day doing exactly what the student did. I have been surprised at how often I thought that the healthiest student response would be to withdraw from the situation. While I do not condone withdrawal in any form and believe there is a variety of more productive alternatives, I could understand why students who were failing would skip classes or smoke marijuana prior to attending some classes. I was surprised at how difficult it was to sit quietly and listen for several consecutive classes with the only breaks being crowded hallways and a noisy lunchroom.

Designers of environments in which adolescents live or learn should carefully consider whether these environments meet basic physical needs. For example, classroom structures and rules should be examined to determine whether they are flexible in allowing students alternatives on days when they do not feel well or experience fatigue. Environments should also be examined to determine the extent to which they provide real physical comfort to students who are expected to perform efficiently over a period of seven hours. Similarly, administrators of residential treatment facilities for behavior-problem adolescents should consider whether their living facilities compound the psychological stress already being experienced by the adolescents involved in their program.

While it is often relatively easy to pinpoint such obvious factors as physical comfort and eating habits, the equally important, but more subtle factors such as the pace and spacing of daily activities are often overlooked. Despite the fact that many students appear capable of coping with the rapid pace found in most schools, behavior-problem students often find the pace more than they can handle.

For example, a special education teacher expressed frustration because one of his behavior-problem junior high school students had experienced a noticeable increase in problems in several of her classes following placement in one additional regular classroom. Since the student was already functioning well in three regular classrooms, the teacher could not understand why the one additional class had created so many problems. An examination of the student's schedule provided a clue to the problem. At the beginning of the school year, the student had been placed in activity classes during third and fourth periods. Soon after the year began she was also placed in a regular English class during fifth period. Following fifth period the student went to a special reading class where she worked in a small group with a very supportive teacher. This schedule provided the student with a place to slow down and discuss any problems that had occurred during her only regular academic class. Then the student had been placed in a regular social studies class second period. Since the student went directly from this class to three consecutive regular classes, she had no time to dissipate any feelings that had been elicited during her new class. Since the new class was one in which the student frequently became confused, she often entered her third period class quite anxious, agitated, and sensitive. As a result, her acting-out behavior increased dramatically in her third, fourth, and fifth period classes.

After examining this situation, the teacher decided to place the student in a first period social studies class. It was further determined that following her first period class the student would return to the resource center and would have an opportunity to discuss the class as well as receive assistance with her assignments. During the first several weeks of this new program, the student frequently expressed that she felt frustrated and nervous. Furthermore, nearly every day she requested assistance in understanding the material covered in class. The value of providing the student with an opportunity to examine her feelings and understand her work was clearly demonstrated by an almost complete cessation of behavior problems in her third, fourth and fifth period classes.

Behavior-problem students are not alone in experiencing difficulties in coping with the fast pace of a school day. Indeed most students become so accustomed to a state of continual input that they are not aware of its effect. However, in order to create a break from the pressures associated with responding to constant external demands, most students develop necessary diversions such as daydreaming, talking to peers as the class begins, leading teachers off task, and beginning to leave class prior to the final bell. While it obviously is not possible to arrange every student's schedule to provide the degree of assistance described above, there are several ways in which teachers can work with students to reduce the tension associated with a fast-paced school day.

One simple solution is to decide upon a specific period of time prior to beginning class when students can sit quietly or talk quietly to their peers. This type of situation is seldom abused when it evolves from a group discussion. However, should a problem arise with students abusing this situation, the solution is simply to make an observation about the situation and discuss the possible alternatives.

A similar solution to the rapid school pace is to provide a brief quiet period prior to class. This approach has worked particularly well with classrooms established for behavior-problem students. Students frequently do not know how to slow themselves down. Consequently, their response to an environment that presents constant challenge is to become increasingly tense until the tension finally explodes in some form of unacceptable behavior. Therefore, the teacher or special educator may want to take several minutes early in the class period and simply ask the students to be silent and attempt to relax. This can be facilitated by playing quiet music and even by providing students with skills in some form of yoga or deep muscle relaxation. Unfortunately, this approach strikes many teachers as silly and as something to be employed only with "problem" or "different" students. However, other than the fact that this approach is much healthier, is a moment of silent meditation different from an adult's cigarette or coffee break?

A quiet time prior to beginning the day's activities is not the only method for assisting students to relax. It is often equally effective to designate the first several minutes of class as a time for having fun. There are numerous activities that can be employed to provide a brief respite from the rigors of a fast-paced day. Some teachers enjoy talking about humorous incidents they have experienced, some like to involve students in guessing the outcome of upcoming athletic events, while others may have students draw lots or throw darts to see who will present their speech or lead a discussion. While it is certainly important to keep such activities within limits and require that students cooperate by focusing on the day's task when the teacher is ready to begin, such activities can have a surprising impact on reducing low-level student disruption.

Need for Safety and Security In suburban neighborhoods as well as in urban environments, situations exist in which students are concerned about their physical safety. Students occasionally experience anxiety associated with such necessary actions as walking to and from school, using the school restrooms, and passing between classes. To the degree that students feel insecure in their environment, they will be less able to function effectively in performing appropriate academic tasks.

While schools normally create environments in which students feel physically safe, there are frequently unknown factors that significantly reduce a sense of psychological safety. An excellent example of this occurred several years ago in a school district in Oregon. The district was concerned both with acting-out behavior among first graders and the fact that these young children often seemed to react negatively to their school experience. Much to the district's credit, they sought the assistance of a group of educational consultants. In examining the situation, the consultants decided to focus on the ratio of positive to negative statements made by teachers. In order to determine the influence of positive and negative statements on students' feelings about school, the consultants simply asked children from each class to answer "yes" or "no" to the question: "Do you like school?"

Figure 2.1. The Influence of Positive and Negative Teacher Statements on Students' Feelings about School

Teacher	Pre 2 weeks after start of school (Sept. 20-27)			Post January 22-24		
	Pos.	Neg.	% of students responding yes to: "Do you like school?"	Pos.	Neg.	% of students responding yes to: "Do you like school?"
1	.72	28	90%	.76	24	90%
2	.34	66	90%	.33	67	20%
3	.66	34	80%	.70	30	70%
4	.69	31	90%	.65	35	80%
5	.54	46	100%	.61	39	20%
6	.80	20	100%	.87	13	100%
7	.22	78	90%	.19	81	20%
8	.64	36	70%	.64	36	40%
9	.79	21	100%	.77	23	100%
10	.92	08	80%	.89	11	90%
11	.52	48	100%	.63	37	60%
12	.73	27	90%	.65	35	90%
13	.45	55	90%	.61	39	80%
14	.67	33	80%	.73	27	80%
15	.58	42	90%	.60	40	70%
16	.51	49	60%	.58	42	10%
17	.76	24	70%	.77	23	70%

(Fredericks, R. Personal Communications. Unpublished research project, Teaching Research, Monmouth, Oregon)

As indicated in Figure 2.1, while student attitudes were generally positive in all classes early in the school year, these attitudes became much less positive for those students who experienced a low rate of positive verbalizations during the first half of the school year. More specifically, in the eight cases in which teachers provided less than 65 percent positive statements, the percentage of students responding that they liked school dropped an average of 48 percent during the first school semester. On the other hand, in the seven classrooms in which 70 percent or more of all teacher statements were positive, students' response to the question of liking school averaged exactly the same after one school semester. This evidence strongly suggests that students respond more positively to environments that are characterized by a relatively high percentage of positive statements. The relationship between this study and Maslow's (1968) concept concerning the need for safety and security is obvious. Students will not experience safety or belonging and will respond less positively to an atmosphere characterized by frequent negative statements and evaluations.

While the above study examined the feelings of primary grade children, several studies involving older students indicate that students' feelings about education become more negative as youngsters progress through the grades. In a study involving a survey of 600 students in grades three through eleven, Morse (1964) found that while

84 percent of third-graders stated that they were proud of their work, only 53 percent of eleventh-graders expressed this belief. Similarly, Cormany (1975) reported that while 64.4 percent of kindergarten children expressed positive feelings about school, only 12.8 percent of sixth-graders reported such feelings. These and other similar findings suggest that schools are failing to provide students with several of their basic needs.

In addition to providing students with a positive environment, it is important to increase their feeling of safety by creating environments that support their emotional needs. Several years ago I observed a poignant example of the importance of creating supportive environments. A girl was walking down a nearly deserted high school corridor. As she approached a group of three girls, she smiled and extended a friendly greeting. As she did so, one of the girls in the group whispered something to the others that elicited considerable laughter. The girl's smile immediately turned to tears, and she continued down the hall with tears streaming down her face. Unfortunately, soon after this incident the final bell rang indicating that all students should be in their classrooms. The girl quickly wiped her eyes and slowly entered her class. However, the girl's ordeal was not yet over. As she slumped dejectedly into her seat, she received a severe reprimand from her teacher for being late. This was immediately followed by several brisk questions regarding her homework. The girl's passive, sullen responses served only to evoke further rebuke. This scene dramatically highlights the need for adults to be sensitive to cues indicating that youngsters may need assistance or may simply need time and space in which to work through their problems.

Student evaluation is another area in which schools frequently fail to provide students with a sense of safety. Students are seldom actively involved in evaluating their own work. In addition, the large numbers of students taught by teachers in secondary schools makes it difficult for teachers to provide personal, individualized feedback to students. Consequently, many students (including those who excel) find grades to be somewhat arbitrary and highly anxiety producing. If educators hope to create school environments that provide students with a sense of psychological safety, they must carefully reexamine their methods of evaluating students' work.

Need for Belonging and Affection   In addition to basic physiological needs and needs to perceive their environment as safe, Maslow (1968) states that they experience a need for belongingness and affection. Most educators would agree that individuals function more effectively in settings that provide these components. However, the basic ingredients necessary for creating such environments are often overlooked. An excellent example of such a situation occurred several years ago when a graduate student and friend of mine expressed concern over the fact that his sophomore English classes were not functioning as well as he had hoped. The teacher noted that it was difficult to involve students in class discussions; attendance was not good; and numerous students were behind in their work. This situation perplexed the teacher because it existed despite the fact that students were seated in a circle, the students indicated that they found the material interesting, the teacher maintained a high positive/negative ratio, and the teacher was a young, dynamic educator.

In examining this and similar situations, it is useful to conceptualize the problem in the following manner. Learning is perhaps best defined as a significant change in an individual's behavior. Since any behavior change alters people's worlds to some degree, it entails risk. People are more likely to feel safe and take risks when they understand their environment. Finally, since other people are an important part of people's environments, it is important that they know those in whose presence they are expected to learn. Given adolescents' intensified self-consciousness and their sensitivity to peer approval, adults should pay particular attention to the importance of creating environments in which students know each other and feel a sense of acceptance and belonging.

With this in mind, I asked the teacher if his students knew each other. He responded that since they had been in class together for several months and many had attended the same junior high school, he was sure they were well acquainted. However, since they appeared to be having real difficulty talking in class, we decided to give the students a quiz to determine how well they knew each other. The results were surprising. Less than 25 percent of the students knew the first names of even half the students in their class.

Based on this finding, the teacher decided to employ several techniques to help his students become better acquainted. In addition to having the students learn all of their classmates' names, the teacher designated every Friday as a day when his classes would be involved in some form of acquaintance or values activity. These activities focused on providing positive peer feedback and increasing self-disclosure. The results of this project were informative and exciting. Data collected before the quiz and three months later showed significant increases in the number of students participating in class discussions, the amount of discussion, student attendance, and percentages of assignments received by the teacher. This incident suggests that knowing their classmates and receiving positive comments from them can have a powerful positive influence on students' classroom performance.

> Positive interpersonal relations among students is necessary both for effective problem solving in groups and for general classroom enjoyment of instructional activity. The psychological safety and security necessary for open exploration of instructional tasks is based upon feelings of being accepted, liked, and supported by fellow students. Class cohesion is based upon positive interpersonal relationship among students. (Johnson and Johnson, 1975b, p. 188)

Need to Experience Respect of Others   The fourth level of human needs outlined by Maslow refers to the need to be respected by others. Many people initially react somewhat negatively to Maslow's inclusion of this need. People tend to believe that individuals should be self-directed and should operate independent of prodding and reinforcement from outside sources. However, while dependency and other-directedness are unproductive when taken to extremes, other people are an important part of a person's environment. Learning is dependent upon the modeling, feedback, and reinforcement provided by others. Even successful, self-actualizing adults find feedback from others helpful and enjoy recognition for their accomplishments. Therefore, while young people should not place an undue emphasis on the opinions of others, their behavior and feelings about themselves are influenced by the behavior of others.

The importance of students perceiving themselves as respected and liked by others has received considerable research support. Davidson and Lang (1960) found that students who perceived their teachers as feeling positive about them had higher academic achievement and more productive classroom behavior. Similarly, Morrison and McIntyre (1969) reported that 73 percent of low-achieving students perceived their teachers as thinking poorly of them, while only 10 percent of high achievers felt this way. While it is difficult to separate cause and effect in such studies, research by Rosenthal and Jacobson (1968) and by Brophy and Good (1970b, 1974) indicates that teacher expectations regarding student performance significantly affect both the quantity and quality of interactions students receive from their teachers, and that this in turn influences student achievement.

Student performance is influenced by peer approval and peer relationships as well as by the quality of teacher-student relationships.

> Although educators generally have not considered student friendships relevant to individual students' cognitive and affective development, our research evidence (Schmuck, 1963; Schmuck, 1966) and experience indicate that they are related. In fact, the friendships classmates have for one another, along with their willingness to help and support one another, represent important ingredients for the enhancement of individual academic achievement. Moreover, learning groups in which friendship and influence are dispersed among many peers have more supportive work norms and are more cohesive than groups in which the friendship and influence processes are hierarchical. Strong relationships with others are not only valuable in themselves; they also can enhance cognitive development in the classroom. (Schmuck and Schmuck, 1974, p. 101)

Considering the importance of peer interactions in providing adolescents with both a support system and a forum for experimenting with a changing self-identity, it is not surprising that positive peer interactions have a significant influence on adolescents' school performance. As educators attempt to create environments conducive to learning and personal growth, they must constantly examine the degree to which these environments meet adolescents' needs for approval from both adults and peers.

Need for Self-Respect   The final need outlined by Maslow deals with self-respect. Maslow stated that higher level needs are based upon and enhanced by the meeting of lower level needs. Consequently, individuals who feel secure, sense that they belong, and consistently receive positive feedback and respect from those around them are likely to possess a higher degree of self-respect.

Research findings consistently support the relationship between a positive self-concept and variables that are directly related to school success. In summarizing the research on the relationship between self-concept and student behavior and academic performance, LaBenne and Greene stated that:

> Empirical and experimental data clearly indicate a direct relationship between the child's self-concept and his manifest behavior, perceptions, and academic performance ... More important perhaps is the fact that most experienced teachers can recite a great many examples in which a student's conception of his abilities severely restrict his achievement, even though his real abilities may be superior to those which he demonstrates. (LaBenne and Greene, 1969, pp. 24-25)

Given the relationship between self-concept and students' academic achievement and behavior, it is important that schools and other institutions that work with behavior-problem adolescents seriously examine their environments to determine whether they are meeting adolescents' basic needs and are thereby providing adolescents with opportunities to develop positive self-concepts. If these needs are not being met, adults should not be surprised when adolescents act out.

Failure to Respond to Cognitive Needs

In addition to attending to the basic needs discussed in the previous section, it is also imperative that schools respond sensitively to both the individual and group variance found in adolescents' cognitive skills. It is quite common for learning-disabled and behavior-problem adolescents to experience considerable difficulty in dealing with abstract concepts. Adolescents differ significantly both in the rate of central nervous system development and opportunities to confront abstract concepts. Therefore, while research suggests that most students begin moving into the formal operations stage between ages eleven to thirteen, there will be considerable variation among students. Consequently, in any given classroom some students will enjoy and easily comprehend abstract material while other students will need to have material related to concrete, practical examples from their immediate environment. When educators fail to provide such concrete examples, they create a situation in which a certain group of students will be unable to understand the material and will subsequently experience failure. When this occurs with any degree of frequency, it is understandable that these students will lose their motivation and will begin to view school as a negative experience.

The importance of providing concrete examples was highlighted several years ago while I was supervising a student teacher. The student teacher was presenting a unit on world powers and the "have-not" nations to a class of juniors and seniors in an upper middle class suburban high school. He presented several excellent lectures, reviewed the material thoroughly, and gave a well-designed examination. Therefore, he was understandably confused and demoralized when the test results indicated that many of the students had failed to acquire the basic concepts he had taught. After discussing the problem with his supervisors, he decided to employ a different approach to teaching the material. He first asked the students to examine their school environment and determine who were the first, second, and third school powers and who were the have-nots. He then asked the students to discuss the interaction patterns that existed between these groups. Following this concrete discussion, he divided the class into four groups. After each group had briefly studied several countries that possessed similar amounts of world power, the groups engaged in a dialogue regarding what goods and services they would be willing to exchange. Finally, the students were presented with a different, but similar examination. The results were striking and rewarding. A large percentage of the students demonstrated a solid understanding of the basic concepts and also indicated that they had enjoyed the lessons. A major reason for the success of the second lesson is that it employed an approach which made the material more concrete while at the same time actively involving the students in the learning process.

Related to problems caused by an overemphasis on abstract concepts is the tendency for schools to employ a passive, noninteractive style of instruction. While some students respond effectively to this instructional style, many students who learn effectively when actively interacting with their environment appear slow and incapable when confronted with a learning environment that is predominantly abstract, verbal, and passive. It is interesting to observe delinquent youngsters who are creative leaders and masters at manipulating their environments, yet who appear dull when functioning within a classroom setting.

Not long ago I shared this observation with a colleague who specializes in discovery learning. His response was to relate a parallel and more specific discovery he had made concerning how different types of students respond to discovery learning activities. He stated that when employing discovery learning techniques, he could with almost unerring accuracy select those students who were the most and least successful in the classroom environment. When asked how he made such discriminations, he stated that the high-achieving students almost always appeared frustrated and annoyed at the discovery approach while the low-achieving students were excited and often successful. His hypothesis concerning the explanation for this behavior was that the successful students had learned to "play the school game" effectively and were frustrated when someone changed the rules. On the other hand, the unsuccessful students found the new activity to be a refreshing change since they were confronted with an activity in which they had not previously failed. In fact, like many delinquent youths, these students were quite adept at this type of analytical, active learning.

The schools' tendency to employ a noninteractive instructional style to teach abstract concepts is compounded by the fact that in many cases teachers are asked to cover too much material too quickly. All too often just as students are beginning to understand new material and its relationship to information they already possess, teachers move on to new, more complicated material. In their haste to cover material, they often fail to provide time and activities that enable students to make the connections necessary for meaningful learning to occur. This situation occurs both within classrooms and in the general approach to organizing the school day.

For example, picture the student who has completed a class in which the teacher rushed through his concluding statements in order to finish before the fast approaching bell. The student leaves the class somewhat confused and valiantly attempting to organize the material. Unfortunately, this valuable process is hindered considerably by the student's sudden realization that he has only three minutes remaining in which to bump his way down two corridors, open his locker while being jostled by passing students, dash down one more corridor, and, out of breath, collapse into his seat seconds before the ensuing bell. As the student begins to regain his composure and attempts to recall the thoughts that had been so rudely interrupted by his race against the clock, he is immediately confronted with a new mental task.

This failure to provide time and activities that enable students to organize their learning has serious implications regarding student motivation. When discussing their high school experience, many outstanding college students note with sadness and anger that they can remember almost nothing of what they learned in many of their high school courses. They frequently recall attempting to determine what questions teachers would ask on an examination and then diligently memorizing facts, which were soon forgotten. Furthermore, these students often state that they did not really understand the material they were learning. Despite the fact that they received excellent grades, they note that they seldom understood the potential practical application of what they had learned.

While these students often found their classes to be boring or confusing, their efforts were reinforced by the grades they received and the competence and power they achieved through successfully playing the school game. These reinforcements were successful in abating the anxiety and frustration associated with a poor learning environment. However, consider the plight of those students who have a similar experience but who have not acquired or refuse to employ the skills needed to successfully cope with a fast-paced, ineffective learning environment. These students are left with a feeling of impotence, incompetence, and confusion. How long can students experience such feelings before they become angry, passive, or simply drop out of school? In his study on rebellion in the high schools, Arthur Stinchcombe (1964) found that, "high school rebellion, and expressive alienation, are most common among students who do not see themselves as gaining an increment in future status from conformity in high school" (Stinchcombe, 1964, p. 49). In further explaining the dynamics of this behavior Stinchcombe states that:

> When a student realizes that he does not achieve status increment from improved current performance, current performance loses meaning. The student becomes hedonistic because he does not visualize achievement of long-run goals through current self-restraint. He reacts negatively to a conformity that offers nothing concrete. He claims autonomy from adults because their authority does not promise him a satisfactory future. (Stinchcombe, 1964, pp. 5-6)

Educators have an obligation to provide instruction that includes adequate time and activities designed to allow students to develop a sense of clarity and competence regarding the material being covered. If they do not provide this, they should expect (and perhaps hope) that students will express their confusion and demand that teachers alter their curriculum and teaching methods.

SUMMARY

Adults are frequently confused and annoyed by the acting-out behavior displayed by adolescents. While understanding this behavior will not make it disappear, understanding does tend to increase patience and serve as the foundation for developing productive interventions.

To a certain extent acting-out behavior is a healthy and natural response to the developmental tasks of adolescence. In addition, these developmental tasks are often compounded by societal factors that block the healthy resolution of developmental tasks and therefore intensify the difficulties associated with making a smooth and productive transition from childhood to adulthood. Indeed, it is not uncommon that adolescents' acting-out behavior is at least partially a response to environments that fail to provide support for basic developmental needs. In such cases adults may need to focus their interventions on either altering unproductive environments or at least providing adolescents with assistance in understanding and coping with these environments.

The Role of Interpersonal Communication in Working with Adolescents

The basic premise of Part II is that positive, open relationships facilitate both learning and personal growth. While many teachers, counselors, and administrators accept this concept, their beliefs are not always transformed into actual day-to-day behavior. There are several reasons why the theory is not put into practice. First, teachers frequently fail to understand the implications of the theories and concepts to which they are exposed. Therefore, for many teachers the idea that improved communication can positively influence student learning and behavior remains in the realm of educational jargon and does not become part of their personal value system. Second, theories and concepts are all too often presented in broad terms, and teachers have difficulty sorting out the specific skills or behaviors that they must employ in order to put theory into practice. Finally, theorists frequently develop their ideas on the basis of idealistic, one-to-one relationships while teachers must work with twenty-five to thirty students at a time. Consequently, teachers frequently become frustrated and discouraged at their inability to successfully employ concepts that experts offer as necessary or useful educational techniques.

Chapter 3 removes the first hurdle to the application of effective communication techniques by examining the relationship between positive, open relationships and adolescents' personality development and learning. Chapter 4 removes the second hurdle by providing specific examples of effective communication skills and when and how to employ these skills. Chapter 5 attacks the third barrier by examining strategies for employing effective communication techniques within the classroom.

All of the communication skills and activities presented in Part II have been employed successfully with adolescents from a wide range of racial and socioeconomic backgrounds and with both "normal" and emotionally handicapped or behavior-problem adolescents. This does not mean, however, that every activity or communication skill must be used in order to work effectively with adolescents. Rather, Part II presents an opportunity to examine the influence interpersonal interactions can have on adolescents and how adults can employ effective communication skills to facilitate adolescent personal growth and learning.

When the facilitator is a real person, being what he is, entering into a relationship with the learner without presenting a front or a facade, he is much more likely to be effective.

Carl Rogers
Freedom to Learn

It seems to the writer that the most important single factor in establishing sound mental health is the relationship that is built up between the teacher and his or her pupils.

Virginia Axline
Play Therapy

CHAPTER
3

The Value of Establishing Open Adult — Adolescent Relationships

THE ADVANTAGES OF OPEN RELATIONSHIPS

Whenever discussions arise concerning the importance of good communication skills as a prerequisite for working with behavior-problem adolescents, someone inevitably asks, "But haven't enough people talked to this type of student already? Don't they need more than just advice or counseling?" The answer to this question is twofold.

First, behavior-problem adolescents probably need more assistance than that provided by contact with concerned adults who are willing to listen to them and provide them with honest, thoughtful reactions to their feelings and behavior. However, regardless of the approach adults take in assisting young people in developing more productive behavior, their willingness and ability to effectively communicate with them is an essential ingredient. As Carl Rogers (1961), Sydney

Jourard (1971), William Glasser (1969), and others have noted, the development of an open, trusting, understanding relationship with a client or student is the first step to effective therapy or teaching. Unless therapists or teachers first establish such relationships, they cannot expect clients or students to take the risks associated with making changes in their behavior. Furthermore, by developing a positive relationship with students or clients, they increase the likelihood that those students or clients will model some of their therapist's or teacher's behaviors and values.

The second point that must be examined in determining whether "more talking" will really help the behavior-problem adolescent revolves around the type of dialogue that has previously been employed with these students. Most behavior-problem adolescents have been involved in a wide variety of adult-child relationships characterized by advice giving, threats, manipulation, abuse, and debate. However, they have seldom if ever been involved in a long-term, two-way relationship characterized by mutual respect, caring, unselfish concern, and productive problem solving. William Glasser stated this point powerfully in his book, *Schools Without Failure,* when he wrote:

> To begin to be successful, children must receive at school what they lack: a good relationship with other people, both children and adults. A child or adult cannot gain a success identity and fulfill his needs through the established pathways because he is lonely. While we may call him by various euphemisms such as "culturally deprived," "disadvantaged," "alienated," "isolated," or even the word I prefer, "uninvolved," his basic problem is that within his family and his community he has not found people to whom he can successfully relate. (Glasser, 1969, pp. 16-17)

Theoretical Evidence

Despite the arguments presented by the numerous writers who have highlighted the value of open two-way relationships, there are many teachers and counselors who state that this type of relationship simply reflects the needs and values of "soft counselor types" and has no justifiable base when working with adolescents. Therefore, prior to a discussion of the specific communication skills that facilitate growth when working with behavior-problem adolescents, it is important to briefly examine a variety of specific adolescent needs and developmental tasks that require or are facilitated by an open, equalitarian, two-way relationship.

Adolescents who are struggling with the conflicts and possibilities created by new cognitive abilities need adult encouragement to question, debate, and challenge. If adults want to encourage higher level cognitive development and creativity in adolescents, they must be prepared to accept the challenge of relationships that include questioning, debate, and conflict. When they hide behind their adult roles or insist that students unquestioningly accept their decisions and parrot correct responses, they are reducing productive disequilibrium and thereby subverting the adolescents' potential for developing higher level cognitive skills and the greater insights associated with these skills.

Similarly, adolescents' growth into higher stages of moral development is dependent upon the disequilibrium and subsequent restructuring associated with continual discussion and increasing amounts of responsibility and independence. If adults sincerely desire to assist young people in moving from lower to higher stages of moral development, they must provide them with alternatives and encourage them to express their opinions. In addition, adults must be willing to model the process of compromise and, when appropriate, to reinforce productive decisions that come into conflict with existing rules or norms.

Anna Freud's (1946) conception of the adolescent as experiencing a major shift in the relative power of the id, ego, and superego also reflects the necessity for engaging adolescents in meaningful, two-way interaction. Anna Freud noted that adolescents experience new drives at a time when they have neither the social sanctions nor social skills to effectively cope with these drives. Freud suggests that adolescents develop a variety of defense mechanisms in order to cope with their increased tension and confusion. This tension could be reduced considerably and the need for energy-draining defense mechanisms decreased if adults would provide adolescents with more frequent and comfortable opportunities for openly discussing and examining issues such as their sexuality, peer relationships, and relationships with parents. In a similar vein, Bronfenbrenner (1970) highlights a powerful reality when he notes that the increasing age segregation (physical as well as psychological) in our society is depriving young people of valuable dialogue and modeling. Adolescents need to realize that even adults do not have all the answers, and that they have concerns and questions about many of the same issues with which adolescents are grappling.

The value of open, two-way relationships in facilitating adolescent development can also be seen in the theories presented by Rank (1945) and Erikson (1968). Rank emphasizes the importance associated with adolescents' need to develop a sense of independence. Certainly this developmental task is greatly enhanced when adults accept adolescents' right to be involved in meaningful, spirited debate concerning decisions that affect them. As Erikson points out, adolescents are struggling first to develop a sense of identity and then to discover means of experiencing this self within meaningful human relationships. Both of these highly important tasks require that adolescents become personally involved with a variety of people and receive feedback concerning others' reactions to their behavior.

Perhaps more than any single theorist, Lewin's (1948) ideas underscore the importance of employing effective two-way communication when working with adolescents. First, Lewin's emphasis on understanding the individual's perception of a situation highlights the necessity for maintaining open channels of communication with adolescents. Since adults cannot read adolescents' minds, and since adults and adolescents are likely to view situations differently, it is extremely important that adults develop and maintain lines of communication that enable adolescents to comfortably provide information regarding their experiences and needs. Behavior-problem adolescents frequently view situations from a different perspective than either adults or other adolescents. Interestingly, these students often know what they need in order to improve a situation. Therefore, it is particularly important that adults encourage them to share their perceptions, needs, and solutions.

Lewin's conceptualization of adolescents as "marginal" people also points to the need for improved communication with adolescents. If adults do in fact confront adolescents with expectations that alternately require child and adult responses, it is important that adults allow adolescents to inform them when this creates anger and confusion. In addition to reducing the tensions between adults and adolescents, such interchanges have the potential for assisting adolescents in clarifying their own conflicts that accompany rapidly changing roles and responsibilities.

There is also a definite relationship between the research and concepts presented by both Mead and Benedict and the value of establishing open communication with young people. Both theorists point to the desirability of associating increased age with increased privileges and responsibilities. This requires that adults increasingly involve adolescents in sincere dialogue about their opinions and ideas and that adults in turn candidly share their ideas and expectations.

Finally, the ideas presented by both Maslow (1968) and Coopersmith (1967) suggest that involvement in open, two-way relationships is a prerequisite to developing positive self-esteem. Both theorists note that some sense of being valued, respected, and cared for is necessary if individuals are to function effectively. It is obvious that adolescents will not develop such feelings in the absence of communication patterns that indicate a sincere interest in their thoughts and feelings.

Perhaps the most effective way to summarize the benefits provided by employing communication skills that foster cognitive, social, and psychological growth is to provide an example in which these skills were successfully employed. Not long ago I visited the classroom of a marvelous man with whom I once taught. The eighth grade students in his class were actively involved in a science project and the room buzzed with noise and interest. As I watched, a boy called across the room to his friend, John, and requested that John throw him the scissors. John immediately obliged and the airborne scissors narrowly missed hitting another student. I watched with interest to see how the teacher would handle the situation. Rather than shouting at John, the teacher walked over to him and put his hand on John's shoulder. He proceeded to share with John the fact that the narrow miss had frightened him because he cared about and felt responsible for the students in his class. He then asked John if in the future he would carry the scissors across the room.

After class I asked the teacher why his intervention had been so calm and personalized. His answer was that young adolescents are involved in so many changes that their egos are very fragile and they personalize almost everything. He went on to state very simply that his goal was to provide the student with information in such a manner that he would be able to hear it. The teacher noted that had he yelled at the student or made an example of him in front of the class, the student's response would very likely have been to focus on the teacher's "mean" behavior rather than to examine his own behavior. The teacher stated that by owning his own feeling and sharing it with the student, he had provided the student with valuable information without making the student defensive. This incident provides an excellent example of a skilled teacher's ability to spontaneously synthesize a working knowledge of adolescent development with practical communication skills. The result of this synthesis was that the teacher was able to respond in a way which facilitated the student's personal growth.

Research Evidence

As is the case with theories, research findings support the value of employing open, warm communication patterns when interacting with adolescents. A variety of studies show that teachers who are perceived as warm and understanding are evaluated as more effective. Brookover (1945) reported that teachers who established closer relationships with students were rated as more effective by both students and employers. Similarly, Hawes and Egbert (1954) and Dixon and Morse (1961) reported that teachers' ability to empathize with students was a major factor in teachers being rated as effective. Using case studies of over seventy teachers, Hearn (1952) found that skills in human relations are important in teachers being rated as effective. More recent studies by Baird (1973), Costin and Grush (1973) and Elmore and LaPointe (1975) have shown that teacher warmth is a major factor influencing positive student ratings. In summarizing research findings regarding adolescents' responses to various teacher characteristics, Conger (1977) stated:

> Taken together, they indicate that adolescents in our culture tend to prefer and to respond more favorably to teachers who are warm, possessed of a high degree of ego strength, enthusiastic, able to display initiative, creative, reactive to suggestions, poised and adaptable, able to plan, interested in parental and community relations, and aware of individual differences in children and oriented toward individual guidance. In contrast, teachers who are hostile or dominating generally appear to affect pupil adjustment adversely. (Conger, 1977, p.375)

Some educators might argue that it is not important whether students or administrators rate a teacher as effective. What really matters is whether students learn the material being presented. Therefore, it is interesting to note that a variety of studies (Aspy, 1969; Hefele, 1971; McKeachie and Lin, 1971; and Stoffer, 1970) indicate that students taught by teachers who possess good interpersonal skills and establish open, warm relationships within the classroom learn more than students taught by teachers who do not possess these characteristics. These research findings provide support for the theoretical conceptualizations that indicate the value of creating learning environments that meet students' personal and developmental needs. It appears that:

> Teachers retain their effectiveness as professional persons only so long as they remain warmly human, sensitive to the personal needs of children, and skillful in establishing effective relationships with them. (Bush, 1954, p.27)

SELF-DISCLOSURE IN ADULT-ADOLESCENT INTERACTIONS

While theory and research support the benefits associated with interacting openly with adolescents, adults often express concern and confusion regarding the extent to which they should respond openly to adolescents. It is, therefore, important to examine the various levels of openness and to consider the payoffs and costs associated with each level.

Levels of Self-Disclosure

It appears that the popularization of encounter groups during the late sixties has led to a fairly widespread misinterpretation concerning the concept of open communication. When talking to parents and professionals about improving communications with adolescents, someone almost always says, "But I don't want to tell them everything about me. Are you saying that we shouldn't keep our personal lives private?" Such statements suggest that openness or self-disclosure is an all or nothing behavior. Fortunately, this is not the case. Self-disclosure falls on a continuum, and people can choose to function at any of several levels of self-disclosure.

One interpretation or level of open communication focuses on the value of almost total openness. If people practice this form of openness or self-disclosure, they will spontaneously share their feelings related to a wide range of issues and will respond candidly to questions concerning their values and beliefs. This type of self-disclosure is characteristic of close friendships or sound marriage relationships.

A second, and perhaps more easily acceptable view of self-disclosure emphasizes the value of sharing responses to events occurring in the immediate situation. When teachers believe in the value of this form of self-disclosure, they will frequently inform their colleagues and students about how they are responding to their behavior. More specifically, a teacher may tell the class, "Your inattentiveness is making me uncomfortable. Can you tell me what is causing the distraction?" Similarly, a teacher may inform a colleague, "I am hurt because you have not smiled at me or talked to me for a week. Can you find time to sit down with me and discuss the situation?" This style of self-disclosure allows people to maintain a large degree of personal privacy and asks only that they share those thoughts and feelings that are elicited by their immediate environment and affect their ability to function effectively and comfortably within that environment. This does not mean that they will not share their feelings about personal matters. Rather, it means that such sharing will be restricted to those environments in which these personal concerns are elicited either by immediate interactions or by the level of trust and commitment that exists within that relationship.

A third view of self-disclosure is that it is an uncomfortable, time-consuming task that has little or no place in educational or other professional settings. When teachers' behavior is based on this premise, they will be unlikely to share their feelings in a work-related setting (and very possibly not in their home or personal life). Since they choose not to share their feelings, their responses to their colleagues and students will be considerably more rule and role bound. Therefore, they are likely to respond to student inattentiveness with discipline, anger, sarcasm or by simply ignoring that the situation exists. Similarly, they are more likely to ignore a colleagues' nonsmiling behavior and possibly discuss his unfriendly attitude with others.

Advantages and Disadvantages of Various Types
of Self-Disclosure

When choosing the degree to which they will respond openly with adolescents, adults should be aware of the advantages and disadvantages associated with the various levels of self-disclosure. Furthermore, they should keep in mind that while their interactions will tend to fall into one of the three styles presented above, they will at one time or another employ behaviors characteristic of each style.

Providing Access to a Variety of Adult Concerns The first, most open style of interaction has the advantage of providing adolescents with a considerable amount of valuable data about how adults view and respond to their world. While adolescents view the rights and privileges possessed by adults as highly desirable, they frequently hold very idealized and inaccurate ideas concerning what it is like to be an adult. By sharing their ideas, values, and feelings about a broad spectrum of personal and social issues, adults can begin to facilitate the more gradual transition from adolescence to adulthood that both Mead and Benedict espouse. Furthermore, adults can begin to break down the barriers Bronfenbrenner outlines when he notes with concern the degree to which an age-segregated society has developed. Openness is important for an adolescent because:

> ... he needs association with others to see what they are, and, by extension, what he might be. As he shapes himself, the characteristics of others are valuable points of reference. From them he acquires a conception of the range of human behavior, a kaleidoscopic view of the possibilities of being. Consciously or unconsciously, he imitates those characteristics which appeal to him, discovering new capacities within himself. (Putney and Putney, 1964, pp. 31-32)

An additional advantage associated with this level of self-disclosure is that it tends to reduce the degree to which adolescents and adults view each other with suspicion and fear. As an individual begins to know another person or group of people, their behavior becomes better understood and more predictable. This in turn tends to increase the individual's feeling of comfort and reduce the anxiety and risk associated with interacting with them.

In discussing this advantage of self-disclosure, I am reminded of a situation I encountered several years ago while working with behavior-problem youngsters. A large chain store was located not far from the school where I worked. As is common throughout the country, the owners experienced considerable difficulty with the large amount of shoplifting that took place in their store. In fact, stealing items from the chain store was one way in which behavior-problem youngsters acquired status. For example, in order to be accepted into one local "gang," a boy was required to steal a specified amount of merchandise within a designated period of time. Admission into another group was contingent upon shoplifting an item larger than a basketball. In discussing their behavior, the boys consistently referred to the fact that nobody would notice the missing items, that the merchandise did not belong to anyone, and that the store was making so much money that it would hardly miss a few items.

Not far from the chain store was a small leather shop where students often stopped after school to talk to John, the owner. John was a relaxed, easygoing man who chatted with the students while he worked and occasionally allowed the boys to work with his tools. The boys knew that John's trade was doing fairly well and that he enjoyed his work. They also knew that John would listen nonjudgmentally to their problems and that from time to time John would discuss his own personal concerns. John was also comfortable leaving his money, tools, and leather within easy reach of the adolescents. Although John worked in a back room behind a beaded divider, he left a small metal box with $40-$60 in cash on the counter in the front room. In addition, the front room contained numerous tools and a considerable amount of valuable leather. However, despite the availability of these items, John never had any money or material stolen.

This situation is a perfect example of the fact that people abuse roles, but seldom abuse people. In working with behavior-problem adolescents I have been impressed by the difference in their behavior when interacting with adults they feel they know and trust as opposed to adults whom they perceive as playing a role. During numerous group discussions in which adolescents have focused upon their feelings concerning teachers, the students have pointed out the importance of seeing their teacher as more than simply a role. In their quest for independence and parity with adults, adolescents need to know that adults see them as important and trustworthy enough to share at least some parts of their personal lives. When teachers, childcare workers and other adults indicate that they are having their personal possessions or institutional materials stolen, it is almost certain that they have not made themselves known to the young people with whom they are working.

As discussed in Chapters 4 and 5, this type of sharing between adults and adolescents and among adolescents can be readily incorporated into most settings in which adults work with adolescents. It is important to note that self-disclosure does not mean that adults must share all of their personal matters. Rather, self-disclosure can involve a fun, relaxed exchange of those portions of their lives that they choose to share and that help those around them to view them as real people.

While there are major advantages associated with an open style of interacting with adolescents, there are limitations and cautions associated with this style. Perhaps the major caution centers around the need for adults to be aware of the degree to which adolescents desire such an open relationship. Adolescents often discuss with disdain teachers who are overly concerned about being their friend and who share extensive personal information instead of teaching. Since adolescents are anxious to become adults, they desperately want to believe that being an adult is different from being an adolescent. When adults act as if they desperately need adolescent support and approval, students frequently lose respect and feel confused and angry. In addition, students understandably wonder why personal information is being shared so freely with people who are often little better than acquaintances. When this behavior is not interpreted as weakness, it is often quite accurately seen as manipulative.

This caution is not meant to imply that adults should not become involved in personal, two-way relationships with young people. There are times when such relationships are desired by adolescents and are highly productive. Extensive, indepth self-disclosure is most appropriate and effective when it occurs in nonclassroom settings (or within courses specifically designed to facilitate such sharing) in which students have requested to have open dialogue, and when adequate time is available for students and adults to become well acquainted. However, even in these situations it is extremely important that adults attempt to clearly separate their needs from those of the adolescents.

A final concern often raised when adults discuss establishing open relationships with adolescents is that students sometimes abuse the privileges connected with an open communication style. This concern highlights an important point about open, two-way relationships. This point is exemplified by a situation involving an attractive, twenty-year-old practicum student who was working in a drop-in counseling center for adolescents. The student was having difficulty because the adolescents with whom she was working began to "take advantage" of her friendly, low-key manner. They refused to follow her directions, acted disruptive when she attempted to gain their attention, initiated inappropriate physical contact with her, and in general displayed varying degrees of discourtesy. The student was concerned because her agency supervisor had informed her that she needed to create more distance between herself and her clients. She was upset because she did not want to be less caring and friendly, and yet she was aware that something needed to change in her interactions with the adolescents.

In examining this student's situation, it is important to focus on the appropriate variable. Too often adults mistakenly assume that if adolescents begin to abuse open relationships, adults must reduce the amount of openness or warmth that they display. There is, however, another variable that is often ignored. Openness and warmth in a relationship do not mean that adults abdicate their own rights and their respect for themselves. In her interactions with adolescents, the practicum student found that she was not asserting her right to be treated with a respect and concern equal to that which she displayed. Therefore, the necessary change was not to decrease the amount of warmth she displayed, but to increase the degree to which she insisted that she be treated with the same courtesy and concern that she provided the adolescents.

An example of a situation in which adult self-disclosure was employed as part of a treatment plan for emotionally handicapped junior high school students may clarify the potential advantages of open communication. Several years ago, the author coordinated a team consisting of two teachers, an aide, and himself. The team received Title VI funding to develop a program for working with emotionally handicapped junior high school students. While our initial interventions focused almost exclusively on contractual agreements aimed at altering the students' behaviors, we soon began to realize that perhaps more than anything else our students lacked an ability to effectively communicate their feelings, wants and needs. Therefore, on those frequent occasions when they were feeling unsuccessful, anxious, and impotent, our students responded in understandable, but often highly inappropriate ways in order to achieve some degree of significance, competence, and power.

In order to gradually alter this situation, we developed a program for teaching our students how to effectively communicate their needs and feelings. In addition to a wide variety of skill-building activities which will be discussed in Chapters 4 and 5, we attempted to have our staff consistently model an open, self-disclosing communication style. Therefore, in addition to teaching and employing the second type of self-dis-closure—sharing feelings about current happenings with those directly involved—we frequently created situations in which our students were able to view us struggling with our problems as team members. One manner in which this was arranged was by simply allowing students who remained after school—either voluntarily or as a logical consequence to their behavior—to observe portions of our daily staffings. While we did not discuss other students or teachers in front of our students, we did air our own disagreements and discuss what we needed from each other. In so doing, we allowed our students to view adults employing productive communication skills to work through important and sometimes rather emotionally charged concerns.

As we continued this policy, we made several interesting observations. First, we noticed that whenever we had an "audience" our communications were clearer and more productive. In a sense, the students' presence forced us to employ our "best behavior." Second, we found that students began to model our actions. We were pleasantly surprised to observe students using phrases and techniques they had heard us employ. Finally, by sharing our concerns and struggles with our students, we became less perfect, more real, and consequently more useful as models. Research (Burnstein, Stotland, and Zander, 1961; Rosekrans, 1967) has found that individuals are more likely to model someone whom they perceive as similar to themselves. Adults cannot expect adolescents to assume that what works for adults will work for them if they see adults as almost totally different people existing in a world governed by different rules. However, as adolescents begin to realize that adults struggle with many of the same issues that confuse and frighten adolescents, they can begin to trust adults more and see them as potential models. As adolescents discover that adults differ more in the processes they employ to solve their problems than in the degree to which problems exist, adolescents will more frequently use adults as models and resources.

It is unfortunate and damaging that adults and young people have so little real, personalized contact. To a large degree young people deal with adults only as roles. They see adults as teachers, counselors, parents, or ministers instead of as real people who laugh, cry, struggle, dream, and search to find their place in a world that sometimes seems frightening and tiring. Therefore, it is no wonder that when confronted with doubt, fear, or pain adolescents so often turn to their peers or to behavioral patterns that adults view as self-destructive. If adults expect adolescents to turn to them for assistance, they must allow adolescents to see that adults also face and cope with problems.

Sharing Reactions to Present Happenings People who have worked as special education teachers, camp counselors, residential treatment staff, or in similar positions that allow close contact with relatively small numbers of adolescents may readily identify with the above discussion. However, classroom teachers who work with as many as two hundred adolescents a day frequently note that such openness and self-disclosure are neither practical nor appropriate. Furthermore, many adults do not feel comfortable sharing their own personal experiences with others.

Fortunately, many of the advantages associated with self-disclosure and open communication can be obtained by simply responding openly and honestly to the situation at hand. Perhaps the major advantage associated with this type of self-disclosure is its potential for eliminating misunderstanding by enhancing a mutual understanding of thoughts, feelings, and behaviors occurring within a particular setting. In addition, this type of interchange allows adolescents to understand adults' feelings and thus enables them to view adults as people instead of roles.

An example of a situation in which this type of self-disclosure resulted in considerable relief to a teacher may serve to highlight the points being made. Not long ago while teaching one of my classes, I noticed that several students had made paper airplanes and were writing notes on them and sending them across the class. My first inclination was to wonder whether my presentation was boring the students. From here my mind wandered to questions about whether the students needed a break, whether the room was too warm, etc. I became aware of the fact that these thoughts were not only distracting my ability to present the material, but also were making me quite uncomfortable. Realizing that the worst that could happen would be that I would receive a negative response to my presentation, I shared my discomfort and annoyance with the class. Much to my surprise the students informed me that they were simply testing me out to see whether I would in fact employ the communication techniques that we had discussed and practiced several days earlier. The students' need to see me "practice what I preached" seemed perfectly legitimate and we spent several minutes discussing how they responded to my intervention and how it might have been improved.

By sharing their reactions to situations as they occur, people can clarify misunderstandings that may exist within a situation. The obvious costs associated with this type of sharing are the risks involved and the time commitment made. However, it frequently happens that people waste more time, expend more energy, and experience more discomfort speculating about others' behavior than they would by actually exploring this behavior.

Another major advantage associated with this form of openness is its potential for providing individuals with valuable feedback. Adolescents require feedback in order to develop a clearer and more mature sense of who they are and how they relate to their environment. Adults do little to assist this development if they respond to adolescents' behavior with immediate authoritarian control. Instead, adults need to provide information regarding how they respond to adolescents' behavior. This information should then be accompanied by efforts to assist adolescents in examining their behavior and its causes.

Perceiving Openness as a "Soft," Time-Consuming Approach   The obvious advantage accompanying this belief about adult-adolescent communication is that in the short run it saves the adult both time and energy. More poignantly, it shields adults from experiencing the risks inherent in an open examination of their behavior. As Carl Rogers stated:

> Very rarely do we permit ourselves to understand precisely what the meaning of his statement is to him. I believe this is because understanding is risky. If I let myself really understand another person, I might be changed by that understanding. And we all fear change. (Rogers, 1961, p. 18)

All people want to see themselves as competent individuals whose behavior is not harmful to others. As Festinger's (1957) theory of cognitive dissonance points out, this is especially true if people have invested considerable time and energy in the behavior in question. No one wants to be informed that a behavior that they have employed for ten years is perceived by others as negative or ineffective.

While a lack of openness may create a certain degree of safety, it has several major disadvantages. First, by refusing to openly discuss their needs and expectations as well as those experienced by adolescents, adults create a situation in which their controlling behavior runs counter to adolescents' basic developmental need for increased responsibility and independence. Thus adults become the adversary and adolescents attempt to subvert what they perceive to be adults' arbitrary behavior. In the long run, it appears that adults expend far more energy in their attempt to control adolescents than they would by engaging in problem-solving dialogue. As a friend of mine once said, "I would rather go home tired from having interacted with students all day than to go home exhausted from having tried to keep the lid on them all day."

There are several additional disadvantages associated with adult-adolescent relationships characterized by authoritarian, one-way communication. First, adolescents are less likely to model adults who employ this type of relationship. If adults have worthwhile skills and values that they wish to transmit to adolescents, they should not employ communication patterns that reduce the likelihood that adolescents will be influenced by what they do and say. Finally, people who are submissive and compliant frequently learn to fear people in authority positions. Unless adults are willing to admit that they want to create a citizenry that is fearful of responsibility and authority, they must not expect adolescents to respond passively to attempts to structure their lives. Nor should adults expect adolescents to behave passively until some designated moment at which they will miraculously be transformed into responsible adults. Rather adults should provide them with ever-increasing access to adult concerns and involvement in decisions that affect them.

SUMMARY

Adults who work with adolescents must make a decision regarding how they will interact with adolescents. When making this decision adults must not only consider their own needs and preferences but also consider the impact their behavior will have upon the adolescents with whom they work. While theories and research suggest that openness is a positive quality within adult-adolescent relationships, each adult must determine the degree to which such relationships should be characterized by openness. When making this decision, it is helpful to consider the advantages and disadvantages associated with various levels of openness. The information presented in this chapter suggests that adolescent development is facilitated by adult-adolescent relationships in which both parties provide the other with immediate and honest feedback concerning their reactions to the other's behavior. In addition, while a high level of personal self-disclosure is not appropriate or desirable in all situations, the transition from adolescence to adulthood can be facilitated by adults establishing open, caring personal relationships with adolescents.

CHAPTER
4

Communication Skills That Facilitate Positive Interpersonal Relationships and Effective Problem Solving

Effective communication is central to all interactions with adolescents. Whether adults' contact with adolescents involves teaching them mathematics or asking them to examine their seemingly unproductive behavior, the results obtained will be significantly influenced by the quality of the interpersonal relationship. Therefore, while communication skills should not be seen as an end in themselves, they are a vital and necessary means to an end.

While many adults who work with adolescents accept and understand the benefits associated with positive, open, two-way communication, they frequently feel frustrated by their lack of training in the area of communication and their subsequent inability to employ effective communication techniques. For example, despite the fact that teachers consistently list discipline problems as a major concern, many schools of education continue to totally ignore or skim over training aimed at assisting teachers to develop effective communication and problem-solving skills. This chapter will attempt to respond to this deficit by examining the major communication skills that can assist teachers in establishing positive, productive relationships with students and colleagues.

The usefulness of this section will depend on the reader's willingness to actually employ these techniques in the classroom or when working individually with a behavior-problem adolescent. Since at least some of the behaviors suggested in the following section will be new to the reader, it will not always be easy to implement them. Consequently, it may prove useful to first try these techniques in a situation that is somewhat safer than with a group of thirty students or when confronted by a screaming adolescent or an irate teacher or parent. Indeed, since the skills outlined below can have a positive influence on any relationship, it might prove enjoyable and productive to first attempt them in interactions with friends and family.

These skills do not carry a guarantee for instant success. Although they are an extremely important factor in facilitating learning, assisting individuals in changing their behavior, and establishing enjoyable relationships, there is no guarantee that the receiver will immediately respond positively, or that behavior-problem students will instantly improve their behavior. In fact, the adolescent (or even an adult) may initially test a person's willingness to consistently employ this style of interaction. Therefore, anyone who plans on employing good communication skills should know their potential advantages and be sincerely committed to consistently using these skills.

There are several major advantages that can be derived from consistently employing the communication skills discussed in this chapter. These include: (1) They enable people to be friendly with and enjoy others, and at the same time allow them to meet their own needs and maintain their integrity within the relationship. (2) They allow people to accept the other person and experience positive attitudes toward them. (3) They enable people to be open, honest and congruent within the relationship. (4) They enable people to understand the other person and to create a situation in which the other person perceives himself as being cared for and understood.

The specific communication skills that enhance the development of such relationships can be divided into two categories: sending skills and receiving skills. Sending skills are those communication skills people use when speaking to another person. Receiving skills are techniques people use to become more effective listeners.

SENDING SKILLS

While different authors have developed various lists, the key sending skills include:

1. Dealing in the here and now. Information is most useful when it is shared at the earliest appropriate opportunity.
2. Talking directly to people rather than about them. This action assures that the message is received more accurately; it also shows respect for the receiver and enables him to provide valuable clarifying information.
3. Speaking courteously. Nothing does more to enhance positive interaction than employing simple courtesies such as "please," "thank you," etc. Contacts with adolescents should include the same courtesies that adults employ when interacting with their adult friends.
4. Making eye contact and being aware of nonverbal messages. If you are talking to someone and looking over their shoulder, your nonverbal behavior makes it difficult for the person to believe that you are really involved in the conver-

sation. Similarly, if a teacher shouts at the class, "I am not angry with you!" they are more likely to respond to the teacher's tone of voice and facial expressions than to the words.

5. Taking responsibility for statements by using the personal pronoun, "I." Sending "we" messages stacks the deck against the receiver. If a person says, "We think that . . ." or "The staff believes that . . . ," they are taking an unfair advantage. Furthermore, since people are experts only about themselves, it appears reasonable that they can accurately share their feelings or beliefs, but must let other people speak for themselves. Also, it is important to express feelings rather than stating opinions or beliefs in the form of "you" messages. Therefore, if a person says, "You are a dominating person," it will likely increase your defensiveness. If, on the other hand, that person says, "I felt very uncomfortable when you interrupted me during the meeting," that person has owned the problem and provided some interesting information.

6. Making statements rather than asking questions. Most questions have an underlying statement behind them. By identifying and sharing the statement the speaker provides the receiver with valuable information. Asking a question puts the receiver on the defensive. For example, if a teacher arrives late to school and the principal asks, "Where have you been?" the teacher is (depending on why he or she is late) likely to feel defensive, annoyed, nervous, or hurt. If, on the other hand, the principal says, "I was really worried because I did not have anyone to cover your class," the teacher has been given some valuable information.

7. Giving specific, descriptive, nonevaluative feedback. For example, when a student's constant talking out is annoying, the teacher might say, "When you talk to your friends while I am talking, it makes me feel bad." Compare this statement to a general, evaluative statement such as, "You are so rude in this class that I can hardly believe it." The former statement provides useful information while the latter borders on name calling.

A closer examination of these communication skills may serve to clarify their value as well as their application to interactions with behavior-problem adolescents.

Dealing in the Here and Now

Feedback is the most useful when it is shared while the situation and the associated feelings are still fresh in everyone's mind. When people discuss behaviors that occurred yesterday or two days ago, they increase the likelihood that they will become embroiled in a debate concerning what really happened. Furthermore, failing to deal immediately with a situation dissipates the benefits associated with sharing feelings. The individual being spoken to can quite legitimately state that since the feelings are not present it makes little sense to talk about past history.

However, although giving immediate feedback is almost always the best policy in dyadic interaction, it may not be the best decision in a group situation. Immediate feedback may be necessary in those instances where the behavior is extremely harmful or disruptive. However, people must always weigh the advantages of giving the feedback against the possibility that it may not be heard in a particular setting at a particular time. For example, if a student is being loud or obscene in front of his friends during lunch, adult feedback, no matter how well presented, may simply stimulate a defensive, challenging reaction. In such situations it is frequently more productive to wait for an opportunity to speak with the student alone. While peer approval is important to all adolescents, it is particularly important to behavior-problem adolescents. These students frequently have had poor relationships with adults and consequently depend more extensively upon their peers for support. Furthermore, it is likely that their peers are more supportive of behavior that runs counter to adult desires. Therefore, it is quite possible that even though the adolescent might respond positively to adult feedback when alone with that adult, he may well challenge the adult in front of his peers.

Talking Directly to People Rather Than about Them

This skill has major implications for working with adolescents. Adolescents, especially those involved in extensive inappropriate behaviors, have a tendency to distrust and question adults. To a certain degree this questioning is part of the normal develop-mental tasks of seeking to develop a sense of independence and establishing a personal identity. However, for the behavior-problem adolescent this questioning has often been accentuated by frequent negative unsupportive interactions with adults.

Given their tendency to question adults and their need for adult approval, it is understandable that adolescents are sensitive to indications that adults are insincere or uncaring. Adolescents often respond angrily to situations in which adults express negative views about adolescents, but fail to share these feelings directly with the adolescents. Several years ago I had an opportunity to experience the power with which adolescents respond to adult "gossip" about adolescents. The situation occurred in a small, rural high school that was confronted with an extreme lack of motivation and considerable acting out by a surprisingly large portion of the student body. Discussions with teachers and students revealed a disturbing, but important, clue about the cause of the problem. It appeared that the faculty lounge was the scene of numerous negative conversations about the quality of students attending the school. Since the faculty lounge was next to a photography lab that students used during the lunch period, students had on several occasions overheard the teachers' discussions. This information had spread throughout the school, and students felt understandably hurt and angry. The only means for improving this situation was to create a series of opportunities for the teachers and students to discuss their feelings and to clarify their needs and expectations.

This situation provides an extreme example of adults' tendency to share their feelings about adolescents' behaviors with adults rather than directly with adolescents. However, there are numerous, less extreme ways in which adults withhold useful feedback from adolescents. For example, when developing intervention programs for behavior-problem adolescents, educators frequently employ staffings in which a wide variety of teachers and specialists get together to discuss a particular student's problem and develop an intervention strategy. While there may be small portions of such staffings from which the student should be excluded, the student being discussed should be actively involved in these meetings. Such involvement tends to serve a variety of functions. First, it increases the sense of both competence and power the adolescent feels. This has obvious positive benefits concerning the adolescent's self-concept. Second, since everyone is the world's best expert on him- or herself, the adolescent's input can provide valuable information concerning what type of educational or behavioral intervention is most likely to succeed. Third, by directly involving adolescents in this process educators enhance the likelihood that the adolescents will have a sense of personal investment in the success of the program. If educators do not involve the adolescents, they set up a situation that forces the adolescents to demonstrate their sense of independence and personal potency by attempting to subvert the educators' manipulations.

The value of involving adolescents in their own behavior change can also be related to Lewin's (1948) concept of the "marginal man." Adults expect adolescents to behave in acceptable, adultlike ways, but treat them as children by assuming that they are not mature enough to be involved in important aspects of changing their own behavior. The confusing message transmitted by this type of adult behavior can do little to assist adolescents in developing a stable, mature, satisfactory self-identity.

There is a final point that is extremely important about talking directly to people rather than about them. People frequently assume that telling someone that their behavior bothers them is a negative, punitive thing to do. However, providing people with feedback concerning their behavior, is in effect giving them a gift—caring enough about the relationship to want to see it maintained and improved. Conversely, a person's talking about others rather than providing them with direct feedback, indicates that the relationship is not meaningful enough to warrant the effort involved in maintaining the relationship.

When examining the hesitancy people often experience in directly and honestly sharing their reactions to others' behavior, it is interesting to ask who they are really protecting. When people decide not to share their positive or negative reactions to someone's behavior, they are often protecting themselves from having to deal with the other person's response to their feedback. When adults work with young people who are experiencing problems, they should not deprive those young people of valuable information simply to protect themselves. This concept applies equally to adults' interactions with colleagues and parents who are working with disturbed youngsters. Adults do the youngsters a real disservice when they fail to productively confront other adults about their interactions with these students. All too often adults' unwillingness to involve themselves in such interactions occurs because they do not want to deal with the discomfort that may be associated with such interactions. By employing the communication skills presented in this section, adults can take a major step in making these interchanges both more productive and more comfortable for both parties.

Speaking Courteously

The sending skill that has the most impact on adolescents' perception of adults is the degree to which adults extend them simple courtesies. Saying "thank you," "please," or "How are you feeling today?" can do a great deal to indicate adults' respect for adolescents. This point was vividly highlighted recently when a graduate student who had raised a family and was returning to teaching, commented that she was amazed at the lack of courtesy shown in the schools. When asked if she was referring to students' lack of respect for teachers, she indicated that she was much more aware of the lack of courtesy that teachers extended to adolescents. At this point someone reminded her that teachers are involved in a tremendous number of interactions each day. Her pointed yet sensitive response to this defense was that she saw clerks at the supermarket responding more courteously to their customers. Every year I have the opportunity of working with between one hundred and one hundred and fifty college students who are teaching or observing in public schools as part of their preservice teacher training. In responding to and analyzing their experiences, their most common critical response relates to the lack of respect that teachers show their students.

These comments are not meant to imply that all or even a majority of teachers fail to offer students the daily courtesies that are so important in maintaining positive interpersonal encounters. However, teachers do often fail to treat students courteously, and this behavior does have a major impact upon student motivation and behavior. Behavior-problem students (and unfortunately a surprisingly large percentage of "normal" students) too often perceive the schools in terms of us against them. Classrooms become either covertly or overtly, and to varying degrees, a battle ground in which the teacher has the artillery and the students counter with guerilla warfare. Although speaking courteously to students (and having students in turn respond courteously to teachers and their peers) is only one step in creating more comfortable, safe, positive school environments, it is perhaps the foundation from which all other changes begin. If teachers do not like, trust, and respond positively to students, it is unlikely that they will employ a broad range of productive teaching strategies that provide students with greater responsibility and serve to assist them in working through the developmental tasks outlined in Chapter 1.

Making Eye Contact and Being Aware of Nonverbal Messages

People frequently respond as much or more to how something is said than to what is said. Students consistently note that they prefer teachers who are enthusiastic and who demonstrate an excitement about their subject matter. Similarly, clients are influenced in important ways by the manner in which the therapist behaves during a counseling session. Most therapists are aware of the fact that when they are more intense and excited, their clients become more alert and energized. Conversely, their being calm tends to have a calming affect on the client. These clinical observations have direct application to adults' interactions with behavior-problem adolescents. When interacting with a highly anxious or emotional student, it is important to remain calm. On the other hand, when working with a very passive, compliant youth, it is sometimes useful to increase the level of interest and intensity. This does not mean that adults must be incongruent and attempt to play a role when dealing with adolescents. However, it does mean that as professionals they can monitor the manner in which they express themselves in order to make more effective interventions with the young people they are attempting to help.

Taking Responsibility for Statements by Using the Personal Pronoun, "I"

There is probably no single communication skill more important than this one. In my work with regular classroom teachers over the past ten years, teachers have consistently stated that increasing their use of this skill had more effect on reducing classroom discipline problems than any other skill or strategy. An understanding of adolescent development provides several reasons why this is the case. First, an "I message" is a prerequisite for establishing a meaningful relationship in which the other person feels cared for and significant. By expressing a willingness to share a part of themselves, teachers indicate that the relationship (and consequently the other person) is of value to them. By sharing part of themselves, teachers break away from what Martin Buber (1958) calls I-It relationships and begin to develop I-Thou relationships, which are characterized by mutual respect and concern. Second, as discussed earlier, openly disclosing their feelings enables teachers to be seen more as individuals and less as a role. Since people tend to abuse roles rather than people, the development of such relationships significantly reduces the likelihood that students will intentionally and maliciously abuse teachers' rights. A third advantage associated with sending "I messages" is that they help to reduce the degree of authoritarian dominance displayed by adults and consequently enable adolescents to experience a greater sense of independence and control over their life space. Finally, the information transmitted by such open communication provides adolescents with much needed information that can assist them in clarifying their values and increasing their cognitive understanding of their environment.

While there are tremendous advantages associated with sending "I messages," there are several dangers associated with employing this skill. First, it is unlikely that adolescents will respond positively to adults' open expression of feeling if they have not previously established a positive relationship with adolescents. I am reminded of a situation that occurred in an adolescent psychology class I taught several years ago. One of the tasks I assigned was for each teacher to employ an "I message" with their students. At the beginning of the class session following the assignment, a teacher noted with anger and concern that when he had tried telling his class that their noisy behavior made him feel uncomfortable, they had intensified their noise and several students had responded by shouting, "Who cares!" This instance highlights an important point concerning open and honest interaction with adolescents. This type of communication will not (and should not) be effective when sporadically employed as a method for controlling adolescents' behavior and meeting the adult's needs. If adults attempt to employ openness in this manner, adolescents will justifiably resent this manipulative ploy and will seize the opportunity to take advantage of adults' momentary vulnerability. "I messages" will be effective only in settings that are characterized by consistent mutual respect and honesty.

There is a second way in which "I messages" are frequently abused. Although sharing information concerning feelings is often useful, it is not useful when people employ communication jargon as a means for disguising subtle put-downs. A common method, often unintentionally employed, is using the word "feel" in place of the words "think" or "believe." For example, when teachers say to a student, "I feel that you are a disruptive factor in this class," they are using a feigned openness to punish the student. The student may believe that he cannot argue with the teacher about an expressed feeling. However, what the teacher has done is disguise his or her real feelings. People feel emotions such as hurt, sadness, pain, anger, and joy. But, people cannot feel that someone is disruptive. They can, however, think that someone is disruptive, describe the behavior that is bothering them, and share the emotions elicited by the behavior.

Two types of "I messages" provide honest and productive communication tools. The first is discussed by Thomas Gordon in his excellent book entitled, *Teacher Effectiveness Training* (1974). Gordon notes that "I messages" have three basic components. First, they inform the student what particular behavior concerns or pleases the teacher. Second, they indicate the tangible effect this behavior has on the teacher. Third, they state the feeling generated by that tangible effect. Therefore, if a student is talking out in class, a teacher might state, "When you talk when I am talking, it makes it hard for me to concentrate, and I am also worried that you are finding my presentation boring."

The second major type of "I message" is one that focuses on peoples' open expression of their needs. When people tell others that they should or must do something, they are usually telling them what they want them to do. Consequently, it is clearer and more honest if people simply state their wants openly. For example, a person may say, "I was hurt by our recent interaction, and I would like some time to discuss what happened." This statement provides more helpful information than if the person said, "You should stop acting that way." Similarly, a teacher may inform a class, "I am concerned about the lack of assignments being completed, and would like to discuss this problem." This statement is different from informing the class that they should stop being so lazy.

Making Statements rather than Asking Questions

When assisting adolescents in solving their problems, adults need to be careful not to bombard them with questions. Questions have several major drawbacks. First, they often make a person feel threatened or defensive. Adolescents frequently indicate that when talking to adults about their problems, they feel like they are receiving the "third degree."

> If I want to communicate with you, I must keep you informed of my feelings. A question often hides my feelings. It is sometimes my attempt to discover your position before I reveal mine, or it sometimes hides a criticism I don't want to risk stating. If I ask you, "Why do you say that" or "Is that what you really think," I show you little of what I am feeling. Instead I put you on the defensive without making it clear what it is in me I want you to respond to. (Prather, 1970)

Second, individuals can be "turned off" by questions that fail to apply to their problem. If adults are consistently off target, adolescents rightfully begin to wonder whether adults really understand them or have been listening to them. Finally, questions have a tendency to structure the conversation and, therefore, may prevent adolescents from dealing with their real feelings.

As discussed in the following section on receiving skills, questions can be replaced by simply listening to the adolescent. Listening often provides access to important information that adolescents seldom share when pressured by constant questions. As mentioned previously, questions can also be replaced by statements. Therefore, rather than ask a student why he did not hand in an assignment, a teacher might say, "I am concerned about your work in class."

This is not meant to indicate that questions are never helpful. There are times when questions are necessary and appropriate tools for helping individuals understand themselves and their environment. More specifically, there are several questions that are particularly valuable when working with adolescents. First, it is helpful to ask adolescents how they are feeling. Adolescents, particularly boys with behavior problems, find it difficult to describe their feelings. Their inability to get in touch with their feelings has major implications concerning adolescents' ability to cope with their environment and alter their behavior. People's interpretations of their environment and consequently their behavior is significantly affected by their awareness of their feelings. For example, when students complain to adults about a teacher, they are focusing attention on the teacher's behavior. While the teacher's behavior may indeed be destructive and in need of change, focusing on this behavior will do little to assist the adolescents to understand themselves and their reactions to their environment. Therefore, rather than focusing on the teacher's behavior, it is useful to ask the students to focus on how the situation makes them feel.

When asked to describe their feelings, adolescents frequently respond that they feel angry. Since anger is a secondary feeling, it is almost always associated with such feelings as hurt, loneliness, anxiety, or embarrassment. Therefore, when adolescents state that they are angry, it is helpful to ask them to identify other feelings they are experiencing. As adolescents are able to gain access to these feelings, they develop a better understanding of their environment. This in turn not only enables them to deal more effectively with their environment, but also provides them with an enhanced sense of competency and potency. Once an adolescent has clarified the feelings that are elicited in a specific setting, it is much easier to pinpoint the environmental factors that are eliciting these feelings. Finally, once pinpointed, it is obviously much easier to attempt to alter these factors, or to deal with the reality that these behaviors cannot be changed.

A second question that helps adolescents is to ask them how they would ideally like the situation to be. Although adolescents have little difficulty expressing dislike for situations, they often experience considerable difficulty specifying how they would like the situation altered. If adults are to assist adolescents in developing a better understanding of their environment, they must assist adolescents in clarifying their needs and wants. The adolescent's life space is characterized by intense, diffuse emotions and confusion caused by an inability to abstractly examine an increasingly complex personal and physical environment. Therefore, it is helpful to assist them to slow down and examine their behavior and others' reactions to that behavior. When adults insist upon providing the answers or attempting to change the environment according to their interpretations of adolescents' needs, adults are developing a dependent relationship that runs counter to adolescents' developmental needs. While it is often more time consuming and frustrating, adults must involve adolescents in making decisions concerning how to alter their environment or their behaviors.

Giving Specific, Descriptive, Nonevaluative Feedback

Adolescents are going through a period of intensified self-consciousness and low self-esteem. Consequently, they have a tendency to take feedback very personally. Thus adults must clearly separate their responses to adolescents as individuals from their responses to adolescents' behavior. The best method for accomplishing this is to make sure that adults clearly pinpoint the behaviors to which they respond positively or negatively. For example, adolescents will likely be hurt and respond defensively to being told that they are acting like children. However, they are likely to accept a statement that indicates that teachers feel frustrated when they give adolescents responsibility for planning a lesson and they come to class unprepared.

While less obvious than in the case of negative behavior, it is equally important to pinpoint the specific behaviors that elicit positive responses. If teachers inform a student that he has been "good" in class, they have given him little useful information. In fact, this form of feedback can have potentially negative consequences. In discussing this issue, Carl Rogers stated:

> Curiously enough, a positive evaluation is as threatening in the long run as a negative one, since to inform someone that he is good implies that you also have the right to tell him that he is bad. So I have come to feel that the more I can keep a relationship free of judgment and evaluation, the more this will permit the other person to reach the point that he recognizes that the locus of evaluation, the center of responsibility, lies within himself. (Rogers, 1961, p. 55)

The type of positive feedback teachers provide students has been shown to influence learning. Page (1958) asked a group of junior high school teachers to provide three types of feedback on exams: (1) grade only, (2) a grade and a positive statement such as "Good exam," "Well written," and (3) statements that provide support, but also identify specific strengths and weaknesses regarding the student's work. Page's results showed that students who received more extensive and specific feedback showed the largest amount of improvement in later tests.

Specific, nonjudgmental feedback is as important in influencing behavior change as it is in enhancing learning. In order to change their behavior, people must deal with finite, observable behaviors. If someone is told that they are obnoxious, there is little they can do to change that quality, since they can only speculate what the person means by the word "obnoxious." However, if someone is told, "I feel anxious when you ramble on during department meetings," they have been given some valuable information. What is bothering the person has been specified, and the specificity enables the individual to check to see whether others perceive them as talking too much at department meetings and whether others are also bothered by this behavior. Adolescents are no different from adults in their need to receive specific, nonevaluative data as a prerequisite to change. A good rule of thumb is: If you cannot pinpoint the behavior, do not give the feedback.

Because they are grappling with serious questions about themselves and their relationship to their environment, adolescents make multiple demands upon adults. Adolescents expect and need adults to serve as models, to productively cope with challenges and questions, to provide them with increasing independence and respon- sibility, and to serve as a source of information and support. These demanding and sometimes conflicting expectations frequently place considerable tension on adult- adolescent interactions. Therefore, it is vital that adults employ effective sending skills in order to insure clarity and stability within such often demanding relationships. If effectively employed, the sending skills described in this section can have a tremen- dous influence on the quality of adult-adolescent relationships.

RECEIVING OR LISTENING SKILLS

Receiving skills are extremely important tools to employ when working with behavior-problem youngsters. When effectively employed, good listening skills can create a situation in which the adolescent feels understood and valued. Equally important is the fact that good listening skills can assist adolescents in getting in touch with their feelings and developing a clear understanding of themselves and their reactions to their environment. While listening skills may be categorized in a variety of ways, the three major listening skills are:

1. Empathetic, nonevaluative listening. This skill is also variously called active listening or paraphrasing. The key concept here is to create a safe, nonjudg- mental setting that allows the speaker to openly express his thoughts and feelings. This expression enables the speaker to reduce the tension and anxiety frequently associated with hiding his feelings. It also enables adolescents to deal openly with feelings rather than expressing feelings through unproductive behaviors. Finally, listening nonevaluatively provides an opportunity for thoughts and feelings to be examined and clarified. The three skills adults can employ to create a situation in which adolescents feel understood include: (1) paraphrasing or active listening, (2) acknowledging, and (3) interpretive percep- tion checking.
2. Perception checking. This skill is employed as a method for determining whether or not people have accurately interpreted someone's statements or behavior. A perception check simply means saying: "This is what I heard you say. Am I correct?"
3. Awareness of personal biases that may influence responses to others. All people have certain biases that have been created by their own experiences and the things they have been taught. For example, if parents consistently informed their children that people can "pull themselves up by their own bootstraps" and those children in fact overcame considerable adversity to reach their current positions, it may be difficult for them to understand why the behavior-problem adolescent cannot do the same thing. Similarly, people who were successful in school and found education to be a rewarding experience, may have difficulty understanding students who perceive school as a frightening, punitive environ- ment.

A more indepth examination of each of these skills will help to clarify their role in working with behavior-problem adolescents.

Empathetic, Nonevaluative Listening

Before discussing the techniques involved in empathetic listening and the reasons why this skill is so valuable in working with adolescents, it is important to note that effective empathetic listening assumes that adults hold certain basic beliefs about adolescents and their feelings. First, they must trust adolescents' ability to solve their own problems. All too often, adults listen to adolescents just long enough to find out what advice to give them. Empathetic listening, when effectively employed, is designed to assist adolescents in developing their own understandings and solutions. Second, adults need to be willing to accept adolescents' feelings and the solutions to problems that may result from adolescents becoming more aware of their feelings and behaviors. Third, adults who employ empathetic listening must be willing to take the time to assist adolescents in working through their problems. Listening, reflecting, and clarifying take much more time and patience than advice giving.

As is the case with good sending skills, the use of empathetic listening does a great deal to assist adolescents in productively working through their major developmental tasks. Increased cognitive and moral development are facilitated by experiencing disequilibrium and struggling to create a new and more sophisticated understanding. Adolescents who question and struggle with their environment develop higher levels of moral thought than those who readily accept adult decisions and values (Podd, 1972). In addition, adolescents must examine and question their values and decisions if they are to develop their own unique identity. Allowing adolescents to explore their own feelings and examine their own behaviors also positively affects their ability to understand and order their life space. Listening nonjudgmentally to adolescents enables them to discuss their uncertainty and to begin to create order and clarity out of their confusion. Finally, it is vital that adolescents have increasing responsibility in solving their own problems. Adolescents will not learn how to solve their own problems if adults constantly provide solutions for them. Young people will not suddenly become effective problem solvers simply because they reach eighteen years of age or graduate from high school.

One of the best examples I have seen of a helping agent failing to employ effective listening skills and consequently violating the personal integrity and blocking the potential growth of an adolescent occurred at a mental hospital. As a staff member finished locking a patient in a security room, a sixteen-year-old male patient came up to him and said, "You shouldn't do that. No one should be treated like that. There must be a better way." The staff member replied gruffly, "If you keep making trouble, I'll throw you in one too!" The young patient's face reflected a powerful combination of fear, sorrow, and confusion as he walked away and said softly, "It just shouldn't be like this."

This scene presented an excellent example of a situation in which good listening skills and effective, two-way communication could have provided a therapeutic learning session for both the staff member and the patient. Instead, the interchange only further confused the client and could understandably have pushed him further into his world of self-designed symbols and meanings. Adults cannot expect adolescents to opt for the adult world and the acceptance of adult values if those values too frequently deny adolescents' integrity and value.

Once adults accept the idea that adolescents can respond productively to empathetic listening, and are willing to spend the time necessary to productively employ this communication skill, the next issue centers on learning how to listen empathetically. This form of listening consists of three subtly distinct skills. When used in isolation, each of these skills has major limitations. However, when sensitively synthesized, they create a highly effective therapeutic tool. The three skills that combine to create effective empathetic nonjudgmental listening are: (1) Paraphrasing or active listening, (2) Acknowledging, and (3) Interpretive perception checks.

Paraphrasing or Active Listening In their book, *Learning Together and Alone*, Johnson and Johnson present seven guidelines to employ this skill. These guidelines are:

General Guidelines for Paraphrasing

1. Restate the sender's expressed ideas and feelings in your own words rather than mimicking or parroting her exact words.
2. Preface paraphrased remarks with "You think. . . ." "Your position is. . . ." "It seems to you that. . . ." "You feel that. . . ." and so on.
3. Avoid any indication of approval or disapproval.
4. Make your nonverbal messages congruent with your verbal paraphrasing, look attentive, interested, and open to the sender's ideas and feelings, and show that you are concentrating upon what the sender is trying to communicate.
5. State as accurately as possible what you heard the sender say and describe the feelings and attitudes involved.
6. Do not add or subtract from the sender's message.
7. Put yourself in the sender's shoes and try to understand what it is he is feeling and what his message means. (David W. Johnson, Roger T. Johnson, *Learning Together and Alone: Cooperation, Competition, and Individualization*, 1975, p. 102. Reprinted by permission of Prentice-Hall, Inc., Englewood Cliffs, New Jersey.)

An example may help to clarify the way to use this listening skill. Several years ago, a friend reported having the following interchange with her nine-year-old daughter. The daughter approached the mother one morning and informed her that she hated the babysitter who had been with her the previous night. At this point, several factors might have prevented the mother from effectively listening to her child. First, she could have responded to the word "hate" and begun a sermon on the fact that the girl should not hate anyone. Second, since she lived in an area where it was difficult to find a babysitter, the mother could have invested considerable effort in convincing her daughter that the babysitter was in fact a very nice girl. Instead, perhaps because she was an excellent elementary school counselor, the mother employed effective listening skills. Her initial response to her daughter was, "You really don't like the babysitter, do you?" The daughter responded by agreeing and noting that the babysitter burned the dinner. Since the babysitter never washed the dishes and the mother had never seen a burned pan, she again had an excellent opportunity to deny and correct the daughter's perception of the situation. Instead, however, she said, "You really don't like the way she does things, do you?" The daughter's response was again to agree and to note that furthermore, the babysitter made the children go to bed early. Since the children were allowed to stay up half an hour later when a babysitter was present, the mother again could have confronted her daughter with her misperception. Instead, she again reflected on the daughter's statement and said, "You really don't like having the babysitter here, do you?" At this point, the daughter responded, "No, and you're gone too much, Mom." By listening nonjudgmentally, the mother had allowed both herself and her daughter access to an important need and a vital issue.

This form of listening has the advantage of assuring the speaker that he has been heard while at the same time allowing the speaker an opportunity to correct the listener if the listener's paraphrasing does not accurately reflect the speaker's meaning. However, when used excessively with adolescents, this form of listening has a major drawback. Since the listener restates the speaker's statement (albeit in somewhat different form), the listener may believe that he is being parroted. Teenagers report that they find paraphrasing demeaning when excessively employed. On several occasions when I have employed too much paraphrasing, I have had adolescents make comments such as "That's what I just said" or "Would you stop mimicking me?" Paraphrasing seems to be more effective when employed with younger children. However, when used with discretion, it is a valuable part of a professional's repertoire of listening skills.

Acknowledging   This form of listening was popularized by Carl Rogers in his work on client-centered psychotherapy. Rather than paraphrasing or interpreting the speaker's statement, the listener indicates his interest by maintaining eye contact and employing such verbal acknowledgments as "Uh-uh," "M-hm," "Yes," "I can see that," and "I understand." Like paraphrasing, this form of listening is least effective when employed in isolation. However, it is an effective listening tool when interspersed with paraphrasing and interpretive perception checks.

Interpretive Perception Checks   Interpretive perception checks are reflective questions the listener asks to assist the speaker in clarifying his thoughts and feelings. While this is similar to perception checking as discussed in the following section, it has been included here because its goal of assisting adolescents to clarify their feelings, wants, and needs is more similar to that of paraphrasing or acknowledging. As mentioned previously, adolescents' increased ability to conceptualize, when combined with a rapidly changing body and increased societal expectations, creates an accentuated amount of confusion in the areas of feelings and values. Therefore, adults must assist adolescents in examining and sorting out these feelings and values.

While paraphrasing and acknowledging help to create an atmosphere in which adolescents can safely examine their feelings and behaviors, these forms of listening do not provide adolescents with interpretations or alternatives that may appear obvious to the listener, but that the adolescent cannot see. When people are struggling with their own problems, they often "cannot see the forest for the trees." Therefore, while it is seldom productive (especially with adolescents) to tell people what their problem is or how to solve it, it is frequently helpful to make comments that assist them to break through their own perceptual limitations. This can be accomplished most effectively by nonjudgmentally and sensitively offering interpretations for the speaker's acceptance or rejection.

Interpretive perception checks, therefore, include such reflective questions as "It's like you . . . ," "It's as though . . . ," "It seems that . . . ," "Are you aware that . . . ," "You mean that . . . ." These statements allow the listener to offer insight while maintaining the focus of responsibility on the speaker. If the adolescent rejects an interpretation, the listener will usually want to employ paraphrasing or acknowledging in order to remain consistent with the belief that the adolescent is his own best expert on himself and is responsible for his own behavior. There are, however, instances in which the listener may want to follow up on an interpretation that has been rejected. If, for example, the adolescent violently rejects an interpretation, it may be useful to make an intervention such as, "You seemed bothered by my comment. Can you get in touch with where that anger came from?"

Sample Interactions   Several examples of adult-adolescent interactions in which the adult employed all three major listening skills may help to clarify these skills. The following interaction is taken from a tape-recorded session with an eighteen-year-old girl who was extremely concerned about the grade she had received in my course.

Student (*angrily*):   I'd like to talk to you about the grade I got in your class.

Teacher: You seem upset about the grade. (*Interpretive perception check*)

Student: I am. I don't think that the grade you gave me was fair.

Teacher: You think the work you did deserved a better grade? (*Paraphrasing*)

Student: Yes. I did all the assignments and I came to class most of the time.

Teacher: M-hm. (*Acknowledging*)

Student: I don't see how you could give me a "C." I got a "B" on one of my papers and I had a "C+" on my final examination.

Teacher: It sounds like you're unclear about how much weight I gave each component. Would you like me to show you how I arrived at the grade? (*Interpretive perception check*)

Student: Well, no, I know that I didn't put a lot of effort into some of the work. It's just that I had a lot of hours this term and I just didn't have time to do my best work, but I did learn a lot.

Teacher: You don't think that your work was really a reflection of what you learned? (*Paraphrasing*)

Student: Yeah. And my grades weren't too good in my other classes and I'm worried about how this will look on my transcript.

Teacher: You mean that you're worried about what a principal or personnel director might think when they see "C's" in several education courses? (*Interpretive perception check*)

Student: Yeah. I mean I really don't think that the grades reflect what I know about the subjects, but they're the only thing that shows.

Teacher: It sounds as if you're worried about what you can do to demonstrate that you really can be an effective teacher. It also seems as if you're having some difficulty because you're taking a lot of classes. Do you want to discuss either of these problems, or do you want to spend some time talking about your grade in my class?

At this point, the student indicated that she really was most concerned about what she could do to show that she was more capable than her record indicated. This opened up the door to several sessions in which the student examined her goals, priorities, and feelings about herself.

Another example that demonstrates the use of all three components of empathetic, nonjudgmental listening occurred with a behavior-problem eighth grade boy. The boy was sent to my office after he had been asked to leave his English class because he defied the teacher's request that he sit down and get to work.

John:	I'm never going back to that classroom. Mrs. R. is a dumb bitch.
Counselor:	You're really upset about what happened in class today. (*Interpretive perception check*)
John:	Ya! That—— ——Jim poked Bill with a pencil and Mrs. R. blamed me for it.
Counselor:	M-hm. (*Acknowledging*)
John:	She's always blaming me for things other kids do and they know it so they do all kinds of things and I get blamed.
Counselor:	So you're getting set up by some of the other kids and Mrs. R. tends to believe them. (*Paraphrasing*)
John:	Yeah, that's right. I don't think the kids in the class like me. (John paused for a minute; his face became pensive and sad.) Ya know, I don't think hardly anybody here likes me.
Counselor:	John, you know there is a difference between liking someone and liking their behavior. I think you know that I like you, but I also get pretty upset at some of your behavior. (*Interpretation and "I message"*)
John:	You mean that kids may not like what I'm doing, and so they pick on me?
Counselor:	That's possible. Are there any other reasons they might pick on you and get you in trouble? (*Clarifying question*)

From here the conversation moved to a discussion of reasons why students tended to pick on John and what payoffs John received from these interactions. Chapter 13 will present several models for involving students in this form of problem solving. The important point being made here is that empathetic, nonjudgmental listening is the first step in problem solving. Problem solving cannot occur until the student feels understood and is able to discover and accept the problem.

Like any new skill, this type of listening may seem somewhat awkward when first employed. Consequently, it is often helpful to initially practice these listening skills in a relatively safe situation such as with family members and friends. Indeed, since these skills are important in establishing any type of positive personal relationship, they can prove valuable in peoples' everyday lives as well as in teacher-student or counselor-client relationships.

As with the other communication skills presented in this chapter, empathetic, nonjudgmental listening is most effective when used at the proper time. In his book, *Teacher Effectiveness Training* (1974), Thomas Gordon makes an important distinction concerning when to employ sending as opposed to receiving skills. Gordon notes that active listening should be employed when the student expresses a concern to the teacher. Therefore, when a student expresses a strong feeling or asks for assistance, the teacher should employ the skills presented in this section. Conversely, Gordon notes that when the teacher is bothered by something, the teacher must "own the problem" by sending an "I" message and employing the skills presented in the section on sending skills.

Several examples of situations in which teachers might be tempted to employ the incorrect skills may help to clarify this point. If a student is carving his name on a desk, most adults would be likely to tell the student to stop or ask the student what he is doing. In this situation, however, the problem is clearly the teacher's. If the student perceived a problem, he would not be carving in the desk. Therefore, the most effective strategy in this situation would be to say to the student, "Your behavior is bothering me," and explain why. If the student responds by apologizing and stopping the behavior, the problem is resolved. The problem arises if the student indicates that he does not care whether his behavior bothers the teacher. When this occurs, the next approach is to tell the student, "I have to share your environment and am responsible for certain aspects of this environment; it is important for us to discuss the problem that arises when you are not willing to respond to my needs." Students seldom refuse to become productively involved in such a dialogue if it is presented matter of factly and without threat. However, should the student refuse to discuss the problem or decide that the problem is still yours, the next step is to bring in a third party—perhaps a counselor, another teacher, or a building administrator—to attempt to clarify the issue. Students do not have a right to disobey logical rules or to make the classroom setting uncomfortable for others. Similarly, adults should not have the right to unilaterally and punitively enforce rules or correct distracting behavior. If valuable learning is to occur, students must understand why their behavior needs to be altered and must be involved in the process of altering it.

Another situation in which adults frequently become confused and employ an unproductive communication approach occurs when an adolescent consistently responds by saying, "I don't know." In such situations, it may initially be helpful to paraphrase the student's statement or to offer an interpretive perception check such as "You sound like you would rather have some time to think about this." However, there will be occasions when behavior-problem adolescents consistently respond in a passive-aggressive manner by refusing to become involved in discussing a problem. At this point it is helpful to send a firm "I message" such as, "When you refuse to work on the problem, I get really frustrated." This can then be combined with an interpretive perception check such as, "When you continually say, 'I don't know,' it seems that you are telling me that you want me to stop trying to help you with this problem. Is that correct?" As noted earlier, when a client is being passive it is sometimes helpful for counselors and teachers to increase their level of intensity. Furthermore, when teachers clarify their feelings and force some form of conflict resolution, they reduce the possibility that students will manipulate them into reinforcing their passivity. If students are unwilling to become actively involved in examining their own behavior, teachers should not continue to reinforce their un-involvement by continuing to apply listening as a strategy for initiating change.

Perception Checking

Perception checking is employed as a means to determine whether a person has accurately interpreted another person's statement or behavior. Unlike interpretive perception checks discussed in the preceding section, the goal of perception checking is to provide the receiver (rather than the sender) with information concerning the accuracy of the message being conveyed. For example, if a group of students are inattentive, a teacher may want to employ a perception check by asking the students whether the material is boring them, is too difficult, or if something else is causing their behavior. As noted earlier, everyone is the world's best expert about himself. Consequently, the only way to find out what someone else's statement or behavior means to them is to ask them. People often act ineffectively simply because they lack important information that is readily available if they would simply ask others about their actions. Therefore, if a teacher changes the topic of her presentation because she perceives the students to be bored when in fact they are hot and tired, she may deprive the students of some valuable learning (and modeling) because she has misinterpreted their behavior.

Another form that a perception check may take is to paraphrase an individual's statement to see whether it has been received accurately. This form of perception check is similar to interpretive perception checks discussed in the previous section in that while it is intended to provide clarity for the receiver, it may also provide new insight for the sender. Therefore, if a student says, "This work isn't worth doing." a perception check might be, "You mean that the work is too simple?" In asking this question, the initial intent is to clarify the meaning for the receiver. However, by requiring that the message be clear, the receiver may assist the speaker in clarifying his own feelings or thoughts.

A final type of perception check can occur when the sender asks the receiver to paraphrase what the speaker has just said. This form of paraphrasing is useful in determining whether students have correctly interpreted instructions. Rather than ask whether anyone has questions concerning the assignment, teachers can ask the students to paraphrase the directions by asking if someone can state what the class has been asked to do and how it will be evaluated. This type of paraphrasing is also useful when working with adolescents who have poor verbal retention skills. Several years ago, I worked with an adolescent who continually failed to benefit from interventions characterized by "I messages," interpretive perception checks, and verbal contractual agreements. Test results indicated that the boy had very poor verbal retention skills. The youngster wanted me to accept him and therefore agreed with my statements and the verbal agreements we made. However, much to my surprise, he understood very little of the important components regarding our discussions. After discovering this limitation, I began to make much shorter, more concrete statements and asked him to paraphrase what I had just said. This new approach made a dramatic difference in both our relationship and the student's behavior.

Awareness of Personal Biases that May Affect Responses to Others

The importance of people's becoming aware of their own biases has received considerable attention since Rosenthal and Jacobson (1968) discovered and popularized what has been called the Pygmalion Effect or self-fulfilling prophecy—the fact that people's beliefs about another person influence their expectations for the other person's behavior, which in turn affects the other person's behavior. Rosenthal's study did not examine how these expectations were transmitted. This question has been extensively researched by Brophy and Good (1970b, 1974). They discovered that teachers' expectations concerning student behavior and academic performance significantly affect both the quantity and quality of student-teacher interaction. For example, Brophy and Good report that:

> Process data have revealed that, when expectation effects are operating, teachers are likely to interact more frequently and more warmly with high expectation students, to observe them more carefully, to attempt to teach them more material, and to reinforce their successes more frequently and/or more intensely. (Brophy and Good, 1974, p. 76)

These findings have both obvious and more subtle implications concerning adults' interactions with adolescents and especially with behavior-problem adolescents. The research indicates that teachers are frequently unaware of the extent of their biases and are to a large degree unaware of the behaviors associated with these biases. Therefore, when working with behavior-problem youngsters, it is important that teachers carefully examine their expectations for and beliefs about these students. At the simplest level, teachers should not work with young people if they do not sincerely believe that young people's behavior is an understandable response to factors that exist and have existed in their lives and that they can, with the help of adults and peers, alter their unproductive behavior. At a somewhat less obvious level, teachers should be aware when their expectations for these adolescents are not a response to valid and reliable knowledge about the adolescents, but rather become based upon their expectations for "this type of student." There is no such thing as "this type of student." Each individual's behavior is a response to his interpretation of his unique life space. Unless people understand that life space and are aware of its positive aspects and potential for growth as well as its significant limiting factors, they cannot effectively facilitate positive growth for that individual.

SUMMARY

Effective communication skills, along with an understanding of adolescent needs and developmental tasks, provide the basis for working effectively with adolescents.

Regardless of how effectively educators develop academic or behavioral programs, their interventions with adolescents will fail unless their communication patterns respond to adolescents' needs to understand their environment and develop a sense of self-respect. Adults' interactions with adolescents will be most effective when they are characterized by listening skills that enable adults to understand adolescents' needs and concerns, and assist them in understanding themselves. Likewise, adults can assist adolescents by employing sending skills that show concern and respect for adolescents, provide clear nonjudgmental feedback, and share some of the ways in which adults, too, struggle with the process of being human.

Adults can work effectively with adolescents without employing all of the skills and activities presented in this chapter. However, their ability to assist both "normal" and behavior-problem adolescents in making healthy, productive adjustments to their environment will be significantly reduced if adults fail to employ communication patterns characterized by openness, mutual respect, courtesy, and specificity.

When considering whether to employ the communication skills described in this chapter, keep in mind that the ability to effectively use these skills when working with adolescents depends to a large degree on the individual's faith in and respect for adolescents. People who do not sincerely believe that adolescents want to solve their own problems, and both desire and are capable of responding maturely to honest, concerned communication should not employ the skills presented in this chapter. Equally important, realize that using these skills will not bring immediate or guaranteed success. These skills are a necessary component in assisting adolescents to understand themselves and alter their behavior. However, adolescents do not always respond positively to adults' use of these skills, and the results of their application are sometimes not immediately apparent.

Perhaps the key questions to ask when deciding whether or not to employ these communication skills are "What is the alternative?" and "What is the cost and payoff associated with employing these skills or rejecting them and employing alternative response styles?" It has been my experience in working with behavior-problem adolescents that employing these skills brings significant gains for both myself and the adolescents with whom I work. Similarly, I have found that when I revert to more authoritarian, controlling relationships, I prevent meaningful growth for both the adolescents and myself.

Anything you can do to increase communication in your class will reduce your need to impose order by authority, and reduce the students' need to rebel against that authority. The class will become more a place for listening and learning, and less a place for fighting and antagonism.

John O. Stevens

Awareness: Exploring, Experimenting, Experiencing

CHAPTER 5

Assisting Adolescents in Developing Effective Communication Skills

As adults begin to improve their communication skills and relate more effectively to their adolescents and colleagues, the question almost inevitably arises, "But what about the adolescents? Isn't it important that they also learn good communication skills?" Adults frequently bemoan the fact that adolescents' interactions are often characterized by cruelty and lack of concern for both peers and adults. Unfortunately, adults also note that they do not know how to alter this undesirable situation. This Chapter will begin by examining the importance of assisting adolescents in developing productive communication skills. This will be followed by a variety of practical strategies for reaching this goal.

The methods discussed in this chapter range from relatively informal procedures for discussing problems with a group to structured activities for teaching communication skills. Therefore, the appropriateness and value of each activity will depend upon the setting in which it is applied and the goals associated with the setting. For example, adults working with behavior-problem adolescents may want to employ most of the activities described in the chapter while classroom teachers may choose to select activities which will facilitate their teaching.

REASONS FOR TEACHING COMMUNICATION SKILLS

As discussed in Chapter One, peers are an extremely important factor within the learning environment. Peer norms and values have a powerful impact on adolescent

68

behavior. Anyone who has taught in a secondary school or worked in a treatment facility for adolescents can recall instances in which adolescents responded in a destructive manner or were prevented from becoming involved in the learning process because of peer pressure. Similarly, anyone who has worked with adolescents— especially young adolescents—can vividly attest to the frequency with which adolescents make cutting remarks to each other or laugh at each other's failures.

Unfortunately, this society does not provide well-planned, formalized instruction in effective, sensitive interpersonal communication. Educators teach reading, mathematics, science, English, etc., but fail to instruct students in the basic sending and receiving skills discussed in the previous chapter. Although it is assumed that these skills will be learned in the home, it is evident that this frequently does not take place. Indeed, all too few adults possess these skills. Even professionals in such communication-oriented fields as education, nursing, and psychology find it necessary to take courses to improve their skills in communicating with others. Similarly, industries and institutions (including schools) spend millions of dollars every year providing training in communication for their employees. Therefore, it should not be surprising that adolescents frequently need assistance in improving these skills. Consequently, if adults want to teach or work with adolescents who possess effective communication skills, they must spend some time and effort teaching and reinforcing these skills.

The importance of teaching these skills was vividly pointed out to me several years ago when I was visiting a high school social studies class. As I observed the class discussion, I was impressed with how well students listened to each other and how smoothly the discussion flowed. This situation was particularly surprising since several of the students in the class were classified as "emotionally handicapped" and normally experienced considerable difficulty in regular classroom environments. After class, I commented that I was impressed with the quality of the discussion. The teacher thanked me for sharing my observation and noted that the discussion I had seen was the result of considerable planning and effort on his part. He informed me that since one of his primary goals was to involve students in discussions, he spent a large portion of the first two weeks in each semester teaching students effective communication skills. He further noted that as students began to understand, accept, and employ these skills, the behavior-problem students began to function more effectively in class. He mentioned that this change was attributable both to the fact that these students actually learned more acceptable ways of interacting with others, and that other students began to give the problem students caring, but direct feedback about their behavior.

This discussion reinforced my experiences in working with emotionally handicapped or behavior-problem students. Programs for behavior-problem adolescents frequently focus almost exclusively on reducing those acting-out behaviors that adults find most annoying and threatening. While it is certainly necessary to reduce these behaviors, equal or greater attention should be placed on assisting these young people in developing skills necessary for functioning effectively in a school environment. Many programs for behavior-problem adolescents fail, not because the behavioral prescriptions are poorly written or the rewards ineffective, but because the students do not possess the basic interpersonal skills necessary for functioning effectively in a school setting. In effect, the intervention programs are putting the cart before the horse. When working with behavior-problem adolescents, educators must incorporate instruction in problem solving and the development of positive communication skills.

In addition to the common sense realization that positive environments are more desirable than environments characterized by negativism, both theoretical conceptualizations and pragmatic considerations point to the importance of developing positive peer interactions. From a theoretical perspective, positive relationships are important for increasing the amount of significance, safety, and respect of others experienced by adolescents. These factors play an important role in creating a positive self-concept and enhancing learning. From a pragmatic point of view, research studies support the concept that learning environments become more productive when students learn to communicate effectively and are encouraged to assist one another.

> These studies suggest that cooperative goal structures produce less anxiety for students and provide a better learning climate, especially for students who are chronically anxious and tense, than do competitive goal structures. . . . Cooperative, as compared with individualistic and competitive goal structures will promote studying behavior and decrease apathetic, non-studying, or disruptive behaviors on the part of students. . . . (David W. Johnson, Roger T. Johnson, *Learning Together and Alone: Cooperation, Competition, and Individualization,* 1975, p. 188. Reprinted by permission of Prentice-Hall, Inc., Englewood Cliffs, New Jersey.)

Having briefly examined several benefits associated with creating learning environments in which students communicate more frequently and positively, the question becomes how to create such environments. Teachers frequently state that while they have a strong interest in developing more positive student interactions, they lack practical strategies for accomplishing this goal.

STRATEGIES FOR DEVELOPING IMPROVED COMMUNICATION SKILLS

Whether working with "normal" or behavior-problem adolescents, the methods for teaching effective communication skills can be divided into seven basic categories according to the types of activities employed and the goals of each activity. These categories are: (1) Helping adolescents become better acquainted with their peers; (2) Instruction and discussion concerning major communication skills; (3) Structured experiential activities designed to improve basic communication skills; (4) Assignments aimed at providing practice in using communication skills; (5) Structured activities designed to improve group membership skills; (6) Processing the group; (7) Role playing. Because it can be effectively employed to assist students in altering a wide range of behaviors, role playing will be presented in Chapter 11. The remainder of this chapter will focus on activities and teacher behaviors associated with the first six methods that can be employed to assist students in establishing positive interpersonal relationships with their peers.

Prior to describing activities associated with each of the categories, it is important to consider when and how these activities can be employed. It is important to realize that the emphasis placed upon improving communication skills and therefore the type of intervention employed will vary considerably according to both the situation and the values and goals held by the adult(s) who are working with the group. For example, it is quite likely that a high school mathematics teacher, regardless of her beliefs concerning the value of effective communication, will employ fewer and less time-consuming activities than someone working with adolescents at a residential treatment facility. More specifically, it is possible that the math teacher might choose to employ several acquaintance activities in order to create a situation in which students are more comfortable with each other and thus more willing to ask questions in class, offer answers, or ask their peers for assistance. Likewise, the teacher may choose to discuss the need for openness in sharing feelings about the class so that students will feel free to suggest that the class format or choice of materials needs to be altered in order to help them learn more effectively. However, it is unlikely that the math teacher would employ activities aimed at increasing the students' skills in employing basic communication skills or in functioning effectively within a small group.

When presented with the activities described throughout this chapter, teachers occasionally comment that the activities seem best suited for small groups and would be difficult to employ in a large group setting. Although most of the activities described in this chapter are less effective when employed with extremely large groups, they are all well suited to groups under forty, and I have personally used each activity with groups of between twenty-five and forty junior high, high school, and college students. Since most schools and residential treatment facilities do not place a major emphasis on learning or living groups larger than forty, the question seems to be not whether these activities work with the size groups normally found in such settings, but whether the adults involved view the benefits of employing these activities as worthy of the time and energy involved. The real issue is not whether the activities can be employed with thirty adolescents, but rather which type of intervention is needed to meet the goals dictated by the setting.

Helping Adolescents to Know Their Peers

If adults expect adolescents to communicate effectively with their peers, it is imperative that they first become acquainted. Individuals who do not know each other have little incentive for communicating in a positive, caring manner. In addition, when adolescents are unfamiliar with their environment, they are much more likely to become passive participants within that environment. Consequently, the first step in developing positive communication skills is assisting the individuals concerned in becoming acquainted with one another. The following activities provide a sample of strategies that can be employed to assist adolescents in becoming better acquainted with their peers.

The Name Chain   A name chain is the most effective method for helping students to learn each other's names. The following steps will help to make this activity run smoothly.

1. Ask the students to be seated in a circle so that each student can comfortably see all of the students in the group.
2. Clearly explain the reasons for being involved in the activity. For example, the teacher might indicate that one benefit of knowing everyone's name is that it increases their knowledge of the environment and thereby makes them more comfortable and more likely to become actively involved. Similarly, the teacher may indicate that knowing other students' names will enable students to greet each other in a more friendly, relaxed manner and this will have a tendency to make both the classroom and the school a more positive place.
3. Ask the students if they have any questions about why they are being asked to do the activity.
4. Explain to the students that each person will be asked to say their first name and tell the group one thing about themselves. They may choose to tell the group something they like to do, something interesting that happened to them recently, how they are feeling, etc. Inform the class that they will be asked to repeat each student's name and the statement they have made. They will begin with the person who spoke first and stop when they have given their name and have said something about themself. For example, the first student may say, "I'm Bob, and I went to the beach this weekend." The next person would say, "That's Bob (or you're Bob), and he (or you) went to the beach last weekend. I'm Sandy, and I enjoy backpacking." Since teachers are faced with the difficult task of learning a large number of names and since having an adult remember their name seems particularly important to adolescents, it is best to have the teacher be the last person to speak. This means that the teacher will be able to list each student's name and what they have shared with the class.
5. Have everyone take a paper and pencil and change seats. Ask the students to start with a designated individual and go clockwise around the circle, writing down each person's name. It is not necessary to have the students list what each student shared.
6. Ask for a volunteer who will begin with the person designated as the starting place and slowly give the name of each person in the circle. This serves as an opportunity for students to check the accuracy of their list and to learn the names of any students they missed.

It is important to provide follow-up for this activity. For example, for several days following the activity the teacher may want to attempt to go around the class and list each student's name or ask for a volunteer to do this. It is important that teachers continue to be aware of whether students are remembering names and that they continue to emphasize the value of knowing names. For example, if students are asked to work in groups, the teacher may suggest that the students make sure they know each member's name before beginning the group activity. Teachers all too often involve students in activities and then fail to follow up with behavior that reinforces the learning derived from and the values implied by the activity.

Know Your Neighbor   A second activity that focuses on students knowing their peers is called "Know Your Neighbor." This activity includes the following steps:

1. Inform the students that the goal of the activity is to assist them in becoming better acquainted with the people in the class. Again, briefly explain the advantages associated with their knowing their classmates.
2. List several items on the board that would apply to students in the class. For example, a list might include such items as: someone who has a birthday this month; someone who can tune their car; someone who is left-handed, etc. Ask the students to add to this list until they have created ten to fifteen items.
3. Have each student copy these items and place a line after each item.
4. Inform the students that each person's task (the teacher should be included) is to move around the room and obtain a signature beside each item from a person who meets the designated criteria. For example, for the item: someone who is left-handed, each student would be required to obtain the signature of a left-handed person. Students should also be told that they cannot have one person sign more than twice.
5. Before beginning, inform the students that the activity is not a race but rather a method for them to become more informed about other students.
6. At the end of the activity, it is useful to ask the students how they felt about the activity, whether they found it helpful, and whether they would recommend that the activity be used in other classes. In addition to providing the teacher with useful information, such questions provide students with a sense of competence and power.

Twenty Things I Like to Do This activity was developed by Sidney Simon (1972) and his associates and has become popular as a values clarification activity designed to assist individuals in becoming more aware of their own priorities and values. This activity can also be used to assist adolescents in becoming better acquainted with their peers. More specifically, it can be employed to assist adolescents in realizing that they frequently have more in common than they realize with peers whom they perceive as quite unlike themselves. Therefore, this activity can serve as a starting point for diminishing the power of cliques which often become negative factors within groups of adolescents.

The procedure for developing this activity is as follows:

1. Discuss the purpose of the activity. Students can be informed that in addition to helping them become better acquainted with several classmates, this activity can help them discover some interesting things about what they perceive as valuable and whether their actions are consistent with their stated values.
2. Hand out a sheet similar to that presented in Figure 5.1 and ask the students to list, in the left column, the twenty things they most like to do. It is important at this point to inform the students that this portion of the activity is for their own use and will not be shared with anyone. It is also helpful to inform the students that twenty is an arbitrary number and that they can list fewer or more activities.
3. When all students have completed their lists, ask them to place codes like those listed in Figure 5.2 in the columns along the top of the paper. Prior to using this

Figure 5.1   Things I Like to Do

Thing I Like to Do	A/P	$3	Fr.	2 yrs.	F	M	Date	S	Rank
1.									
2.									
3.									
4.									
5.									
6.									
7.									
8.									
9.									
10.									
11.									
12.									
13.									
14.									
15.									
16.									
17.									
18.									
19.									
20.									

Figure 5.2   Possible Codes for Use with Things I Like to Do Activity

Symbol	Directions
A/P	Mark an A for activities done alone, P for activities done with people.
$3	Place a $ across from each activity that costs more than $3.
Fr	Mark an Fr for each activity you would want your boyfriend/girlfriend to have on their list.
2 yrs.	Check those you would list 2 years ago.
F	Mark an F for those your father would put on his list.
M	Mark an M for those your mother would put on her list.
Date	Write the approximate date you last did each activity.
S	Mark an S for those activities you learned in school.
Rank	Number the top five (1-5), the ones you like to do best.

activity, it is important to develop categories and corresponding codes that are appropriate to the interests of the participants.

4. Ask the students to place the appropriate symbol in the box across from the corresponding activity. For example, the letter *A* should be placed in the column across from those activities which the student normally does alone.

5. Ask that the students turn their sheet over and list (in any order) the five activities which they most like to do. At this point be sure to inform the students that this list will be shared with other students and that they should list only activities which they are willing to show to their peers.

6. Ask the students to look around the room and choose one individual whom they believe is most likely to have the most items on their list similar to those on their own list. In essence they are being asked to choose the person whom they perceive as having interests most like their own. It is important to emphasize that they should select only one person and that it does not matter if that person is selected by several other people. In fact, it is quite common that five or six people will choose one individual.

7. Inform the students that they are to compare their list with the person they choose (not with the student or students who choose them) and to simply write down the number of items that were identical or nearly identical to those listed by that individual. For example, if they have listed running as an activity and the person they choose has listed jogging, this can be counted as one item in common. It is useful to inform the students that if they have any questions concerning whether two items are in fact similar enough to count, they should consult the teacher.

8. When all students have completed this activity, have the students choose an individual whom they think has the least number of items in his or her top five similar to their own. It is important to state that this does not mean that they do not like the student, but merely that they see that student as having interests very different from their own. Once the students have chosen this student, they should follow the same procedure as with the first choice.

9. When all of the students have indicated that they have completed the task, the teacher should draw a chart similar to that shown in Figure 5.3. The chart is

Figure 5.3   Form for Tallying Results from Comparing Students' Interests

Number of Similar Interests

	0	1	2	3	4	5
Student chosen as being most similar						
Student chosen as being least similar						

completed by asking how many students had no activities in their top five which were similar to the person they chose as most likely to share their interests, how many had one in common, etc.

10. Once the chart has been filled in, the teacher should ask the students to interpret the data. The data often indicate that adolescents have nearly as much in common with those whom they thought were dissimilar to themselves as they do with those they thought were most similar. If, however, the data indicate something different, the teacher should be ready to point out the advantages this suggests for getting to know other people.

Dyads   This acquaintance activity simply involves providing adolescents with an opportunity to spend several minutes getting to know someone with whom they are not well acquainted. This activity is most beneficial when it provides adolescents with an opportunity to interact both with peers whom they would like to get to know better and peers whom they might initially not choose to meet. The specific methods for involving students in this activity are listed below.

1. Explain the reasons for employing the activity. Inform the participants that the activity simply provides them with an opportunity to sit down and talk to several peers whom they do not know well. Be sure to provide the students with an opportunity to question and discuss the activity.
2. Ask the students to stand in a circle so that they can see all members of the group. Then ask the students to look around the group and see whether there are people whom they would like to get to know better. This may be a person whom they have not met but would like to meet or a person whom they know a little and would like to get to know better. At this stage in the activity it is helpful to point out that picking someone does not mean you want to date them or become their best friend. It simply means they are a person whom you do not know well.

3. Suggest that each person determine several people whom they would like to meet since the person they choose may be chosen by someone else. At this point it is helpful to state that a situation sometimes arises where the last few people remaining already know each other. This situation can be handled in two ways. First, these individuals can simply form dyads and get to know each other better. Second, these adolescents can each join a dyad which includes two people whom they do not know well. Since the activity is much less effective if groups become larger than three, it is important to limit the group sizes.

4. Prior to having students make their selection, inform them that their task is simply to spend four or five minutes getting to know the person they choose or who chooses them. At this point it is useful to tell the students that they can learn something about themselves by paying attention to the way in which they choose or are chosen. For example, if they turn their back slightly, look at their feet, and think, "I'm not very interesting, no one will choose me," they may be creating a situation in which they are less likely to be chosen. It is also important to inform the class that since this is not an easy task they may have a tendency to take the easy way out by choosing their best friend. It is helpful to point out that while this may in fact be easier, they may be cheating both themselves and other students of some interesting learning.

5. Inform the students that they can now choose someone and that they will be called back together in approximately five minutes.

6. Approximately one minute before their time is up, inform the students that they have about one minute to complete their conversation.

7. When the students are once again in the large group, ask them how the activity went and how they felt. Allow several minutes for this discussion and then, unless they found the activity to be very difficult and do not want to try it again, ask them to once again look around the group and choose a person whom they would like to get to know better. Depending on the time available, the leader's goals, and the students' interest, this process can be repeated any number of times. If the students indicate that the activity was difficult and they do not want to continue, it is important to follow up by asking what they found difficult. It is possible that their difficulty stems from such factors as well-formed cliques that need to be dealt with in order to create an open, safe environment.

8. One interesting alteration that teachers and group leaders find beneficial is to have the students select someone whom they might normally not get to know. It is important to indicate that this does not mean that they do not like the person, but simply that that person might be a little more difficult for them to approach. It is helpful to provide the students with examples and for teachers to share their own concerns about meeting certain types of people. For example, the leader might note that when he was in high school, he was not athletic; and therefore, he found it difficult to approach "jocks." He might also note that people tend to have difficulty approaching someone they have never met or who has interests different from their own. While this version of the activity is more

difficult for adolescents, it does have considerable payoffs in reducing tensions and expanding the pattern of student interaction.

Guess Who   A final acquaintance activity used by a number of secondary teachers provides students with an opportunity to discover how well they know their peers. The steps for setting up this activity are:

1. Briefly describe the activity to the students and elicit their willingness to take part in the activity.
2. Ask students to write brief (two- or three-line) statements about themselves, which can include facts about their personal history, family, hobbies, etc.
3. Collect all of the autobiographical statements.
4. Ask each student to take out a piece of paper and pencil. Read each description and ask the students (the teacher should also be involved) to write down the name of the student who they believe wrote the description.
5. After all the descriptions have been read, reread the descriptions and ask the authors to identify themselves. The students should be asked to indicate on their list whether they made the correct choice. Upon completing the task, students can be asked to indicate the number of their peers whom they correctly identified. These results can be used to initiate a discussion concerning the degree to which class members have become acquainted. ·
6. An interesting alternative to this activity is to have students write brief statements that include one false statement about themselves. The class can then be given the student's name and personal description and asked to decide which statement is false. This activity can be performed by the entire group or can be developed as a contest between two groups.

The activities described are only a sample of activities available for teachers or other professionals who are interested in assisting adolescents with whom they work to become better acquainted. There are numerous books available that include a variety of additional activities. These include Stanford and Roark's *Human Interaction in Education* (1974), Johnson's *Reaching Out* (1972), Canfield and Well's *100 Ways to Enhance Self-Concept in the Classroom: A Handbook for Teachers and Parents* (1976), Castilla's *Left-Handed Teaching: Lessons in Affective Education* (1974), Johnson and Johnson's *Joining Together: Group Theory and Group Skills* (1975), and a wide variety of books by Sidney Simon and his associates including *Values Clarification* (1972), and *More Values Clarification: Strategies for the Classroom* (1975).

Some teachers will respond to the use of acquaintance activities by noting, correctly, that many students learn perfectly well in the absence of such activities. However, an understanding of adolescent development indicates that learning is likely to be enhanced by increasing friendship patterns within a classroom. Furthermore, the students who function effectively within a classroom are often those who have established friendships within the class or who receive considerable adult reinforcement and support for their efforts. Behavior-problem adolescents frequently fail to fit into either of these categories. Therefore, they are apt to benefit somewhat more from these types of activities than are the more successful students. Nevertheless, most, if not all students will perform more effectively in classrooms characterized by increased student acquaintance.

Although knowing someone is certainly an important ingredient in feeling comfortable around them and communicating effectively with them, there are situations in which poor communication exists between people who are well acquainted. Anyone who has taught or worked with adolescents in a residential treatment facility has observed numerous instances of negative interactions between adolescents who know each other quite well. Therefore, if adults expect adolescents to respond in caring, productive ways when interacting with their peers, adults must do more than merely assist them in becoming better acquainted.

Instruction and Discussion concerning Communication Skills

When working with adolescents, the most effective strategy adults can use is to be open and clear about their goals and expectations. Consequently, any attempt to facilitate the development of positive, courteous communication within the classroom should begin with a discussion concerning the reasons for desiring this form of interaction. It is important that students be actively involved in this discussion. For example, it is useful to ask students what types of courtesies they would like to see in the classroom and why these seem important. The easiest and most expedient means for creating such a list is to simply write them on a large piece of butcher paper. The use of butcher paper allows the teacher to save the original list and refer to it later if there is a need to reinforce the fact that the class decided upon the desirability of employing certain communication skills.

Once the group has discussed the need for positive, supportive interactions within the classroom, the teacher can ask the class if they would be willing to spend some time discussing these skills in more detail and practicing them by becoming involved in several activities and assignments. If the teacher has involved the class in developing the list and discussing the necessity of positive interactions, students will almost always respond enthusiastically to the opportunity to improve their skills. If, however, the students express some hesitancy, this provides an excellent opportunity for involving students in a discussion concerning how they want the class to function and how much responsibility they are willing to take for the operation of the class. If adolescents choose not to become involved in initial activities aimed at improving student-student and teacher-student interactions, this decision creates the possibility that this issue will surface later and can be dealt with when it is a more immediate issue. The section on processing a group will outline the methods that can be employed in dealing with such situations.

Assuming that the students do agree to devote some time to developing communication skills that will make the classroom a more comfortable working atmosphere, the next step is to briefly outline the sending and receiving skills presented in Chapter 4. This outline provides students with a clear overview of the specific skills that are related to the concerns they have listed, and also provides an opportunity for students to add any additional skills that they believe have been omitted. Once these skills have been presented and discussed, it is helpful to provide an activity or assignment aimed at improving the students' ability to apply each skill. Several of the communication skills presented in Chapter 4 can be most productively highlighted by candid discussions regarding their application to the present environment. The remainder of this section will be devoted to these skills. The following sections will provide examples of activities, assignments, and teacher behavior that can assist students to better understand and more effectively use the remainder of the skills.

Staying in the Here and Now   While it is possible to develop activities that highlight the importance of most, if not all, of the communication skills listed in Chapter 4, there is a danger in developing activities for the sake of having activities. Some concepts either do not lend themselves well to activities or are so directly related to real adolescent and teacher concerns that they can be examined more effectively through the use of candid discussions. The value of dealing in the here and now is one such concept.

As is almost always the case, the most effective way to begin such a discussion is to ask students to list situations in which it is important that they receive immediate feedback and why they find this helpful. If this discussion does not begin to focus on issues related directly to the immediate environment, the teacher can begin to make these connections by indicating situations in the present environment in which it is important for the teacher to receive immediate feedback. For example, an effective teacher would rather know immediately if students are having difficulty understanding the material than not find out until a large percentage of the class does poorly on an examination. Similarly, competent teachers would rather hear immediately if students are having difficulty with the form of instruction or the style of teacher-student communication. It is sometimes difficult to receive such feedback immediately and directly. However, it is much more difficult (unless the goal is to deny the feedback) to hear about it "through the grapevine" or from student feedback solicited at the end of the term.

Once teachers discuss several reasons why they would appreciate immediate feedback, students will usually begin to discuss their reasons (if they have not already done so). Students may focus on such topics as the importance of knowing where they stand concerning grades, how the teacher is feeling about their participation in class, or where they stand on their particular treatment program. One of the major problems in residential treatment centers is the sense of impotence and fear experienced by adolescents who are unsure about what their treatment entails, why it exists, or where they stand in relation to certain levels or criteria for improvement. Adults can take a major step in developing greater personal safety and enhancing self-concept by continually providing adolescents with specific information regarding these concerns.

Once these concerns have been brought forth, the next issue is to begin to examine the means for implementing immediate feedback. This discussion is frequently instigated most comfortably by beginning with a relatively bureaucratic, less interpersonal issue such as grading. From there, the discussion can move to the types of interaction that enable individuals to provide nonthreatening, nonpunitive feedback to others concerning changes they would like them to make. This discussion obviously relates directly to the use of such skills as sending "I" messages and making perception checks (skills that can be practiced by students and modeled by adults).

Reducing the Impact of Personal Biases by Clarifying Expectations and Needs   Adult-adolescent interactions are frequently characterized by negative stereotyped biases on both sides. Adolescents, particularly those experiencing behavior problems, frequently view adults with skepticism and distrust. Since these adolescents have only sporadically succeeded at receiving significant reinforcement from the school system or adults, they have not developed positive perceptions and attitudes regarding adults.

Similarly, teachers frequently have negative feelings about behavior-problem students. These feelings arise from several sources. No one likes to be constantly interrupted in class or to have to spend a significant amount of class time dealing with behavior problems. Most secondary teachers are trained in their subject matter and find it generally interesting and worthwhile. It is frustrating to constantly have to put teaching aside in order to deal with discipline problems. There are also more subtle reasons for negative responses to behavior-problem adolescents. Their apparent disinterest in the subject matter and their disdain for what appear to be reasonable rules provide a challenge to teachers' values. Students' acting-out behavior forces teachers to either covertly or overtly examine their curriculum and teaching styles. This examination may range from teachers who openly discuss these issues with students to teachers who spend considerable energy protecting the correctness of their values and behaviors by belittling the adolescents. In either case, the challenge provided by problem students is time consuming and energy draining and may therefore create some resentment.

Given these biases or personal filters that exist for both adults and adolescents, it is extremely useful to begin a class or a student's stay at a residential treatment facility with a candid discussion of each party's wants, needs, and expectations. It is valuable for the adult to know how the adolescent perceives adults and which adult behaviors have particularly positive or negative valence for the adolescent. It is not uncommon for major blowups to occur when an adult behaves in a manner that seems completely acceptable to a majority of the other adolescents, but which one adolescent perceives as abusive, rude, or punitive. The frequency of such situations can be significantly reduced by initially providing an opportunity for all parties to discuss how they need to be treated if they are to feel comfortable and safe and therefore respond positively in the environment.

It is important that teachers also share their needs and biases. Adolescents frequently see adults as applying rules and expectations that are unclear and inconsistent. If adults discuss what types of behaviors they feel are helpful in creating a good learning or growth environment and explain their rationale for including these, they can help adolescents better understand their environment. As discussed in Chapter 1, adolescents are struggling with the instability associated with a rapid change in their life space. When adults clarify their expectations and biases, they provide adolescents with a sense of order and stability that increases adolescents' sense of safety and potency.

Adolescents (even behavior-problem adolescents) are seldom as uncaring and uncompromising as adults view them. While they may have difficulty consistently demonstrating a level of concern and stability with which adults are comfortable, adolescents can be receptive to adults' needs when they are presented clearly and sensitively. One advantage of communication skills such as "I messages" and various levels of self disclosure is that these skills enable adults to provide adolescents with important information concerning adult wants and needs without attacking the adolescent.

It is important to keep in mind that discussing these issues is no guarantee that the associated problems will immediately vanish. Adults cannot expect one-trial learning when dealing with complex tasks that involve a high degree of personal involvement. Expecting adolescents with behavior problems to consistently employ these skills after they have been discussed is analogous to expecting adults to improve their golf or tennis swing after a brief discussion with their playing partner. Change requires frequent nonthreatening feedback and continual practice.

Finally, teachers must be careful not to create a self-fulfilling prophecy by assuming that behavior-problem students are "too far gone" to benefit from discussions such as those described in this section. Acquisition cannot always be gauged by performance. While adults' interventions may initially appear to have limited effectiveness, they may come to surprising fruition later when other variables have changed or other aspects of the treatment program have enabled the adolescent to demonstrate skills that have previously been too threatening or have simply been superseded by more pressing issues.

Structured Experiential Activities Designed to Improve Basic Communication Skills

While not all communication skills can be taught using structured experiential activities, this approach has several advantages. Because students actually practice the skills, it is easier for them to become comfortable with these skills. People can do something more easily when they have practiced it than when they have simply discussed it. Practice enables people to receive feedback on their performance and to ask questions about the new behavior. Furthermore, since the skill can be practiced in the same environment in which it will be employed, there are fewer problems with generalization. Paraphrasing, perception checking, and giving specific, behavioral descriptions are examples of three skills that can be taught most effectively using structured experiential activities.

Paraphrasing Perhaps no communication skill has been as widely practiced as that of paraphrasing. In situations where a number of individuals are involved in discussions, the application of this skill can have a major impact on improving communication. The most common and productive method for teaching this skill includes the following steps:

1. The teacher should briefly describe or have the students list some of the difficulties that arise when a number of people are involved in a discussion.

These may include: individuals interrupting each other; people being so busy thinking about what they want to say that they do not listen to what others are saying; and people not responding to the previous speaker's statement, but starting out on a new tangent. Once these issues have been raised, the teacher can inform the class that by practicing paraphrasing, the teacher and students can become more aware of these problems and more able to prevent them from occurring during class discussions.

2. The students should be divided into triads (if possible, the teacher should be included) and one individual in each group should be designated the observer.

3. The teacher should inform the remaining two students in each group that they will be involved in discussing a topic of mutual interest. It is often helpful if the teacher has developed a topic or list of possible topics. The two students are then asked to have a discussion on the topic. However, the students are informed that before they can speak, they must first paraphrase what the other student has just said. Before proceeding, the student must receive a nod from the speaker indicating that the paraphrasing contained the essence of the speaker's previous statement. The observer's task is to make sure that the statements remain brief enough to be accurately paraphrased and that a student does not take his turn at speaking until he has accurately paraphrased the other student.

4. As is frequently the case after giving directions, it is helpful to ask the students if they can paraphrase the directions. Allow the students approximately five minutes for their conversations.

5. At the end of five minutes take some time to discuss how the students felt about the activity. At this point it is useful to integrate student comments into teaching points such as the difficulty people often experience in really listening to other people.

6. Following this discussion have the students switch roles so that the observer has an opportunity to experience the paraphrasing aspect of the activity.

7. An extremely important aspect to employing activities such as this is the teacher's ability to make the connection between the activity and actual classroom or group behavior. Therefore, each activity should conclude with a discussion concerning the application of the activity to classroom behavior and a decision on how the group can respond when the skills are not being employed. For example, at the end of this activity the teacher might ask the class what they thought would be the most effective method for pointing out situations in which people were not listening effectively to each other. By making this process open to class discussion, the teacher significantly reduces the possibility that students will be hurt or resentful if the teacher or another student notes that they seem not to be listening to or interrupting others.

One interesting follow-up to practicing paraphrasing is to occasionally ask the students to employ the skill as part of regular class discussions. For example, prior to discussing a particularly controversial or emotionally laden topic, the teacher might ask the class if they would be willing to paraphrase the previous speaker before stating their opinion. It is also helpful to allow this request to be made by either the teacher or a student when a discussion starts to become disruptive.

Perception Checking With most concepts, real understanding comes only after the individual has actually experienced the principles associated with the concept. The following activity assists adolescents in understanding the concept that all people see situations somewhat differently and therefore often misinterpret others' statements and actions.

1. Briefly discuss the difficulties all people experience in accurately interpreting what others mean. This may be enhanced by asking students to relate instances in which something funny or significant happened as a result of their misinterpreting someone's statement.
2. Have students break into dyads and sit facing each other.
3. Ask each group to choose one person who will begin the activity by making a statement which has several possible interpretations. At this point, it is important to provide the students with several examples of such a statement. For example, if I say, "I am tired today," it could mean that I did not sleep well last night, I was up too late, or I have had a hard day. Likewise, if a student says, "I like this class," it would mean that his girlfriend is in the class, he likes the subject matter, or he likes the teacher.
4. Inform the second person in each group that their task will be to say, "You mean that . . . ," followed by what they think the person means by his statement. They are to ask this question until they receive a total of three "yes" responses from the person who made the statement.
5. Tell the students that when one person has made three accurate interpretations, they should switch roles and go through the activity again.
6. When the activity is completed, it is important to discuss the implications this skill has regarding the classroom or group situation. For example, it can be noted that if students are unclear about an assignment, they should express this by employing a perception check in the form of "You mean that . . ." Similarly, students can be informed that there will be instances when the teacher will employ this skill in order to determine why they are responding in a particular manner. It is helpful for them to realize that when the teacher employs a perception check it is simply the teachers' attempt to better understand what they are communicating by their behavior.

Behavioral Descriptions One of the most difficult communication skills is providing others with specific feedback about their behavior without placing a value on, or assigning motives to, the behavior. For example, if a student is looking out the window while the teacher is speaking, it is easy to assume that he is not paying attention and to make a comment such as "John, if you don't pay attention, you're going to have real trouble on the test." What the teacher has done in this situation (besides possibly embarrassing and alienating John) is to make an assumption that since John was looking out the window, he was not paying attention. The teacher's interaction with John would be much more productive if the teacher spoke with him alone and made a statement such as, "John, I noticed you were looking out the window during our review session. I am concerned that you might be having some problem with the material. Is that the case?" In this situation the behavior is clearly separated from the interpretation, and the teacher checks to see whether the interpretation is correct.

While discussions can assist students in understanding the difficulty of simply describing behavior, the following activity can facilitate this learning.

1. Discuss the problems associated with misinterpreting others' behaviors. Students can be encouraged to relate situations in which someone made an inaccurate assumption about them based on a misinterpretation of their behavior.

2. Since students sometimes find this activity difficult, it is important to clearly discuss the fact that its goal is to help them become more skilled in simply describing behaviors as opposed to linking behaviors and motives.

3. Ask the students to choose four or five (depending on the number of students) students with whom they feel comfortable. Have the groups sit in a circle.

4. Inform the participants that their first task will be to simply describe their current behavior. At this point, it is helpful for the leader to model the skill by describing his own behavior. For example, the leader might say, "Right now I am talking to the group; I have my hands folded across my chest; my left leg is slightly in front of my right leg." After modeling the task, inform the participants that they should each briefly describe their behavior.

5. When the groups have completed this task, mention that the more difficult task is to describe someone else's behavior without making some interpretation about what they are thinking or feeling. At this point, choose a student who will feel comfortable being used as an example and briefly describe their behavior. For example, you might say, "Sally is sitting with her hands folded on her lap; she is looking at me; she has both feet on the floor." At this point it is helpful to point out that while it is tempting to guess what she is thinking (e.g., she is interested and attentive), the only thing people can do with accuracy is describe the behavior and inform her how they feel when she behaves in that manner. Having modeled the task and discussed its purpose, ask each student to describe the behavior of the person sitting to their immediate left.

6. When the students have completed the activity, they should be given time to discuss their reactions to making behavioral descriptions. Following this discussion it is important to draw the connection between the skill-building activity and communication patterns within the classroom. For example, teachers might state that it is helpful when students inform them of things they do that bother the students. Also, if teachers are to change these behaviors, students must provide teachers with specific feedback. For example, it may be interesting, but not extremely helpful for a teacher to be told, during a class session, "You are intimidating." However, if students are more specific, "You did not smile, and you asked questions in an unusually sharp tone," the information is specific enough so that the teacher can change his behavior. Similarly, students' indicating that a test was too hard provides very little information. More specific information concerning what portions they found difficult and what created the difficulty is needed.

Structured experiential activities have the advantage of enabling adolescents to actually practice a skill and develop a sense of what it feels like to employ the skill. The disadvantage of such activities is that they tend to present the skill in a rather structured form, which reduces the likelihood that the skill will be generalized to other settings. One strategy for increasing the likelihood that skills will be employed in other settings is to teach them in conjunction with specific assignments that ask students to try the skills in a variety of settings.

Assignments to Provide Practice in Using Communication Skills

There are three types of assignments that can assist adolescents in developing and actually employing effective communication skills: (1) written practice, (2) attempting the skill and reporting the results, and (3) keeping records of how often they and others employ the skills.

The first two types of assignments should be related and can be used to teach such skills as sending "I messages", employing active listening, making a statement rather than asking a question, or employing paraphrasing. For example, in the case of making a statement rather than asking a question, adolescents can be given a list of commonly asked questions and asked to change them to statements. Such a list might include such questions as: Are we almost done? Will this test count? Do we have to watch a film tomorrow? All of these questions would provide the listener with much more information if the sender could clearly put them in the form of a statement. For example, students might turn these questions into statements such as: "We've been discussing this for a long time and I am ready for a break. I am concerned about how much this test will affect my grade. We've watched a lot of films lately. Could we do something else tomorrow?"

Written assignments can be coordinated with assignments that encourage students to actually practice a communication skill. For example, if students have changed "we" or "you" statements into "I messages," they can be asked to send several "I messages" during their daily interactions with people and record both their statement and the response they receive. The results of this assignment can then be shared and discussed at a future meeting.

The third type of assignment—collecting frequency data—can be employed for increasing students' awareness of their own behaviors and the behaviors of others. These assignments ask students to actually record the frequency with which they and others employ certain communication skills. For example, students might be asked to record instances in which students and the teacher used certain courteous statements. When giving this type of assignment, it is helpful to first have the class develop a uniform coding sheet. In the case of courteous statements, the class might use a chart like that shown in Figure 5.4. When developing this type of assignment, it is important to emphasize observing positive behaviors. While it is sometimes useful to structure observations that pinpoint both positive and negative behaviors, it is usually better not to focus exclusively on negative behaviors.

Figure 5.4   Tally Sheet for Monitoring Courteous Comments

Days of the Week

		Monday	Tuesday	Wednesday	Thursday	Friday
	Please					
	Thank You					
Courteous Comments	Excuse Me					
	Friendly Greeting					
	I'm Sorry					

Several examples may serve to clarify the procedures and highlight the advantages associated with this type of assignment. One of the most commonly employed and positive assignments aimed at increasing positive student interaction is the use of secret pal notebooks. In setting up this assignment, each student draws the name of a student in the class. The students are then asked to observe the student whose name they have drawn and to write down specific things that student does or says that relate to the skill being studied. One week is an effective amount of time to ask students to record the behavior. Behaviors being observed might include courteous statements, assisting another student, and instances of paraphrasing. At the end of the week each student receives a notebook that provides him with feedback about his positive behaviors throughout the week.

A second example of a data collection assignment was presented to me several years ago by two graduate students who were teaching in a suburban junior high school. The teachers had developed the assignment in order to alter what they described as extremely negative peer interactions, which occurred in the halls between classes. The teachers introduced the assignment by having open discussions with their students concerning the quality of interactions in the halls. During the discussions students consistently stated that their negative remarks were made in response to negative comments they received from other students. Realizing that the negativism was an excellent example of a vicious circle, the teachers asked their students if they would be willing to keep data on their hallway interactions with peers. When the students readily agreed, the teachers assisted the students in developing the uniform data

Figure 5.5   Tally Sheet for Monitoring Negative or Positive Student Statements

Days of the Week

	Monday	Tuesday	Wednesday	Thursday	Friday
Me					
Them					

collecting system shown in Figure 5.5. The students were asked to simply make a mark in the column labeled *them* each time someone said something negative to them and to mark in the column labeled *me* each time they made a negative comment to someone else. The teachers then spent several minutes developing examples of comments that would be coded as negative and comments that were basically neutral and, therefore, should not be coded. It was agreed that the students would collect data for one week and that on the following Monday, the classes would tally and analyze the data. Since each teacher taught approximately one hundred and fifty students and there was only a slight overlap in students taught, nearly 220 students were involved in the assignment.

The data indicated a clear relationship between the number of negative comments given and received. As students reduced the frequency with which they made negative comments, the number of negative comments they received diminished significantly. In order to check the reliability of the students' data, the teachers tallied student behavior at designated times and places each day. The teachers' results substantiated the accuracy of the students' data.

The students indicated that they thoroughly enjoyed the assignment, and follow-up data collected by the teachers indicated that the behavior changes were maintained over time. In reflecting on the assignment, the teachers noted that they might have obtained similar results by asking students to tally positive rather than negative comments. Although it is best not to focus on negative behavior, there are two reasons why the focus on a negative behavior did not create a negative reaction. First, students were counting their own behavior as well as their peers'. Therefore, the emphasis was less on "what they are doing to me" than on "how we are responding to each other." Second, a natural outcome of the activity was that students were able to observe a significant decrease in negative interactions. This provided a positive focus despite the fact that negative responses were being tallied.

Structured Activities to Improve Group Membership Skills

All of the skills and associated activities presented earlier in the chapter help individuals function more effectively within a group setting. However, there are instances in which teachers or group leaders may wish to focus directly on skills needed to make task groups operate more effectively. These skills are more sophisticated and setting-specific and are not as likely to be taught as an initial strategy for working with behavior-problem adolescents. Nevertheless, there are instances in which focusing on these skills can serve to alleviate problems that arise during group meetings or small group work.

There are two commonly employed and interrelated approaches to assisting students in improving group membership skills: (1) involving students in structured group activities that highlight problems frequently experienced by groups, and (2) coding behaviors that facilitate and/or block effective group functioning. A wide range of structured activities has been developed to assist students in becoming aware of the problems associated with group problem solving. Johnson and Johnson's *Joining Together: Group Theory and Group Skills* (1975) and Stanford and Stanford's *Learning Discussion Skills Through Games* (1969) provide descriptions of a variety of such activities.

The second approach (which is frequently employed in conjunction with student involvement in a structured group activity) focuses on students becoming aware of specific group member behaviors that enhance and hinder effective group work. The most common method for familiarizing students with these skills is similar to the methods presented earlier in this chapter for teaching more general communication skills. Students are first introduced to these skills or asked to develop a list of skills. Next, the skills are more specifically defined and students may be asked to participate in activities that enable them to practice these skills. Coding systems such as those shown in Figure 5.6 and Figure 5.7 can then be devised and students become involved in observing groups in action and tallying group members' behaviors. Finally, students are provided with opportunities to analyze and discuss the resulting data.

Processing Interactions in a Group Setting

The first five approaches to teaching communication skills, as well as the role playing discussed in Chapter 11, all depend upon creating somewhat structured, unspontaneous opportunities for examining and practicing effective communication skills. The method presented in this section focuses on responding to communication problems as they arise. This method is based on the principle of modeling and depends initially upon the adult's ability to sensitively employ effective communication skills in responding to classroom situations and students' needs. Educators frequently point to the desirability of responding to the opportunity for employing the students' immediate needs and concerns as a primary motivational tool. Anyone who has worked with adolescents is aware of the frequency with which communication

Figure 5.6   Group Process Feedback Form

	Group Member				
Maintaining Behaviors	Amy	Bob	Tim	Sally	Carl
1. Encourager of Participation 2. Harmonizer and Compromiser 3. Tension Reliever 4. Perception Checker 5. Evaluator of Emotional Climate 6. Process Observer 7. Active Listener					
Task Behaviors					
1. Information Giver 2. Opinion Giver 3. Information Seeker 4. Opinion Seeker 5. Starter 6. Direction Giver 7. Summarizer 8. Consensus Taker 9. Problem Outliner 10. Energizer					
Blocking Behaviors					
1. Withdrawing 2. Sarcasm 3. Punishing Remarks 4. Dominating 5. Clowning 6. Defensiveness 7. Attacking 8. Judgmental Evaluation 9. Irrelevancy—off-task stories					

difficulties arise. By responding to these situations as they occur, teachers have an excellent opportunity to demonstrate the importance and efficacy of effective communication skills.

Unfortunately, teachers frequently fail to respond to the emotions involved in teacher-student and student-student interactions. In fact, Flanders and Amidon (1967) reported that only .005 percent of classroom verbal interactions were related to acceptance of feelings. If teachers acknowledge the fact that emotions influence learning, it appears that they must increase the extent to which they respond to the emotions inherent in classroom interactions.

There are three types of interactions to which adults can respond when making spontaneous observations about the communication patterns being employed within a group. First, they can respond to interactions between two individuals. For example, when adolescents "put down" their peers, adults can share their feelings about the interchange or they can ask the student who was put down how he is feeling. The latter intervention should not be attempted until group members have become familiar with the communication skills outlined in this chapter and existing group norms support their use.

Figure 5.7   Observation Form for Monitoring Positive Group Behaviors

When a student uses one of the skills, write his or her initial in the box beside that skill.

Listening Skills				
1. Paraphrasing				
2. Perception Checking				
Contributing to the Discussion				
3. Contributes an idea or suggestion				
4. Asks a question about the topic				
Sending Skills				
5. Says how she/he is feeling				
6. Describes the group's behavior				
Group Facilitation Skills				
7. Encourages participation by another member				
8. Makes summary				
9. Reinforces on-task statements				
10. Asks how group members are feeling about the group's position or progress				

Second, adults can process interactions that occur between themselves and an individual adolescent. For example, adults may be faced with an incident in which they believe that their behavior has made an adolescent uncomfortable. In this instance, adults can model both perception checking and courteous behavior by first asking whether the adolescent was in fact hurt and, if this is the case, apologizing for making the statement. Similarly, when adults are annoyed at an adolescent's behavior, they can employ an "I message", specifically describe the behavior which is bothering them, and politely request that the individual change the behavior. When working with groups of adolescents, there are numerous opportunities for employing this type of modeling.

An important point that is often overlooked in processing interpersonal interactions is that certain types of dyadic interactions are best handled outside of the group setting. For example, when teachers are bothered by an adolescent's constantly talking to a peer while they are talking, it may be less threatening to the adolescent when the teachers share their feelings in private. When interacting with adolescents it is important to choose communication skills and situations that optimize safety and respect for the needs of the individual. Since adolescents are sensitive about their peers' reactions, solving an individual issue in a group setting frequently creates a situation in which the adolescent is more acutely aware of peer responses than the adult's attempts at conflict resolution.

The third type of interaction to which adults can respond when making observations about a group's communication patterns is the larger group process. When people are aware of and respond to pervasive patterns of communication, they can avoid the disadvantages associated with solving individual conflicts within a group setting, while at the same time deal with issues that affect more students and have major implications concerning effective group functioning. Several examples may help to clarify this process. Consider a situation in which a group discussion is characterized by numerous instances of interruption and group members' failure to respond to the previous speaker's statement. In this situation a useful intervention would be to ask the group if the group members can describe the pattern occurring in their communication. If the group has previously discussed effective communication skills, group members will almost always point out their shortcomings and even suggest possible strategies for improving the situation.

Similarly, imagine a situation in which students are expected to work on an assignment and a large number of students are off task and noisy. This situation exemplifies the importance of considering options and examining the advantages and disadvantages associated with each option before making an intervention. For example, one option would be to threaten the students by telling them that the material will be on an examination and that if they continue to act the way they are, they will fail the exam. Like most forms of punishment, this response has the advantage of normally creating an immediate and temporary termination of the bothersome behavior. An obvious disadvantage of this response is that it does not address the cause of the problem. Furthermore, this type of response reduces the adolescents' sense of competence and power and therefore tends to create a you versus them situation.

A second response that could be employed in this situation would be to ignore the disorder and assume that it is just "one of those days." One advantage of this response is that it does not require involvement in the situation and therefore requires far less risk taking and energy. Several disadvantages are that students are not productively involved in learning and a "laissez faire" attitude may be interpreted as ineffectiveness or disinterest.

A third alternative is to request the students' attention, make an observation (behavioral description) about the classes' behavior, share any feelings elicited by their behavior, and ask the students to share their observation and suggestions concerning their behavior. While this response requires some risk, it has numerous benefits. By involving students, teachers open channels of communication that might lead to receiving useful information concerning such instructional factors as the clarity of their directions, the materials being used, and the degree to which students were prepared for the assignment. Students might also respond by apologizing for their behavior or explaining why they are so disruptive. In any case, students have been given responsibility that is clearly theirs and teachers have opened up a tremendous source of potential information and ideas.

When discussing the pros and cons of processing individual and group interactions with adolescents, teachers frequently note that this task requires considerable time and energy. Whenever I hear this topic being discussed, I am reminded of a statement a veteran teacher made to me during my second year of teaching in the public schools.

The teacher noted that working with adolescents was a very demanding task. He stated that it is inevitable that anyone who spends all day with adolescents will return home tired. However, he noted that, depending upon how teachers interact with adolescents, the fatigue tends to take two different forms. The first form he described as best expressed by the teacher who closes his classroom door and sighs "Whew, I held them in line for one more day. I hope I can do it again tomorrow." The second form of fatigue he believed was based on having processed interactions all day. In analyzing the long-range effects of the two types of fatigue, he noted that the former was often accompanied by anxiety, worry, and self-doubt while the latter was frequently associated with positive feelings.

In the final analysis, employing good communication skills as a means for dealing immediately with group problems requires that adults must be willing to respect students, risk receiving feedback, and concentrate on modeling effective communication skills. It also means that they must be willing to spontaneously take class time for developing a more safe and productive learning environment. These appear to be efforts and risks that any concerned, competent professional must make when working with adolescents.

When presented with the benefits associated with processing group interactions, adults frequently respond that they are not qualified and do not feel completely comfortable employing this method. It is certainly true that teacher training programs and psychology departments frequently fail to teach practical skills for interacting with adolescents. Nevertheless, there are several ways that teachers can improve their skills in group processes. As indicated earlier, adults can practice these skills in safer interactions with friends and family. In addition, many colleges, churches, and continuing education programs offer experientially oriented courses that enable adults to develop and practice communication skills in a relatively safe and structured setting. Teachers and other professionals can also employ these skills in professional interactions such as one-to-one contacts with colleagues or in faculty or staff meetings. These kinds of experiences should gradually create a situation in which it becomes comfortable to employ these skills in a spontaneous group situation.

SUMMARY

A major cause of adolescents' unproductive behavior is that adolescents often lack skill in effectively communicating their needs and wants. Neither the home nor social institutions provide adolescents with adequate skill development in communication and problem solving. Consequently, any attempt to assist adolescents in effectively coping with their environment must include a well-conceptualized and thoughtful approach to teaching these skills.

The first step in teaching effective communication skills is to assist adolescents in becoming acquainted with their peers. This initial intervention is necessary in order to establish a sense of safety that is prerequisite to any significant risk taking and learning. Once adolescents have become acquainted, instruction in communication skills can be approached through a variety of means. The methods described in this chapter include direct instruction and discussion, structured experiential activities, homework assignments, and spontaneously modeling effective problem solving. When effectively employed, these methods can significantly increase adolescents' communication skills and this in turn will have a major impact on adolescents' ability to function productively in a wide range of environments.

PART

III

Creating School and Classroom Environments that Reduce Behavior Problems

As discussed earlier, adolescents are in the midst of a time characterized by rapid personal change. While this time period is seldom exempt from conflict and questioning, the degree and form of anxiety and challenge are significantly influenced by the social institutions with which adolescents come into contact. Indeed,

> "One of the prevailing assumptions which Americans have learned to take for granted is that anxiety is a product of inadequate adjustment. This may be the case, but it is equally likely that anxiety reflects inadequacies in the pattern to which the individual attempts to adjust." (Putney and Putney, 1964, pp. 7-8)

Consequently, a major factor in working with behavior-problem adolescents involves examining their environments and attempting to make these environments more responsive to adolescents' psychological and developmental needs.

Before embarking on this unit that provides educators with ideas for altering school environments and instructional strategies, it seems logical to briefly examine the rationale that supports such changes. My experience as both a teacher and consultant suggests that at least a significant minority of secondary teachers firmly believe that it is the students and not the school or staff that need to change.

Those who would support placing the responsibility solely upon the problem student point to the fact that a significant majority of students report having basically positive attitudes toward school. Indeed, surveys such as that reported by Bachman (1970) suggest that a large percentage of secondary students have basically positive attitudes toward school. However, while schools are providing a satisfactory experience for many adolescents, surveys also indicate that a significant portion of adolescents do not find school a meaningful or positive experience. Each year nearly one million students (approximately one-quarter of the potential graduates) drop out of school. In 1975 the cost of school theft, assault, and vandalism was over $500 million. These facts indicate that schools are failing to meet the basic educational needs of a significant and important minority of adolescents.

The recent awareness concerning the need to provide a positive educational experience for all youngsters has highlighted the fact that the schools have often failed to work effectively with less fortunate, less gifted, and less passive/receptive students. Legislation aimed at alleviating this problem has increasingly focused on the importance of incorporating these youngsters into the mainstream of the educational process rather than educating them in isolation. This decision will provide a real challenge to our schools. While no one can expect schools to provide a positive experience for every student who enters their doors, there is room for improvement. If educators sincerely desire to provide a productive educational experience for as many students as possible, they must consider making substantive changes in their approach to educating adolescents.

Despite the fact that it will require considerable thought and energy to create school environments that provide an atmosphere more conducive to learning for a wider range of students, this approach has several definite advantages when compared to interventions that focus entirely upon assisting adolescents to change their behavior.

One major advantage associated with examining the conditions under which behavior-problem adolescents are asked to learn is that this approach focuses on factors that have potential benefits for many adolescents. As educators alter school environments in the direction of responding more effectively to adolescents' needs, they will provide more productive learning settings for all students. Parents and teachers frequently complain that too much time and money is expended helping behavior-problem students, while not enough attention is paid to the more "average" student. When educators focus their initial interventions for behavior-problem students on environmental factors that benefit all students, they respond to this legitimate concern.

A second advantage of examining environmental factors is that it more clearly separates seriously disturbed students from students who are experiencing developmental or situational problems. A significant amount of adolescent misbehavior is a response to environments that fail to meet important and legitimate needs. When the educational environments respond effectively to these needs, educators will be better able to determine which students are really in need of intensified, specialized assistance. Possibly educators will discover that there are far fewer seriously disturbed adolescents than they had anticipated.

This approach has special implications for counselors, special educators, and psychologists. If educators create school environments that effectively meet students' needs, they will reduce a wide range of possible causes of adolescent misbehavior. Thus specialists can more confidently focus on other—usually more indepth—variables and possible treatment styles. As the situation exists in most schools today, specialists have considerable difficulty separating that portion of the problem that belongs to the adolescent from the part that belongs to the school. In his book, *Schools Without Failure* (1969), William Glasser commented on this focus for intervention when he stated:

The traditional psychiatric-sociologic approach is ineffective because it assumes that school problems are almost entirely a reflection of individual personal problems, poor home environment, poverty, and racial discrimination. In contrast, it is apparent to me and to most of the educators I work with that, although external environmental conditions are bad for many children, there are factors inherent within the education system itself that not only cause many school problems but that accentuate the problems a child may bring to school. (Glasser, 1969, p.8. Reprinted by permission of Harper & Row, Publishers, Inc.)

A third advantage of focusing initial interventions on improving adolescents' environments is that this approach facilitates adolescents' eventually assuming greater responsibility for their behavior. When adolescents are forced to function in environments that fail to meet their legitimate psychological needs, they will respond to adult disapproval of their behavior by criticizing adult behavior. However, when school environments respond sensitively and effectively to adolescents' needs, educators find it much easier to confront adolescents with their responsibility for their unproductive behavior.

A final reason for altering adolescents' environments as an initial and major step in changing their behavior deals with the personal history of adolescents who are experiencing serious school difficulties. Adolescents who experience serious behavior problems frequently come from homes that have failed to provide them with the types of adult-child relationships that meet basic personal needs and subsequently facilitate growth (Ahlstrom and Havighurst, 1971; Bandura and Walters, 1959; Duncan, 1971; McCord, McCord, and Zola, 1959). Similar factors are found among school dropouts (Cervantes 1965a, 1965b). When compared to students who complete high school, dropouts view their home environments as less supportive and more negative.

Unfortunately, school dropouts and students with behavior problems find the school environment similar to their home environment. They are less involved in school activities, see the school as less supportive, and find themselves struggling in a system that fails to meet such basic needs as significance, belonging, and security. Therefore, if educators want to assist these adolescents in successfully coping with school environments, they must first focus on creating environments that support adolescents' basic needs. If educators do not create these environments, they cannot expect these students to remain in school or respond positively to the school environment. Indeed, it would be a sad commentary upon the state of their mental health if these students responded passively to yet another environment that they perceived as frightening, confusing, and unsupportive.

Part III will examine ways in which school environments and teaching strategies can be altered to more effectively meet adolescents' needs and thereby reduce failure and acting out. As indicated in Chapter 1, adolescents must work through a variety of developmental tasks. Examining adolescents' environments with the intent of focusing on how to facilitate each one of these tasks would present an awesome chore. There are, however, several basic needs which, when met, provide a solid foundation from which adolescents can begin to effectively cope with their environment and take responsibility for their own growth. These needs are best expressed by Maslow's (1968) hierarchy of needs and Coopersmith's (1967) belief that self-esteem is based on experiencing a sense of significance, competence, and power. Part III will focus on ways schools can structure adolescents' experiences so as to maximize the degree to which these needs are met. When viewed in isolation, some of the methods presented in this section may seem insignificant as factors that can assist in coping with behavior-problem adolescents. However, they build upon each other to create a vital foundation. Without this foundation, interventions such as behavioral contracts will seldom succeed.

The methods presented throughout Part III vary widely; not every method or idea will fit every educator's personal style or educational philosophy. It is not necessary to employ every method. What is important is that educators become increasingly aware of whether schools, classrooms, and residential environments are structured so as to meet adolescents' basic needs.

Strategies described in the following chapters often will respond to several needs. Indeed, it is to be expected that effective teaching strategies will have a variety of positive effects. Nevertheless an attempt has been made to describe teaching strategies in connection with the need that is most directly affected by the specific strategy. Chapter 6 provides a variety of ideas for increasing the degree to which adolescents experience a sense of significance and belonging in school settings. Chapter 7 considers methods for providing adolescents with an increased sense of competence. Finally, Chapter 8 outlines strategies for assuring that adolescents experience a reasonable amount of control over their school environment.

CHAPTER
6

Establishing a Sense of Significance and Belonging

As noted in Chapter 2 students who perceive themselves as liked by their teachers and peers tend to achieve better in school. Similarly, adolescents who perceive themselves as playing a functional role within their school are much less likely to drop out of school than are students who are uninvolved in school activities. Gump (1966) reported that despite comparable grades, home environments, and IQs, marginal students in small schools are much less likely to drop out of school than are marginal students in larger schools. Since there are fewer students available per activity in smaller schools, marginal students in small schools are more likely to become involved in school activities and therefore experience a greater sense of being needed.

Recently, a suburban high school in Portland, Oregon asked each student to complete a School Climate Survey. Figure 6.1 indicates how the 818 respondents answered those questions that referred to feeling a sense of significance or belonging.

An examination of these results shows that on only four of the twelve items did more than half of the students respond in the positive direction and on only one of the twelve items did over 75 percent of the students respond positively. Furthermore, only 27 percent of the students indicated that they "felt wanted and needed at this school." Therefore, it is not surprising that only 33 percent of the students indicated that they were "generally enthusiastic about coming to school."

99

Figure 6.1   School Climate Survey: Items relating to the
Degree of Significance Experienced by Students.
(Used by permission of Edward A. West.)

Questions Asked	% Yes	% No
I know at least one teacher very well.	76%	24%
When I have a problem, I know someone I can go to.	65%	35%
When a student comes along who has special problems, this school works out a plan to help this student.	62%	38%
I feel teachers respect me regardless of the kind of grades I make.	55%	45%
In this school I am treated as a person rather than simply as a student.	48%	52%
I have an opportunity to discuss things that are important to me.	45%	55%
I am recognized for my special talents, abilities, and interests.	43%	57%
I receive special encouragement when I need it.	41%	59%
I can think of three positive things about myself a teacher has told me recently.	41%	59%
I feel that teachers understand my needs and interests.	34%	66%
I am generally enthusiastic about coming to school.	33%	67%
I feel wanted and needed at this school.	27%	73%

In his book, *Schools Without Failure* (1969), William Glasser speaks pointedly to the issue of students feeling needed and involved when he writes:

> To begin to be successful, children must receive at school what they lack: a good relationship with other people, both children and adults. A child or adult cannot gain a success identity and fulfill his needs through the established pathways because he is lonely. (Glasser, 1969, pp. 16-17. Reprinted by permission of Harper & Row, Publishers, Inc.)

He goes on to state that:

> They can't make better choices, more responsible choices, unless they are strongly and emotionally involved with those who can. In education, involvement may start with one person, be he teacher, counselor, or administrator, or it may start with groups of children or even with a whole class. Both in psychiatry and in school, teachers and therapists too often stand aloof from children; they do not get emotionally involved; they are not warm, personal and interested; they do not reveal themselves as human beings so that the children can identify with them. Thus they fail to alleviate the loneliness of the many children who need human warmth so desperately. Only in a school where teacher and student are involved with each other and equally involved with the curriculum through thinking and problem solving does education flourish—an education that prepares students to live successfully in the world. (Glasser, 1969, p. 19. Reprinted by permission of Harper & Row, Publishers, Inc.)

HELPING STUDENTS KNOW AND INTERACT WITH
THEIR PEERS

With this background in mind, the problem becomes determining what educators can do to increase the degree to which students experience a feeling of significance and belonging within a school or institutional setting. One method educators can employ is to create situations in which students know their peers and the adults in their environment. This can be accomplished by employing acquaintance activities (described in Chapter 5) and by teachers employing a reasonable amount of self-disclosure. Students' feeling of involvement can also be enhanced by seating students in a circle or other seating arrangement that enables them to see each other. Similarly, teachers can employ small group work that allows students an opportunity to interact with peers and to be more actively involved in the learning process. It is difficult for students to feel needed or involved when the teacher is consistently the focus of attention and almost all classroom interactions are directed at the teacher.

When discussing the use of a circle, square, or U-shaped seating arrangement, teachers frequently note that at first students find this type of arrangement uncomfortable. In addition, they note that there are occasionally one or more students who pull back from the circle or refuse to sit in the circle. There are several explanations for this type of student behavior, and these explanations highlight several advantages of a more inclusive seating arrangement. First, students' hesitancy is to some extent a natural response to something new. Many students have not experienced a classroom in which they were seated in a manner that facilitated peer interaction. Second, both this type of seating arrangement and the use of group work have definite implications concerning the value and role of students. Making students more accessible to each other implies that students should be more active in and responsible for their own learning. It is much harder to hide in a circular seating arrangement or in a small group than in the more traditional row arrangement. Students may find this new definition of their value and role frightening. This anxiety and discomfort is not surprising. Most students have spent most of their school years involved in relatively passive learning from which they could easily escape. Expecting active involvement creates a significant amount of disequilibrium that is necessarily accompanied by some confusion and anxiety. However, if adolescents are to feel that they are a meaningful part of a classroom, they must not be allowed to sit unobtrusively in the corner.

The fact that some students may balk at becoming more actively involved in class activities provides an excellent opportunity for teachers to express their concern for such students. Teachers can involve such students (either individually or as a group) in discussions aimed at clarifying both for themselves and for teachers why they are expressing a need to be uninvolved and outside the group. As a result the student may choose to remain outside the group for a period of time. However, this decision, when made by the student and accompanied by an awareness of what this decision means, provides the student with a feeling of significance, competence, and power. Compare this to a situation in which students are ignored and their right to remain alone is granted without any dialogue. Adults who have worked with adolescents are aware that the quiet, removed behavior is sometimes a cry for help, a request to be assisted in making the difficult move outward and toward others. Adults must be willing to create environments and make contacts that reinforce such steps toward growth.

DEVELOPING APPROPRIATE EXPECTATIONS

Directly related to the concept of involving students in the classroom is the fact that research indicates that teachers respond differently to high- and low-achieving students. In their book, *Teacher-Student Relationships: Causes and Consequences* (1974), Brophy and Good summarize a wide range of research that indicates that teachers' interactions with high-achieving students are more encouraging and positive than those with low-achieving students. More specifically, teachers tend to call on high-achieving students more often, wait longer for highs to respond to questions, respond more supportively to incorrect or partially right answers from highs, reinforce highs' correct answers more, and demand more of highs. The research presented by these authors clearly indicates that teachers tend to both directly and indirectly tell high-achieving students that they are more important, valued members within the classroom.

These findings should not be viewed as a condemnation of teachers. Anyone who has taught knows how easy it is to slip into the situation of letting the "better" students carry the class. Instead, these findings should serve to make teachers more aware of the subtle ways in which low-achieving or behavior-problem students begin to experience a lack of significance and belonging in the classroom. In some ways, this realization places the teacher in a double bind. While teachers do not want to ignore poorer students, neither do they want to place these students in a position of embarrassment by asking questions that the students cannot answer. Again, the best approach to solving this problem is to share this concern (individually, in a small group, or with the entire class) with the student(s) and develop a plan for involving the student(s) in a manner that is comfortable both for the teacher and the student(s).

An excellent example of the surprising and positive results of such an interaction was reported to me by a high school Spanish teacher. The teacher had for some time been concerned about a second-year Spanish student, named Sally, who was doing very poorly in class. Sally was extremely quiet and never volunteered answers. On those rare occasions when she was asked questions, she invariably muttered something incoherent, and the teacher quickly provided the answer or moved on to another student. The teacher became increasingly concerned about Sally's behavior and her related failing grades. Finally she decided to become more involved with Sally. She began by saying "Hi" to Sally in the halls and greeting her at the door each day. When this approach appeared to have limited effect on Sally's classroom behavior, the teacher decided to schedule a conference to discuss the problem with her. The teacher began the conference by sharing her observations about Sally's classroom behavior and expressing her concern. However, much to the teacher's surprise, Sally's response was loud and clear, "It's your fault, you never call on me in class!" Following a discussion of this issue, they agreed that the teacher would ask Sally more questions and that Sally would be responsible for attempting to provide an audible response to each question. The results were amazing. Sally's work improved markedly. Despite the fact that she had failed the first nine-week grading period, Sally's work earned her a "C" for the semester grade.

Certainly every instance will not turn out as satisfactorily as this one. However, adults have so little to lose and so much to gain through openly expressing their concern for adolescents and involving them in discussions aimed at examining adults' expectations and adolescents' needs. While there are several minor barriers to creating this type of dialogue, these can be readily overcome. One problem many teachers express is that this type of discussion requires some time alone with the student and that such time is difficult to find during a school day that is tightly scheduled for both the teacher and the student. One answer to this problem is simply to employ at least some classroom activities that do not involve constant teacher attention. For example, when students are involved in group work, individual research, or watching a film, the teacher can schedule times to talk individually with students who are uninvolved or unproductively involved in class.

A second concern expressed by some teachers is that they do not feel comfortable with this form of confrontation or problem solving. There are several ways to deal with this situation. First, if the student is willing, it may be helpful to ask a counselor, another teacher, or another student to assist in facilitating the discussion. This can make the interchange flow more smoothly, and it can provide teachers with an opportunity to increase their own skills by watching someone who is more comfortable and skilled at handling this type of dialogue. Another way for teachers to increase their skills in this area is to take courses or inservice training that focuses on topics such as problem solving or interpersonal communication. Most courses covering such topics provide a wide range of opportunities for role playing and other experiential activities that can assist teachers in improving their problem-solving skills.

EMPLOYING EFFECTIVE COMMUNICATION SKILLS

Although it is included within all other methods for increasing students' sense of significance and belonging, the value of employing effective communication skills cannot be overemphasized. There is no single factor that has more potential for expressing concern and respect for others than the way in which people speak and listen to others. By employing some degree of self-disclosure, adults indicate to adolescents that they value adolescents enough to share some of their thoughts, feelings, and concerns. By employing open sending skills, adults indicate to adolescents that they respect their ability to be involved in candid, two-way adult interactions. Finally, by employing the listening skills outlined in Chapter 4, adults indicate that adolescents' input is valued and that adults respect their ability to be actively involved in solving their own problems.

A final point about the effect of communication skills in providing students with a sense of significance relates to teachers' use of courteous remarks. Anyone who has worked as a waiter or waitress is aware of the effect courtesy has on making a person feel important and valued. When courtesies are lacking in such situations, the relationship becomes one in which people treat each other as roles rather than as people. Similar situations occur when adults work with adolescents. Since, like the patron at the restaurant, society affords teachers more authority and power than the adolescents with whom they work, it is easy for teachers to occasionally slip into communication patterns that lack the courtesies they would afford their peers. Such slips inevitably reduce the degree to which adolescents experience a sense of being valued.

RECOGNIZING STUDENTS AND THEIR ACCOMPLISHMENTS

In this section I would like to share two instances I have seen that highlight the value of recognizing students and their accomplishments. The fact that anyone who has worked with adolescents for any period of time can cite similar instances reinforces the importance of attending to this issue.

Several years ago, I attended a staffing on a particularly troublesome eighth grade boy. After listening to considerable discussion concerning how difficult the student was to motivate, I was relieved to hear a counselor ask whether anyone was having a successful experience with the student. Much to everyone's surprise, a teacher responded that he was having few problems with the student. The surprise turned to humor when one of the teachers pointed out that the teacher who was experiencing no difficulty was by far the largest teacher in the school. Fortunately, the counselor probed further and asked the teacher if he was doing anything special to which he might attribute his success. The teacher responded that he had noticed that the student seemed to need a lot of attention. Therefore, he had decided to greet the student at the door each day by saying, "Hi Larry," and touching the student. He followed this by finding three opportunities each day to compliment Larry, say his name, and touch him. The teacher reported that since he had initiated this program, he had observed a significant improvement in Larry's behavior. After hearing this information, Larry's teachers decided to each find opportunities to acknowledge Larry and to comment upon his positive achievements. While Larry did not become a model student, teachers reported a marked change in his attitude and behavior.

An incident that highlights the value of acknowledging students' accomplishments was reported to me by a student teacher. The student teacher had been experiencing considerable difficulty with a particularly rowdy junior boy. The boy frequently interjected humorous off-color remarks, refused to follow reasonable teacher requests, and made negative comments to other students about the student teacher. By openly sharing with the student the discomfort his behavior was causing her and asking him what could be done to improve the situation, the situation had been improved considerably. However, the real change came when the student teacher attended several of the student's wrestling matches. When the student realized that the teacher was interested not only in his classroom performance, but also in something that was important to him, his behavior changed dramatically. Obviously not all situations with behavior-problem adolescents can be solved so readily. However, instances such as this point to the importance of developing what Buber (1958) termed *I-thou* rather than *I-it* relationships. When adolescents perceive adults as being concerned only with their own needs and interests, adolescents are likely to respond in kind. If, on the other hand, they see adults as genuinely interested in them, they are more likely to behave in ways that support adults' needs and interests.

There is a 16mm film entitled *Cipher in the Snow* that depicts a junior high age boy who dies one day on the way to school. The film presents episodes from the boy's life that highlight the fact that this boy simply received so little caring—had so little significance—that he lost his will to live. While the story is fictional and the episodes stylized, the point is powerful. All people need to experience a sense of belonging, a feeling of being valued and important to at least one other individual. While most people do not die from a lack of significance, almost all people find ways to defend themselves from feelings of worthlessness. Some people choose to achieve, some rebel and strike out, others become passive, some take their own lives. There is no guarantee that providing problem adolescents with a greater sense of significance will make a major change in their behavior. This may or may not happen. However, any long-term change in their behavior must ultimately have as its base a sense of worth and belonging.

Figure 6.2 I Am Present

My happiness is me, not you.
Not only because you want me to be what I am not.
I cannot be happy when I change
Merely to satisfy your selfishness.
Nor can I feel content when you criticize me for not thinking your thoughts.
Or for seeing like you do.
You call me a rebel
And yet each time I have rejected your beliefs
You have rebelled against mine
I do not try to mold your mind.
I know you are trying hard enough to be just you.
And I cannot allow you to tell me what to be
For I am concentrating on being me.
You said that I was transparent
And easily forgotten
But why then did you try to use my lifetime
To prove to yourself who you are.

From the Introduction:
  Michelle! You were with us for such a short time before choosing that fog swept beach to continue on your way. It was July, 1967, and you were only 20.

CREATING POSITIVE PHYSICAL ENVIRONMENTS

While often overlooked, the quality of the physical environment that adults provide for adolescents says a great deal to them regarding adults' feelings toward them. It is difficult for someone to feel valued when they are placed in working or living conditions that blatantly reflect a lack of concern for their comfort or health.

Given the importance physical environments can play both in enhancing productivity and creating a sense of being valued, it is surprising that most secondary school classrooms are so uncomfortable, drab, and uninteresting. I recently visited a high school classroom in which a teacher had taught five or six periods a day for over twenty years. The room was almost completely devoid of color or decorations of any kind. Thinking that the teacher might simply prefer a very bland environment, I inquired as to whether he preferred this type of environment. Somewhat to my surprise, I was informed that he enjoyed a variety of contemporary painters and that he enjoyed growing plants. In fact, the room in which he worked at home was quite well decorated. While his behavior was undoubtedly influenced by social conventions and expectations as well as by the classrooms he had experienced as a student, his classroom nevertheless reflected a lack of excitement about and commitment to what took place in that room. If teachers expect students to value what goes on in their classrooms and to see the classroom as an important place, they must treat their classrooms as if they were valued and interesting environments. There are a variety of ways to create more lively and comfortable classrooms. Classrooms can be decorated with plants, posters, and mobiles. Since students spend a considerable amount of time in a classroom, it seems only natural that they should be actively involved in decorating the room. Students are almost always interested in becoming involved in this task and will usually work after school in order to create a more interesting classroom. Much to most teachers' surprise, adolescents often enjoy creating interesting bulletin boards, which add color to the room. Perhaps even more important is the sense of commitment and involvement that accompanies having been actively involved in decorating a room.

While most secondary school classrooms are rather striking examples of uninteresting environments, most school cafeterias provide even more obvious examples of physical environments that fail to respond appropriately to students' physiological needs. Most teachers will attest to the fact that students frequently return from lunch periods quite excited and tense. People need only eat in most school cafeterias to understand why this occurs. Despite what people know about the physical advantages associated with eating slowly in a peaceful atmosphere, educators provide students with a noisy, crowded environment.

While it is obviously difficult to change such situations given the current structure and funding of most public schools, there are practical changes that can be made. Some schools have altered cafeterias by replacing long, institutional tables that seat eight to sixteen students with small tables that seat only four students. When covered with checkered tablecloths, these tables help to create a warm environment that tends to elicit quiet talk and vastly improved manners. A similar approach to solving the problems associated with noisy, crowded cafeterias has been the creation of small cafes run by home economic students. On those occasions when I have eaten in such settings, I have been impressed with the degree of calmness with which students leave such cafes. The students who had eaten in such settings appeared far better prepared to become productively involved in learning than did those leaving a standard school cafeteria.

Schools are certainly not alone in their failure to provide comfortable physical surroundings for adolescents. Unfortunately, the majority of programs for delinquent and seriously disturbed adolescents provide limited amounts of physical comfort or personal space. Most juvenile prisons and residential treatment facilities find it necessary to pack a large number of young people into a small space. Similarly, living quarters for such youngsters are too often sadly lacking in privacy or comfortable furnishings. Most adults who would define themselves as functioning effectively would experience considerable discomfort and possible regression to less productive behavioral patterns if they were asked to live in housing similar to that provided for problem youth. Unfortunately, this situation reflects current societal values and priorities and will most likely continue for some time. However, when working with adolescents who must live in such environments, the least adults can do is acknowledge the difficulties associated with such conditions and do their best to improve these environments as much as possible within the limits imposed by inadequate funding.

SUMMARY

Almost everyone feels more comfortable and more able to perform effectively when they are surrounded by conditions that indicate that they are accepted, liked, and valued. Although some individuals can accept the challenge of functioning effectively in less safe and favorable conditions, the developmental and educational experiences of behavior-problem adolescents intensify their need to receive support and acceptance when confronted with demands for academic performance or changes in behavior. Since the creation of more supportive learning environments will have a positive impact upon all adolescents, it seems logical that educators should, whenever possible, work to create environments that provide adolescents with a sense of comfort, safety, and significance.

While there are numerous approaches to creating such supportive environments, this chapter has focused on five strategies. These strategies include (1) helping students to know and interact with their peers, (2) developing appropriate expectations, (3) employing effective communication skills, (4) recognizing students and their accomplishments, and (5) creating positive physical environments. Chapters 7 and 8 will examine educational strategies that support these approaches through more actively involving students in the learning process.

CHAPTER
7

Creating a Sense of Competence

As mentioned in Chapter 1, seeing oneself as competent and respected by others is a basic ingredient in the development of a positive self-image. Almost all persons have experienced the difference in the way they feel and behave when they feel competent in a situation as compared to when they perceive themselves as unable to cope with the situation. Similarly, anyone who has worked in an organization is aware of how people are influenced by the overt as well as covert messages that indicate the degree to which the organization respects and involves its members. When people are treated with respect and given responsibility and trust, they tend to apply themselves more intensely and feel a greater sense of commitment and loyalty to the organization. Conversely, when people are carefully monitored and treated with suspicion, they tend to find ways to subvert the system. In a sense, they are "getting back" at people for not giving them the respect they believe they deserve.

A useful scheme for presenting this concept was developed by McGregor (1967). McGregor noted that there are two basic ways of viewing people and that these views strongly affect the manner in which managers (or principals, teachers, parents, etc.) arrange environments, solve problems, and interact with others. The first manner of viewing people McGregor labeled "Theory X." Theory X maintains that people are by nature passive and resistant and must, therefore, be provided with consistent direction and prodding. Theory X states that human behavior is basically extrinsically motivated and that people will work only when they receive measurable rewards for their behavior or punishment for their failure to respond appropriately. Under this theory, people are seen as basically dishonest and unable to be actively involved in decision making.

McGregor labeled the second manner in which to view people as "Theory Y." Theory Y assumes that people are by nature curious and exploratory. Individuals are viewed as having a high degree of intrinsic motivation. Consequently, people can be expected to take action when the activities available provide them an opportunity to learn something that appears interesting and meaningful to them. Theory Y therefore stresses that individuals can be actively involved in their own learning and decision making.

McGregor's conceptualization concerning the two ways to view human nature and motivation has significant implications for working with adolescents. Adolescents are extremely sensitive to the responses of those around them. Indeed, a major portion of the developmental tasks of adolescence are direcly related to becoming viewed and treated as competent individuals. Since they are in the process of developing a sense of who they are, adolescents are understandably sensitive to what adults' words and behaviors say about them.

Given the immediacy and intensity of their striving for developing a sense of competence and independence, it is not surprising that adolescents respond negatively when, operating from Theory X, adults provide them with environments that deny the importance of their involvement and their input. This chapter and the following chapter on providing adolescents with some sense of control over their environment will examine ways in which teachers can structure their classrooms and interactions with adolescents in order to more effectively meet adolescents' need for competence and independence.

INFLUENCING COMPETENCE THROUGH EXPECTATIONS

While an individual's feeling of competence might ideally be based solely upon personalized, internal criteria and evaluation, people are to some extent dependent upon other's opinions and judgments as a guidepost in determining their success and even their worth. Since adolescents are searching to discover their own sense of worth and identity and are to a large extent still dependent upon adults, it is not surprising that they are sensitive to the values and evaluations implied within adults' judgments and expectations. Therefore, when working with adolescents adults must be particularly sensitive to the ways in which their expectations influence their own behaviors in ways that transmit judgments, which in turn significantly influence adolescents' feelings and behaviors.

Expectations Influence Perceptions, Interpretations, and Behaviors

A vivid example of an interaction that characterizes the manner in which adults send messages to adolescents concerning their competence and trustworthiness occurred while I was supervising a student teacher. As I walked into the faculty lounge, I met the student's cooperating teacher. The teacher informed me that the student teacher had had an excellent learning experience the previous day. He proceeded to inform me that the student teacher had discovered that he could not trust students and that if he gave them an opportunity, they would take advantage of him (Theory X). He noted that the student teacher had given the students some freedom and that when he went to check on them he found that they had taken advantage of him. He suggested that I talk to the student teacher and informed me that the incident was not a reflection on the student teacher's ability, but was simply due to his inexperience in working with adolescents. He suggested that I watch the next class period carefully since this class had been the one with which the student teacher had experienced the problem.

As I entered the class, the student teacher completed filling out his attendance slip and moved to the front of the class. He informed the class that prior to starting the day's lesson, he would like to share his feelings about an incident that had occurred the previous day. He proceeded to inform the class that he was angry and disappointed with the manner in which several students had behaved the previous day. He noted that since the film he had shown was of below average quality, he had given the students a choice of watching the movie or going to the library to work on their class projects. He commented that he was angry because when he went to the library to see if the students needed any assistance, a number of students were not in the library. He stated that while there might be good reasons to explain this situation, the students' behavior had placed him in a rather bad position. Finally, he informed the students involved that he would like to speak with them after class.

As I listened to this young prospective teacher, I was struck by one major difference between his perception and that of his cooperating teacher. The student teacher indicated that he had gone to the library to see if he could be of assistance to the students. He had not gone down to check on them. He assumed that most, if not all, the students would be working on their projects (Theory Y).

When working with students, it is vital that teachers sincerely anticipate that the students will succeed and that teachers communicate this expectation to them. Research clearly points to the powerful effect that teacher expectations have on student learning and behavior (Brophy and Good, 1974). As these authors indicate:

> Expectations tend to be self-sustaining. They affect both perception, by causing the teacher to be alert for what he expects and to be less likely to notice what he does not expect, and interpretation, by causing the teacher to interpret (and perhaps distort) what he sees so that it is consistent with his expectations. (Good and Brophy, 1977, pp. 391-392)

In further describing how expectations tend to influence teacher behavior, Good and Brophy state that:

> When a teacher's initial perception of a student's ability and motivation is inaccurate, the teacher is likely to treat the student as if he were somewhat different from what he actually is. In time, such teacher behavior may move the student in the direction of the original (and erroneous) expectation. Even accurate expectations can be self-defeating if they are inflexible. The teacher may correctly perceive a student as a low achiever; however, if the teacher sees this as an unchangeable condition, he may assign the student tasks that are interesting and time-consuming but not geared to raising the student's achievement level. (Good and Brophy, 1977, p. 384)

More specifically, research findings clearly indicate that teachers do, in fact, subtly communicate their expectations to students. Specifically related to the area of competence, these findings indicate that teachers ask many more questions of students whom they view as high achievers. In addition, teachers ask high achievers many more questions that require a complex response while reserving the simple, factual questions for students whom they view as low achievers. Even more important, however, is the fact that teachers wait longer for high-achieving students to answer a question and are likely to respond to an incorrect or partially correct answer from a high-achieving student by providing some form of hint, encouragement, or reinforcement. Conversely, when low-achieving students fail to respond or respond incorrectly, teachers are more likely to immediately call on another student or provide the answer themselves. Therefore, low-achieving students learn that much less is expected of them. A comparison of response patterns of low-achieving students in various grade levels shows that as they become older, low-achieving students become increasingly less involved in the classroom. It is quite possible that these students have learned that teachers do not expect them to respond and that they can hide within the classroom by simply not responding.

When working with behavior-problem adolescents, teachers must therefore guard against developing and communicating expectations that create self-fulfilling prophecies. Rather, teachers must respond to students in ways that clearly indicate their respect for the students as individuals and their belief in their students' potential to change. In working with behavior-problem adolescents, I have been amazed at the power of this single factor. Adolescents see adult distrust variously as an indication of dislike, aggression, ignorance, and arrogance. When adults indicate their suspicion, distrust, or skepticism, they strike a particularly sensitive chord in adolescents. Understandably, adolescents respond like anyone who is attacked. They become defensive, counterattack, flee, or—worst of all—give in and accept adults' definition of them.

Developing High Expectations

While having high expectations sounds good in theory, adults who work with behavior-problem adolescents frequently point to the fact that when they let down their guards and give these adolescents responsibility, adolescents frequently abuse that trust. This concern is valid and must eventually be confronted by anyone working with problem youngsters.

Someone Must Take the First Step in Showing Trust   When people wish to change the form of interchange in any interaction, someone must go first in letting down his guard. Interpersonal interactions can be compared to an arms race between two nations. As long as both parties keep up their shields and continue to stockpile munitions, no progress will be made toward resolving the conflict. One party must be willing to take the risk to lower their build-up of defenses in hope that the other party will follow. The analogy applies to adults' interactions with adolescents. Someone must be willing to change the pattern of interaction, to take the risk of saying, "Okay, if you think you can handle this, I trust you enough to let you do it." When adults do this they may find that, somewhat to their surprise, the other party is relieved by the possibility of dismantling some of their arsenal and subsequently becomes more receptive to requests. There is no guarantee that this will happen. However, the possible benefits are considerable.

High Expectations as a Motivational Factor   Another point associated with trusting adolescents to competently handle situations refers to the old adage that "you can't succeed if you don't try." Certainly people must always consider the possible negative consequences (both for the adolescent and others) that might accompany failure. However, programs for behavior-problem adolescents all too often structure out any real opportunities for demonstrating and being reinforced for relatively major changes in behavior. Most programs operate on the basis of providing reinforcement for small, relatively superficial behavior changes. This is not to say that in many instances reinforcing gradual increments of change is not necessary or desirable. Nevertheless, attitudes, expectations and motivation have a significant influence on behavior. Adolescents often possess the ability to display appropriate behavior, but do not do so because of their feelings about their environment. Anyone who has worked with behavior-problem adolescents has observed numerous examples of extreme differences between these youngsters' knowledge and skill acquisition and their performance. As adults work to bring about changes in the environment and adolescents' attitudes about their environment, adults may want to provide them with opportunities to display major behavioral changes. When adults allow adolescents opportunities to display only small increments of behavior change or change in very limited areas, adolescents may interpret this action as manipulation or lack of respect. Adolescents respond negatively to either of these possible interpretations. It is, therefore, possible that in at least some instances the subtle messages implicit in structured behavioral programs may prove to be a deterrent to productive growth for adolescents.

An interesting perspective on the motivational potential of high expectations is presented in Kleinfeld's (1972) study of teacher behavior with Indian and Eskimo students who were experiencing difficulties associated with moving from a rural to an urban school. Kleinfeld found that teachers were most successful when they combined a personal interest in and warm relationship with their students with high expectations. Her findings indicated that teachers who failed to incorporate one or both of these ingredients were unsuccessful in working with these students. In summarizing her findings, Kleinfeld stated that:

> ... The essence of the instructional style which elicits a high level of intellectual performance from village Indian and Eskimo students is to create an extremely warm personal relationship and to actively demand a level of academic work which the student does not suspect he can attain. Village students thus interpret the teacher's demandingness not as bossiness or hostility, but rather as another expression of his personal concern, and meeting the teacher's academic standards becomes their reciprocal obligation in an intensely personal relationship. (Kleinfeld, 1972, p. 34)

Failure Can Facilitate Learning   An important point related to trusting adolescents with meaningful responsibility and opportunities to display change is that in many instances failure experiences are a prerequisite to learning. If an adolescent's implicit or explicit statement is, "I could do that if I had the chance," then adults have much to gain by providing the chance. If the adolescent succeeds, both the adult and adolescent have gained confidence in his ability to effectively handle another situation. If the adolescent fails, both adults and adolescent can examine the reasons for the failure and perhaps break the task down into smaller units or teach the skills necessary for success.

However, if adults inform the adolescent that he cannot attempt the task, they are setting up a power struggle that, even if adults win, has several negative consequences. This situation indicates a basic lack of trust and respect for the adolescent. Adolescents are likely to respond to this perceived denial of their competence by finding other—often less appropriate—opportunities for displaying their competence. A similar problem associated with not allowing adolescents to attempt constructive activities that they feel they are prepared to handle is that they will frequently attempt to demonstrate their power by subverting those activities that adults choose for them. It appears that adults would be much better off if they allowed adolescents to attempt the behaviors and assume the responsibility that they believe they can handle. Although adults may need to develop reasonable safeguards and checkpoints to monitor their attempts, the efforts expended in this direction are potentially productive while the effort expended in controlling adolescents' resentful behavior is frequently destructive.

Preventing Possible Harmful Effects   The obvious question now becomes: What about the situation in which the behaviors that adolescents want to perform are potentially harmful to the adolescents or to others? The key issues here are whether a real danger does exist and whether the possible gains are great enough to risk some loss. Certainly there will be times when an adolescent cannot be permitted to attempt an activity. However, in many if not most instances the dangers are not as great as adults would like to believe and can be significantly reduced if adults develop a well-planned program. While Chapter 13 will present a variety of models for developing behavior change programs for adolescents, an example may help to clarify the point being made here.

Consider a situation in which a student believes he can succeed in a particular teacher's class. The student has had a history of talking back to teachers, refusing to follow teacher requests, and skipping classes. The teacher with whom the student wishes to be placed has high expectations for students and tends to be quite negative with students. It is also known that the adolescent involved has difficulty responding well to negative verbal statements made by adults. Finally, the counselor involved has spent considerable effort in establishing a positive relationship with this teacher and convincing him that problem students in the building need some degree of additional assistance. This final goal has been only tentatively reached.

In this instance, no real danger exists for the student, the teacher, or other students. The question then becomes whether the possible gains outweigh the potential losses. While this is obviously a subjective judgment, the potential for making the "right" decision can be enhanced considerably by following a pattern that should be employed whenever an adolescent wishes to attempt a task about which adults have some reservations. First, the behaviors that the adolescent will have to employ should be carefully examined. It is helpful at this point to include the classroom teacher in this discussion and to focus on developing specific, observable behavioral expectations. Once this has been accomplished, the counselor should sit down with the adolescent and discuss whether he believes he can perform the specific behaviors that have been outlined. At this point the counselor should raise any concerns and should examine the possible consequences associated with both the success and failure of the program. If the decision is reached that an adolescent will attempt the task being considered, the next step is to develop a method for conflict resolution within that environment. It is extremely important that all parties involved are included in developing this plan. In the case presented above, the teacher, the student, and the counselor should list numerous specific problems that might arise and reach a consensus on specific methods for coping with these potential problems. This step is analogous to the trapeze artist's employing a safety net. Adults often accept adolescents' decisions to attempt behaviors and develop no method for handling small failures that almost inevitably arise when someone attempts a difficult task. When adults fail to provide such a safety net, they are in some ways setting the youngster up to fail.

This brings up a very subtle, but extremely important point related to working with adolescents. Since their failures may sometimes "prove an adult's point," adults must be careful that they do not subconsciously develop programs that have a high probability for failure. Adults must be sure that the adolescent's success is more important than their own need to perceive themselves as knowledgeable predictors of behavior. Although this may appear to be a minor point that presents an overly critical view of adults, all people have a need to be competent. This need can be subtly, yet powerfully keyed when working with adolescents in a conflict situation. When an adolescent tells adults that they are wrong, and unfair, and that he should indeed be allowed to perform a specific task, adults can easily slip into a response (often not consciously acknowledged) of "Okay, you can try it, and when you fail you'll see that I was right."

Once adults have maximized the possibility of success by developing a safety net, the final step in aiding adolescents in attempting a new task is to develop a schedule for monitoring the student's progress. In the case of the student taking a course from a demanding teacher, it would be useful to schedule periodic conferences in which the counselor, the student, and the teacher discuss how the student is functioning in class. Conferences like this provide an opportunity to discuss and reclarify expectations and to examine how the safety net strategies are functioning.

Teachers must become aware of their own response patterns, and they must work with students to develop realistic and mutually accepted ways to increase students' classroom involvement. The method presented for helping a student to succeed in a demanding class provides a useful model for working with individual students to develop a program for increased student involvement. The next section will focus on the need to more actively involve all students in the learning process.

INCREASING ACTIVE STUDENT INVOLVEMENT
IN THE LEARNING PROCESS

While there are numerous ways in which adults communicate their respect or lack of respect for students, perhaps the most powerful message is found in the extent to which they involve students in activities that directly affect them. Regardless of what adults may say to adolescents concerning their respect for adolescents' rights and skills, the real message is communicated by adults' behaviors and the extent to which they actively involve adolescents in the learning process.

In addition to the message implied by actively involving adolescents in the learning process, it is also important to realize that active participation is an important and even necessary prerequisite for learning for many adolescents. Consequently, when this ingredient is missing, many students will be unable to achieve success and will therefore not obtain the sense of competence associated with successful school achievement.

The Need for Increased Involvement

While research highlights the fact that low-achieving students are noticeably uninvolved in classroom learning situations, a wide range of research indicates that students in general often play a relatively passive role in the classroom. In summarizing his early findings, Flanders (1963) stated his "rule of two-thirds." This rule states that (1) within classrooms someone is talking about two-thirds of the time, (2) about two-thirds of that time the teacher is the person talking, and (3) about two-thirds of the teacher's talk is spent in giving directions, expressing facts and opinions, or criticizing students. Further analysis of Flanders' findings shows that:

> In studies of seventh grade social studies and eighth grade mathematics classes, Flanders found that the teachers in superior classes talked only slightly less than the teachers in the other classes, 50 to 60 percent of the time; but that only 40 to 50 percent of their teaching was directive. In other words, the teachers whose classes had constructive attitudes and scored higher on content achievement were more flexible than others in the quality of their verbal influence.
>
> By contrast, the analysis of classes below average in constructive student attitudes and in content achievement showed that their teachers spoke over 75 percent of the time, and that over 75 percent of their talk was devoted to giving directions, expressing opinions and facts, and occasionally, criticizing students. For these teachers, the rule of two-thirds becomes the rule of three-fourths plus. (Ryan and Cooper, 1975, p. 210)

Employing a different coding system, Bellack et al. (1966) observed fifteen high school classes and found results similar to those presented by Flanders. Bellack's findings suggest that classrooms are dominated by teacher talk that focuses on factual, subject material. In fact, it appears that the students' primary role is to respond to teachers' commands and questions.

Results similar to those presented above were found by Gallagher (1965). When studying the types of questions employed by teachers, Gallagher found that even in classrooms for gifted children, nearly 50 percent of all questions asked were cognitive memory questions, i.e., questions that required the students to reproduce already learned material.

These and other studies point to the lack of involvement that adolescents experience in school classrooms. The picture the research paints of a typical secondary classroom is one in which students are receivers of information and regurgitators of prepackaged ideas. This tendency to minimally involve students—and then nearly 50 percent of the time on a superficial basis—has real implications concerning students' feelings of competence.

The type of classroom interaction described above may provide opportunities for demonstrating competence to those students who possess good auditory retention skills and who can receive reinforcement by doing well on examinations. Unfortunately, there are many students who find this form of classroom structure uncomfortable and replete with failure. Discussions with such students reveal their dislike for situations in which they must sit as passive recipients of information that they frequently can neither understand nor relate in any meaningful way to their current life experiences. As discussed in Chapter 2, students' acting-out behavior is often related to the fact that they see no reason to accept a role of uninvolvement and continued failure when they see no concrete benefits being derived from such a role. As a high school student wrote:

> But how about interest? This is obviously the most important part of the discussion, for if the individual student feels that he cannot make a meaningful contribution to the learning process, he will reject it. This is where dropouts and disillusionment come from. The traditional lecture format with the instructor telling the pupils that "such and such is true" without any justification is a disaster. (Divoky, 1969, p. 97)

When confronted with a situation characterized by uninvolvement and failure, students have three options. First, they can continue to grapple with an environment in which they feel incompetent and impotent. For adolescents who have experienced failure for a number of years, it is unlikely that they will view their chances of success as worthy of further struggle. A second option open to adolescents who are experiencing failure and frustration is to accept the fact that they cannot succeed and to blame themselves for their failure. However, no one wants to view him- or herself as a failure at something that society values as highly as education. Furthermore, to accept the entire blame for their failure is not realistic. Most behavior-problem students have been confronted with home and/or school experiences that have intensified or even caused their existing difficulties.

The final option available to students who feel uninvolved and unsuccessful is to strike out and blame their teachers and school for their failure. While this approach does not assist students in creating a more successful school experience, it does enable them to transfer the source of blame and at the same time frequently involves them in behaviors that bring about their removal from the failure setting.

Teachers must expect that when they fail to show students respect by actively involving them in the learning process, discipline problems will arise. Anyone who has sat through a lengthy meeting in which they have had no involvement knows the feelings and attitudes this elicits. Adolescents experience such situations much as adults do. They feel bored, annoyed, angry, restless, and insulted. They also respond as adults do. Some accept the situation and remain attentive. Some play the game and feign interest while allowing their minds to wander to more exciting things. Others find ways to subtly undermine the ongoing task and are highly critical of the environment in which they have been forced to passively participate. Finally, some leave the environment, and others openly rebel against it.

This relationship between classroom management problems and active student involvement was highlighted by a series of studies conducted by Kounin (1970). Kounin compared the classrooms of teachers who were noted for having few classroom management problems to those of teachers who experienced serious and consistent classroom management problems. His results indicated that the difference in the behaviors of the two groups of teachers lay less in their ability to deal with serious behavior problems as they arose than in their ability to successfully avoid such problems. Specifically, Kounin found that the successful teachers were much more effective in keeping students actively involved in the learning process. Their pacing and classroom structure created fewer times in which students waited or were passively involved. In addition, Kounin found that the successful teachers were more aware of and continually monitored student responses and behaviors. Therefore, rather than allowing incidents to get out of hand, these teachers continually responded to the classroom process.

Part II has presented the skills necessary for responding effectively to students' negative responses. The remainder of this chapter and the following chapter will focus on teaching strategies that can increase active student involvement in the learning process. As Kounin found, when these two sets of skills are combined, classroom management problems are drastically reduced.

The Influence of Student Seating and Classroom Arrangements on Student Involvement

People who attend sporting events or concerts are aware of the increased attention and energy level that occur when they are able to obtain front row seats. Being near the action tends to create a sense of involvement and commitment that is reflected in greater interest. When people are seated near the performers, they are less likely to become engaged in conversation; the performance seems to have a greater impact.

Since the teacher is the major source of information and reinforcement in most classrooms, it seems reasonable to assume that students seated near the teacher will be more involved in on-task behavior and will receive greater benefit from the instruction. In examining the effects of student seating on students' classroom behavior in first, sixth, and eleventh grade classes, Adams and Biddle (1970) found that nearly two-thirds of on-task student talk was generated by students who sat either in the front row or in the row directly in front of where the teacher stood or sat. This finding is not surprising since these researchers also found that the teachers whom they studied spent nearly 70 percent of their time in front of their classes.

Other studies support these findings. For instance, Delefes and Jackson (1972) found that teachers tend to call on students seated near the front and center areas of the room and only infrequently call on students seated in the back or on the periphery. Similarly Schwebel and Cherlin (1972) report that students seated near the back of the class are less likely to stay on-task when given in-class assignments and are less attentive during class activities. Finally, Daum's (1972) study concerning the effects of altering student seating arrangement within the classroom suggests that teachers can improve student achievement by placing students in a position where they are closer to the focus of instruction.

Therefore, it appears that the amount of teacher talk is not the only variable that influences student involvement and reduces students' sense of being a meaningful part of the classroom environment. Indeed, it appears likely that teachers' willingness to allow students to continually sit on the periphery of the class may be a subtle yet powerful form of negative expectation. Students soon learn that by seating themselves in the back row and on the sides of the classroom they can escape much of the attention that is focused on their more involved peers who are seated nearer the teacher. Unfortunately, teachers are often either unaware of such patterns or justify their existence on the basis of not wanting to embarrass students who are unprepared or who feel uncomfortable speaking in class. However, by accepting this behavior, teachers are indirectly communicating their belief that these students are less important and/or less capable than students who choose to become more involved. Therefore, while it may not be effective or helpful to merely call on these students more often, Daum's (1972) study suggests that it may be productive to seat them closer to the center of instruction.

There are numerous methods for reducing the degree to which certain students become isolated from the focus of instruction. First, teachers can simply arrange a seating chart so that less involved students are seated near the front of the classroom. While this change may be effective, it also has the disadvantage of frequently creating resentment as well as reducing the involvement of those students who had previously been seated near the teacher. A second option available to teachers is to create a classroom structure that provides all students with equal access to the focus of instruction. This can be accomplished by employing a circular or U-shaped arrangement as well as by employing small group activities. A third approach to involving isolated students is to ask them to discuss the situation and to suggest and explore a variety of methods for increasing their involvement in the classroom. This latter approach has the advantage of responding to adolescents' needs to understand their environment and to be actively involved in making decisions that influence their behavior.

Monitoring Student Involvement

Another method for increasing student involvement is simply to insure that every day all students are involved in some way in the classroom. There are several ways to monitor student involvement. One method is to make a simple checklist that includes each student's name and a coding system to indicate the manner in which each student participates (Figure 7.1). Another method for monitoring student involvement is to

Figure 7.1   Form for Monitoring Student Class Involvement

Student's Name	Questions Asked		Answers Given		Responses to Peers			
	Procedural	Academic	Objective	Abstract	Academic		Social	
					+	−	+	−
Bill								
Sally								
John								
Sam								
Mary								
Ann								
Brian								
Justin								
Cindy								
Alicia								

ask students to keep a similar record of their classroom participation. This record can periodically be handed in and can serve as useful information at teacher-student conferences. By placing the responsibility for data collection on the students, teachers indicate their respect for the students' ability to monitor their own behavior. This format has the additional advantage of taking teachers out of the role of "Big Brother" and placing them into a role where they assist students in examining information they have collected.

A third method for coding classroom involvement is to have a colleague visit the classroom and collect data on the teacher's interactions with students. While this situation requires a positive, supportive relationship between the parties involved, it has tremendous potential. The fact that both parties are trained professionals, increases the likelihood of accurate data collection and a serious, creative, and productive examination of the data. The following incident provides an excellent example of the advantages associated with this type of data collection.

Several years ago I had the opportunity of working with a group of teachers who decided to meet regularly to discuss ways to improve their teaching. One approach they decided to employ was that of visiting each other's classes. One of the first teachers to request a visit was a first year social studies teacher who stated that she was concerned about class involvement. She indicated that it seemed that a few students did most of the talking in her class. Several classroom observations indicated that her perceptions were accurate. In fact, four students did slightly over three-quarters of the on-task talking in her class. Fortunately, the observations also indicated several possible causes of this phenomenon. Results obtained from using a modification of the Brophy-Good coding system (Brophy and Good, 1970a) that codes the teacher's as well as the students' behavior, indicated that the teacher was asking almost entirely factual questions and that she directed a majority of these questions at four students who were seated directly in front of her podium. Since the teacher had requested this information and it was presented to her in a supportive atmosphere, she was able to accept the results without becoming overly defensive. Furthermore, her colleagues offered several useful suggestions concerning the classroom arrangement and the teacher's questioning strategies. These suggestions served as a springboard for several constructive changes for the young teacher. Follow-up results showed that student participation had increased markedly.

A final method for collecting data concerning student involvement is to tape record class sessions. Tape recordings can be coded to examine such factors as the percentage of teacher versus student talk, the types of questions being asked, and whether certain students are dominating classroom discussions. An interesting and somewhat humorous example of the benefits of tape recordings was told to me by a special education teacher who provides consultation to classroom teachers. The consultant had been asked to assist a teacher who was having considerable difficulty with classroom management. After several visits, the consultant and the teacher decided to tape record several class sessions. As they were listening to one of the sessions, the teacher said, "Hear that loud noise? How can students be expected to concentrate with that type of noise going on?" The consultant asked the teacher if she knew who was making the noise. When the teacher indicated that she did not, the tape was rewound and played again. This time the teacher realized that the loud noise to which she referred was in fact her voice. This awareness opened the door for considerable change in both the amount and type of teacher talk in the classroom. Follow-up data indicated that these changes were associated with increased student involvement and a significant decrease in minor disruptive student behavior.

Teaching More than Facts

In addition to monitoring the amount and type of both teacher and student behavior, it is important to examine the curriculum to determine whether it involves students in a meaningful way. A large percentage of student acting-out behavior is the result of learning environments that fail to involve the learner and/or to relate the material in a meaningful way to the learner's current life space.

> When it comes to motivating school achievement, it appears that the type of learning structure is by far the more important factor, with grades playing a secondary, even negligible role. (Covington and Beery, 1976, p. 117)

There are a number of ways to conceptualize the various levels at which teaching and learning occur. The most simple and functional conceptualization seems to be one that divides teaching and learning into the four levels of facts, concepts, generalizations, and values. At the facts level, students are asked to learn basic information that provides the basis for other levels of learning. At the concepts level, students learn the relationships between facts and discover general themes that can be derived from the facts. At the generalization level, students are asked to employ these concepts by interpreting situations or solving problems. At the values level, the students are directly involved in relating the concepts to their own values and behaviors. Several examples may serve to clarify these levels.

If a teacher is focusing on the topic of ecology, the facts level might include a study of the various types of pollution, and the history of pollution and pollution legislation. The concept level could include discussions concerning issues such as man's relationship to his environment, the multiplicative nature of technological advancement, individual versus collective rights, and short- versus long-term goals. The generalization level might ask students to develop legislative proposals that would protect the environment without significantly affecting the economy. It might also involve students in planning an ecologically sound community, given certain information concerning population, geography, and weather. Finally, the values level might ask students to examine their own behavior concerning ecology. For example, they might be asked to develop and have students and teachers fill out a questionnaire on individuals' behavior associated with such ecological concerns as waste, pollution, and recycling.

When presented with the desirability of including these levels, teachers often indicate that their subject matter is not conducive to this form of instruction. In their book, *Clarifying Values through Subject Matter* (1973), Harmin, Kirschenbaum, and Simon provide examples of this type of instruction for twenty different subject matters. While the authors do not include the generalization level in their conceptual schema, they do provide an excellent list of ideas related to the facts, concepts, and values level. Finally, their discussion of the values levels provides teachers with fifteen types of activities that can be used to involve students in examining their values in any curriculum area.

When working with teachers who are experiencing difficulties with classroom management, I have consistently found that discipline problems occur most frequently when teachers focus almost exclusively on the facts level. An obvious reason for this situation is that learning factual material involves students in a very limited way. Adolescents are developing the ability to deal with abstract thought and to solve problems by first examining a variety of possible alternatives. When teachers ask them to deal primarily with factual information, they are functioning in opposition to a major developmental task. In addition, teaching at a factual level usually involves a larger percentage of teacher talk; or, in the case of programmed material, limited interaction of any kind. As Kounin's research indicates, when students are not involved in the learning process, discipline problems are much more likely to occur.

In contrast to the disadvantages of teaching primarily at the factual level are the benefits associated with teaching at the higher levels. An excellent example of this form of teaching occurred in a modern problems class I visited. This example illustrates the important point that a teacher does not need to proceed systematically from facts to concepts to generalizations to values. The classroom was one in which a student teacher was presenting a lesson on the United Nations. The class had previously studied the history of this organization. The teacher began his lesson by dividing the class into groups of five. Each group was then given the five square game. This game provides each group with a variety of puzzle pieces. When properly distributed, the pieces can be arranged so that each group member has a square in front of them. However, the pieces are designed so that there is only one combination that enables all five members to make a square. A variety of other combinations will allow several members to make a square, but will prevent all members from building a square. The goal of the game is for each group to arrive at the situation where each group member has a perfect square in front of them. The major rules of the game are that no talking is allowed and that while a group member can give away one or more pieces, no one can take a piece or signal to have a piece given to them. These rules are intended to put a premium on observing others' needs and being willing to give up something of value for the eventual greater good of the group.

The students worked feverishly at this task for approximately half the period. By that time several groups had finished and two other groups were blocked by members refusing to break up their squares in order to open new combinations for the group. At this point, the teacher asked the students to put aside their task and form one large circle. He began the discussion by asking students to discuss how they felt about the activity and to examine their own behaviors during the exercise (values level). Students listened carefully as their peers talked about their experiences. After approximately fifteen minutes of discussion, the teacher asked the class how this activity related to the United Nations (generalization level). A number of students offered the idea that when individuals or nations protect their private interests, this adversely affects the goals of the larger group (concept level). Students were then asked to list specific instances in which this had occurred both in the United Nations (facts level) and at their school (values level).

The student on-task level throughout the class period was 98 percent. This fact would not have been as striking had the class not included three students who were labeled "emotionally disturbed" and who spent part of their school day in a special resource room. In addition, the class contained a high percentage of low-achieving students who were viewed as behavior problems. This example is not meant to infer that students will in every case respond positively to this form of classroom instruction. It does, however, indicate that behavior problems can often be prevented by actively involving students in lessons that they can relate to their own experiences.

While it is important to employ a variety of levels when developing a lesson or curriculum, students can become actively involved at all levels, including the accumulation of facts. The following incident dramatically highlights the advantages of this instructional strategy.

The situation occurred when a young teacher expressed his concern about presenting a lesson on the various types of cancer. The teacher indicated that he was especially concerned about a student who consistently made flippant, off-color remarks during class. He noted that he had had a serious confrontation with the student earlier in the year and that ever since then the student had been a distracting factor in his classroom. This situation was accentuated by the fact that the student was known to be a gang leader and students either followed his lead or accepted his remarks. The teacher was sure that this student would have a variety of distracting remarks to accompany a lecture that included the topics of breast, prostrate, and cervical cancer.

In order to reduce the likelihood that this would occur, the teacher decided to employ group competition as a strategy for teaching the lesson. The teacher divided the class into two groups and worked with one group while a colleague worked with the other group. Each teacher took ten minutes to cover designated facts concerning three different forms of cancer. After the ten minute mini-lectures, each group had five minutes to teach the other group everything they had learned. Following this, each group had ten minutes to study everything they had learned about the six forms of cancer. The final ten minutes of the class was set aside for a quiz covering the material. In order to enhance students' motivation, the test scores were totaled for each group and it had been decided that the team with the lowest average score on the quiz would bring treats for the winning team.

This competitive activity was highly successful in meeting its goal. The behavior-problem student was on task during virtually 100 percent of the period. In fact, not surprisingly, he took a leadership role in organizing his group and keeping other students on task. Even more interesting, however, was the fact that this behavior tended to generalize to subsequent class periods. As the teacher increasingly involved students in the learning process, the behavior-problem student continued to respond appropriately during class sessions. By more actively involving students, the teacher provided an opportunity for the problem student to demonstrate his competency in organizing and motivating group activity. This in turn made the student feel more positive both about the class sessions and his role as a class member. The result was a significant reduction in inappropriate behavior. As Maslow notes, unproductive behavior is a person's response to the inability to meet basic needs. When opportunities for meeting these needs are provided, individuals will almost always decrease their unproductive behavior.

There is one exception to the association between teaching entirely at the facts level and increased discipline problems. It is sometimes possible (in fact many teachers design their teaching around this principle) to reduce acting out by creating a highly structured, fact-oriented learning environment. This type of teaching strategy is usually based upon the assumption that students desire the rewards the teacher can disseminate (usually grades) and will behave in a manner that maximizes the possibility that they will receive these rewards. Therefore, if quietly paying attention and learning facts are followed by successful test performance and the related reinforcement of high grades, students will sit quietly and learn facts.

There are, however, several obvious problems associated with this approach. First, this approach is only effective with those students who view the teachers' reinforcers as both desirable and attainable. However, not all students will respond positively to this type of instruction. When this situation arises, the teacher is forced to employ punishment as a means for maintaining control. Unfortunately, this changes the focus from a positive form of motivation to a negative and repressive means of control. In addition, this latter form of control is dependent upon the students' fearing the punishers that teachers have at their command. However, as most secondary teachers know, reinforcers and punishers that work with elementary children are frequently ineffective with adolescents. Therefore, a major problem with presenting a teacher-centered, fact-oriented curriculum to adolescents is that teachers have relatively few tools for assuring that adolescents will respond positively to this structure and material. Furthermore, since this form of teaching runs counter to several major developmental tasks, it is understandable that only a few students—those who want teachers' reinforcers and are willing to compromise themselves in order to earn them—will respond positively to such learning environments. If teachers insist on employing this type of teaching, they must expect confrontation and conflict.

Responding Spontaneously to Student Interests

Another strategy for reducing inappropriate student behavior by responding to students' needs to be recognized as competent deals with the way teachers respond to off-task student talk. Anyone who has taught adolescents has experienced situations in which student conversation has drifted far from the topic under discussion. One way of dealing with this situation is to send an "I message" and inform the students, "Your off-task behavior is making me uncomfortable and I would appreciate your refocusing on the task." This type of intervention might also include a request for information concerning the cause of their response to the task. Perhaps the assignment was not clear, the task was easy and has already been completed, or the assignment was similar to one that they were given in another class.

Another method for dealing with this type of situation is to incorporate the students' discussion into the subject matter. A situation which exemplifies this approach was recently reported to me by a high school English teacher. The teacher had assigned each student the task of writing a short story. While he was discussing short stories, three students in the back of the room became involved in a lively discussion about the relative merits of alcohol versus marijuana. Instead of cutting off their conversation, the teacher asked how the use of these drugs would influence the characters in their short stories. Since two of the students were writing stories in which the main character committed a violent crime, the teacher directed the discussion toward the need to build believable characters. The teacher asked the students to consider whether their characters would more likely be heavy drinkers or smokers. When the discussion was over, the students listened to the remainder of the teacher's presentation. When the teacher provided the students with class time in which to work on their short stories, the three students were observed hard at work.

In this situation the teacher responded to the interests expressed by the students. By doing so, the teacher indicated his respect for the students. At the same time, by relating the students' interests to the topic being discussed, the teacher indicated his respect for the relevancy of the subject matter. Students' concerns are very real and powerful to them. By incorporating students' concerns into the material being presented, teachers indicate their respect for students while attempting to stretch students' perspectives and integrate new skills into their approach to dealing with their interests. While it is certainly not possible to fit all student discussions into the subject matter, the payoffs are such that teachers should be aware of any opportunities to do so.

Peer Teaching

One of the most effective means for involving students in the learning process is to have students teach other students. This process responds positively to a variety of student needs. By actively involving students in the instructional process, teachers respond to students' needs to feel a sense of competence and potency. By reducing their domination of classroom activities, teachers indicate their respect for students' knowledge and ability to control their own environment. At the same time, teachers respond to students' needs to experience a sense of independence and to be involved in meaningful interactions with their peers. Allowing students a more active role in the teaching process also tends to reduce their status as marginal people. When teachers dominate classrooms and expect students to sit quietly, be polite, and learn, they place students in a classic bind of being dependent and childlike in one respect and competent and adult in another. It is not surprising that students find this role confusing and often annoying. Finally, if teachers want to provide a gradual transition to students from being passive to being more dominant and responsible, teachers must increasingly involve adolescents in their own learning.

In addition to the theoretical benefits associated with increased student involvement in the teaching process, research findings point to the advantages of this form of instruction. When summarizing the research comparing the effectiveness of traditional competitive learning environments versus situations in which students work together and teach one another, Johnson and Johnson wrote:

> There is, then, considerable evidence that the most desirable goal structure for promoting achievement in problem-solving (as well as information recall) tasks is a cooperative one. When working on problem-solving tasks within a cooperative goal structure, students are also learning how to problem solve, how to cooperate, and how to join with other individuals to solve a common problem or to accomplish a common task. (David W. Johnson, Roger T. Johnson, *Learning Together and Alone: Cooperation, Competition, and Individualization*, 1975, p. 193. Reprinted by permission of Prentice-Hall, Inc., Englewood Cliffs, New Jersey.)

Equally as important is the fact that a variety of studies indicate that students display more positive attitudes toward learning when they are involved in cooperative as opposed to competitive learning situations. (Crombag, 1966; Dunn and Goldman, 1966; Haines and McKeachie, 1967; Wheeler and Ryan, 1973).

When presented with the theoretical advantages and research results supportive of giving students a more active role in teaching their peers, many teachers respond with skepticism. Teachers often note that since students do not possess the prerequisite knowledge, they cannot be expected to teach others. It is therefore important to examine the wide range of ways in which students can be involved in teaching their peers.

Large Group Discussions   Perhaps the simplest form of peer teaching can be found when students are involved in class discussions. When discussions involve a wide range of students and when students employ good communication skills, discussions can be an excellent strategy for enabling students to share their ideas and develop a sense of involvement and competence.

This strategy can be extended by allowing students who possess special knowledge or have a special interest in a given topic to facilitate the discussion on that topic. This method can be carried still further by asking all students to take responsibility for designated topics and assisting students in developing the subject matter expertise needed to lead a discussion. There is no question that allowing students this amount of responsibility requires considerable risk as well as planning. Furthermore, students must feel comfortable in a classroom setting before this type of instruction can be effective. However, this type of instruction has real potential for increasing student involvement and feelings of competence while at the same time reducing student boredom.

Peer Tutoring Another method for involving students in the teaching process is to allow students to assist each other during periods in which students are involved in individual work. There are several advantages associated with this form of instruction. First, it prevents the more capable students from becoming bored or restless. These students can become involved in teaching material to peers who are experiencing more difficulty comprehending the material. Some educators and parents may say that this is unfair to better students in that it prevents them from continuing on to advanced work. However, most educators have experienced the truth associated with the concept that the best way to learn the real essence of material is to teach it to someone else. By working with other students, advanced students have an opportunity to develop a more complete understanding of the material.

A second advantage to peer tutoring is that it provides more individuals who are available to assist students, so that students do not have to wait long periods of time in order to receive assistance from the teacher. In addition, students who do not find it comfortable to work with the teacher are provided with an opportunity to acquire assistance from someone else. A third advantage associated with peer teaching deals with the positive feelings students develop when they become a valuable and influential part of their environment. Peer tutoring allows students to step out of their traditional role of passive participants and into a role of a valuable and active contributor.

I observed an excellent example of peer tutoring while observing a young teacher presenting an art lesson to a group of eighth grade students. The teacher was working with a particularly difficult class. The class included several students whom the school had termed behavior-problem students as well as a very withdrawn emotionally handicapped boy. The teacher indicated that she was somewhat concerned about the day's lesson since she had a very limited background in the material she was presenting. In addition, she noted that the last period of the day on a particularly nice spring day was not the ideal time to be teaching eighth graders a concept as difficult as depth perception. With this introduction, I was prepared to observe considerable chaos and to have numerous opportunities for observing the teacher's skills in dealing with behavior problems.

The teacher began the lesson by briefly reviewing the material she had presented the previous day. She appeared comfortable responding to a variety of student questions. On one occasion, a student pointed out a major flaw in something she had presented. The teacher indicated that she did not see his point and asked the student if he would be willing to come up to the board and clarify his point for both her and the class. The student did so, and the class responded politely to his brief instruction.

After perhaps ten minutes of instruction, the teacher indicated that the students should continue working on their assignments. She noted that some students were finding the tasks more difficult than others and suggested that when they had a problem, they find another student to help them. As students began working on their projects, the teacher circulated around the room answering student questions and reinforcing students' work. It soon became apparent, however, that she could not possibly answer all the questions that were being fired at her. When this occurred, her interventions changed from direct work with students to serving as a clearing center for resources available within the classroom. As she moved around the room, she made comments such as "Why don't you ask John, he does a real good job with two-point perspective." "It might help, Bill, if you could explain to him why you . . ." "I really appreciated your helping, Sue. You did a really good job of teaching because you helped him to discover the answer for himself."

As I observed the class, I was impressed with the extremely high percentage of on-task behavior displayed by the students. In addition, the teacher's role as facilitator freed her to spend a considerable amount of time with her most severely disturbed student. Since she had structured student responses to be positive and supportive, student interactions throughout the class period were extremely positive. In addition to assisting each other, students frequently showed their work to their peers and almost always received either compliments or constructive suggestions.

In examining the dynamics of this class period, it is interesting to recall Postman and Weingartner's (1969) statement that teachers should perhaps teach subjects outside of their area of academic preparation. When teaching subjects they understand extremely well, teachers often do all the teaching, while the students are forced into the role of passive learner. On the other hand, when teachers are learning the material or are somewhat unsure about the content, it may be easier to allow students to become involved as co-learners and team teachers. While it may appear that material is covered more slowly (and perhaps more noisily) when using this format, the theoretical considerations and research results presented earlier in this section point to a wide range of advantages associated with this form of instruction.

An important point that is often overlooked when asking students to instruct other students is that teachers must first assist students in developing instructional skills. Most people have at one time or another suffered through a course in which the instructor knew his material but lacked the teaching skills needed to effectively communicate his knowledge. Since most students have seen predominantly infor-mation-giving types of instruction, it is not surprising that when they are asked to assist their peers, they tend to provide answers rather than giving assistance that helps the other person develop their own answer. Therefore, if teachers expect peer teaching to be effective, they must spend time discussing and demonstrating such basic instructional strategies as asking clarifying questions rather than providing answers, giving specific feedback rather than global evaluative statements, and reviewing to determine whether the learner has mastered the material. Depending upon the amount of peer instruction teachers employ, this instruction can range from simply discussing the teaching act with students and eliciting their ideas to extensive role playing and video taping.

Small Group Work Large group discussions and peer tutoring are only two of the many methods that employ some form of peer instruction. Providing students with assignments to be completed in small groups is another form of peer teaching. As with any teaching strategy, there are certain dos and don'ts associated with small group work. Perhaps the most important ingredient in effective small group work is developing some form of accountability. If students believe that they will not be held accountable for their work, small groups become ideal settings for discussing such peer group concerns as sporting events, dances, and dating. Therefore, it is important that any small group assignment include some form of written and/or verbal presentation of the group's work.

When using small groups as an instructional strategy, it is important to spend time discussing how groups function. It is helpful to discuss the various roles that group members can play and to indicate which roles tend to help and which hinder effective group functioning. If small group work is employed regularly, it is helpful to occasionally ask a group member to observe the group and provide some feedback to the group regarding how it functioned during the observation period.

One further caution should be made when discussing the use of small groups. Students sometimes see small groups as a strategy teachers use to "keep from teaching." This perception is validated when teachers continually use small group time as a time to grade papers, have a cup of coffee, or carry out coaching duties. When using small groups, it is important that the teacher be actively involved in observing and participating in the groups. It is helpful also to explain to students the rationale for using small groups to accomplish a particular instructional goal. It is a good idea to involve students in determining—or at least approving—the type of activity to be employed in reaching any instructional goal. There are several advantages associated with this process. By involving students in this decision, teachers increase the likelihood that they will take an active part in the activity. It is also quite possible that students will present thoughtful reasons why a particular activity is not conducive to obtaining a particular goal. Students are indeed the world's best experts on themselves, and they often possess information that enables teachers to determine which teaching methods are most conducive to student learning. For example, students may inform teachers that they are involved in small group work in several other classes and that at this point in time this mode of instruction would not enhance student motivation.

Cooperative Work on Examinations Another form of peer instruction involves students in assisting each other in studying for examinations. Students frequently find examinations to be competitive, anxiety-provoking events. This view of tests can be altered by creating situations that reinforce the concept that tests are noncompetitive events that simply provide students with indications of how well they understand the material they have been studying. Teachers can encourage this view of tests by structuring class time for students to work together to prepare for tests. By encouraging this form of studying, teachers indicate that the goal of the test is not to "beat" other students, but rather to determine how well students have learned the material.

An additional strategy for creating a more cooperative, learning-oriented view of tests is to inform the students that their score on an examination will be determined by averaging the scores of those who are assigned together. When employing this type of scoring for the first time, it is important that teachers discuss their rationale with the class and ask for their input. This step is important because adolescents have become accustomed to viewing tests as competitive tasks, the goal of which is to obtain a high grade. Therefore, it is best to initially employ group scoring on relatively minor examinations that students view as having only a small effect on their grades.

SUMMARY

Both the acting-out and withdrawal behavior characteristic of behavior-problem adolescents is influenced to a large but undetermined degree by the fact that these youngsters do not view themselves as competent, respected, involved, or important. When adolescents view themselves as unable to demonstrate competence and receive respect through accepted channels, they may strive to achieve competence through means that adults describe as undesirable, antisocial, or unproductive.

If schools are to provide adolescents with a sense of competence and respect, they must begin by viewing behavior-problem youngsters not as frightening adversaries, but rather as students who can be trusted and who, when given appropriate support and instruction, can behave responsibly and achieve academically. The establishment of high, realistic, mutually determined goals is a major component of any program for behavior-problem adolescents.

In addition to establishing reasonable goals, school programs must provide behavior-problem adolescents with an opportunity to become actively involved in the learning process. Perhaps to a larger degree than their more passive and high-achieving peers, behavior-problem adolescents benefit from and respond to instruction that actively involves the learner in dealing with realistic, concrete issues. When teachers fail to provide this type of instruction, they create a situation in which they are to a large extent responsible for the fact that a certain percentage of their students will fail, act out, or drop out.

The first portion of this chapter examined the impact of expectations and ways in which teachers can examine and alter their expectations and the behaviors that are influenced by these expectations. The second half of the chapter focused on methods for assisting students in developing a sense of competence through active involvement in the learning process.

Thus, low motivation, negative self-attitudes, and failure are largely the result of improper learning conditions. According to this learning-theory analysis, we should be able to alter a student's failure rate by changing the conditions of classroom learning and, as a consequence, increase his motivation to succeed. Actually there is considerable experimental evidence on this point.

Martin Covington and Richard Beery

Self-Worth and School Learning

CHAPTER
8

Developing a Sense of
Potency and Self-Respect

INCREASING STUDENTS' SENSE OF RESPONSIBILITY

The schools' failure to provide adolescents with a sense of understanding and controlling their environment often plays a major role in increasing the behavior problems displayed by students. In describing American education in his book, *Crisis in the Classroom: The Remaking of American Education* (1970) Charles Silberman wrote:

> More important, schools discourage students from developing the capacity to learn by and for themselves; they make it impossible for a youngster to take responsibility for his own education, for they are structured in such a way as to make students totally dependent upon the teachers. Whatever rhetoric they may subscribe to, most schools in practice define education as something teachers do to students, not something students do to and for themselves, with a teacher's assistance. (Silberman, 1970, p. 135)

Speaking more directly to the situation in secondary schools, Silberman wrote:

> Because adolescents are harder to "control" than younger children, secondary schools tend to be even more authoritarian and repressive than elementary schools; the values they transmit are the values of docility, passivity, conformity, and lack of trust. (Silberman, 1970, p. 324)

The results of a survey conducted in 1977 at a suburban high school in Oregon (Figure 8.1) tend to substantiate Silberman's statements. The survey indicates that while students do experience some sense of control over the courses they take, they do

Figure 8.1   School Climate Survey: Items relating to the
Degree of Power Experienced by Students. (Used by
permission of Edward A. West.)

Questions Asked	%Yes	%No
I am encouraged to develop self discipline and to control my own learning.	79%	21%
I can partially determine what I study.	71%	29%
I have the opportunity to make some decisions about what and how I learn.	69%	31%
I have enough opportunities to choose subjects that I like.	59%	41%
I can change my school program if it is not right for me.	57%	43%
I can make some of my own decisions about how to learn.	53%	47%
I can voice a concern openly.	50%	50%
My parents' opinions are valued by the school.	45%	55%
When I don't understand something, most teachers will adjust their class activities to help me.	42%	58%
I have influence on the decisions within the school which directly affect me.	26%	74%
I feel that if I think a program or school policy needs changing, I can have some effect in getting those changes made.	26%	74%

not feel capable of influencing the basic rules or format within which they must live
seven hours a day for three years.

Probably, the most overriding developmental task for adolescents is the need to
develop a sense of independence and to establish a sense of their ability to take
responsibility for themselves. Without this growth, adolescents cannot make a smooth
and productive transition from a state of dependency to a role as healthy, productive
adult members of society. Consequently, it is vital that, despite the fact that they will
sometimes falter, adults provide adolescents with opportunities for practicing self-
direction, autonomy, and responsibility. When adults fail to provide these opportunities, they operate from McGregor's Theory X. Since adolescents are struggling to
develop a sense of independence, they will understandably rebel at being treated like
second-class citizens who require constant direction and prodding. It is therefore
imperative that educators carefully examine their school and classroom environments
to determine whether they provide adolescents with a sense of potency and
responsibility.

A frequent response to recommendations that adolescents be given more responsibility is that they do not know how to handle this responsibility. If this is the

case—and it often is—then it is a sad commentary on educational institutions. If adolescents misuse or abuse responsibility, it is because they have had too few opportunities to experience self-direction and responsibility. When discussing this issue, William Glasser has written that:

> We teach thoughtless conformity to school rules and call the conforming child "responsible." Although he may be conforming, he is not necessarily responsible. Responsibility is learned only by evaluating the situation and choosing a path that a person thinks will be more helpful to himself and to others. (Glasser, 1969, p. 22. Reprinted by permission of Harper & Row, Publishers, Inc.)

As Kohlberg (1971) and others have noted, schools tend to function at lower levels of moral development. Students are seldom asked to seriously examine the school's structure and rules with the expectation that they will be actively involved in changing them. Neither are students consistently reinforced for acting upon their own beliefs concerning the correctness of their behavior and the impact it will have on others.

The points presented above are not intended as a generalized criticism of the public schools. There are some schools and many teachers who encourage students to handle increasing responsibility and who provide the structure and types of relationships that support students in their efforts to become more self-reliant. However, education has a long way to go before schools provide adolescents with meaningful and frequent opportunities to experience a sense of control over their environment and therefore develop the increased self-esteem and academic achievement that accompanies this experience. If teachers hope to reduce the number of adolescents who achieve below their potential and who behave destructively, teachers must increase the degree to which students experience a sense of control over their school environment.

> Students who feel that they can influence other students, their teacher, and the activities in their classrooms feel good about themselves, feel good about school, and achieve at levels consonant with their intellectual abilities (Schmuck, 1966). Unfortunately, student influence depends a great deal on the teacher's behavior and the structure of the curriculum. In too many classrooms students influence learning activities only in spite of the teacher's actions and the curriculum structure. Students who feel powerless and unable to make a personal mark upon their classes tend to be unhappy with school and usually do not perform up to their intellectual capabilities as indicated by I.Q. scores. (Schmuck and Schmuck, 1974, pp. 108-109)

The remainder of this chapter will focus on strategies that teachers can apply for increasing the amount of control and responsibility students experience. As suggested throughout this chapter, this focus does not imply that students should be given total control over their learning environments. Especially during early adolescence, students want and need guidance and structure. However, structure can be provided in ways that incorporate meaningful student input and therefore facilitate students' developing skills in becoming responsible for themselves and their environments.

INVOLVING STUDENTS IN DECISION MAKING

One relatively simple but important method that can be used to increase the likelihood that students will initially feel an increased sense of potency in their classroom is to begin each new semester or term by discussing teachers' needs and expectations and allowing students to present theirs. Thus teachers do more than simply inform students that they expect the class to be quiet and they expect assignments to be handed in on time. Rather, teachers discuss such issues as (1) how they view their role as teacher, (2) what responsibilities they will take and which they would like students to take, (3) how they view their relationships with students, (4) what form of instruction they hope to employ and why, (5) how they hope to see students interact in the classroom, and (6) what method of evaluation they plan to employ. In addition to presenting their beliefs, it is extremely important that teachers encourage students to respond to teachers' ideas and to discuss their beliefs concerning how they learn best.

It is quite possible that students may initially experience some difficulty in responding to this request for information concerning what qualitites they find most conducive to learning. My own experience with students in junior high, high school, and even college is that they are initially surprised and somewhat skeptical about being asked to present their needs and concerns. In fact, many students indicate that this is a new experience and that they have never really thought about what helps them to learn. There are additional reasons students may not provide an immediate, sophisticated response. It is possible that the students do not agree with some or much of what teachers have presented, but they have learned not to question adults' statements. It is also possible that the students need some time to consider the issues being raised. Indeed, despite the fact that teachers have studied the characteristics of productive learning environments and have had their development as a primary responsibility throughout their teaching careers, many teachers would have difficulty presenting an immediate and concise statement about what they believe to be the most effective methods of teaching and evaluation.

It is easy to see why students have a tendency simply to agree with teachers' thoughts about learning and evaluation. While this may provide an easy solution and may even be a boost to teachers' egos, there are several disadvantages associated with accepting their initial compliance. People tend to become more enthusiastically involved in activities that they have chosen as compared to those that have been chosen for them. Because adolescents are struggling to develop a sense of independence and to define themselves as capable, responsible individuals, they often respond more critically than adults to situations that are thrust upon them, and they are likely to criticize and subvert activities that they have no role in developing. When individuals are involved in developing an activity, they may be critical of the activity, but it is unlikely that they will subvert the activity. Instead, their criticism is more likely to take the form of reexamining their decision and developing alternative approaches to the situation.

> Research shows that the quality of work, the degree of pride in the final product, and even one's willingness to undertake the work in the first place, all increase when individuals are taken into the leader's confidence; and that resistance is a common reaction among individuals who are not first consulted about what it is they are to do. . . . (Covington and Beery, 1976, p. 124)

It is therefore important that teachers begin classes, group work, or other long-term activities involving adolescents by structuring the situation so that adolescents provide input concerning their wants and needs and make an initial commitment to the goals and methods being presented.

When working with students who are experiencing behavior problems, it is often useful to schedule an individual conference with each student to develop mutually accepted expectations concerning academic performance. Students who display behavior problems in a classroom setting almost always do so because they cannot succeed at or see no value in the tasks presented. Consequently, they experience the classroom as boring, anxiety provoking, or embarrassing. Their response to these feelings is variously to become aggressive, to remove themselves from the environment, or to involve themselves in behaviors that are more comfortable for them. These behaviors usually include talking to other students, making off-task comments, wandering around the room, or complaining about class activities and assignments. While teachers may find these behaviors distracting and unacceptable, they are understandable in that they prevent students from having to face tasks that they did not choose and they do not feel they can successfully complete.

Imagine yourself forced to spend six hours a day in a situation where you understood very little of what was being discussed. Further imagine that you knew you would be evaluated on your ability to comprehend the material and that if you accepted the values of the institution, the evaluation you received would be an important criteria in determining your success in the institution as well as in later life. Finally, imagine that your family and peers placed limited value in your succeeding at the tasks presented in your classes. Given this situation, how would you act?

Most people probably would either remove themselves from the situation or would passively or actively reject the material and the associated values. Indeed, an acceptance of the material and values presented would be an acknowledgment of the individual's ineptness and inadequacy.

Continue imagining yourself in the situation described above. Now imagine that someone sat down with you and asked you what your goals were and what material you thought you could learn. Imagine how you would feel if they admitted that they sometimes went too fast and that they realized that the material as they presented it was not always clear. How would you feel if they stated that they would like to see you succeed and that they would be willing to work with you to create a situation whereby you could have a successful experience?

Research (Alschuler, 1969; Homme, 1970; Lewin, Dembo, Festinger, and Sears, 1944; Lovitt and Curtiss, 1969) clearly indicates that student motivation and achievement are enhanced when students are allowed to work toward clearly specified, realistic goals. In fact, when students work toward individually developed goals rather than competing against their peers, they tend to choose realistic goals that are beyond their current performance level yet clearly within reach (Lewin et al., 1944).

> A number of other studies confirm that clearly stated objectives lead to increased achievement and that it is the anxious, failure prone student who benefits most from such clarity. (Covington and Beery, 1976, p. 105)

It is very important during goal setting conferences for teachers to guard against talking down to students or indicating that they do not think the students can do the work. It is often best to begin such conferences by simply asking the student how he feels about the classes and the material being covered. If he states that the format and material seem fine, the teacher can express his pleasure with the student's response and indicate that if he becomes uncomfortable or upset at any time, the teacher would appreciate his coming to see him so that any necessary adjustments can be made.

If a conference occurs as a result of student failure or misbehavior, the teacher can acknowledge that the student's behavior may well be a response to the fact that the class is not meeting his needs. Teachers can reduce their defensiveness and increase students' willingness to compromise by not blaming them and by acknowledging that some changes may need to be made in the assignments or class structure. Adolescents do not act out without cause. It is possible that the causes are too deep seated or too far removed from the classroom for teachers to have any influence. However, teachers cannot make this determination until they have done everything possible to make the classroom setting one in which they can expect the student to respond positively.

A frequent response to suggestions that teachers hold conferences to allow problem students to express their needs is that this practice requires an excessive amount of time or that it is impossible to hold conferences with every student and that behavior-problem students already receive a disproportionate amount of attention. In examining these concerns, it is interesting to note which takes more time—a conference with a problem student or continual disruption of class time because the student cannot cope with existing class structures. Furthermore, conferences can be scheduled during times when students are involved in activities that are not teacher directed. For example, teachers can schedule conferences while students write papers, are involved in group work, or assist each other in preparing for examinations. Finally, while it is true that behavior-problem students do require more attention, it is also true that many of the other students find the environment comfortable and reinforcing without needing additional assistance.

When working with behavior-problem adolescents and their teachers, I have consistently been impressed with the extent to which problems can be reduced by providing these students with an opportunity to be heard and to have the power to make necessary and reasonable changes in their environments. Adolescents do not want to act out or fail. Indeed, they personalize failure experiences more intensely than most adults do. Therefore, teachers will often notice dramatic improvements in adolescents' behavior and achievement after they have taken the time to discover what environmental factors are eliciting the adolescents' unproductive behavior and what teachers can do to create an environment which responds sensitively to adolescents' needs and abilities.

DISCUSSING CURRICULUM DECISIONS

A second and closely related method for providing students with a sense of understanding and controlling their classroom environment is to provide them with clear explanations regarding why teachers ask them to learn the material. When asked why they are learning material, students all too often respond that they are learning it because they want good grades so they won't be "hassled" by parents, so they can graduate from high school and therefore find a better job, or so that they can go to college. While these may be realistic reasons, they are not reasons that most concerned educators would prefer to hear. Furthermore, these reasons for learning do not affect students who do not plan on attending college or whose parents do not care how they function in school. These reasons for attending class, studying, and behaving appropriately are based on extrinsic motivation. They fail to tap adolescents' interest in understanding themselves and their world. When students give such reasons, they are expressing that the material lacks real meaning. When this meaning is absent, students do not experience a sense of understanding or controlling their immediate environment. Rather, they are responding to the need to "play the game" until the time when they will be given some degree of control. As one adolescent stated:

> School is just like roulette or something. You can't just ask: Well, what's the point of it? . . . The point of it is to do it, to get through and get into college. But you have to figure the system or you can't win, because the odds are all on the house's side. (Silberman, 1970, pp. 146-147)

When talking to a group of summer school students, I heard a seventeen-year-old girl who had dropped out of school and recently returned, state similar concerns when she noted that so much of her schoolwork had seemed totally unrelated to her life. She went on to state that this made her feel that she was not a part of school and that it was doing something to her rather than for her or with her. She happily noted that her summer school teacher not only explained why the class was covering material, but also related the material to current issues that the students read about in the newspaper. She remarked that even the Spanish American War made sense when she could see that some of the same issues existed today. During this same discussion, a sixteen-year-old boy indicated that he had studied certain parts of history three times. He commented that no one had ever asked him if he had studied the material before. He noted that it seemed ridiculous for the school to kick him out of school simply because he did not attend sessions that were boring.

Most adults have sat through meetings in which they were presented with material that did not affect them. Recall your response to such meetings. It is likely that you resented having to attend the meeting. It is also possible that you or some of your colleagues talked quietly to each other or made derogatory remarks about the quality of the meeting. How different is this situation from what many students experience in the classroom? It might prove interesting to observe yourself and your colleagues during faculty or staff meetings. You might find that some of the behavior you observe is characteristic of behavior-problem students.

Adolescents, too, need to understand why they are asked to do something. Furthermore, the material teachers present to them should relate in some way to their present existence. If teachers fail to provide this relevance, adolescents will rightfully feel a sense of impotence and confusion. Unless they see obvious future payoffs for tolerating this sense of impotence and confusion, they will understandably react passively or negatively to classroom situations.

... with increasing frequency from grade one through the end of graduate school, much of
what is required is either totally or partially irrelevant to the world around them as they see it.
Thus both excess memorization and increasing irrelevance cause them to withdraw into failure
or to strike out in delinquent acts. (Glasser, 1969, p.30. Reprinted by permission of Harper &
Row, Publishers, Inc.)

Providing the connections between curriculum and adolescents' experience of the
world is not always an easy task. However, it is a major task associated with competent
teaching. Knowledge for the sake of knowledge cannot possibly be meaningful to
young people who are struggling to define themselves and their relationship to their
environment. Knowledge aimed at understanding their environment helps them to
develop a greater sense of control over their lives.

There will undoubtedly be times when adolescents will respond negatively to even a
well-planned curriculum that involves them in meaningful activities. However, these
frustrating times will be far fewer than if teachers present adolescents with prepackaged knowledge that they cannot relate to their lives. Furthermore, when students
fail to respond to a meaningful curriuclum, teachers are in a position to provide them
with valuable feedback. When students fail to respond to a poor curriculum, they are
providing teachers with valuable feedback.

The material on teaching at the fact, concepts, generalization, and values levels
presented in Chapter 7 provides an excellent model from which to develop a
curriculum that responds to adolescents' needs. As educators develop this type of
curriculum, it becomes much easier to explain to adolescents the reason for studying
the material.

A final point related to discussing the curriculum with students is that this is most
effective when it is a frequent occurrence. In fact, it is desirable to set aside several
minutes at the start of each day to outline the day's activities and related goals. When
students understand what they will be doing and why they will be doing it, they are
much more likely to become productively involved. At the same time, students may
provide teachers with useful suggestions concerning how they can alter their lessons.

REQUESTING FEEDBACK FROM STUDENTS

One of the most obvious means for providing students with a sense of competence and
power is to ask them to provide feedback concerning how they view various aspects of
the learning environment. Before examining various methods for obtaining feedback
from students, it is important to examine several factors that tend to reduce adults'
willingness to ask students for feedback.

Overcoming Concerns Related to Student Feedback

One concern teachers often express is the fear that the feedback will be critical. It is
likely that a portion of the feedback will be critical. No one can work with a large
number of people without occasionally behaving in ways or making requests of others
that receive a negative response. However, it is useful to keep in mind that the value of

feedback is to a large degree dependent on how many people give the same type of feedback. For example, if only three students inform me that I lecture too much, that is interesting data that I may choose to discuss individually with those students. However, if 120 out of 140 students give me the same feedback, I have been given some very useful information that I should attend to.

Another helpful thought to keep in mind when contemplating the feedback teachers might receive is that adolescents are themselves very sensitive about receiving negative feedback. In fact, there is probably no issue on which they can have greater empathy than that of receiving criticism. Because of this, adolescents tend to be fairly gentle when responding to teachers' requests for feedback. This does not mean that they never abuse such opportunities. Nevertheless, if teachers have treated them fairly and with respect, they will do the same when giving teachers feedback.

It is also helpful to keep in mind that when asking for feedback, teachers will almost always receive a considerable amount of positive feedback. When they protect themselves against receiving critical feedback, they also reduce the channels available for receiving positive feedback. People who have worked with adolescents for any length of time have experienced the warm feeling that comes when a student thanks them for a good class, expresses appreciation for their help, or makes a positive change in his or her life while teachers are helping the student to change. While it certainly should not be the goal of requesting feedback, this process can increase the amount of positive responses teachers receive.

An additional point to keep in mind when deciding whether to risk asking for feedback is that it is better to receive criticism immediately than after the fact when teachers can do nothing to alter their mistakes. For example, concerned, competent teachers prefer to receive critical student feedback after three weeks compared to hearing through the grapevine that students who took their class found it to be boring or found the teacher to be unconcerned. A similar advantage associated with frequently requesting feedback is that problems can be dealt with before they become major issues. By providing students with opportunities for expressing their likes and dislikes, teachers decrease the likelihood that students will experience discomfort or failure to the point that they begin to withdraw or to disrupt the class.

A final thought about feedback is that it can be viewed as a gift. If teachers inform someone that he has done something that they like, they are obviously giving him a gift. However, if teachers give someone feedback about behaviors that make them uncomfortable or angry, they are also giving him a gift—by providing him with information which will help him to improve his relationship with them as well as with others. This shows more concern and caring than continually rejecting the person or discussing their shortcomings with others.

Considering the Value of Feedback

A second statement frequently made by teachers is that students possess neither the knowledge nor skill to provide adults with useful feedback. While students may need assistance in developing the skills needed to give helpful feedback, there can be no question concerning whether they possess the necessary knowledge. The aim of educational institutions is to assist students in acquiring useful skills and knowledge. Therefore, students are the consumers of teachers' educational interventions. While testing and statistical analysis can provide useful data concerning the results associated with certain types of teaching, students must tell teachers whether they are providing environments that the students experience as positive, motivating, safe, etc. To deny the value of adolescents' input is to deny their ability to function as critical thinking, sensitive, concerned individuals. When teachers view adolescents as incapable of providing useful feedback, they are making a damning statement about the educational system. The educational system has failed miserably if after seven or more years in the system, a student cannot be expected to critically analyze something about which he has extensive cognitive and affective data. Even more significantly, a rejection of student feedback indicates teachers' lack of respect for students. If teachers do not respect students' ability to comprehend their environment, they will certainly present them with curriculum and teaching strategies that fail to do justice to their potential skills. If teachers do not respect adolescents enough to value their feedback, it is questionable whether those teachers can teach them effectively.

Although adolescents possess the knowledge base from which to provide teachers with useful feedback, they often lack skills in presenting the feedback in a clear, helpful manner. There are several steps teachers can take to assist students in providing them with useful feedback. Prior to asking for feedback, teachers can provide students with guidelines for giving feedback. Several important criteria for giving feedback include:

1. Feedback should be descriptive rather than evaluative. It is most helpful when people tell someone how his behavior makes them feel.
2. Feedback is most useful when it is specific rather than general. People need to tell the person the specific observable behaviors to which they respond positively or negatively.
3. Feedback should focus on behaviors that the receiver can change. It is useful to inform someone that they lecture too much. It is not helpful to inform them that their age makes it impossible to communicate with them.
4. Feedback is most helpful when it is given at the earliest convenient opportunity.
5. Positive feedback is as helpful as negative feedback. While it helps to know what people do that bothers others, it also helps to know what others like.

Students can also be given opportunities for practicing giving feedback. One method for improving their skills is to give them written samples of unproductive feedback and ask them to change these into helpful statements. Another method is to ask them to discuss situations in which they have given or would currently like to give someone feedback. They can be helped to examine these situations and develop positive methods for giving feedback.

Methods for Obtaining and Processing Student Feedback

Perhaps the best method for assisting students in providing teachers with useful feedback is to develop a structured approach to obtaining feedback. For example, rather than simply asking for general impressions, teachers can develop questionnaires that focus the students' attention on specific areas on which teachers would like feedback. If teachers want feedback on specific topics such as their grading policy, the amount of homework they assign, the quality of their material, or the type of classroom activities they employ, they should devise instruments that ask students to respond in a structured manner to questions concerning these topics. Instruments for receiving useful student feedback are like good examinations. In developing both types of instruments it is important to begin by developing specific ideas concerning the type of information teachers want students to present or analyze. The next step is to develop questions that focus students' efforts on responding to the designated information. These questions should be written in such a way that student responses will clearly indicate their knowledge of the topics being covered. Finally, the results should be analyzed in a manner that provides specific data regarding both individual and group responses. Figures 8.2 and 8.3 provide examples of two forms that can be used to assist students in providing helpful feedback. Additional methodology and forms can be found in *Diagnosing Classroom Learning Environments* (1966) by Fox, Luszki, and Schmuck.

Once teachers have asked students for feedback concerning their teaching and the quality of the learning environment, it is vital that teachers discuss the results with their students. Asking students to provide feedback will only increase student alienation and distrust if teachers fail to respond to their input. A useful approach for responding to student feedback is to present students with the combined class responses. Sharing the compiled results with students enables students to put their feedback into perspective. For example, a student may realize that since the rest of the students responded positively to an existing policy, it is unlikely that the policy will be changed in response to his suggestion. Once the data has been presented, it should be employed as a stimulus for a discussion concerning changes that may be desirable in light of the feedback.

Figure 8.2 Weekly Evaluation

Please answer these questions honestly.

---

1. On a 1-5 scale, please rate your week.
   1 (very poor, low)   2   3   4   5 (very good, high)

2. Name one new thing or skill you learned this week.

3. What experience made you feel good about this week?

4. What experience made you feel uncomfortable?

5. What special thing happened to you this week that seemed important?

6. If you could change something about the week, what would it be?

7. If you have any suggestions for next week, please let me know here.

8. Other comments:

Figure 8.3 Classroom Evaluation Form

Complete each sentence by honestly describing your feelings/thoughts about this class.

1. The high point of this week was_____

_____

2. I enjoy this class most when _____

_____

3. I enjoy this class least when _____

_____

4. One thing the teacher could do to make this a better class would be to _____

_____

5. The most positive thing about the way we are graded is _____

_____

6. The thing I like least about the way we are graded is _____

_____

7. One thing I can do to make this class better for me is_____

_____

8. When I am in this class I feel _____

_____

Responding productively to student feedback does require time and effort. However, the payoffs are well worth the effort. By asking students to assist in evaluating their learning environments, teachers provide them with a feeling of being able to influence their environment. Teachers also indicate that they respect students' position as well as their ability to provide teachers with useful information. In the process, teachers can assist students in developing useful skills in providing feedback. Finally, teachers may find that students' feedback provides them with information that can make their classrooms more positive and exciting places.

INVOLVING STUDENTS IN THE EVALUATION PROCESS

When discussing their school experiences, a large percentage of adolescents indicate that the area of evaluation and grading creates a real sense of impotence and anxiety. Students realize that grades are an indication of the degree to which they have been successful in the school setting. For some adolescents, grades are closely linked to approval and rewards from parents. Other adolescents see grades as a necessary stepping stone to important future goals. Even those students who refuse to work and have apparently given up react to grades. For these students, teacher evaluation is often the potential punishment associated with trying. Many of these students unconsciously operate on the supposition that if they do not try, they cannot fail.

This point was poignantly demonstrated to me several years ago while working with an extremely disturbed junior high school boy. Test scores indicated that the student had above average potential as well as skills that placed him nearly at grade level.

Nevertheless, the student refused to attempt any school work and never brought paper and pencil to class. He justified this behavior by indicating that the work was easy and that he did not have to take notes, do assignments, or take tests in order to learn the material. Behavioral contracts had almost no effect on altering this boy's behavior. Discussions with his parents revealed that they were extremely anxious for him to succeed and that they critically analyzed any work that he took home. Since the boy's father was well known, teachers also held rather high expectations for this boy. The boy's response was simply to deny the value of school work. If no one could see his work then no one could evaluate it.

Evaluation is often perceived by students as a battle of wits between teacher and student. Since student competence is to a large degree judged by performance on teacher-assigned tasks and examinations, teachers have an obvious advantage in this battle. Therefore, it is not surprising that students resort to guerilla warfare in order to succeed. Cheating, studying only the material they think will be on the exam, and cramming material they know they will soon forget are examples of guerilla tactics employed by students.

Unfortunately, even those students who succeed at achieving success on examinations often fail to experience the positive feelings associated with achieved competence. Because much of the evaluation employed in schools requires students to employ guerilla tactics, students are frequently aware that the related learning is short lived and superficial. The learning is not integrated into their own attempt to understand their world and is therefore disjointed and incongruent with their natural attempts to order their life space. Consequently, studying for traditional examinations frequently leaves the adolescent with a sense of incompleteness, personal dishonesty, and lack of integrity. Adolescents cannot always verbalize these frustrations. However, their dislike for and criticism of much of school evaluation is based much more upon this discomfort than on the laziness to which teachers so often attribute their dissatisfaction. Indeed, the fervor with which adolescents approach living and personal relationships points to the excitement that learning holds for them.

Since grades have a powerful impact on students, it is surprising that educators do so little to involve students in the evaluation process. If teachers want to provide students with a sense of controlling important portions of their school environment, they must involve them in a meaningful way in evaluating their work. As is the case with student involvement in the teaching process, there are a number of ways in which adolescents can become meaningfully involved in the grading process.

Discussing Evaluation Procedures with Students

A good first step for increasing student involvement in evaluation is to discuss this topic with the class. This does not necessarily mean that students will make major decisions related to evaluation. However, it is important that students are clear about teachers' policies and that they understand the reasons behind teachers' decisions. It is also possible that students may provide teachers with helpful ideas concerning their methods of evaluation. For example, students might indicate that they would prefer an examination to a journal that was assigned. If several other teachers have assigned journals, they may find this form of evaluation tedious at that point in time. Similarly, students might note that they would prefer several small exams rather than one large examination. If this is acceptable to the teacher, she has provided students with an opportunity to influence their environment, and it is likely that this will positively affect student motivation. If, on the other hand, teachers have definite reasons for giving one large examination, their explanation will serve to clarify their course goals and their beliefs about the learning process. This clarification will allow students to better understand their role in the classroom, which should enhance the students' sense of potency and feeling of security.

Individual Conferences

A second method for involving students in the evaluation process is the use of individual conferences. Conferences provide teachers with an opportunity to discuss individual student concerns regarding testing and grading. There will be instances in almost every class where the grading policies developed for the entire class will be inappropriate for one or more students. This will be especially true when a decision has been made to base grading on absolute standards (such as a percentage) or norm-referenced grading (grading based on comparing a student's performance with those of his classmates). In responding to this issue, Good and Brophy noted:

> We have argued that success is necessary if students are to maintain positive self-views and involvement in assigned school work. To use a grading system based upon absolute standards, but standards that are unattainable for some students, will guarantee that these students will give up and expend only minimal efforts in pursuing course work. To use norm-referenced comparisons will also guarantee that some students will reduce their time and effort in the course (for example, those who do poorly on the first exam). (Good and Brophy, 1977, p. 473)

Individual conferences enable the teacher and student to develop evaluation methods and grading standards that provide students with a feeling that the goals are realistic and attainable. This will most often take the form of employing a criterion-referenced evaluation format in which an individual's performance is determined by the degree to which the individual has learned predetermined skills or concepts. This type of evaluation enables students to focus on developing specific skills rather than on competing with other students or attempting to reach impossible standards that apply to all students.

When confronted with the possibility of students developing their own evaluation criteria, teachers often note that students will develop criteria that are too lenient. Research findings tend not to support this contention. When working toward individual learning goals, students tend to choose moderate, yet challenging goals (Lewin et al., 1944). In addition, when students develop their own criteria for success and reinforcement, they learn more effectively than when these criteria are established by a teacher (Lovitt and Curtiss, 1969). Students are aware of the amount of reinforcement their efforts deserve. In fact, students are not motivated by teacher praise if the praise is associated with performances that fall below the student's personal standards (Marston, 1968; Gergen, 1971). Given an opportunity, students can develop realistic goals and evaluate their performance fairly.

Benefits of Students Evaluating Student Performance

Another means for increasing students' sense of potency is to involve students in evaluating their own work and work produced by their peers. There are several negative implications connected with teachers having sole responsibility for evaluating students' work. First, this implies that the teacher is the sole source of legitimate knowledge within the classroom. Second, in those cases where the work could be checked by students, it can imply that students cannot be trusted. Finally, giving teachers sole responsibility for grading implies that work is done for the teacher or for the grade that the teacher has the power to dispense. Involving students in evaluating their own work or providing feedback regarding their peers' work reduces the degree to which these implications become part of students' assumptions about learning.

Student involvement in evaluation has several positive effects. First, it has the effect of increasing the likelihood that learning will be intrinsically motivated. If students are involved in evaluating the quality of their own work, the focus is switched from pleasing the teacher to satisfying themselves. Second, when students evaluate their own or their peers' work, they must have a working knowledge of the goals that the work is meant to accomplish. If teachers involve students in the evaluation process, they must spend time discussing the goals associated with their assignments and tests. These explanations will significantly increase the degree to which students understand the reasons they are doing their work. As Carl Rogers (1969) wrote in his book, *Freedom to Learn:*

> The evaluation of one's own learning is one of the major means by which self-initiated learning becomes also responsible learning. It is when the individual has to take the responsibility for deciding what criteria are important to him, what goals he has been trying to achieve, and the extent to which he has achieved these goals, that he truly learns to take responsibility for himself and his directions. For this reason it seems important that some degree of self-evaluation be built into any attempt to promote an experiential type of learning. (Rogers, 1969, pp. 142-143)

A third advantage associated with allowing students to evaluate their own work is that teachers increase the opportunities for students to receive meaningful feedback that they can clearly understand. Feedback on students' work too often includes simply a grade or the word "good" placed beside a particular answer or paragraph. This type of feedback has little meaning other than that directly associated with extrinsic motivators. Critically evaluating their work against explicit, clear criteria provides students with specific meaningful feedback. Finally, evaluating their own work is seldom as threatening to students as having someone evaluate their work. Most people have experienced the feelings associated with completing a task and then deciding that certain parts needed improvement. Consider for a moment the difference between these feelings and those that you experience when someone else examines and evaluates your work. The former evaluation is less anxiety producing while at the same time having real potential for providing useful corrective feedback.

Developing Peer and Self-Evaluation

There are a variety of ways in which teachers can involve students in evaluating their own learning. One form of self-directed evaluation that enables adolescents to experience a sense of achievement and to maintain a sense of integrity is to simply ask them to express in their own words what they have learned. As discussed previously, teachers frequently present adolescents with so much material in such a short time that they do not really understand the material they have supposedly learned. Setting aside time to examine and discuss what they have learned and what it means to them provides adolescents with an opportunity both to integrate and evaluate their learning.

There are several methods for putting this theory of evaluation into practice. One method is to ask students to keep a notebook in which they record what they are learning. Class time can be provided for writing, and the teacher can examine these notebooks periodically in order to determine whether students are in fact under-standing key concepts. These notebooks also provide an excellent opportunity for individualizing instruction. Teacher's responses to students' journals can provide students with individualized feedback and instruction. Notebooks can also provide teachers with valuable feedback concerning the degree to which student learning is consonant with the teacher's instructional goals.

Another method for allowing students to integrate their learning is to facilitate class discussions centered around what has been learned and how it can be applied. By giving students primary responsibility for such discussions, students will be required to clarify for themselves what the learning has meant to them. Again, observation of such discussions can enable the teacher to ascertain the extent to which students have comprehended the material. Anyone who has taught knows that the best test of one's knowledge of material is how effectively it can be presented to others. Asking students to demonstrate their competency by privately responding to questions deprives them of the opportunity to experience an extremely valuable learning activity.

In addition to requesting that students summarize and analyze their learning experiences, it is also possible to meaningfully involve students in evaluating their responses to more traditional methods of evaluation. For example, after having completed an examination, students can be asked to outline the strengths and weaknesses of their own responses or those written by their classmates. This procedure can be facilitated by the teacher leading a discussion directed at highlighting the key concepts that should be included within each answer. Once these concepts have been clarified and possibly written on the blackboard, it is easy for students to provide themselves or their classmates with constructive evaluative feedback.

This form of student involvement has the dual advantage of facilitating knowledge acquisition and providing students with fairly extensive and immediate written feedback. Given the fact that most secondary teachers work with between one hundred and two hundred students, it is understandable that teachers often cannot provide students with extensive written comments concerning their work. Further-more, teachers often find that it requires several long evenings and perhaps a weekend of work in order to adequately respond to students' work. Consequently, students often receive delayed feedback that arrives long after the class has begun dealing with a new concept. Based on what educators know about the value of immediate and specific feedback, it appears that there are real advantages connected with students evaluating their own work or that of their peers.

A Synthesis of Teacher and Student Evaluation

The comments presented above are not intended to negate the value of evaluation from outside sources. Teachers have information and a sense of perspective that make their evaluative input useful and necessary. However, the manner in which teacher evaluation is presented can dramatically influence its value. Consider the difference between the following methods of evaluation. In the first situation the student is presented with an essay examination. After completing the exam, the student waits several days before receiving the results. When they arrive, the results indicate that out of a possible ten points on each question, the student received six points on question one, eight on question two, and nine on question three. The student further learns that his answer to question three was excellent and that he received a B on the exam.

Now consider the student who completes the same examination and spends time in a large group discussion directed at outlining the major points associated with each answer. The student is then asked to examine his answers and to list the strengths and weaknesses of each answer. Following this, the student is asked to score each answer on a one to ten scale. Several days after completing this task, the student receives an indication of the teacher's (or another student's) response to his examination. The evaluator has assigned each answer a numerical value and has added reactions to the answers and to the student's reactions to his answers. If the teacher's numerical evaluation or comments differ significantly from the student's, the student is asked to have a conference with the teacher to discuss the differences.

In comparing these forms of giving feedback, it is obvious which provides students with better understanding, a greater sense of worth, and more control over their environment. Also, it seems obvious that the latter method has much greater potential for increasing students' skills in such areas as critical thinking, personal responsibility, and self-evaluation. If teachers expect students to find learning to be an exciting, useful process, teachers cannot eliminate them from the evaluation process. The two are intricately intertwined. Effective learning cannot occur in the absence of a sound, clear evaluation procedure.

PROVIDING CONSTRUCTIVE STRUCTURE

While it is extremely important that adolescents be involved in making decisions concerning issues that directly affect them, it is also important to realize that adolescents need and want limits and structure. Young adolescents are experiencing rapid biological, cognitive, and social changes. Although their world is intense and exciting, it is also characterized by new dimensions of confusion, anxiety, self-analysis, and decision making. Consequently, young adolescents have a need to experience a sense of stability and certainty. By providing clear rules and adequate structure adults provide an important ingredient in assisting adolescents to experience feelings of safety and power.

At the same time that adults acknowledge adolescents' need for structure and order, they are faced with adolescents' real need to explore new ideas and challenge old beliefs. Challenge and experimentation are important ingredients in adolescents' search for establishing a healthy identity. When confronted with the apparently conflicting concepts of providing structure while at the same time accepting and even reinforcing questioning and challenges, it is little wonder that many teachers consider junior high school the most difficult and demanding teaching assignment; and parents often express strong feelings of frustration and impotence when attempting to guide their junior high aged children.

When attempting to develop an approach to working effectively with young adolescents, research and theory in parent-child relationships provide a useful perspective and suggest a productive direction. Parenting styles have frequently been divided into the three categories of authoritarian, democratic, and laissez faire. Simply stated, an authoritarian style of interaction is based upon the adult attempting to control the adolescents' behavior so that it conforms to fairly rigid standards of conduct. Furthermore, in such situations the control is generally perceived by the adolescent as arbitrary and is maintained by punishment or threats of punishment (Baumrind, 1968). At the other extreme, a laissez faire style of parenting refers to situations in which adolescents are allowed to unilaterally make a wide range of decisions concerning their own behavior. Somewhere between these two extremes lies the democratic parenting style in which parents maintain ultimate responsibility for the adolescent's behavior while at the same time providing an open forum for discussion, explanation, and compromise.

It is interesting to note that a wide variety of research and theory points to the frequent negative effects that accompany both the authoritarian and laissez faire styles while highlighting the positive results associated with democratic child-rearing techniques (Ahlstrom and Havighurst, 1971; Bandura and Walters, 1959; Elder, 1963; Glueck and Glueck, 1950; Mead, 1970; Tait and Hodges, 1962). These research findings strongly support the value of developing a style of working with adolescents that blends structure and support with flexibility, open dialogue, explanations, and conflict resolution. There is no question about the fact that adolescents need adult guidance in creating environments that are clearly organized and in which rules and expectations are readily understood. On the other hand, it is equally important that adolescents become increasingly involved in creating the rules, discussing the expectations, and evaluating the results. The methods for creating environments that incorporate a healthy blend of structure and freedom are based upon using the communication skills described in Part II to assist in gradually instituting the teaching methodologies outlined in Part III. The remaining sections of the book will consider interventions that can be employed with those adolescents who are unable to respond effectively, even within environments that consistently meet their developmental and psychological needs.

SUMMARY

A major developmental task of adolescence involves the gradual acquisition of skills and self-esteem that enable youngsters to establish a sense of independence and autonomy. Adolescents have a strong need to understand and influence their environment. Unfortunately, schools all too often provide adolescents with limited opportunities for meeting these needs. Indeed, significant numbers of adolescents seem to view schools as confusing places in which they have little or no ability to influence their environment.

This chapter has examined several strategies that teachers can employ in order to increase the extent to which adolescents understand and feel they can control their school environment. These strategies include discussing school structures, expectations, and materials with students; allowing students to provide feedback concerning their responses to the learning environment; and actively involving students in evaluating their own learning. The chapter concludes with a brief discussion concerning the necessity of creating school environments that provide a productive synthesis of freedom, responsibility, and structure.

The strategies presented in Part III provide methods for creating school environments that meet adolescents' needs and provide students with a positive learning environment. It is unlikely that any teacher would choose to employ all of the strategies presented. Neither should the ideas presented here be viewed as an exhaustive list of ways to create healthier learning environments. A useful task that can assist teachers in employing the basic concepts presented in Part III is to create a list of activities or structures within the classroom that facilitate and that block feelings of significance, competence, and power. Classroom management problems will begin to dissipate as teachers are able to add items to the former list and alter classrooms to reduce the latter list.

When combined with the use of effective communication skills, the principles presented in Part III will eliminate many of the behavior problems that teachers experience when working with adolescents. However, there are a small percentage of adolescents whose problems are such that they will behave disruptively even when provided with a positive environment. Part IV will focus on counseling techniques that can be employed with these adolescents.

Strategies for Assisting Adolescents in Developing Productive Behaviors

Unfortunately books and workshops aimed at assisting professionals in working with behavior-problem adolescents have often focused on techniques for altering youngsters' behaviors without first examining adolescents' needs and the environments to which adolescents are being asked to adjust. In response to this common oversight, the first eight chapters of this book have focused on understanding adolescents and creating both productive adult-adolescent relationships and healthy learning environments.

However, factors other than current situational variables often play a major role in determining adolescents' behavior. Behavior-problem adolescents often act inappropriately because they have not developed attitudes and skills that enable them to respond productively to the demands associated with even the best learning or living conditions. Similarly, behavior-problem adolescents have often developed defense mechanisms that prevent them from being aware of their unproductive behaviors and the negative consequences associated with these behaviors. Therefore, interventions aimed at helping behavior-problem adolescents will often need to focus on the individual as well as on environmental factors. Part IV will present a variety of intervention strategies aimed at assisting adolescents in becoming more aware of their behavior and more able to employ behaviors that meet their needs while at the same time eliciting positive responses from those around them.

The techniques presented in this section are intended for use with adolescents whose behavior problems are such that they cannot be altered by the environmental interventions presented in Parts II and III. Therefore, these techniques are more likely to be employed by specialists such as psychologists, counselors, and special education personnel. Nevertheless, teachers can employ many of the ideas presented in this section. In fact, with the current emphasis on mainstreaming, teachers will increasingly find themselves required to work with behavior-problem students within a regular classroom setting. An understanding of the concepts and skills presented in Part IV will enable the classroom teacher to deal more effectively with behavior-problem adolescents and to work with specialists in implementing productive behavior change programs.

Throughout Part IV an emphasis has been placed on actively involving adolescents in changing their behavior. When adults attempt to control adolescents' behaviors, they act in direct opposition to their need to be independent and to experience a sense of significance, competence, and power. Furthermore, unless adults involve adolescents in examining and altering their own behavior, it is unlikely that they will develop skills that will enable them to transfer their learning to new environments. In the final analysis, the adult's task is to assist behavior-problem adolescents to become more aware of their behavior, its impact on others, and the consequences resulting from their behavior. At the same time adults must help these youngsters to develop skills (alternative behavioral responses) that will enable them to meet their needs while employing behaviors that allow them to interact positively with others.

Chapter 9 presents the basic concepts that provide the framework for developing effective behavior change programs with adolescents. The remaining three chapters focus on three forms of intervention that can be employed to assist behavior-problem adolescents in developing more appropriate and acceptable behaviors. Chapter 10 presents a variety of strategies for assisting adolescents in increasing their awareness of their behaviors and others' responses to these behaviors. Chapter 11 presents a variety of models for employing behavioral counseling techniques with adolescents. Chapter 12 provides information on when and how to employ contracting with behavior-problem adolescents.

Philosophically, there is little question about the desirability of extending autonomy and freedom of choice to everyone; the problem is determining when and how much. The ability to act independently and make wise and appropriate choices is learned just like any other facet of behavior . . . A child needs not only experience, but the right kind of experience. And he needs a wise guide who can steer him clear of danger and who encourages, prompts, and reinforces behavior that is adaptive and successful.

Garth Blackham and Adolf Silberman

Modification of Child and Adolescent Behavior

CHAPTER
9

Basic Concepts Associated with Developing Effective Behavior Change Programs

Before examining a variety of specific methods for assisting adolescents in changing their behavior, it is important to consider several important concepts regarding the development of behavior intervention strategies. Like theories of adolescence, these concepts provide an invaluable foundation for developing successful behavior change programs. In the absence of an understanding and application of these concepts, behavior change strategies can become mechanical tools that are ineffective and/or destructive as often as they are effective and productive. However, when these basic tenets are understood and applied, behavior change strategies can become humanistic tools that assist adolescents in developing more desirable and appropriate behaviors while concurrently enhancing self-esteem and increasing their sense of personal integrity and responsibility.

THE THERAPEUTIC RELATIONSHIP

An examination of the social and family backgrounds of problem adolescents will show the importance of establishing a therapeutic relationship characterized by

151

stability, trust, and mutual respect. The majority of adolescents experiencing serious behavior problems come from environments in which security, mutual concern, and respect have been lacking. When describing the social background of delinquent youth, Conger notes that:

> Increases in delinquency, as well as in other adolescent difficulties, appear most likely to occur where a sense of community solidarity and the integrity of the extended family has been most seriously disrupted. . . . Furthermore, within the suburbs, increases appear to be greatest in communities and among families characterized by a high degree of social and geographic mobility and a lack of stable ties to other persons and social institutions. (Conger, 1977, p. 578)

The family backgrounds of behavior-problem adolescents also tend to be characterized by a lack of security and stability. As discussed earlier, the family backgrounds of problem adolescents are frequently characterized by discipline techniques that are either very lax and indifferent or overly strict and harsh. The importance of the quality of family interaction is highlighted by the fact that the relationships existing within the home appear to be more important than whether the family has stayed intact. Youngsters coming from unbroken homes characterized by hostility or apathy appear to be more likely to become involved in delinquent acts than adolescents raised in broken homes characterized by their warmth and supportive atmosphere (Ahlstrom and Havighurst, 1971).

The lack of involvement and support that behavior-problem and socially withdrawn students experience in their home and community tends to be compounded by the alienation and failure they experience at school. As discussed earlier, the school experiences of students who eventually drop out of school are frequently characterized by failure and uninvolvement both in the classroom and in school-wide activities.

As a result of the lack of security, support, and involvement found in their experiences within the community, school, and family, behavior-problem adolescents tend to have low self-esteem and to experience difficulty in establishing meaningful, mutually satisfying relationships. When describing the personality characteristics of delinquents, Conger states that:

> Many of these traits appear defensive in nature, reflecting impaired self-concepts and feelings of inadequacy, emotional rejection, and frustration of needs for self-expression . . . According to their own self-concepts, delinquents are undesirable people; they tend not to like, value, or respect themselves . . . In particular, they appeared to feel less capable of establishing close personal relationships with either peers or adults, especially the latter. (Conger, 1977, pp. 580, 582)

Evidence clearly points to the fact that adolescents who experience emotional and behavior problems have been seriously limited in the availability of productive, supportive, indepth relationships with adults. Moreover, in addition to their needs for security, support, and guidance that stem from varying types and degrees of social deprivation, these young people also experience several developmental needs that enhance the importance of the therapeutic relationship. Paramount among these needs is the need for a safe, secure environment in which personal concerns associated with increasing self-awareness and self-consciousness can be explored. In addition, adolescents experience the need for a relationship in which realistic limits are established, clearly explained, and allowed to change as the adolescents' understanding and skills expand. This last point is extremely important. While adolescents desperately need a relationship characterized by support, trust, and warmth, they also need to know that adults have enough respect for themselves and the rights of others that they will not ignore or accept adolescent behavior that is harmful to others. Adolescents need to work with adults who will continually attempt to assist them in developing attitudes and skills that support behaviors that are productive for both the adolescent and those around him.

If adults fail to develop therapeutic relationships characterized by safety and support, they cannot expect adolescents to risk examining and changing their behaviors. Regardless of how effectively adults develop contracts or attempt to teach skills, unless they first develop a positive relationship they will be confronted with the same type of manipulation, defensiveness, or withdrawal that has characterized the adolescent's previous interchanges with adults.

BEING RESPONSIVE TO NORMAL DEVELOPMENTAL TASKS

When making a decision concerning which type of intervention strategy to employ when working with an adolescent, it is important to carefully examine the extent to which the intervention facilitates or blocks developmental needs. More specifically, behavior interventions employed with adolescents must respond to adolescents' needs to: (1) experience a sense of significance, competence, and power; (2) experience a sense of structure and order; and (3) focus on current, concrete issues and behaviors.

As mentioned in Chapter 1, adolescents experience an intensified self consciousness as well as an interest in and ability to become involved in more indepth relationships. These changes create a situation in which adolescents experience a need to be involved in relationships that are characterized by mutual respect, warmth and concern. Therefore, as noted in the previous section, it is important that any intervention aimed at assisting adolescents in altering their behavior should include supportive and meaningful contact with adults. Writers such as Rogers (1961), Jourard (1971), Maslow (1968), and Glasser (1969) have attempted to describe the qualities within the therapeutic relationship that maximize personal growth and stimulate a willingness to change. These ingredients include realness or genuineness, unconditional positive regard, empathic understanding, and mutual self-disclosure. Since these ingredients all support a feeling of significance, they are vital to an effective therapeutic relationship with behavior-problem adolescents.

Since a major developmental task for adolescents is establishing a feeling of competence and personal potency, any approach to working with adolescents must provide adolescents with an opportunity to experience a sense of involvement and personal responsibility. At the same time, however, it is important to keep in mind that adolescence is a period of rapid cognitive and physical change. Even for the adolescent who is involved in successful, positive experiences, this change is understandably accompanied by some confusion, anxiety, and frustration. For the adolescent who is confronted with school failure, family turmoil, and peer rejection, the adolescent years can become a nightmare of confused values, confused goals, and feelings of anxiety and frustration. Furthermore, while early adolescence is a period during which most individuals begin to develop an ability to manipulate abstract concepts and to respond more effectively to an extended time perspective, there is considerable variation in the age and rate at which individuals develop advanced cognitive skills (Dulit, 1972). Since adolescents who experience considerable learning and behavior problems are apt to be somewhat delayed in the development of advanced cognitive skills, they may experience particular difficulties in dealing with abstract, unstructured situations. Therefore, counseling strategies that adults employ in working with adolescents must also provide them with a sense of stability and structure around which they can begin to rebuild their world. If adults provide too little structure they fail to supply adolescents with the necessary benchmarks around which to structure their newly developing insights and skills. At the same time, however, they must be careful not to provide too much structure. Too much structure creates a situation in which adolescents cannot experiment and develop a sense of who they are and what they can do.

Within the therapeutic relationship the adult's role should be one of assisting adolescents in examining their behaviors, establishing realistic goals, and developing the skills needed to achieve these goals. For example, the girl who is experiencing conflict with her mother should not only be asked to examine this situation within the therapeutic environment, but should also be asked to work on developing skills that will help her to interact more effectively with or make a healthy break from her mother. Similarly, while the boy who is involved in violent interchanges with his teachers should be assisted in examining the factors that elicit this behavior and the consequences associated with this behavior, the sense of competence associated with understanding this situation should be accompanied by the more dramatic competence associated with developing skills that enable him to better control himself and his environment.

Research (Middleton and Snell, 1963) indicates that discipline that adolescents view as either authoritarian or permissive is associated with a lack of closeness between the parent and the child. In summarizing his findings on the effects of various parenting styles Elder (1962) stated "In essence, child rearing structures which represent considerable adolescent participation in self-direction appear least provocative of rejection feelings" (p. 260). These findings suggest that adolescents prefer adult-adolescent relationships characterized by a blend of meaningful adult involvement and active adolescent participation. Indeed, it is precisely this type of relationship that provides adolescents with a sense of being supported while simultaneously being perceived as capable of influencing their own behavior.

Since most educators and therapists have successfully mastered large amounts of abstract material, it is reasonable to assume that the majority of professionals in these fields are among those adults who possess the ability to effectively manipulate abstract concepts. Unfortunately, professionals often fail to realize that their students and clients may not possess sophisticated skills in abstract thinking. This oversight is often accompanied by adults applying therapeutic interventions that seem exciting and appropriate, but only cause greater confusion for adolescents. Therapeutic interventions that center on insight or reason appear most likely to suffer from this misdirection. Therefore, before employing developmental, rationale-emotive, or other insight-oriented interventions, adults should carefully consider the adolescent's ability to comprehend and generalize the concepts being presented.

In working with behavior-problem adolescents, I have been consistently impressed by the fact that interventions that are associated with significant changes in behavior almost always include a major emphasis on current behaviors and feelings. In fact, when more cognitive, abstract interventions are successful, it is almost always because they have incorporated a major emphasis on specific behaviors. For example, programs that employ a transactional analysis model are seldom effective when their major thrust is toward cognitive understanding. However, such programs can be quite effective when they involve adolescents in actively employing the concepts through role playing and assignments.

Based on the above discussion, it is obvious that one of the major reasons why so many interventions with behavior-problem adolescents fail is that they contain major components that are in direct opposition to normal developmental tasks. I had the opportunity to observe an excellent example of this concept when I first began working with emotionally handicapped adolescents in a school setting.

The program I was asked to direct had previously operated on an extremely structured, behavioristic model. For example, one technique employed in the program was to set a timer at random intervals. If all students present in the room were on task when the timer sounded, the class was given a bonus point. A designated number of bonus points enabled the students to receive a special privilege. Another technique employed was to reinforce completion of assignments with a coke. A coke machine had been installed in the room to facilitate the dispensing of these reinforcers. While the use of these techniques was accompanied by an increase in both on-task behavior and the number of assignments completed, the year-end results showed limited changes in the students' behavior outside the confines of the special classroom. Furthermore, while on-task behavior and completed assignments increased slightly, there appeared to be no major decrease in the amount of inappropriate and aggressive behavior displayed by the students. Considering that students were provided with individualized academic material and considerable individual attention, it was surprising that acting-out behavior continued at a fairly high level.

In examining the program, it became apparent that it failed to respond effectively to a number of important adolescent needs. First, students were not meaningfully involved in deciding what behaviors needed to be altered or how these behaviors would be altered. Students were allowed to make only token decisions such as what reinforcers would be provided. While several of the seventh grade students (who very likely were just beginning to develop formal operational thought, higher levels of moral reasoning, and to experience a need for independence from adult authority) responded quite well to this tokenism, many of the older students appeared insulted by the adult control and manipulation. These older students appeared willing to "play the game" when they were interested in obtaining the rewards. However, their behavior appeared calculated, and neither their attitudes nor their behavior showed significant changes. In evaluating this program, it appeared that a primary reason for its lack of success was that the program failed to respond to the students' need to be seen as competent and able to control meaningful parts of their environment. These adolescents were certainly not so naive as to believe that they could do what they pleased. They did not expect—and in fact probably did not want—complete control over their environment. Nevertheless, these adolescents expressed a desire and a need to be meaningfully involved in a program whose primary goal was to change their behavior. Problem adolescents need adults to listen to them, give them feedback concerning their behavior, help them to learn skills, and assist them in controlling their behavior. They do not need and will seldom accept having adults make unilateral decisions about how to structure their lives. Furthermore, even on those occasions when they are bribed or forced into unquestioningly following adult guidelines, this type of intervention seldom brings about significant long-term behavior changes.

A second area in which a major developmental need was blocked concerned the area of peer acceptance. By isolating the students in a room that was obviously very different from other classrooms (no other classroom had carpeting, a two-way mirror, and a coke machine), the program created a situation in which the students became even more different from their peers. While attempting to alleviate differences in the areas of off-task behavior and work completed, the program enhanced the differences in the more important (to the students) areas of personal freedom, use of time, and privileges received. Consequently, the special room became known as "the goon room," and the problem students became even more isolated from and feared by the majority of their peers. Since the isolation and associated labeling reduced the sense of significance, competence, and power experienced by the "special students," these students frequently intensified their acting-out behavior in order to demonstrate their competence and power.

The above discussion paints a rather negative picture of behaviorally based interventions with adolescents. These comments may appear overly critical in light of the fact that a wide range of studies (Cohen, Goldiamond, and Filipczak, 1973; Jesness, DeRisi, McCormick, and Wedge, 1972; Karacki and Levinson, 1970; and Phillips, Phillips, Fixsen, and Wolf, 1971) indicate that adult-directed behavior modification programs can be effective in altering specific unproductive adolescent behaviors. However, these studies almost universally fail to examine generalized or long-term behavior changes. As discussed in Chapter 12, behavior contracts can be very effective in assisting adolescents to make important immediate changes in their behavior. However, if adults wish to assist adolescents in developing responsibility, personal competence, and positive self-concepts, it is extremely important that adults' therapeutic interventions respond to adolescents' developmental needs by actively involving them in the development and evaluation of treatment programs. As discussed in Chapters 10 and 11, there are a variety of creative and highly successful approaches to assisting adolescents in terminating specific unproductive behaviors and replacing these with socially acceptable behavior. A key ingredient in all of these interventions is that the adolescent is actively involved in all phases of the program. Adolescents must be meaningfully involved in determining the behaviors that need to be terminated or learned, the performance criteria, and the methods for changing the behavior. By involving adolescents in ways that support their natural developmental tasks, adults greatly enhance the likelihood that the results will be positive and that they will be incorporated into the individual's long-range behavioral repertoire.

When discussing the value of involving adolescents in their own behavior change program, adults frequently point out that at certain times and with certain types of adolescents it is simply not possible to involve the adolescent in major decisions. When making this point, adults often confuse the concept of active involvement with allowing the adolescent to make the decision. It is certainly not possible to allow a court committed youngster to have complete control over when and under what conditions he will be released. Similarly, it is seldom productive to allow an angry student to decide what behaviors are acceptable within a classroom setting. However, in both of these cases it is nearly as unproductive to have the adult unilaterally make the decision. If adults expect adolescents to make meaningful changes in their attitudes and behaviors, they must involve them in ways that maintain their integrity by acknowledging their ability to discuss and evaluate their own behavior. When I provide adolescents with these opportunities, I am consistently impressed with their enthusiasm for becoming involved and the rigor with which they evaluate their own behavior. While this does not mean that they immediately alter their behavior so as to fit their goals, their involvement does create a sense of personal worth and an associated motivation that significantly enhance the potential for change.

IDENTIFYING AND RESPONDING PRODUCTIVELY TO EMOTIONS

People who have worked with emotionally handicapped adolescents are aware of how often an effective contract or a decision reached during a counseling session is subverted by a strong feeling. Students often explain their unproductive behavior in terms of feelings: "I knew what to do, but I got angry," or "I really did want to have a good day, but I got so frustrated." The frequency of such statements suggests that students' feelings are an important variable influencing their behavior.

Feelings can be compared to the lubricants put in cars. Regardless of how mechanically sound and how well tuned the engine, it will boil over or blow up if the amount and quality of lubrication used is not attended to. Feelings serve a similar function for people. No matter how physically sound or well trained they may be, their behavior can become dysfunctional if they cannot effectively channel their emotions. The athletic coach is well aware of the importance of emotions. Many physically gifted athletes do not make the starting team because they cannot successfully cope with the emotions associated with competition, teamwork, pressure, and success. Similarly, numerous less gifted athletes become outstanding performers because they can use their emotions to make optimum use of their physical gifts.

Like the gifted athlete who cannot perform under pressure, behavior-problem adolescents often suffer from an inability to effectively cope with their emotions. When discussing the emotional characteristics of children with learning and behavior disorders, Gardner (1977) states that:

> ... when comparing these children and youth with "normal" peers without a history of excessive failure, the following points should be kept in mind:
> There are fewer aspects of the child's environment which produce positive emotional reactions . . .
> There are more aspects of the child's environment which produce negative emotionality . . .
> There is greater likelihood that the child will engage in intense and disorganizing episodes of negative emotionality . . .
> The usual events which produce positive emotional responses in most children, or which are neutral, may in fact become cues for negative emotional reactions. . . .
> Minor sources of irritation or frustration may produce unusually strong emotional reactions . . .
> There are more negative self-referents depicting emotional reactions . . .
> There are more negative and fewer positive referents depicting emotional reactions toward others and things . . .
> The child may have a more limited range of emotional reactions or he may demonstrate difficulty in discriminating the appropriateness of various emotional reactions. . . . (Gardner, 1977, pp. 405-407)

The fact that emotions do strongly influence adolescents' behavior makes it vital that behavior-change programs include a component that assists adolescents in responding productively to their emotional responses. Since behavior-problem adolescents often have defenses that limit both access to and understanding of their emotions, it is important that adults begin by helping adolescents to identify their emotions. Once this task has been accomplished, the next step is to assist adolescents in developing skills that enable them to respond productively to their emotions.

FOCUSING ON POSITIVE BEHAVIORS

Adolescents who are experiencing behavior problems have almost always had a history of failure. Consequently, these youngsters experience more negative feelings about themselves than do their more successful peers. In addition, there are usually many more environmental conditions that elicit negative feelings in behavior-problem youngsters. Because of this situation, it is important that, whenever possible, adults direct behavior interventions at reinforcing new, desirable behavior on the part of behavior-problem adolescents.

> The major focus of educational program efforts designed to deal with problem behaviors should be on strengthening those desirable learning and behavior characteristics which will compete with, and eventually replace, undesirable patterns. (Gardner, 1977, p. 334)

While a positive focus is desirable when working with children of any age, there are at least five reasons why it is particularly important when working with adolescents. First, from a purely pragmatic point of view, it is often necessary to focus on positive behaviors when working with adolescents. Negative consequences are much more difficult to employ with adolescents than with children. For example, while many children will accept isolation, adolescents are much more likely to refuse to obey an adult's request to accept a time-out situation. Similarly, while it is relatively easy to ground a child, it is often difficult to place home restrictions on an adolescent who is angry and feels unfairly treated. A second reason for focusing on appropriate behaviors when working with adolescents is that adolescence is a period when youngsters are struggling to develop a sense of identity. Consequently, adolescents are sensitive to criticism and frequently react defensively to implications that there is something wrong with their behavior. By focusing on positive behaviors, adults indicate their respect for adolescents' skills rather than emphasizing their deficiencies. Third, adolescents are attempting to demonstrate their competence. Asking them to employ positive behaviors sometimes taps their desire to demonstrate their competence. Fourth, adolescents are striving to obtain a realistic sense of independence and control over their environment. A focus on terminating unproductive behaviors is often perceived by adolescents as an adult's attempt to control their behavior. However, a request that the adolescent display an alternative behavior may be perceived as an opportunity to demonstrate an ability to control their own behavior. Finally, an emphasis on positive behavior is more likely to respond to higher levels of moral development than is a focus on controlling negative behavior. More specifically, the emphasis on positive behavior may highlight Kohlberg's stage three (maintaining good relations), five (social contract) or six (individual principles of conscience) while the emphasis on negative consequences will usually focus on level one (punishment and obedience), two (instrumental hedonism) or four (law and order). Since adolescents are developing higher levels of cognitive ability and desire to be treated like adults, it seems appropriate, whenever possible, to employ interventions that focus on higher levels of moral development.

MAINTAINING HIGH EXPECTATIONS

With the possible exception of situations in which behavior must be controlled immediately in order to protect an adolescent or those around him, it is always desirable to begin with the intervention that is least restrictive and allows adolescents the maximum responsibility. Such interventions are responsive to developmental needs, and also prevent the legitimate criticism and defensiveness stemming from programs that require adolescents to respond on moral and skill levels below their current attainment. Furthermore, there is no harm in basing initial interventions on the assumption that an adolescent can function at a higher level than he is really capable of. It is relatively easy and almost always therapeutically sound to move toward a more structured intervention by presenting an adolescent with his failure in functioning effectively in a less structured program. This leaves the adolescent with the goal of moving from the more structured program back to a program that places greater responsibility on the adolescent.

For example, consider the situation that occurs when a behavior-problem seventh grade student first enrolls in a junior high school. With few exceptions, the best (and often most accurate) initial assumption should be that the youngster's development or the change in the school environment has created a situation in which the youngster can function in a supportive regular school environment. If this assumption proves false, the adolescent's school program should include gradual increases in the amount of structure. In terms of the format presented in this book, the program should move from productive communication and a careful examination of the learning environment, to self-observation and awareness programs, to behavioral counseling, to contracting, and finally to special school placement.

The importance of focusing initial interventions at a level that reflects high expectations is also supported by a large body of research concerning the powerful impact adult expectations have on student performance (Braun, 1976; Braun, Neilsen, and Dykstra, 1975; Brophy and Good, 1974). Studies (Brophy and Good, 1974; Rosenthal and Jacobson, 1968) suggest that student behavior tends to move in the direction of teacher expectations. It appears that positive expectations and the adult behaviors accompanying these expectations can have a positive effect on student performance. The effectiveness of such an approach was highlighted by the Kleinfeld (1972) study discussed in Chapter 7. Recall that Kleinfeld's research involved work with Indian and Eskimo students who were having adjustment problems following their move to an urban environment. Kleinfeld's research indicated that these students adjusted better and learned more effectively when their teachers combined active interest in the students with demands that slightly exceeded the students' beliefs concerning their own abilities. Since behavior-problem students are similar to Kleinfeld's students in that they lack academic skills and often experience a feeling of social isolation, it seems likely that the same teacher variables will be effective in assisting their successful learning and social integration.

SPECIFICITY IN DESCRIBING BEHAVIORS

When employing a behavioral intervention, it is important that the behaviors be presented in terms of specific, observable actions. Furthermore, it is important to specify the exact expectations regarding the frequency with which the behavior is to occur. For example, a student will understandably be confused or overwhelmed by a contract that indicates that he must be "good" everyday in class if he is to remain in the class. It is much easier to comprehend a contract that states that he must bring a pencil and a notebook each day, must remain in his seat unless otherwise directed, and must turn in each assignment the teacher lists on the board. Most behavior-problem students want and need some degree of structure—provided that the structure exists within a positive environment that includes realistic expectations. The specificity provided by a well-written behavioral program meets adolescents' needs for concrete rules and for structure within an often confusing and frightening environment. Structure also provides adolescents with limits and order that are necessary prerequisites to obtaining some degree of success and subsequently a feeling of competence.

The specificity found in an effective behavioral intervention program is often equally helpful for the adults involved. Teachers and parents frequently become quite emotional when dealing with a behavior-problem adolescent. Consequently, when initially asked to describe a problem, teachers often provide general, emotional descriptions, such as, "This is the most disruptive student I have. He is always causing a problem." Similarly, parents often make statements such as, "I simply cannot control him. He has no respect for us." While these statements provide an indication of the adults' frustration and need for assistance, they are almost useless in providing adolescents with information concerning the behaviors that adults believe must be altered. It is extremely important that adults be able to clearly describe the specific behaviors that are creating a problem as well as the specific behaviors that they would like to see the adolescent display. When parents and teachers are asked to list the specific behaviors that they need an adolescent to emit, they are often surprised both by the difficulty they experience in creating such a list and how relatively short the list is.

COLLECTING DATA ON OBSERVABLE CHANGES
IN BEHAVIOR

There are a variety of reasons why data collection is an important ingredient in any effective behavior change program. First, data provide important information that serves as the basis for continuing or altering an intervention strategy. More specifically, data are necessary because they decrease the likelihood that educators' perceptions and subsequent behaviors will be biased by their own needs. As Festinger (1957) found in his study on cognitive dissonance, individuals have a tendency to view as positive those activities in which they have invested considerable time and energy. People do not want to acknowledge that their time and energy have not produced meaningful results. Therefore, in the absence of data, it is likely that depending on the circumstances, adults will perceive greater or lesser changes than actually occur.

Several years ago, I worked with several junior high school counselors who were concerned about the fact that teachers often informed them that students acted less satisfactorily following visits to the counseling office. While the counselors did not believe that they were facilitating positive behavior changes in every student who visited them, they were quite certain that students were not increasing their acting-out behavior following visits to the counseling office. In order to clarify this situation, the counselors agreed to ask teachers to specify the type of student misbehavior that elicited the students' referral to the counseling center. Based on this information, a small sample of students were observed prior to and following their visits to the counseling center. Since the building had two-way mirrors in each classroom door, it was possible to observe students without influencing the classroom interactions.

The data indicated that students emitted less frequent negative behavior following counseling sessions. However, in many cases the decrease in acting-out behavior, while significant, was relatively small in absolute terms. Based on this data, it appeared likely that because teachers expected major changes in student behavior following counseling, teachers in fact viewed inappropriate behavior as increasing when students returned from counseling and continued to exhibit an inappropriate behavior. This finding suggests that unless educators collect specific, objective data, they will sometimes interpret as ineffective an intervention program that is having a gradual but significant impact upon a student's behavior.

Regardless of whether teachers' expectations lead them to perceive more or less change than actually occurs, data provide an objectivity that enhanced both accountability and flexibility. A number of years ago when I first began working with emotionally handicapped adolescents, the individual responsible for evaluating our project made a statement I will always remember. We had just completed a discussion in which I had informed him of my intention to employ a wide range of environmental, interpersonal, and behavioral interventions in working with emotionally handicapped junior high school students. Much to my surprise he indicated that he was not concerned about whether my interventions included the currently espoused behavior modification techniques. Rather, he was concerned that I kept accurate data that clearly indicated the success or failure of the interventions. He concluded by stating that while behaviorism and behavioral techniques would in the future probably become less rigidly applied, the key concept that behaviorists had introduced was the importance of collecting specific behavioral data.

In addition to their value in providing direction for intervention strategies, data respond to several important adolescent needs. Data provide adolescents with a concrete, observable, short-term reinforcer. Like many of us, behavior-problem adolescents become discouraged when their attempts to change their behavior are not immediately and completely successful. Presenting adolescents with specific data concerning their progress enables them to see that their efforts are paying off. This information provides them with an important source of competence and power. Data are especially important for behavior-problem youngsters since they frequently operate at a more concrete cognitive level and tend to have difficulty responding to delayed gratification. The specificity and immediacy of behavioral data help these adolescents understand their behavior, while simultaneously providing immediate reinforcement.

An excellent example of the value of data collection was presented by Rosenberg (Gray, Graubard, and Rosenberg, 1974) in his work with behavior-problem junior high school students. Rosenberg and his colleagues taught behavior-problem students to reinforce their teachers' positive behavior as a means to improve teacher-student interaction. Results showed that students remained involved in the project and had positive results only when they kept accurate data concerning the results of their intervention.

SYNTHESIZING BEHAVIORISM AND HUMANISM

Therapeutic interventions that respond to the central themes of both behavioral and dynamic/humanistic psychology are more likely to be successful than those that are based upon concepts from only one paradigm. It is helpful to keep in mind that similarities do exist between the basic concepts underlying both behavioral and psychodynamic paradigms. Individuals operating from both the behavioral and psychodynamic point of view believe that emotionally handicapped or behavior-problem adolescents are the product of ineffective socialization. Whether people believe that the problem adolescent has been reinforced at the wrong time and for the wrong behaviors, had inappropriate modeling, or not been provided with basic psychological support, most psychologists would agree that behavior-problem adolescents lack skills that enable them to cope effectively with their environment. Therefore, while they often differ in their approaches to assisting adolescents, all adults in the helping professions would agree that one of their major goals is to assist the youngsters with whom they work in developing a repertoire of behaviors that will help them in interacting more effectively with their environment.

Given the fact that professionals from a wide range of disciplines and theoretical backgrounds experience some success in reaching this goal, it appears reasonable to assume that each form of intervention has something valuable to offer. Therefore, when professionals employ an intervention strategy that focuses on a narrow interpretation of the variables that are important in changing behavior, they often ignore valuable and even necessary variables. For example, when employing counseling strategies that focus almost exclusively on providing adolescents with a caring, understanding, trusting relationship, educators often fail to respond to adolescents' need for structure as well as their need to develop observable skills that will elicit positive responses from others. Thus they often fail to provide the problem adolescent with the skills necessary to create a sense of competency and power. Likewise, when adults focus exclusively on behavioral approaches to changing adolescents' behaviors, they often ignore adolescents' needs to be involved in the change process, to understand adults' intentions and procedures, and to experience a relationship characterized by trust and mutual respect. Such shortcomings create a situation in which the adolescent may not experience a sense of significance or power.

In summarizing the synthesis of humanistic/psychodynamic and behavioristic techniques, the basic humanistic/psychodynamic concepts are: (1) attending to the importance of the therapeutic relationship, (2) maintaining flexibility in determining whose behavior will be altered, (3) establishing dialogue between all parties involved in the behavior-change process, (4) emphasizing behavior changes directed at improving interpersonal interactions, and (5) considering the adolescent's developmental needs when developing a behavior-change program. The key behavioristic components include: (1) focusing on observable, objectively defined behavior, (2) collecting data, (3) working with a limited number of behaviors at any given time, (4) providing immediate feedback of results. When consistently employed, this synthesis provides an exciting, flexible methodology for assisting adolescents in developing behaviors that are more acceptable to others and more beneficial for the adolescent.

VIEWING INTERVENTIONS AS A REPARENTING PROCESS

When working with problem adolescents, it has helped me to perceive my task as assisting these individuals in learning to parent themselves. To varying degrees, behavior-problem adolescents did not have their basic needs met during childhood. Neither did they develop the social skills that enable them to receive positive reinforcement from a wide variety of sources. As children, these individuals were limited in their ability to control their environment. However, as adolescents they are capable of learning skills that enable them to establish meaningful relationships and to receive a variety of the reinforcements that their environment offers to their peers.

With this in mind, the adults' task becomes one of creating environments (including their relationships with adolescents) that enable them to meet some of the needs that have not been previously met. In doing this, adults are simultaneously creating an environment that provides enough safety and security to enable adolescents to experiment with new behaviors. Equally important, however, is adults' task of assisting adolescents in developing a new repertoire of behaviors. Like good parents, adults in the helping professions will initially need to allow some dependency and may have to take responsibility for providing much of the emotional support and many of the behavioral controls. However, as is so important in parenting, it is necessary to allow youngsters to find increasing amounts of emotional support from a widening group of people. Similarly, adolescents must be allowed to gradually assume increasing amounts of control over their own behavior. By following this procedure, problem adolescents will gradually become more able to parent themselves. They will begin to develop the sense of security and skills that enable healthy adults to obtain the psychological support and physical possessions that are necessary for a healthy existence in our society.

SUMMARY

Intervention strategies aimed at altering adolescents' behaviors are often based on a rather narrow conceptual foundation. Behavior-change programs all too frequently stem from a relatively limited understanding of one theoretical position. Programs designed in this manner often appear successful in that they are frequently associated with limited, short-term changes in behaviors. However, if the goal is to assist behavior-problem adolescents in becoming functional, healthy members of society, adults cannot be satisfied with programs whose results are incomplete and short lived. While such programs may satisfy those adults who referred the adolescent and whose primary goal is the temporary cessation of a particularly annoying behavior, adults do adolescents a disservice if they accept this limited definition of success.

This chapter has presented several basic concepts that must be considered when developing effective behavior-change programs. Programs that do not respond to all of these concepts can be effective. However, a well-conceptualized program that brings about significant long-term results will almost always include major components that respond to each of the concepts outlined in this chapter.

One of the central themes of the humanistic behavioral approach, . . . and indeed perhaps the ultimate goal of education, is to insure that a child learn increasingly varied and complex skills of self-management. With these skills the child or adolescent is in a position to self-influence those behaviors which will be most enhancing to him.

William Gardner

Learning and Behavior
Characteristics of Exceptional
Children and Youth: A Humanistic
Behavioral Approach

CHAPTER
10

Self-Observation and Self-Awareness as Behavior Change Strategies

Even the child raised in a supportive, healthy environment experiences an increase in self-consciousness, conflict, questioning, and anxiety during the adolescent years. While adolescence has perhaps been exaggerated as a period of inevitable and almost overpowering stress and confusion, it is nevertheless a reality that adolescents growing up in a complex, changing society will experience varying degrees of confusion and anxiety. Adolescents not only are suddenly able to comprehend the problems and multiple value-laden issues within both their own immediate environment and the larger society, but also are simultaneously bombarded with media, peers, and adults espousing a variety of methods for resolving these value conflicts. The increased tension and anxiety associated with the adolescent years create varying amounts of disruption in the adolescents' psychological equilibrium. Small amounts of this disruption are healthy and facilitate the development of higher order cognitive skills and higher levels of moral development. However, since large amounts of disruption create discomfort, the individual understandably employs psychological mechanisms aimed at reducing this discomfort.

While all adolescents experience some psychological disequilibrium, adolescents who are experiencing major adjustment and behavior problems experience disequilib-

165

rium to a much larger degree. As noted throughout this book, these youngsters often find themselves in home and school environments in which their basic needs are not being met. Furthermore, as they develop cognitive skills that enable them to more carefully examine the match between their own behaviors and skills and those that are accepted by the majority of adults and peers, they become increasingly aware of their position as unacceptable and isolated individuals. Because this awareness is in direct conflict with their need to experience a sense of acceptance and competence and to develop a positive self-image, it is understandable that problem adolescents both consciously and unconsciously attempt to alter or ignore at least some of the incoming data that attest to their failure. The term *defense mechanisms* has been used to describe the various responses that individuals employ to reduce the anxiety and discomfort associated with large amounts of psychological disequilibrium (Dollard and Miller, 1950; Freud, 1946). Figure 10.1 provides a list of the major defense mechanisms employed by adolescents. For the purpose of this chapter, the important issue associated with adolescents' use of defense mechanisms is that their use frequently prevents behavior-problem adolescents from developing an awareness of their own behavior and the impact it has on others.

A powerful example of an adolescent being unable to acknowledge his own behavior involved an extremely volatile ninth grade boy whose major problem centered around his frequent violent outbursts with peers and adults. The youngster almost always denied his aggressive behavior; and on those occasions when he was able to acknowledge his inappropriate behavior, he either ran away from school or

Figure 10.1 Defense Mechanisms Commonly Employed by Adolescents

Mechanism	Definition
Repression	The removal of uncomfortable memories or thoughts from conscious awareness.
Denial	The insistence by the individual that events which obviously occurred, did not occur.
Projection	Ascribing one's own thoughts or actions to another person.
Displacement	Placing one's appropriate and legitimate responses and feelings about a person or situation onto another individual or situation.
Rationalization	Creating socially acceptable reasons for one's behavior when the real reason may not have been as acceptable.
Withdrawal	Directly avoiding environments or people which one finds uncomfortable.
Regression	Employing a response which was more appropriate at an earlier stage of development.
Intellectualization	Responding in a cognitive, abstract, generalized, impersonal manner to issues which stem from obviously personal concerns.
Asceticism	Choosing behaviors or a life style which ignore a variety of basic physical and/or developmental needs.
Aggression	Responding in an aggressive, unacceptable manner in order to avoid dealing with the anxiety associated with more acceptable behaviors.

vehemently placed the entire blame on others. This behavior reached its climax in an incident that began when the student responded angrily to a female staff member's request that he return to his seat. When the teacher calmly but firmly repeated the request, the student became enraged and threw a handful of tacks in the teacher's face. Fortunately, the teacher was not hurt. However, despite the fact that other students verified the student's behavior, he vigorously denied having thrown the tacks. In addition, his parents also maintained that the incident was a trumped-up charge that was the result of the teacher not liking their son and wanting to be rid of him.

This incident could have intensified the student's pathology and behavior problems had it not been clearly captured on a video tape that was operated behind a two-way mirror. When confronted with this information, both the student and his parents were forced to accept the reality of the boy's behavior and the consequences associated with this behavior. Viewing the tape and accepting the month-long expulsion that followed seemed to have a powerful effect on the student and his parents. Upon returning to school, his behavior improved dramatically, and he showed a willingness to examine and take responsibility for his behavior.

If people accept the idea that awareness, motivation, and personal responsibility are necessary and desirable factors in any program aimed at assisting someone in changing their behavior, it seems logical that the first step in behavior change involves creating awareness. Since adolescents have a strong desire to see themselves as competent and accepted, it is not surprising that providing them with concrete evidence concerning their inappropriate behavior often serves as a strong motivator for significant behavior change. Similarly, providing adolescents with evidence of their ability to become involved in productive behavior can provide the motivation for significantly increasing the frequency of such behaviors.

When considering the advantages associated with increasing adolescents' awareness, it is important to keep in mind that increased awareness can lead to immediate changes only in those behaviors that already exist within adolescents' behavior repertoire. However, it is possible that the adolescent does not possess the skills necessary to produce the desired behavior changes. In such cases, awareness may serve as an important motivating factor. However, this awareness must be accompanied by methods aimed at assisting the adolescent in developing the skills necessary to respond productively.

INDIVIDUAL SELF-MONITORING

Having adolescents monitor their own behavior is perhaps the most ideal approach to creating an increased self-awareness. Since self-monitoring meets adolescents' needs to control their own behavior, it is usually met with less resistance and defensiveness than approaches that employ peer or adult monitoring and feedback.

While they are most often used with younger children, countoons are in excellent example of a self-monitoring instrument. A countoon (Figure 10.2) consists of a picture depicting the youngster's inappropriate behavior and two pictures of the youngster behaving appropriately. Beside the pictures is a calendarlike list of numbers. The student is asked to place an "X" through a number each time he emits the

WHAT I DO

Figure 10.2 Countoon

behavior being considered. For example, if the behavior under consideration is talking in class while the teacher or another student is talking, the student may be asked to simply cross out a number each time he emits this behavior. It is also possible to focus on a positive behavior. For example, if the teacher and student determine that the student often fails to raise his hand when he wants to talk, the student could be asked to cross out a number every time he raises his hand and does not talk unless called upon.

As mentioned above, this form of data collection works best with younger adolescents. While this technique is often effective with seventh grade students, older students find the countoon figures "childish" and will often refuse to be seen with, let alone mark, a countoon. The fact that this form of data collection can be effective with young adolescents was reinforced for me when a graduate student decided to employ a countoon with a particularly rowdy seventh grade boy. The boy was extremely disruptive during class and his most troublesome behavior was his constantly talking to other students during class. Whenever the teacher shared her feelings about this behavior with the boy, he responded by stating that she was picking on him and that he seldom talked to other students during class. After some discussion the student agreed to settle the issue by recording the number of times he emitted the behavior each day for a period of one week. The teacher's baseline data showed that the student averaged thirty-eight different conversations each day. The teacher indicated that she would be pleased if the student reduced the number of conversations to half that amount. Surprisingly, the results showed that the student initially reduced the behavior to zero. During the first three days the student was not involved in a single in-class conversation. Data from the following two days showed an increase to two and four conversations. Follow-up data collected during the following two weeks demonstrated that the behavior had been maintained at a low frequency. The highest count during the follow-up period was seven conversations.

In analyzing this intervention, it seems likely that the student decided to prove his competence and power to the teacher by controlling his own behavior and proving her wrong. Certainly teachers cannot expect every student to have this reaction. Some students would flatly reject the idea of counting behavior, while others might manipulate the situation by becoming involved in a conversation that lasted the entire period. Nevertheless, in many instances adolescents will respond positively to an opportunity to control their own behavior and indicate to an adult that they are not as irresponsible or disruptive as the adult seems to believe.

Countoons are only one method for assisting adolescents in monitoring their own behavior. A variety of studies have demonstrated that student awareness based on students recording their own behavior can bring about significant changes in adolescents' behavior. Broden, Hall, and Mitts (1971) reported two cases in which increased student awareness was associated with significant positive behavior change. In one case an eighth grade girl reported having difficulty staying on task during her history class. When discussions with the school counselor failed to alleviate the problem, it was determined that the girl would record the amount of time she was on task during her class. Data collected by an independent observer indicated that the girl's attending behavior increased from 30 to 80 percent during the periods in which the student collected data on her behavior. In the second case presented in this study, talking out behavior was decreased significantly when a student recorded his talk-out behavior.

In a study that focused on eliminating a vocal tic in an eighteen-year-old boy, Thomas, Abrams, and Johnson (1971) taught the boy to employ a hand counter to tally the number of times the tic occurred. The results indicated that the counting was accompanied by a rapid decrease and eventual elimination of the tic. In a similar study Hutzell, Platzek, and Logue (1974) used self-awareness developed through tallying the occurrence of behaviors to significantly reduce both head jerking and a guttural barking sound emitted by an eleven-year-old boy.

SELF-MONITORING ON A CLASSWIDE BASIS

While self-monitoring has generally been employed as an intervention strategy with individual adolescents, it can serve as an extremely effective method for altering group behavior. An excellent example of group self-monitoring involved a young eighth grade math teacher. The teacher sought assistance because she was concerned about the fact that her class wasted large amounts of instructional time due to their difficulty in settling down when they entered the class. The teacher's baseline data indicated that it took an average of nearly nine minutes before all the students were ready to begin working. After some deliberation, the teacher decided to bring this issue to the students' attention and seek their advice concerning a solution to the problem. With some assistance from the teacher, the students decided to create a large chart on which they could record the amount of time it took them to become completely settled each day. After creating a list of five specific, observable behaviors defining "becoming completely settled," the class decided that their goal should be to "be completely settled" when the bell rang each day. Fortunately, the teacher was aware of the importance of making changes in small increments and thereby avoiding impossible goals. She, therefore, informed the class that she would be extremely pleased if they could be settled and ready to work two minutes after the bell sounded. After agreeing upon this goal, the next task facing the class was to determine how the data should be collected. The students stated that they wanted to be responsible for monitoring their own behavior. The students decided that they would borrow a watch from the physical education department and that each day a different student would be responsible for timing the class and marking the results on the chart. Finally, the class agreed that the program would last for two weeks.

Following the initiation of the program, the class never required longer than one minute forty-five seconds to settle down. Perhaps more importantly, follow-up data recorded a month after the project was terminated indicated that the behavior had been maintained. In examining this project, several factors appear to have contributed to its success. First, students were actively involved both in making the decision and collecting the data. Second, the program included a clear description of the desirable data, focused on an obtainable goal, and incorporated an observable data display. The success of this program appears to have been enhanced by the fact that it included a majority of the components associated both with a humanistic and a behavioral approach.

A student teacher with whom I worked decided to employ her own, simplified version of the strategy employed by the eighth grade math teacher. The teacher, a young-looking college senior, was working with a rather exuberant eighth grade choir. Despite frequent requests for silence and several discussions with the choir, the students continued to create a noise level that was noticeably above what the teacher considered desirable. Finally, the teacher asked the class if they would be willing to simply keep a tally of the number of times she had to ask them to "be quiet" each day. The students readily agreed. The teacher then informed the students that during the past several days she had counted the number of times she had said, "Be quiet," and that it had averaged sixteen times a day. The students decided that this was indeed too many times and that they could significantly reduce this number.

The teacher reported that following this agreement, the noise level in the class was significantly reduced. Students were frequently heard reminding each other to "quiet down" so that the teacher would not have to say, "Be quiet." As would be expected, the teacher used this phrase much less often.

IMPROVING INTERPERSONAL RELATIONSHIPS
THROUGH SELF-MONITORING

In addition to aiding students in changing inappropriate classroom behaviors, self-monitoring can be employed to improve the quality of interactions that exist within a school setting. As discussed in Chapter 2, the percentage of positive statements made in a setting can dramatically influence students' feelings about that environment. Furthermore, as indicated in Chapter 5, it is possible to significantly increase the amount of positive student-student interaction merely by asking students to keep a record of the times when they interact positively and negatively with their peers. Similar strategies can be employed to alter adult-adolescent interactions.

An example of improving interpersonal relationships through the use of self-monitoring involved a junior high school student who frequently responded to adults in an argumentative, critical manner. The young man frequently failed to comply with reasonable adult requests, often argued minor points with adults, and was openly critical of a wide range of adult behaviors. When asked to examine his behavior, the young man noted that his behavior was merely a response to the negative statements made to him by adults and that he should not be expected to change unless the adults changed. The student also complained that the problem was worse at home than at school. Therefore, since the parents were involved in a school-based parent group and were interested in improving their relationship with their son, it was decided that the initial intervention would take place at home rather than at school.

In order to obtain baseline data, the boy was asked to keep a tally of all negative statements his parents made to him over a three-day period. Similarly, the parents were asked to tally the negative statements their son made to them during the same time period. Following the baseline period the family met together to discuss the results. Both parties seemed surprised at the large number of negative remarks that they had apparently emitted. Since both parties agreed that it seemed desirable to decrease the number of negative comments being made at home, they decided to continue the data collection process. The next step in this process involved asking the boy to record each instance in which he made a negative statement to his parents as well as each instance in which he perceived his parents as making a negative statement to him. As a method for insuring the reliability of his tallies, the parents were asked to record the same data. In order to further increase reliability, the youngster and his parents agreed upon a list of common negative statements.

The results of this second round of data collection indicated that both the boy and his parents had drastically reduced the number of negative comments made. Since the ultimate goal of the intervention program was to develop a positive relationship between the boy and his parents, the next step was to ask the family to continue their coding behavior but to code positive statements made and received. The family was asked to develop a list of positive statements and to inform each other of statements that they particularly liked to hear. While no baseline data were collected during this intervention, the family expressed their pleasure with what they perceived as a refreshing improvement in both the quantity and quality of positive statements made in the home.

An interesting variation of self-monitoring as a method for improving relationships was presented by Gray, Graubard, and Rosenberg (1974). In their study, behavior-problem students were informed that they would be taught how to alter their teachers' behavior. The students were initially asked to tally the number of positive and negative comments they received from their teachers. Once baseline data had been obtained, the students were taught methods for reinforcing positive contacts initiated by their teachers. For example, when a teacher assisted a student with his work, the student would express his gratitude to the teacher or indicate his excitement concerning the new learning. The students also learned appropriate ways to inform teachers that the teacher's statement or behavior had not been helpful. Once their training was completed, the students proceeded to collect data on the number of positive and negative teacher comments they received while applying their newly acquired skills. The results were striking. The number of negative statements received dropped to near zero, while the number of positive statements increased nearly four-fold. After five weeks, the students were asked to stop employing their newly learned behaviors. The results showed that this change in student behavior was associated with a rapid and significant decrease in positive teacher comments and an accompanying increase in the number of negative teacher comments.

When considering the use of an intervention strategy based on student data collection, it is obvious that student motivation and impulse control are major factors. There are certainly some behavior-problem adolescents who would refuse to collect data such as that described in the previous paragraphs. Similarly, some behavior-problem adolescents would agree to collect such data, but would have difficulty remaining objective when negative interactions occurred. While strategies outlined later in this chapter will focus on more appropriate interventions for such youngsters, it is important to remain open to the possibility that adolescents may possess the ability to control their own behavior and collect their own data. This type of intervention has the obvious advantage of providing adolescents with opportunities for experiencing a sense of competence and power.

INCREASED TEACHER AWARENESS: MODELING
THE VALUE OF AWARENESS AND CHANGE

Discussions of self-observation often overlook the possibility of adults modeling the self-monitoring process. While this method is more easily employed in small, self-contained groups such as those found in residential treatment facilities and self-contained classrooms, it is possible to use this strategy in regular classrooms. By demonstrating that monitoring one's behavior is acceptable, fun, and can lead to positive changes, adults can model a productive behavior and can thereby help to establish a norm that enhances the acceptance of such behavior.

I can still recall my first opportunity to model the value of self-monitoring. The opportunity arose when a student approached me after class and indicated that I had said, "You know" forty-nine times during the class period. The student indicated that the behavior distracted him and suggested that I stop using the term. The next day I discussed this issue with the class and discovered that most of the students found the behavior to be somewhat annoying. As a result of this discussion it was determined that I should attempt to count the number of times I made this statement. When I indicated that I anticipated some difficulty in simultaneously teaching and tallying my behavior, the class decided that a student in the back of the class would raise his hand each time I said "you know." It was also decided that another student would tally the number of times the hand was raised, and that the daily results would be placed on a large chart at the front of the room. The results of this intervention were both immediate and long lasting, and to this day I seldom use those words.

In examining this intervention, it is likely that the public display of the results provided an additional incentive for my altering my behavior. The benefits associated with publically displaying an individual's self-observations were studied by McKenzie and Rushall (1974). These researchers incorporated this approach in a program designed to reduce inappropriate behavior among members of competitive swim teams. Their results suggest that a public display of self-recordings facilitated behavior change in both children and adolescents.

VIDEO AND AUDIO TAPING

Video taping provides an excellent opportunity for increasing adolescents' awareness of a wide range of behaviors. Since neither video nor audio taping requires active participation by the adolescent during the data gathering phase, it can be employed with adolescents whose initial motivation for change is limited. Another advantage associated with video taping is that it allows the individual to examine a wide range of subtle, nonverbal behaviors. Adolescents can be provided with an opportunity to observe their mannerisms, gestures, and other behaviors of which they are often unaware. Video and audio taping also provides the observer with an instant replay of the situation as it actually occurred. Therefore, the selective perceptions precipitated by adolescents' biases and needs can be pointed out as they compare what actually transpired to their perception of what occurred. This concrete, unalterable depiction of a situation provides behavior-problem youngsters with an opportunity to examine ways in which they manipulate and are manipulated by others. Another advantage of taping is that it allows adolescents an opportunity to examine an emotionally laden situation at a time when their emotions are dissipated. This enables them to view the situation much more objectively and enhances the possibility that they will examine the situation in an open, nondefensive manner.

Video and audio taping works particularly well with adolescents because they are in the process of examining their behaviors and the impact these behaviors have on others. The focus on, "Who am I?" and "How do others perceive me?" makes adolescents particularly sensitive to feedback that provides them with an honest, unalterable view of themselves in interaction with others.

When discussing the use of video taping, teachers and special educators often note that a major limitation centers around the likelihood that the problem adolescent will not demonstrate his inappropriate behavior in front of a camera. There are several reasons why this concern is unnecessary.

First, while adolescents' concern with self-image does enhance the likelihood that their behavior will improve when they know they are being video taped, the recording equipment soon becomes an accepted part of the environment and the behaviors that initially created a problem often return. Second, and more important is the fact that if the presence of a video tape camera can indeed terminate the unproductive behavior, adults should normally be delighted to employ this technique. Behavioral psychologists note that a major goal of behavior modification strategies is to allow individuals to eliminate unproductive behaviors so that they can receive the natural reinforcements that the environment provides for productive behaviors. Behavior contracts are frequently designed to alter adolescents' unproductive behaviors so that they can be replaced by more appropriate behaviors that can then be reinforced. If a video or audio tape can be employed to reach this end, adults should certainly employ this relatively simple intervention.

An example of a situation in which a video tape camera facilitated this procedure occurred when I was working with a particularly disruptive eighth grade boy. The boy frequently disrupted classes by talking out, poking his peers, and getting out of his seat. These behaviors had proved resistant to a variety of behavioral counseling procedures as well as several behavior contracts. Therefore, it was decided that a video tape would be made of the boy's behavior; and that the boy, myself, his teacher, and his parents would view the tape. Since the student constantly denied that his behavior was disruptive and yet refused to monitor his own behavior, it was our hope that the video tape would at least force him to acknowledge his behavior. From here we hoped to instigate a self-monitoring program.

Given the intensity and frequency of the student's behavior, we were surprised when the student demonstrated almost totally appropriate behavior during the first day of video taping. However, since we had been attempting to bring about this behavior change for several months, we decided to reinforce this behavior if it occurred the second day. The teacher and several peers were asked to provide the student with a variety of positive statements if his behavior continued to be acceptable. The student behaved extremely well the second day and consequently received a considerable amount of social reinforcement. Since the student seemed pleased by this change of events, we decided to intensify this positive bombardment by allowing him to view the tape. While viewing the tape we frequently pointed out positive behaviors and asked him how he felt about the situation. In addition, we frequently asked him to describe how he thought his teacher and classmates felt and what responses he was evoking from them. At the end of the session we informed the student that if he would like, we would schedule a conference so that his parents could observe the tape that would be made the following day. When the student responded enthusiastically, we were convinced that we would have at least one more productive day in class. As expected, the student behaved remarkably well the following day and late that afternoon his parents joined us to observe his tape recording.

We continued the tape recording for ten school days. While the student's behavior was not uniformly acceptable, it showed a vast improvement (Figure 10.3). Also, on those days when he displayed considerable unproductive behavior, we took the opportunity to observe the behavior with him and asked him how he felt observing this behavior and how he felt about others' reactions to his behavior.

Since the video tape equipment was needed elsewhere and we believed it had served its purpose, we moved from video taping to self-monitoring. The self-monitoring maintained the behavior at levels near that obtained during the second week of video taping.

When using video tape recordings to increase awareness and examine inappropriate behaviors, it is important that the data be presented to the adolescent in a sensitive manner. In most cases it is desirable to inform the adolescent(s) that the purpose of

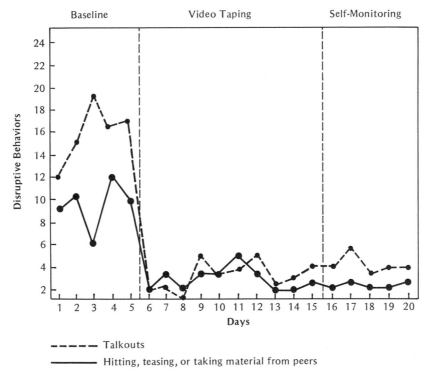

Figure 10.3 Behavior Change Associated with an Intervention Program Involving Video Taping and Self-Monitoring

the tape recording is to provide them with information concerning their behavior. There will, however, be situations in which it is desirable that the adolescent not know that he is the focus of the video taping. For example, if the tape recorder is available for only a short period of time or if it is known that the adolescent is skilled in manipulating his environment, it may be necessary to create a cover story regarding the equipment's use.

Once tape recordings have been obtained, it is important that they not be used in a punitive manner. There is a tendency to use recordings that capture inappropriate behavior in an "Okay, now we've proved it" manner. While this may be necessary at a future time, the tapes should initially be employed as a means of assisting adolescents to examine their behavior. Bear in mind the fact that adolescents want to develop a positive self-image, want to control their own behavior, and want to be accepted by others. When adults begin their interventions by focusing on their evaluations of adolescents' behavior and the consequences adults plan to associate with that behavior, adults direct their energies against adolescents' developmental needs rather than allowing these needs to work for them. Therefore, when viewing or listening to tape recordings with adolescents, an emphasis should be placed on asking them to describe what they are doing or saying, and asking them questions that focus on: how they are feeling as they observe or listen to the tape, what factors influenced their behavior, how others responded to their behavior, what they might have done differently, and how this alternative behavior might have influenced the responses they received from others.

An example of employing this format occurred with a group of behavior-problem junior high school students. Several times each week were set aside for meetings that included all students who spent any portion of their school day working in a resource area. The purpose of these meetings was to allow student input into the operation of the resource area while at the same time assisting the students in developing improved interpersonal and problem-solving skills. After several moderately successful attempts at processing these group meetings, we decided to video tape the sessions. The video tape enabled us to place greater responsibility on the students by providing them with an opportunity to observe and evaluate their own behavior. This evaluation was then used as a springboard from which the students could begin to develop rules to more effectively govern their behavior and consider alternative responses to replace those that were obviously interfering with the smooth functioning of their meetings. Results based on pre- and post-observations indicated that video tape analysis was effective in reducing such disruptive group behaviors as interrupting, hitting, withdrawal, and put-downs.

One final point concerning video taping is the value of capturing students when they are involved in productive behaviors. As noted earlier, adolescents who are experiencing behavior problems frequently have low self-images. The acting-out or withdrawal behavior displayed by these adolescents is often an attempt to demonstrate some form of competence and power to hide their perceived incompetence. Since a major task in working with these youngsters involves assisting them in learning that they can perform and be reinforced for acceptable, productive behaviors, it is important to assist them in recognizing their ability to perform desirable behaviors.

Video taping behavior-problem adolescents while they are involved in productive behaviors allows adults to show adolescents that they can perform successfully and can receive positive responses from others.

An example of this use of video taping involved an eighth grade boy who was referred because his classroom behavior was characterized by inattentiveness, lack of completed assignments, and constant complaining about the difficulty of the work he was assigned. Observations showed that the boy's on-task classroom behavior was below 25 percent. Because of his academic difficulties, the student was temporarily placed in a resource center during his language arts and social studies classes. Several days after he began working in the resource center he was video taped during a forty-minute period in which he emitted 100 percent on-task behavior. Immediately following this period the student was asked if he would like to view the tape recording. The student enthusiastically accepted the invitation and sat spellbound watching himself study. After he had watched nearly half an hour of this tape, he asked if his mother could see the tape. He was informed that she would be invited to view the tape with him.

As is often the case with interventions occurring within natural environments, it was impossible to determine the exact effect the boy's viewing this and subsequent tapes of himself had on his positive study behaviors. Nevertheless, the boy's on-task behavior showed significant increases following this intervention; and when he returned to his regular classroom, his on-task behavior stabilized at nearly 80 percent. While some of these changes were undoubtedly due to changes in his academic program, at least some of the changes seemed attributable to his realization that he could stay on task.

Although audio tapes do not provide the amount of data available on video tapes, they are easier to use and can prove effective in assisting adolescents to become aware of a limited range of behaviors. More specifically, audio tapes can be used to give adolescents concrete, objective information concerning verbal behaviors such as talking out, profanity, making polite verbal requests, etc. Like video tapes, audio tapes provide an opportunity to objectively examine and evaluate behavior at a time when the individual's emotional state permits a clearer and more productive analysis.

STOP ACTION

Stop action is a strategy that can be used to produce some of the advantages of video taping. The goal of stop action is to increase adolescents' awareness of their behavior. Unfortunately, unlike video taping, stop action cannot hold the behavior until it can be examined in a more objective, less emotional setting. Stop action is employed by creating a situation in which the adolescents involved agree to stop or freeze immediately upon hearing a designated word or sound. When initially establishing the format for this intervention, it is important to emphasize that the intent of this activity is not to catch students behaving inappropriately. Therefore, it is important that no negative consequences be associated with students being involved in inappropriate behaviors when they are asked to freeze. Instead, students should be informed that the sole intent of the activity is to assist them in gaining greater awareness of and control over their behavior.

There are several methods for choosing both the behaviors on which the adolescents will focus and the manner in which these behaviors will be examined. One approach is quite similar to a countoon. Each individual is asked to choose one unproductive behavior that causes them particular problems or one positive behavior that they want to increase. This behavior is then specifically described either pictorially or in written form and placed on the students' desks. When the teacher asks the students to "freeze" or "stop action," students are asked to make a mark indicating whether or not they were involved in the behavior described on their charts. A somewhat different approach to employing stop action involves asking the students to simply stop and record exactly what they were doing each time the teacher requests that they "stop action."

While this approach can prove very useful in assisting adolescents in becoming aware of their behavior, it does have several limitations. First, the method works most effectively with younger adolescents or with older adolescents who have a strong motivation for examining and changing their behavior. Second, since this activity involves—or at least draws the attention of—all those present, it is most appropriate in a setting in which most or all of the individuals are focusing on changing their behavior. Therefore, while a teacher might employ this strategy in a classroom setting, this method is most effective when used in a resource center for behavior-problem students or in a residential treatment facility.

WRITTEN RECORDINGS

Adolescents frequently find themselves in environments that do not provide them with time for slowing down and examining their learning or behavior. Adolescents frequently move from one tense, anxiety-provoking situation to another until they finally withdraw completely, become involved in mildly disruptive behavior, or explode in what may appear to adults as an irrational, unprovoked display of emotionalism. When working with behavior-problem adolescents, it is therefore important to structure opportunities for them to slow down, examine their responses to their environment, and if necessary release tensions and frustrations.

The use of logs or journals is one method for helping adolescents to relax and dissipate anxiety while at the same time providing them with an opportunity to increase their awareness of their environment and the manner in which they react to this environment. This is such an obvious method for increasing behavior awareness while reducing tension that it is surprising how seldom this approach is employed. In reflecting on this situation, it seems that all too often adults underestimate the cognitive skills and motivation for competence that behavior-problem adolescents possess. Consequently, adults often mistakenly assume that they must facilitate change either by manipulating adolescents or in some other way circumventing techniques that focus primarily on self-directed awareness and analysis. Assisting adolescents in becoming more aware of their behavior is often more time consuming than developing a behavior contract. Furthermore, self-awareness activities may not bring about short-term results that are as dramatic as those associated with a well-conceptualized contract. However, because analyzing their own behavior responds to most of the normal developmental needs of adolescence, it is a potentially effective intervention with many adolescents.

Written recordings can be used in a variety of ways and in a variety of settings. In school-based programs for emotionally handicapped adolescents, journals can be used to assist students in adjusting to courses into which they are mainstreamed. Since behavior-problem students are usually excluded from classes because they could not behave appropriately and could not do the work, it is to be expected that re-entry into regular classes will be accompanied by considerable anxiety. Therefore, as students are placed into regular classrooms, they should, whenever possible, initially be provided with some free time following each class. This free time can be used by the students to slow down and examine what occurred during the class. For example, the student may be asked to record (either in writing or on audio tape) how he acted and how others responded during a particular class. When discussing students' log entries, teachers should reinforce instances in which students were able to clearly define specific behaviors and feelings. Students should be encouraged to accurately and specifically define what occurred, how they felt, how others responded, and what alternative behaviors they could have employed.

I recently observed a situation in which the use of logs could have assisted a group of adolescents in coping more effectively with a school setting. The adolescents involved were boys who lived in a group home and attended the local junior high school. Most of the boys had a long record of serious delinquency and had been away from public schools for a considerable amount of time. It was, therefore, under-standable that the boys would experience some discomfort and difficulty in adjusting to a public school environment.

When the boys began to experience serious problems in the school setting, the group home staff decided to set aside the last period of the school day as a time when a staff member from the home would go to the school and hold a group meeting with the boys. The purpose of this meeting was to involve the boys in a discussion of their school day and to examine ways in which they might have behaved differently. While the boys seemed to accept and even enjoy this last period group session, it appeared to have little effect on their school behavior. An examination of these results suggests several reasons why this intervention was unsuccessful. First, the session occurred at the wrong time. The session would have been much more beneficial if it had occurred during the middle of the day. This change in schedule would have enabled the boys to examine situations occurring early in the day while the impact was still immediate. Of equal importance, a midday session would have provided the boys with an opportunity to release emotions and to consider productive behaviors that they could employ during the remainder of the day.

A second problem with the session was that it did not require the students to record their responses in any form. As anyone who has worked with delinquent adolescents knows, rap sessions aimed at discussing school can easily deteriorate into generalized complaint sessions in which the students do not take responsibility for seriously examining their own behavior. Consequently, it is important to incorporate some form of log or data analysis into such a session. This procedure helps adolescents to slow down and take their task seriously. It also provides adolescents with something concrete to examine and compare with earlier entries or data. While adolescents will obviously prefer a rap session and may initially balk at any form of writing, the payoffs associated with requiring some observable record keeping exceed the initial resistance to such a program. Since behavior-problem adolescents frequently lack skill in analyzing their own behavior and others' reactions to that behavior, it is often necessary to initially provide them with a format for recording this information. Figure 10.4 provides an example of a form that can assist adolescents in this task.

In addition to lacking the skills needed to examine their feelings and behaviors, many behavior-problem adolescents lack writing skills that would enable them to record their reactions. In cases where adolescents possess very poor writing skills, behavior can be analyzed using structured discussions. When working with adolescents who possess limited writing skills, it is important to provide them with log forms like the one presented in Figure 10.4 that enable them to record their reactions with a minimum of writing.

In addition to aiding adolescents in developing an increased awareness of their feelings, behaviors, and alternatives within such general situations as classes and living groups, logs can be effective tools for dealing with specific crisis situations. This point was poignantly and somewhat embarrassingly pointed out to me a number of years ago

Figure 10.4   Behavior Analysis Form

Choose a particular class period or incident about which you have strong feelings. Please take a minute to analyze this situation by completing this form.

1. What did you do? Be specific.

2. How did you feel?

3. What did the other person/people do? Be specific.

4. How do you think the other person/people felt?

5. What was the result? What happened to you?

6. What could you have done differently in order to make things work out better? Be specific.

7. What could the other person/people have done differently to have made things work out better? Be specific.

when I first began working with behavior-problem adolescents. Since I believed in the value of having adolescents examine situations in which their behavior had caused problems, it was not uncommon for students to be sent to my office for a discussion when their behavior had been highly inappropriate. While the students were often upset upon their arrival at my office, they nevertheless found this environment more comfortable than that which they had just left. Therefore, it is not surprising that I began to have frequent visitors to my office. After perhaps a month during which I was inundated with problem-solving sessions in my office, a colleague who frequently had sensitive insights into areas in which I was blinded by my own values or involvement, pointed out that not only was I reinforcing the students' inappropriate behavior but also I was taking considerable responsibility for their behavior. He suggested that prior to seeing me, the students should be required to first evaluate their behavior and examine possible alternative behaviors. Furthermore, he suggested that whenever possible this evaluation should take place in the environment in which the inappropriate behavior occurred. This process was discussed with the students; and it was determined that if a student was involved in a disruptive behavior that warranted disciplinary action, the student would be asked to evaluate the situation either in essay form or by employing a behavior analysis form. It was further determined that if either the teacher or student believed that this analysis could not take place within the setting in which the problem had occurred, the student would be sent to a resource center to complete the task. Once the task was completed, the student was provided with an opportunity to discuss the situation with the teacher or with a special education staff member. The results of this change were striking. Acting-out behavior decreased dramatically and problem-solving sessions with students became much more student centered.

Interestingly, this procedure is equally effective as a method for dealing with conflict between two or more individuals. When two students are involved in a conflict, it is often effective to ask each individual to complete a behavior analysis form. Once they have completed this task, the students can be asked to meet together without an adult. The students are simply informed that they are to reach an agreement and present their solution in writing to an adult. While this format can be extremely effective, it obviously has several limitations. For example, this format is inappropriate when considerable anger exists even after each individual has evaluated his behavior. It is also inappropriate when one individual possesses a noticeably larger amount of power and influence and has a history of using this influence. In such cases an adult mediator is necessary.

Regardless of how adults structure the use of logs or other devices used to assist students in evaluating their behavior, the process has several major benefits. First, it allows adolescents to slow down and examine the situation in which the difficulty has occurred. Second, the process places primary responsibility on the adolescent and thereby responds to the need for self-direction, competency, and power. Finally, the process provides a relatively high degree of structure. As discussed earlier, adolescents are often confused and frightened by their inability to understand their environment or control their behavior. In such cases structure provides a sense of relief and calmness.

STRUCTURED ANALYSIS OF INTERPERSONAL INTERACTIONS

The popularity of materials that attempt to explain human behavior and personal interactions has opened up a relatively new and interesting approach to using increased awareness to change adolescents' behavior. Theories like Transactional Analysis, Rational Emotive Therapy, Assertive Training, and a variety of material on interpersonal communication have enabled skilled adults to teach adolescents the basic concepts of human interaction and to subsequently ask adolescents to employ these concepts in examining their own behavior. The most common approach to employing human relations and self-awareness models as a method for assisting adolescents to improve their behavior has been to combine group instruction with individualized analysis and assignments. This approach usually follows a fairly standard pattern.

During the first several sessions, the adolescents are taught the basic concepts involved in the particular model. As soon as the adolescents have become familiar with the terminology and basic concepts, they are asked to apply these to their daily interactions. In order to make this transition, adolescents are asked to choose a situation in which they have experienced considerable difficulty when interacting with a specific person. The adolescents are then asked to as accurately as possible write a transcript of what occurred during this exchange. These transcripts are then brought to the group meeting and are discussed and analyzed by the group. The purpose of this analysis is to assist the adolescent in understanding the interchange and developing an alternative set of behaviors that could be employed in similar interactions.

Regardless of which conceptual model is used, this type of intervention has several major advantages as a strategy for working with adolescents. Perhaps most important is the fact that this approach responds to a wide range of adolescents' developmental concerns. This approach responds to adolescents' needs to: (1) understand themselves and their interactions with others, (2) become responsible for their own behavior, and (3) constructively criticize and analyze adult's behavior. In addition to responding to a wide range of adolescent needs, this approach has real potential for improving adolescents' interactions with adults. As adolescents begin to understand the dynamics of interpersonal relations and take more responsibility for the quality of their interactions, they frequently become viewed by adults as more mature, positive individuals. This alteration of adults' perceptions can play an important role both in improving adult-adolescent interactions and altering adolescents' behaviors.

PEER FEEDBACK

Adolescence is a period in which feedback from peers plays an important, if somewhat exaggerated, role in assisting individuals in developing a personal identity. Adolescents are highly sensitive to and powerfully influenced by peer feedback. While this is true for adolescents at all ages, it is particularly true for young adolescents.

Given adolescents' sensitivity to peer influences, feedback from peers can serve as a powerful tool for enhancing self-awareness and subsequently facilitating behavior change. Perhaps the most powerful example of the impact of peer feedback occurred when I was working with a seventh grade boy who was in danger of being expelled from school because of his constant low-key acting out. Jim's (a fictitious name) behavior was perhaps more mischievous than aggressive, and he was almost constantly being referred to the office for behavior such as pulling girls' hair, snapping girls' bra straps, wandering around the room, stealing other students' materials, pulling chairs out from under students, and placing tacks on chairs.

In order to understand Jim's behavior, it is important to know that he was an only child whose father had left when he was quite young. Jim was a somewhat overweight, unathletic boy of average intelligence. He was not particularly successful at any activity other than disrupting classes and had almost no friends either in or out of school.

When we first began working with Jim, we attempted to alter his behavior through the use of behavior contracts. It was initially agreed that Jim would receive designated reinforcements whenever his behavior during a class period showed a specified reduction in the number of acting-out behaviors. Since Jim was unwilling to monitor his own behavior, it was necessary to have an aide monitor his behavior. Unfortunately, despite developing what appeared to be sound contracts with viable reinforcers, Jim's behavior changed very little (Figure 10.5). After several such failures, it became apparent that the reinforcements Jim had agreed upon could not possibly match the peer attention he received for his acting-out behavior. It seemed that Jim's sense of significance, competence, and power could be more effectively met through his ability to annoy and frustrate teachers than by his ability to alter his behavior.

With this possible explanation in mind, we decided to talk to Jim's classmates in an

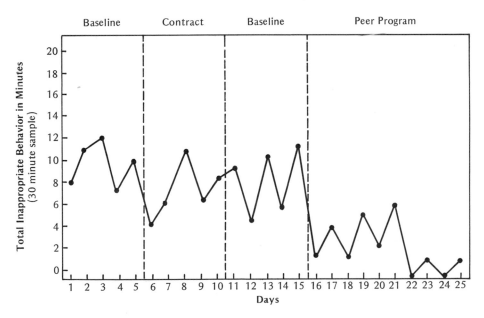

Figure 10.5 Time Sample Data for Student Involved in a Peer Change Program

effort to obtain their ideas and cooperation. When asked whether he wished to be present during the discussion, Jim indicated a strong desire to be elsewhere. Since we believed it would be valuable for Jim to hear what his peers had to say, we informed him that we would video tape the discussion and that we would like him to view the tape. Jim agreed to this compromise, and both his mother and teacher gave their support to the idea of discussing the problem with his classmates. Since Jim's behavior was the most extreme during his language arts class, it was determined that the intervention should begin there.

The class discussion was begun by simply informing the students that we were concerned about Jim's behavior and asking them if they would be willing to help us work out a plan to help Jim. As has inevitably been the case when I have made such requests, the class expressed a real interest in helping Jim. As our discussion progressed, it became apparent that Jim was being heavily reinforced because he provided diversity and humor in a class that the students otherwise viewed as very dull. In fact, one student commented that Jim was a little like the funny advertisements during a boring television show. However, while the students indicated that they found certain portions of Jim's behavior entertaining, a number of students indicated that they did not like his behavior and that it was annoying and sometimes even dangerous. Once the students had offered this information, we attempted to make the class aware that while Jim's behavior was entertaining, the reinforcement they gave him was a major reason why he continued to act as he did. Therefore, we noted that they were at least partially responsible for the fact that he was in serious trouble with the teacher and principal. As the students began to appreciate this point, they became eager to assist in helping Jim change his behavior. Several students suggested that the class ignore Jim's "bad" behavior, and one student pointed out that the students should be nice to Jim when he improved his behavior. Another student suggested that when Jim's behavior became "very bad" any member of the class should be able to request that Jim be asked to leave. If the majority of the class agreed, Jim would be required to go to the principal's office for the remainder of the class. With these student suggestions as a foundation, it was not difficult to develop a specific program in which students agreed to ignore designated behaviors, to inform Jim how other behaviors made them feel, and to provide Jim with reinforcement when he had a good day. Reinforcers included saying "thank you," "giving five" (slapping hands), talking to Jim in the hall, asking him if he needed help with his work, and sitting with him at lunch. The program also involved allowing the students whom Jim bothered or hurt to request that the class vote to exclude Jim for the remainder of the class period. Immediately following the class meeting, Jim was asked to observe the tape. While his responses understandably ranged from real hurt to excitement, his general reaction appeared to be one of serious thoughtfulness.

The data collected on Jim's behavior are shown in Figures 10.5 and 10.6. Since the teacher was unwilling to collect data on specific behaviors, her recording consisted of simply indicating those days on which Jim's behavior was disruptive to the point that he was required to leave the class (Figure 10.6). Other data (Figure 10.5) were obtained by taking fifteen-minute time samples twice a day. As the data indicate, peer feedback was highly effective in changing Jim's behavior. Apparently peer acceptance

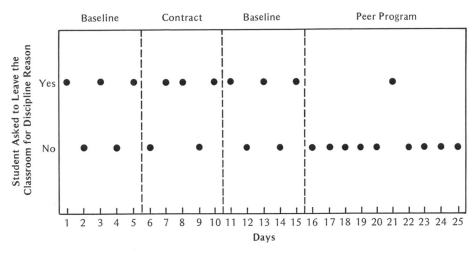

Figure 10.6 Teacher's Data for Student Involved in a Peer Change Program

was the most important reinforcement for Jim and any intervention that failed to take this variable into account was likely to fail.

Peer feedback can be employed in a variety of ways other than class meetings and highly structured interventions. However, since peer feedback is emotionally laden and requires considerable personal involvement, it is most often used and is most effective in relatively small groups in which adolescents know each other and experience a sense of support and safety. One method for creating such environments within the school setting is to develop small groups that meet once or twice a week for the purpose of helping students adjust to the school environment.

In order to create a safe, supportive environment that will increase productive sharing and risk taking, it is important to begin a group by employing acquaintance activities aimed at assisting students in becoming more familiar with their peers (see Chapter 5). As students become familiar with each other, groups can be used to provide students with a wide range of both positive and critical feedback. Positive feedback can be provided by any number of approaches. One common method is to ask one student to be the center of attention and ask each student to make one positive statement about that student. Another method is to have each student make a small booklet with one page for each group member. The students sit in a circle and the books are passed around the circle. As they receive each individual's book, students write one specific positive statement about that person. At the end of the exercise each person will therefore have a book that includes a positive statement from each member of the group.

Another method for providing positive feedback is to ask group members to observe their peers during the time between meetings and write down one positive behavior that they observe each group member emit. These observations can be shared with the group at its next meeting. Similar results can be obtained by drawing names so that each group member is responsible for observing and recording positive behaviors emitted by one of their peers. At a designated time each group member can give his or her list to the individual whom he or she observed.

While positive feedback is important and should always be included when providing adolescents with peer feedback, it is also important that adolescents be provided with information concerning specific behaviors to which their peers react negatively. When assisting adolescents in providing this type of feedback, it is extremely important to first provide them with skills concerning how to give feedback (See Chapter 4). For example, when giving negative feedback, it is important that students focus on specific behavior, deal only with behaviors that the individual can change, and whenever possible provide the individual with an alternate behavior that would be more positively received. One method that is useful in assisting adolescents in providing critical feedback to their peers is to ask them to describe both a behavior to which they respond positively and one that they find hinders their interaction with or feelings toward the person involved.

Since adolescents are often hesitant to give feedback that may be perceived as negative and also often respond with anger or hurt when given critical feedback, it is important that adults model giving thoughtful critical feedback and carefully facilitate activities that involve negative feedback. Therefore, when working with behavior-problem adolescents, it is not advisable to initially divide a group into dyads or small groups when focusing on critical feedback. Given adolescents' concern about peer status, peer feedback can, when properly structured, be an effective strategy for creating awareness and subsequently affecting behavior change. However, the adults involved must be careful lest this powerful tool be destructive rather than constructive.

ADULT FEEDBACK

Chapter 4 includes an extensive discussion of the skills needed to provide students with helpful feedback. However, a discussion of increasing student awareness would not be complete without mention of the role adults can play in creating such awareness. Adults are in a unique position that makes their feedback valuable to adolescents. As adolescents begin to seek independence from their parents, they search for other adult models. Since many behavior-problem adolescents have experienced parental relationships that were characterized by hostility, rejection, or disinterest, it is only natural that they will look to other adults both as models and parent surrogates. This transference not only enables the adolescent to resolve conflicts that may have existed with parents but also enhances other adults' ability to serve as meaningful models. While it is true that all of these factors are more pervasive and powerful when working with young adolescents, it is important to realize that many behavior-problem adolescents are functioning at developmental levels characteristic of much younger ages.

There are a wide range of methods available to those adults who are willing to become involved in providing adolescents with productive feedback. The important point is that this feedback must be specific, must provide the adolescent with acceptable alternative behaviors, and must be presented in a positive, safe environment. As discussed previously, this feedback can be provided by making process observations, sending "I" messages, employing interpretive perception checks, and discussing realistic expectations. An additional approach that works well with youngsters who are involved in self-observation programs is for the adult to collect data on the same behavior the adolescent is observing. For example, if the student is collecting data on the number of times he talks out without permission, the teacher and student can agree to have the teacher also count these behaviors. Following the observation period, the teacher and student can compare their results, and the teacher can reinforce the student both for accuracy and improved behavior.

Chapters 11 and 12 will present a wide variety of additional methods that adults can use to assist adolescents in understanding the positive and negative aspects of their behavior. The key point being presented here is that adolescents are often receptive and responsive to adult feedback that is thoughtfully and skillfully presented. Consequently, adults do adolescents a real disservice when they fail to incorporate consistently constructive adult feedback as a major component within a treatment plan.

Questions that Can Increase Adolescents' Awareness

The majority of strategies presented in this chapter have focused on rather structured methods for helping students better understand their own behavior. However, when working with behavior problem adolescents, there are numerous occasions when it is important that youngsters become aware of their behavior or emotions at times when they are not involved in a structured behavior awareness program.

When these situations occur, it is important that adults combine empathic, nonevaluative listening with questions aimed at assisting adolescents in focusing on their feelings and behaviors. Since adolescents are frequently rather emotional at these times, it is helpful to initially diffuse some of this emotion by employing active listening or interpretive perception checks. If the adolescent appears willing to listen, yet seems defensive or emotional, it is a good idea to elicit his cooperation in the process of examining the situation. This can be done by simply asking him if he would be willing to discuss how he is feeling and attempt to work out a solution. Once he has made this commitment, there are several questions that can assist him in developing an increased awareness. These questions include: (1) How are you feeling? (2) Can you describe what you were doing? (3) Are you aware of why you started to act that way? (4) How were other people reacting to your behavior? (5) How do you think other people were feeling? (6) What did you want to happen? (7) Did your behavior help that happen? (8) What could you have done/do to make what you want occur? (9) What do you want to do now?

An example of an exchange with a fifteen-year-old boy may help to clarify the manner in which these questions can assist adolescents in becoming more aware of their behavior.

John: (standing up in a group meeting and walking over to a staff member) You son-of-a-bitch, you can't take away his privileges! You don't have any proof.

Staff Member: You think that's an unfair decision, a cheap shot?

John: I sure as hell do. It's unconstitutional. If we had any legal rights you couldn't get away with that kind of shit.

Staff Member: John, this seems really important to you and I'm willing to talk about it. However, first I'd like to stop a minute and look at what just happened.

John: What do ya mean?

Staff Member: Before we talk about the decision, I'd like you to look at what just went on between you and me. Will you agree to do that?

John: Ya, I guess so. But I wanna talk about the decision.

Staff Member: That's fair. I'd really like to see if you and I can work this out. Are the rest of you willing to let us have the time and help us out if we get stuck?

Group: (The group members give positive acknowledgements ranging from a tentative, "Ya, why not" to a positive, "Sure that's what we're here for.")

Staff Member: Okay, John, how are you feeling right now?

John: I'm pissed off.

Staff Member: Okay, you're pretty angry. Anything else?

John: (following a brief pause) No. I'm just angry.

Staff Member: If I were in your shoes, I might be a little scared. Like if that can happen to him, it can happen to me and that's a little scary.

John: Ya maybe, but I don't feel afraid.

Staff Member: Can you tell me what you did when you got angry?

John: Sure, I jumped up and ran over and stood in front of you.

Staff Member: Okay. Do you know how your face looked and what you were doing with your hands?

John: No. (pause) Well I guess my face looked mad and I don't know what my hands were doing.

Staff Member: Can anyone help him out? Did anyone see what his hands looked like?

Group Member: Ya, his hands were clenched like he might hit you.

Staff Member: Okay. Thanks Jim. John, why do you think it's important to know what you were doing?

John: I don't know. Maybe because, oh hell, I don't know.

Staff Member: That's okay. Does anyone know why it might be important to know what your body is doing?

Group Member: Ya, maybe it would let him know how you might feel. Like if his fists were clenched you might be ready to hit him.

Staff Member: Okay. John, how do you think I was feeling when you came over here?

John:	I don't know. Why don't you tell me?
Staff Member:	Fair enough. I was worried that things might blow up and I was real nervous because I didn't want to get into a fight. Can you understand why I might have felt that way?
John:	Ya, I guess so.
Staff Member:	John, what did you want to have me do? What did you want from me when you came over?
John:	I wanted you to get off Bill's back. I wanted you to change your mind and not ground him.
Staff Member:	Okay, that's a fair request, but did your getting mad and running over here help make that happen?
John:	(pause) Ya, you said that we could talk about it.
Staff Member:	You're right, but what do you think would happen if you did that at school or with your dad?
John:	I'd get hassled. My old man would probably belt me.
Staff Member:	Ya, I think you're right. Most teachers and a lot of students would get real uptight if you did that and you'd have a big hassle.
John:	I don't care. They'd have it coming.
Staff Member:	Maybe so, maybe not, but would it help get them off Bill's back?
John:	(pause) No, I guess not. We'd both probably get hassled worse.
Staff Member:	Ya, I think you're right. What could you have done that let me know you were angry, but didn't start a hassle that made things worse?
John:	(pause) I don't know. I guess I could have not blown up.
Staff Member:	Anything else?
John:	Naw, I don't know. I was really angry.
Staff Member:	Okay, can anybody help us out? What can you do when you see something that you think is wrong and you want to change it?

At this point the group spent several minutes discussing possible alternatives. When these appeared to be exhausted, the staff member suggested that before talking about the issue of Bill's grounding, they role play the situation and see if they could come up with a good way to handle requesting such a discussion. The group members agreed and several members role played the situation.

The major advantage to employing focused questions as a method for increasing awareness is that this process enables adults to respond immediately to a wide range of situations. In addition, this approach allows adults to focus on a wide range of behaviors and emotions rather than being limited to behaviors for which they have previously developed a behavioral program.

One reason this interchange went quite smoothly is that the boys knew that part of the reason for having group meetings was to talk about their feelings and their behaviors. At the first group meeting the staff had discussed the goals for group meetings, had provided examples of what might happen, and had asked for input and eventual agreement from the boys.

SUMMARY

Behavior-problem adolescents often possess a limited awareness concerning the exact nature of their unproductive behaviors and the effect these behaviors have on others. This lack of awareness significantly limits their ability to alter unproductive behaviors. Therefore, in order to involve adolescents in the process of changing their behavior, it is imperative that adults begin by assisting them in developing increased awareness in this area.

Fortunately, since adolescents have a need to be accepted and to develop a personal identity that includes a sense of interacting effectively with others, they will often alter behaviors that they realize are alienating others. In addition, adolescents experience a strong desire to be viewed as competent and independent. Adolescents want to understand and control their own behavior. Consequently, they almost always respond with interest to activities that aid them in better understanding themselves. Furthermore, once they become aware of behaviors that significant others view as inappropriate, they will often choose to demonstrate their competence by taking the initiative in changing these behaviors.

Given these developmental factors that suggest that adolescents are motivated to examine and control their own behavior, it appears that creating increased self-awareness is a logical first step in instigating a behavior change program with adolescents. This chapter has provided a variety of methods that can be employed to assist adolescents in developing an increased understanding of their behavior and others' reactions to that behavior.

The counselor must help the client describe how he would like to act instead of the way in which he currently acts. The counselor must help the client translate his confusions and fears into a goal that the client would like to accomplish and which would begin to resolve the client's problems. This can be accomplished by focusing on specific behaviors in the client's present situation.

John Krumboltz and Carl Thoresen

Behavioral Counseling:
Cases and Techniques

CHAPTER 11

Employing Behavioral Counseling with Adolescents

Like behavior modification, behavioral counseling places a major emphasis on developing specific, observable goals and collecting data to determine the degree to which these goals have been reached. However, unlike behavior modification programs that often employ a token economy or other contingency management program in which adults determine the behaviors to be reinforced, the reinforcement schedule, and even the reinforcers, behavioral counseling places an emphasis both on considerable client involvement and on the use of behavior change strategies ranging from negotiated contracts to sensitivity training.

When a counseling goal is finally formulated in behavioral counseling, it must meet three criteria: (1) It must be a goal desired by the client; (2) The counselor must be willing to help the client achieve this goal; and (3) It must be possible to assess the extent to which the client achieves the goal (Krumboltz and Thoresen, 1969, pp. 1-2).

A basic tenet of behavioral counseling centers on the importance of shared decision making. Both the student/client and the adult must accept and agree upon the goals associated with the behavior change program. Behavioral counseling centers around negotiating and clarifying mutually acceptable goals and cooperative planning in developing the method for bringing about behavior change. While the counselor may initially have considerable responsibility for assisting the client in focusing on behaviors in need of change and developing methods for altering those behaviors, the final decision rests with the client. Furthermore, as the client begins to develop increased skills in analyzing situations and developing behavior change strategies, the counselor becomes much less salient in the counseling relationship. However, at no time does the counselor attempt to develop a sense of distance or reflexive uninvolvement. It is always clear that the counselor is interested and actively involved in examining specific behaviors and their outcomes. In discussing the major components of a behavioral counseling program, Krumboltz and Thoresen (1969) note that "The general ideal, whether it is self-actualization or self-realization, needs to be analyzed into specific actions desired by each client so that the counselor and the client know where they are going and when they get there" (Krumboltz and Thoresen, 1969, p. 2).

This chapter will include a variety of approaches for working with adolescents within a behavioral counseling paradigm. It would be impossible to present every behavioral counseling model or every interpretation of each model. Instead, I have presented those intervention strategies that have been most effective in my work with behavior-problem adolescents. These approaches can be altered and expanded upon as they are employed in ways that fit different individuals' personal style and meet the individual needs expressed by different groups of clients and students.

GLASSER'S BEHAVIORAL COUNSELING MODEL

Perhaps more than any single individual, William Glasser has provided the leadership in developing and popularizing techniques for employing behavioral counseling with adolescents. Glasser has developed and trained professionals in several different step-by-step approaches to assist youngsters in controlling and taking responsibility for their own behavior. The particular model presented here is often termed "Reality Therapy." This method is especially useful for teachers or other adults who need to work out a solution to a problem, but have a somewhat limited amount of time. This approach does not require extensive evaluation of the situation, nor does it require formal data collection. Nevertheless, it does emphasize examining specific behavior, actively involving the adolescent, and evaluating the outcome. The eight major steps outlined by Glasser are: (1) be warm and personal and be willing to get emotionally involved, (2) deal with present behavior, (3) help the person make a value judgment, (4) work out a plan, (5) get a commitment, (6) don't accept excuses, (7) don't punish, and (8) follow up.

The first step has been emphasized throughout this book. Adolescents are more likely to model (Bandura and Huston, 1961; Elder, 1963) and to accept direction from (Elder, 1963) adults whom they perceive as personally and actively involved with them. Since adolescents experience a strong need for significance and acceptance, it is understandable that they will respond more enthusiastically to adults who display warmth and who are willing to establish meaningful, two-way relationships with them.

The second step serves the purpose of assisting the adolescent in focusing on specific behaviors. Rather than dealing with possible causative factors such as others' behavior, the weather, or the fact that it is a "bad day," the adolescent is asked to describe what he did. When working through this step, it is important to be aware of any tendencies for turning this step into an inquisition. Therefore, rather than asking,

"Okay, what did you just do?" it is more effective to ask, "Are you aware of what you were doing just now?" or "What do you think you did that made Mrs. Smith send you down to my office?"

There will obviously be times when adolescents will balk at describing their behavior. At this point, it is helpful to ask the adolescent if he would be willing to listen to an adult's interpretation of his behavior. If the counselor was not present when the problem arose, the counselor can volunteer to serve as mediator while an adult or peer who was present attempts to describe the adolescent's behavior.

While adolescents almost always agree to examine their behavior, there will be instances in which they will indicate an unwillingness either to discuss their behavior or to listen to someone else's interpretation. At this point it may be helpful to indicate to the adolescent that his refusal creates a problem while at the same time detracting from his power to work out a solution. The following sample dialogue suggests how this intervention might be handled.

John: I don't know.
Counselor: You mean that you aren't sure what you did that might have upset Mrs. Johnson?
John: Ya.
Counselor: Okay, would you be willing to sit down with Mrs. Johnson and listen to her so that you could understand what upset her?
John: I don't care what upset her. That's her problem. She's always getting bent out of shape over nothing.
Counselor: John, if you are not willing to look at what happened so we can work out a solution, then what do you think we should do?
John: I don't care. That's your problem.
Counselor: John, the problem is that if you won't help me work out a solution, then you end up with whatever solution Mrs. Johnson and the vice principal decide upon. I respect your ability to solve your own problems, and I would like to see you have some say in working things out. Does that make sense?
John: Ya, I guess so. (pauses) Okay, what do you want me to do?
Counselor: It would help me and I believe it would help you if you could explain what happened in class today.
John: Okay, I. . . .

Since students want to be viewed as competent and want to control their own behavior, they can often be convinced that examining their own behavior is a necessary prerequisite for being included in decisions which will directly affect them.

The third step in Glasser's model involves asking individuals to evaluate the results of their behavior. Glasser suggests that this can be facilitated by asking questions such as "Did this behavior help you?" and "Did it help other people?" Another approach is to ask the adolescent to list the payoffs and the costs associated with the behavior. While this step can be worked through verbally, it is often productive to ask youngsters to make a list of the ways in which their behavior helped and hurt them.

The process of writing something down requires somewhat more time and energy, and the results seem to be better thought out and more meaningful to the adolescent than verbalized statements.

The fourth step centers on the adolescent's developing a plan or an alternative approach for dealing with the situation in which the problem occurred. A plan may range from something as simple as sitting apart from a group of friends to something as complicated as becoming involved in family counseling. The key concept within this step is that the adolescent plays a major role in developing the plan. While the teacher or counselor may provide suggestions or ask critical questions concerning the plan, the plan must be developed and accepted by the adolescent.

If the fourth step has been effectively resolved, the fifth step is a formality. In the fifth step, the adult simply asks the adolescent if he is willing to try this plan for a designated period of time. It is very important at this point to establish a time at which the adolescent and adult involved will get together and evaluate the results of the plan. For example, the teacher might ask that the student drop by during lunch on Friday so that they can chat briefly about how the plan is working.

The sixth step is sometimes misinterpreted. The concept of not accepting excuses does not mean that the adult does not listen to the adolescent's concerns about a plan that has failed. However, it does mean that the adult places the responsibility back on the adolescent. This can be done by indicating that he has developed the plan and noting that if the plan is not working it should be reevaluated and another plan devised. For example, assume that a student has decided that he will avoid conflict with a teacher by accepting the teacher's criticism and recording his feelings in a journal that will be shared with the counselor. If after several days the student is sent to the office for talking back to the teacher, it is important not to spend an extensive amount of time listening to the student's reasons why he was unable to control his behavior. Instead, it is more productive to remind the student that he developed the plan and suggest that he reexamine the plan and decide whether something else needs to be done. By focusing on behavior and placing the responsibility on the adolescent, adults can prevent themselves from becoming involved in unproductive sympathizing or debating while simultaneously indicating their respect for the individual's competence and placing the source of power squarely back on him.

The seventh step reflects the importance of not being punitive either when discussing the initial problem or examining an unsuccessful plan. Adolescents experience enough pain and self-derogation in connection with conflict or failure situations. Adults should not be fooled by the bravado or apparent lack of concern often projected during times of stress. Except in the case of extremely hardened or emotionally disturbed adolescents, this behavior simply hides the hurt or anxiety associated with yet another problem. Punitive statements only add another layer to the wall many problem adolescents feel they must place around themselves. Absolutely nothing is gained by punitive remarks and they violate the first step in Glasser's counseling procedure.

The eighth and final step deals with the importance of following up on any plan that has been made. As mentioned earlier, it is important to designate a specific time and place for discussing the results of the plan that has been developed. It is also useful to find some opportunity prior to this meeting to make contact with the adolescent and check on how the plan is working. This follow-up serves two important purposes. First, by taking time to check with adolescents, adults indicate their concern for them and interest in their situation. Second, since almost all plans require that adolescents attempt a new, more positive behavior, it is important that adults provide immediate positive reinforcement when adolescents emit the behavior. If adults wait several days before reinforcing the new desirable behavior, they should not be surprised when the old behavior reappears. Unproductive behaviors exist because they meet some need or receive some form of reinforcement. If adults want to replace these with new, more productive behaviors, they must provide frequent reinforcement for the new behaviors.

Example

An example may help to bring together and clarify the various steps Glasser outlined. Several years ago, I saw a ninth grade student who was referred because he was constantly disruptive during his social studies class. When asked to describe why the teacher had told him to leave the class, the boy indicated that he and two of his friends occasionally mimicked the teacher, threw paper wads at other students, and talked during class. When asked to make a judgment about his behavior, the student listed the payoffs as: (1) not having to listen to a boring lecture, (2) getting attention from other students, (3) being accepted by his friends, (4) not having to do the work in class, and (5) coming to the counseling office rather than being in class. The costs listed included: (1) not passing the class, (2) turning off some students, (3) getting in trouble at school, which meant getting hassled at home, and (4) getting a bad reputation. After discussing these payoffs and costs, the student agreed to a plan in which he would not sit next to his friends.

When I checked with the student the following day, I discovered that he had barely escaped being told to leave class that day. When asked to evaluate his plan, the student indicated that when he had seated himself across the room from his friends, they had come over to join him. He indicated that he did not want to alienate his friends by asking them to leave, and as a result they all became involved in many of their familiar behaviors.

At this point, it occurred to me that the central issue in this situation might revolve around the student's inability to understand the material being presented in class. If this were the case, it seemed unlikely that future plans would be successful since improving his behavior would mean that the student would have to confront his inability to cope with the subject matter. When presented with this hypothesis, the student indicated that he did not find the material "over his head." Examination of achievement test scores verified the student's perception.

The next step was to again ask the student to make a value judgment concerning his behavior. This time the student was asked not only to evaluate his behavior, but to seriously determine whether he was committed to altering this behavior. When the student indicated that he sincerely wanted to improve his grades in social studies, he was asked to consider alternative plans. At this point he acknowledged that the key to his difficulties in this particular class centered around the peer pressure from his two friends. He concluded that any viable plan would have to include a program for breaking up this group. Given this information, I suggested that since it was difficult for him to solve the issue alone that it might be productive for the three boys to meet with me to discuss the problem. I indicated that if it would make him more comfortable, I would approach the problem from the teacher's point of view rather than asking him to confront his friends. He appeared relieved at this suggestion, but also indicated that he was willing to carry his share of the load by remaining firm in his belief that things needed to change.

The meeting with the three boys proved to be extremely productive. While the other boys were somewhat less concerned about doing well in class, they nevertheless seemed relieved at the possibility of extricating themselves from a situation that committed them to acting out. The boys agreed to support each other in improving their behavior and grades in the class. Both short- and long-term follow-up indicated that the boys' behavior had improved dramatically and that their academic work had also showed considerable improvement.

There are several distinct advantages associated with employing Glasser's model. First, as mentioned earlier, it is a relatively simple model that does not require a great deal of time. Consequently, it can be employed by teachers, child-care workers, aides, or other staff who do not have large blocks of time in which to become involved in more indepth, time-consuming counseling procedures. Second, it follows a step-by-step outline; and therefore, lends itself to systematic analysis and evaluation. If a particular intervention proves to be unproductive, the teacher can systematically examine each step in order to determine why the intervention failed. Finally, as with all behavioral counseling models, Glasser's model places much of the responsibility on the client. Not only does this situation respond appropriately to a wide range of adolescents' developmental needs, but it also increases the likelihood that the new behaviors will generalize to other settings.

AN ALTERNATIVE STEP-BY-STEP MODEL

In employing a behavioral counseling format, I have found it useful to have several available models from which to choose. Different models seem to work more effectively with different clients and within given time dimensions. The model presented in this section is one that can be used when time limitations are not a major factor. This approach is also effective with clients whose cognitive skills are somewhat limited and who have difficulty dealing with the concept of long- and short-term consequences. The basic steps to this model require that the counselor and client determine the: (1) undesirable behavior, (2) causes of this behavior, (3) payoff associated with this behavior, (4) costs associated with this behavior, (5) appropriate behavior to replace the old behavior, (6) methods for accomplishing the new behavior. The two examples offered in this section indicate how this model can be employed with a wide client population. The first example deals with a fifteen-year-old delinquent boy. The second example examines work done with a severely handicapped twenty-one-year-old man.

Example Number One

The client in this case was a bright, handsome, athletic fifteen-year-old boy named Sam (a fictitious name). While I had worked with Sam in a school setting, the intervention discussed here occurred over a year after I had left Sam's school. Sam's mother initiated the contact and asked if I would be willing to talk to Sam. The mother indicated that Sam had run away from home and refused to return. She also noted that Sam was flunking all of his classes and that she was concerned that he was involved in considerable drug usage.

The first meeting with Sam focused on listening to his side of the story and determining whether he was interested in changing his behavior. He indicated that he was willing to consider some changes in his behavior. The next step was for Sam to examine which behaviors he saw as most unproductive. The behaviors that Sam finally listed in this category included his angrily leaving home, his poor grades, and his behavior on the streets. The latter category included extensive fighting and drug usage.

Once the unproductive behaviors had been outlined, Sam was asked to list the possible causes of these behaviors. A focus on causes is not normally considered part of a behavioral intervention program. The advantage associated with including this category is that it provides an opportunity for adolescents to express their feelings while at the same time providing some valuable insight into what they perceive as the environmental cues and reinforcers. If adults expect to assist adolescents in developing functional behavior change plans, they must have a solid understanding concerning adolescents' perception of their own environment. This understanding must include both an understanding of the adolescent's feelings and the cause and effect variables that they perceive as being most important.

In discussing the causes of his behavior, Sam placed a major emphasis on the fact that his mother was no longer living with his father, that she expected him to take care of the house and babysit his younger brother, and that he did not like the fact that his mother's current boyfriend acted like a father in expecting Sam to obey his rules. Considerable time was spent in allowing Sam to focus on the feelings elicited by his parents' separation, his mother's demands, and his relationship with his mother's friend. It became clear that Sam was experiencing considerable hurt, rejection, and fear. Since feelings do influence behavior, it was important that Sam be given assistance in acknowledging and understanding his feelings. If these feelings had not been examined and associated with behaviors, it is likely that when these feelings were elicited in the future, they would again interfere with his ability to cognitively choose the most productive behaviors. In addition, by having his feelings accepted and legitimized, Sam began to feel more in control and less "crazy." As he began to accept that his feelings were not "wrong," he began to feel better about himself and be less defensive about his behavior. This in turn freed him to more critically analyze the behaviors in which he was engaging.

The next step in examining Sam's behavior involved asking him to list the payoffs and costs associated with the unproductive behaviors he had listed. Sam did not hesitate in listing "punishing his mother" as the most important payoff. He also listed the freedom he was experiencing and the fact that he did not have to see his mother's boyfriend or be responsible for chores around the house. As disadvantages or costs associated with his behavior, Sam listed: (1) he would not graduate from high school, (2) he was not feeling well physically, (3) he had alienated most of his friends at school, (4) his grandparents were upset with him, and (5) he did not like some of the behaviors expected of him by the gang members with whom he associated.

Several sessions were devoted to discussing the payoffs and costs associated with Sam's current, unproductive behavior. Following these discussions, Sam decided that the costs did in fact outweigh the payoffs, and that he was interested in examining alternative behaviors that might meet his needs without incurring such high costs. At this point, he was asked to list possible behaviors that could replace those in which he was currently engaging. Sam took this task seriously and developed a list that included: (1) joining the armed services, (2) staying with a friend, (3) living with his maternal grandparents, and (4) going back home following some negotiations with his mother. It was decided that Sam should investigate one alternative between each weekly session and that the session would be devoted primarily to examining the advantages and disadvantages of that alternative. Sam rejected the first alternative because he felt the time commitment required by the armed services was too long for him to accept. He rejected the second alternative because his friend's father frequently became violently drunk and the living conditions in that home were consequently quite undesirable. Sam had considered the third alternative to be the most desirable. However, when he met with his grandparents, he was informed that they believed he should be living with his mother, and that they did not want to be involved with him until he decided to return home. This visit had a strong impact on Sam. He greatly admired his grandfather and was surprised and hurt by the response he received from his grandparents. Perhaps more than anything else, this response led Sam to decide to follow the last alternative.

The problem then became how to develop a plan so that Sam's needs could be met within his home environment. After rejecting several rather unlikely solutions such as sending his mother a list of ultimatums that she would sign and return, Sam agreed that he and his mother should each develop a list of needs and expectations and that they should meet with a counselor to develop a compromise. Sam's mother enthusiastically agreed to this decision. After several sessions, a workable compromise was developed, and Sam returned home. He and his mother continued in counseling for several months at gradually increasing intervals. While their relationship was not always smooth, Sam lived at home until he graduated from high school.

Example Number Two

This case was reported by a student in a behavioral counseling seminar. The student was employed as a counselor at a shelter home for handicapped adults. The client was a twenty-one-year-old mentally retarded, cerebral palsied man. The man expressed

Figure 11.1 Behavioral Counseling Program with a Twenty-One-Year-Old Severely Handicapped Client

Unproductive Behavior	Cause *(What makes me do it?)*	Cost *(What I lose because of my behavior)* / Payoff *(What do I get from it?)*
Suspicious of people— does not meet people or spend time with people	Rejection and hurt in past	Cost: Does not make friends and is lonely Payoff: Avoid relationships and don't get hurt
Too friendly to people physically—feels they back away from close-ness	Anxious for friends Deafness might contribute European background of more frequent touching might contribute	Cost: People seem to be offended Payoff: It is nice to touch people
Overly friendly (verbally) on first meeting with people	Anxious to please and make friends	Cost: People back away Payoff: None
Conversation usually at formal, superficial, stilted level	Afraid to risk revealing self	Cost: Don't deal with genuine feelings Payoff: Less worry about being rejected
Can't take kidding	Feels it is directed towards him, was laughed at as a child and in previous work situation	Cost: Alienation, bitterness Payoff: None

Appropriate Behavior to Replace Old	Methods of Accomplishment
Establish trusting relationships Make more contact with people	Build friendships slowly with "safe," accepting people. Homework assignment on charting contacts.
Establish appropriate distance when interacting with people	Distance exercise with counselor. Observations of others who have successful friendships. Practice distance with accepting people. Role-play in appropriate behavior. Homework assignment on charting contacts. Feedback from counselor on personal reaction to touching.
Establish appropriate verbal responses	Same as above, except feedback from counselor on reaction to verbal overfriendliness.
Deal more at feeling level	Group sessions to increase affective communication. Feedback from counselor on her reactions to conversations.
Take self less seriously	Role-playing. Practice in safe real-life situations. Cognitive data from counselor on how men in our society often express affection (and hostility) in a kidding way.

concern over several issues related to social contacts. Figure 11.1 provides a summary of five behavioral counseling programs carried out over a nine-month period. The student's data indicated that each of these interventions was not only seen as successful by the client, but also resulted in positive behavior changes.

The model presented in this section provides an opportunity to blend a systematic, behavioral approach with discussions concerning the client's needs and feelings. The model can be effectively employed with a wide range of clients and does not require sophisticated abstract reasoning skills by the client.

FOCUSING ON LONG- AND SHORT-TERM PAYOFFS AND COSTS

The model presented in this section is most effective with adolescents who are willing and able to examine their behavior and its consequences and who have the ability to conceptualize fairly extensive time dimensions. Consequently, this form of behavioral counseling is most effective with young people who possess average or above average intelligence as well as a reasonable amount of impulse control. However, even when working with more impulsive youngsters, this model can provide a valuable starting point. Even if this approach is initially ineffective, this fact can provide adolescents with valuable information concerning the extent to which they can be responsible for their own behavior-change program. Furthermore, the model can be employed effectively in the latter stages of therapy as adolescents become more able to control their own behavior. A side benefit associated with this model is that it can provide the counselor with valuable information about adolescents' ability to conceptualize their problems, deal with extended time dimensions, and take responsibility for their own behavior.

The model (Figure 11.2) involves adolescents in examining the short-term and long-term payoffs and costs associated with their behavior. In cases where a distinct behavior choice exists, this model can be extremely useful in assisting adolescents in

Figure 11.2   Payoff-Cost Model of Behavioral Counseling

	Short Term	Long Term
Payoffs		
Costs		

making a choice between the two behaviors. When the initial task is to evaluate an unproductive behavior, the counselor can focus on the model as presented in Figure 11.2. Once the adolescent has carefully examined this behavior and decided that some alternative behavior would be more productive, the counselor can begin to focus on short- and long-term payoffs and costs associated with several alternative behaviors. The two examples presented next indicate the manner in which this model can be employed.

Example Number One

This case involved a thirteen-year-old girl, named Kathy, who was seen in individual therapy at a private counseling center. Kathy was referred to the center because of her extensive truancy, school failure, and consistently being "beyond parental control." Results of testing at school and the clinic showed that Kathy scored slightly below average in intelligence, and that she scored nearly three years below grade level in reading.

Early counseling sessions with Kathy indicated that she was experiencing a strong need to be accepted. Unfortunately, the group of boys with whom she was spending much of her time were not attending school and were quite heavily involved in drug usage and petty theft. While she had not yet become involved in these behaviors, Kathy was missing numerous classes to be with these boys. Furthermore, Kathy's desire to be with her delinquent friends was causing serious family problems. Kathy frequently became involved in heated arguments with her parents concerning what she considered to be unreasonably restrictive curfew hours. This situation had been intensified by the fact that Kathy had on several occasions remained out several hours past the designated curfew. Her parents had responded to these violations by strongly suggesting that Kathy might have to leave home and live with relatives in a town several hundred miles away.

In analyzing her behavior using the model presented in this section, Kathy listed the payoffs and costs shown in Figure 11.3. An examination of Figure 11.3 highlights several recurring themes found when working with adolescents.

First, adolescents frequently focus on short-term effects to the almost complete exclusion of long-term effects. Second, adolescents often appear to ignore the short-term costs connected with their behavior. This denial of short-term costs is often accomplished by projecting the blame for any such costs upon another agent. In the case under consideration, Kathy blamed her parents' lack of concern and love for the most powerful short-term cost associated with her behavior. By blaming her parents for the fact that she might be asked to leave home, she successfully denied her responsibility for the short-term negative consequences. A final concept highlighted by this case is the tendency for payoffs to include both direct payoffs and payoffs that are based upon the avoidance of an undesirable situation or task. For example, in this case, having friends and being in exciting situations were the direct short-term payoffs while avoidance of a difficult school experience was the avoidance-based, short-term payoff. When working with adolescents, it is important to help them identify and

Figure 11.3 Payoff/Cost List Developed by Kathy

	Short Term	Long Term
Payoffs	1. Getting out of boring classes 2. Doing something exciting 3. Having friends 4. Feeling important	1. Becoming an independent person
Costs	1. Parents are angry 2. Having to leave home 3. Being "hassled" by teachers 4. Flunking classes 5. Losing some friends from school 6. Possibility of getting caught 7. Developing a "bad" reputation	1. Not graduating frm high school 2. Getting caught and having that on her record 3. Getting "hooked" on drugs 4. Ruining her relationship with her parents

discuss both types of payoff. Only in this way can adults assist them in developing a complete picture of their behavior and its consequences.

Returning to Kathy's specific case, the cost/payoff model was employed as a means to motivate Kathy to work with her parents. Kathy had been focusing almost exclusively on the short-term payoffs and had denied the short-term costs by blaming her parents for her problem. Therefore, in order to convince Kathy that compromises with her parents might benefit her, it was necessary that she take a more realistic look at the costs and payoffs connected with her behavior.

After working separately with Kathy for several sessions, Kathy agreed that she was ready to meet with her parents to discuss possible agreements that could lead to a reduction in their conflicts. After several sessions the family agreed that Kathy could go out after dinner on week nights until nine o'clock twice a week. It was also agreed that she could go out until 10:30 p.m. on Friday and Saturday nights as long as she informed her parents where she was going. In turn, Kathy agreed that she would stay home after dinner for three nights a week and either work on homework or participate in family activities. Kathy further agreed that if she was not home on time or if she left home after dinner more than twice a week, she would lose the privilege of going out the following weekend.

The results of this intervention were somewhat surprising. Kathy's behavior improved dramatically over the next two months. She began to attend school more regularly, her schoolwork improved, and she did not break her contract with her parents. These results appear to be due to two major factors. First, like so many adolescents, Kathy's attraction to a destructive peer group was more a response to the lack of a relationship at home than the positive draw of the peer group. As Bronfenbrenner has stated,

> the peer-oriented child is more a product of parental disregard than of the attractiveness of the peer group—that he turns to his age-mates less by choice than by default. The vacuum left by the withdrawal of parents and adults from the lives of children is filled with an undesired—and possibly undesirable—substitute of an age-segregated peer group. (Bronfenbrenner, 1970, p. 102)

As Kathy began to spend time at home and become involved in the increasing number of family activities organized by her parents, she began to need her peer group less. This decreased dependency in turn freed her to become more selective in choosing peers with whom she would spend time. A second factor contributing to the positive results of this intervention is that Kathy learned that she could serve her own purposes more effectively by interacting openly with her parents than by rebelling against them.

Example Number Two

A second case study in which a payoff/cost model was effective involved a seventeen-year-old high school senior whom I will call Sally. Sally came for counseling because she was extremely distraught about her relationship with her boyfriend. She initially expressed concern over the fact that her boyfriend seemed almost totally dependent upon her. Sally appeared interested in breaking up with her boyfriend, but indicated that whenever she suggested they date other people, he became extremely depressed and hinted that he would commit suicide if she broke up with him.

In analyzing her situation, Sally listed the payoffs and costs seen in Figure 11.4. After a careful examination of her list and the feelings associated with this list, Sally decided that it was important for her to change her relationship with her boyfriend. Understandably, however, Sally had serious concerns regarding her ability to effectively cope with her boyfriend's depression. In order to increase the likelihood that Sally could carry out her decision and reach her goal, it was decided that several counseling sessions would focus on teaching Sally skills for responding to her boyfriend's manipulation. Role playing was employed for desensitizing Sally to her boyfriend's remarks and assisting her in developing a repertoire of responses that allowed her to show her concern while remaining firm in her decision to change the relationship. Sally reported being pleased with the results of her interchanges with her boyfriend, and follow-up indicated that both parties were adjusting well to the change.

As in the previous case, it was necessary to combine the payoff/cost model with another behavioral counseling model. Since the payoff/cost model is primarily cognitive and does not in itself include a skill-building component, it is seldom successful when employed as an isolated intervention. However, by assisting adolescents in examining the consequences of their behavior, this model forms a foundation for concurrent interventions while at the same time providing adolescents with a tool that can be used in future conflict situations.

CLARIFYING EXPECTATIONS AND PROCEDURES:
A MODEL FOR MAINSTREAMING OR READMITTING
THE BEHAVIOR-PROBLEM STUDENT

I have found the model presented in this section to be the most successful approach for working with behavior-problem adolescents within a school setting. This model can also be effectively employed in a residential treatment setting as well as in family counseling. The key components in this plan are an emphasis on clarifying expectations and the concept of negotiation. In addition to its effectiveness as a behavioral

Figure 11.4 Payoffs and Costs Listed by a Seventeen-Year-Old
Girl Regarding Remaining with Her Boyfriend

	Short Term	Long Term
Payoffs *Behavior #1* *(Remaining in the* *relationship)*	1. Always having a date 2. Not having to worry about being lonely 3. Avoiding dealing with his manipulative depression 4. Not having to go through the difficulties of establishing a new relationship	None
Costs	1. He totally dominated her time 2. She could not develop new relationships which interested her 3. The energy spent on the relationship was affecting her grades	1. Passing up good relationships which might lead to marriage 2. Flunking school and not receiving a college degree 3. Becoming trapped in a long term relationship which did not meet her needs
Payoffs *Behavior #2* *(Breaking up)*	1. Freedom to enjoy new relationships 2. More time and energy for studying 3. Being more honest with herself and her boyfriend	1. Opportunity to establish a good long-term relationship 2. Graduation from college 3. Learning how to deal with manipulation
Costs	1. Having to confront her boyfriend 2. Having to deal with his manipulative depression 3. The occasional loneliness and hurt associated with establishing new relationships	None

intervention, this model has the added advantage of serving as an ideal precursor to the development of behavior contracts. This section will focus on applying this model as a behavioral counseling tool without the use of an associated contract.

In working with behavior-problem adolescents, I am continually impressed by the frequency with which they indicate a rather dramatic lack of understanding concerning the specific demands being placed upon them within various portions of their environment. These youngsters all too often view their home and school environments as characterized by very generalized and confusing expectations and rules. Interestingly, this situation often occurs even when the expectations and guidelines appear quite clear to siblings and classmates who are not experiencing major behavior problems. A careful consideration of the situation reveals several possible explanations for the confusion often experienced by troubled adolescents.

First, most behavior-problem adolescents experience low self-esteem and feelings of inadequacy (Ahlstrom and Havighurst, 1971; Conger and Miller, 1966; Gold and Mann, 1972).

Delinquents are significantly more likely than nondelinquents to perceive themselves, consciously or unconsciously, as "lazy," "bad," "sad," and "ignorant." According to their own self-concepts, delinquents are undesirable people; they tend not to like, value, or respect themselves. In addition, their self-concepts are confused, conflictual, contradictory, uncertain, and variable. (Conger, 1977, p. 580. Reprinted by permission of Harper & Row, Publishers, Inc.)

Since the establishment of a satisfactory identity is a major developmental task during adolescence, it is understandable that adolescents who are experiencing major difficulties in this area will find their world rather confusing and unclear. The anxiety associated with a low self-concept impairs troubled adolescents' ability to effectively analyze and respond to their environment. Behavior-problem adolescents very often spend considerable amounts of psychological energy defending and coping with an impaired self-concept. This situation creates a selective perception that often excludes information that is picked up by peers who are more confident and secure within their environment. It is, therefore, often necessary to assist behavior-problem adolescents in clarifying and gaining some sense of control over their environment.

A second major reason for the confusion often experienced by behavior-problem adolescents is the fact that these youngsters have experienced relatively few positive experiences that can serve as guidelines to clarify what behaviors are acceptable and will be reinforced. In the absence of these benchmarks, and lacking a relatively stable and acceptable self-image, behavior-problem adolescents operate in an environment that is not clearly defined. When people do not clearly understand their environment, their behavior is more likely to be characterized by passivity or extreme actions— behaviors that are characteristic of behavior-problem adolescents.

Adults often feel badly when adolescents cannot function within their home or classroom. Unfortunately, in order for adults to reduce their feelings of inadequacy associated with not having interacted effectively with troubled adolescents, they often shift the blame to the adolescents. Instead, adults need to assist both themselves and adolescents in defining needs and expectations. This procedure can provide adults with a sense of accomplishment and order while simultaneously assisting adolescents to better understand and thereby function more effectively in the classroom or home. Figure 11.5 presents an outline of a procedure for establishing clear expectations and altering environmental structures in order to enable adolescents to meet reasonable expectations. The remainder of this section will include a detailed description of these procedures.

While the procedure outlined in Figure 11.5 can be employed in family, institutional, and school settings, the discussion in this section will focus on school interventions. It is important to keep in mind that this procedure can be effectively employed without the assistance of a third party. However, since it is usually helpful to work with a third party when applying this procedure for the first time, the procedure will be described as it would be applied with a third party.

Step One

The first step centers on assisting the teacher in specifically describing those student behaviors that are causing major problems. It is important to listen empathically while

Figure 11.5 A Model for Clarifying Expectations and Procedures as a Means for Mainstreaming or Readmitting the Behavior-Problem Student

Step 1: Teacher lists the problems as she perceives them
a. problems should be stated in terms of specific observable behaviors
b. if possible data should be collected
1. data help determine if the behavior requires intervention
2. data provide a base from which to determine if an intervention is effective

Step 2: Teacher lists expectations
a. stated positively
b. include 1-5 goals
c. goals are observable and measurable
d. goals include the minimum level of acceptable behavior

Step 3: Teacher lists what she is willing to do in order to enhance the likelihood that the expectations can be met

Step 4: Student lists the problems as he perceives them
a. problems should be stated in terms of specific observable behaviors

Step 5: Student examines the teacher's list of problems and determines what behaviors do in fact occur and create a problem

Step 6: Student examines the teacher's list of expectations and indicates those which he can and cannot meet

Step 7: The student lists what he needs in the class in order to meet the teacher's expectations
a. needs must be stated in terms of specific observable behaviors
b. stated positively
c. include 1-5 needs
d. include the minimum level of acceptable behavior

Step 8: Student lists what he is willing to do in order to enhance the likelihood that the teacher's expectations can be met

Step 9: Teacher examines the student's statements concerning:
a. which teacher expectations can be met
b. what needs the student has
c. what the student is willing to do

Step 10: Student and teacher meet and develop a plan which states each party's responsibilities
a. responsibilities are listed in terms of specific observable behaviors
b. responsibilities are stated positively
c. responsibilities include a minimum level of acceptable behavior

Step 11: Teacher and student develop a safety net plan
a. plan lists what each party will do if he or she believes the other has violated the agreement

Step 12: Evaluation
a. includes periodic conferences to examine the program's progress
b. includes specific data collection when possible

the teacher expresses the emotions associated with working unsuccessfully with a problem student. Not only does this catharsis allow the teacher to diffuse her emotions, but active listening indicates concern and is important in establishing rapport. However, once the teacher has expressed her concerns, it is important to begin to focus on specific, observable behaviors. This step is particularly important since the teacher's list will eventually be shared with the student. If the teacher indicates that the student is "totally disruptive" and the worst student she has ever had, this will devastate or anger the student without providing him with specific behaviors that can be changed. As noted in Chapter 10, it is important that behavior-problem adolescents receive feedback concerning their behavior. However, it is also important that they be able to differentiate between the acceptability of their behavior and their own self-worth. By providing them with specific feedback about their behavior, adults can indicate that they accept adolescents but cannot accept certain behaviors.

The process of specifically defining behavior aids teachers in pinpointing the student actions that they find most bothersome. For example, on several occasions when I have asked teachers to specifically define the behaviors that bothered them, they discovered that the student did not act as badly as they had thought. They began to realize that their frustration with the student stemmed from a combination of the student's low-level disruption and the student's apparent disinterest in the subject matter. This clarification enabled the teacher to consider changing the focus from removing the student from class or drastically altering the student's behavior to focusing on ways to assist the student in more effectively coping with the academic material presented in class.

Step Two

The second and perhaps most important step involves the teacher's establishing a list of realistic, specific, positively stated expectations for the student. Teachers often indicate that they will allow a behavior-problem student back in class if he will "improve his behavior" or "stop acting out." In addition to being extremely general, these demands are stated in rather negative terms. A basic principle of behavioral counseling is to, whenever possible, focus on positive goals. Therefore, rather than demanding that a student stop talking in class or stop coming to class unprepared, it is more desirable to request that a student listen quietly while the teacher is talking or come to class with paper and pencil.

In addition to providing the student with a clear set of expectations, this step creates an opportunity for teachers to clarify their minimum standards regarding student behavior. Since secondary school teachers are trained in a subject matter that they enjoy and usually view as important, it is quite easy for them to slip into unrealistically high expectations concerning student interest and performance. This step enables them to moderate these expectations while at the same time maintaining standards that are necessary for maintaining a productive learning environment.

When developing expectations, it is important to keep the number as small as possible. A student who is experiencing difficulty in class will understandably be overwhelmed by a list of ten requirements. My experience indicates that five expectations is the maximum number behavior-problem students can effectively cope with. The optimum number seems to be three.

Step Three

The last step that occurs during the initial contact(s) with the teacher is the teacher's input concerning the possible steps she can take to alleviate the problems and assist the student in meeting her expectations. When covering this step, it is helpful to ask the teacher to examine how she interacts with the student and if there are ways in which her responses might become more supportive. Similarly, the teacher may be encouraged to investigate the possibility of individualizing her curriculum in order to accommodate the student's needs or abilities.

Steps Four and Five

It is possible to skip steps four and five (the student describes his perception of the problem and validates or clarifies the teacher's description) and move directly to step six. For example, if a student has been suspended from a teacher's class or is preparing to return home from a stay in a residential treatment center, the important decision may be to discuss whether the youngster can meet the demands that will be made upon him when he reenters the classroom or home environment. Since steps four and five focus on negative issues, a point can be made for avoiding them whenever possible. In cases where the student has been removed from the home or classroom environment for a period of time, it seems both pointless and potentially harmful to delve into old problems.

While it is important to carefully determine whether or not to include these stages, they do have several definite payoffs. First, step four provides adolescents with an opportunity to express their own feelings and thoughts. This indicates adults' respect for adolescents and provides them with a sense of competence and power. Second, this step may provide adults with useful information that they could not acquire in step one. While this information may surface during step seven, it is more direct and clear when dealt with separately.

Step five also has the advantage of indicating respect for the student and providing the student with a sense of power. By discussing the problem in some detail, adults increase the likelihood that adolescents will clearly understand the issues involved. In addition, step five involves adolescents in acknowledging the problem. Unless adolescents acknowledge that a problem exists and agree upon the nature of the problem, it is unlikely that they will become meaningfully involved in any problem-solving activities. Indeed, if adults define the problem unilaterally, adolescents will often do their best to subvert adults' efforts.

Step Six

Step six is extremely important and should be given adequate time. If teachers expect adolescents to function comfortably and effectively within a classroom, it is imperative that adolescents themselves believe that they can perform the tasks required of them. Therefore, it is important that behavior-problem students be given an opportunity to examine the teacher's expectations and indicate any which they feel are unreasonable. This does not mean that these students have the power to eliminate any expectations that do not meet their fancy. However, it does mean that further discussion and perhaps some degree of compromise needs to take place regarding these expectations.

For example, assume that a teacher includes an expectation that the student be on time to every class, turn in every assignment, and not talk to other students when either the teacher or a student is talking. It is possible that in examining this list a student might indicate that he attends physical education prior to the class being discussed and that it is extremely difficult to go from the gym to his locker and still make it to class on time every day. Similarly, the student might legitimately ask what happens if one of his peers begins talking to him just as the teacher glances in his direction. This could be perceived as his being involved in talking to another student. It is important to provide behavior-problem students with an opportunity to discuss such issues prior to making a final agreement concerning expectations.

Step Seven

It is important to provide students with an opportunity to discuss what they need in order to perform effectively within a home or classroom environment. As in the case of teacher expectation, it is important to assist adolescents in describing needs positively and in specific, observable terms. For example, when asked what they need in order to meet a teacher's expectations, behavior-problem students often respond with statements such as, "I need her to get off my back" or "I need him to stop hassling me." While these responses are certainly expressive of the students' dissatisfaction, they do not provide useful information that can be discussed with the teacher. Therefore, when students are critical of teachers, adults need to assist students in describing specific teacher behaviors that may need to be altered.

An example of such a situation occurred not long ago when a student stated that he needed the teacher to stop hassling him. When asked to clarify this request, the student indicated that the teacher frequently asked him in front of the class why he had not completed his assignment. When asked if this meant that he would rather be reminded privately about overdue assignments, the student indicated that what he really needed was help in understanding the work. This led to the student's listing a need to have the teacher available during class or after school to provide some individual assistance. This final expression of the need was much clearer and more positive than the student's initial statement.

Step Eight

This step provides students with an opportunity to take responsibility for their own behavior. If a student is motivated to change and believes that a teacher's expectations are reasonable, it is quite possible that the student will agree to many if not all of the teachers' requests. This is especially apt to occur if the student is impressed by what the teacher has stated she is willing to do in order to assist the student in meeting her expectations.

While it is always reinforcing to hear students indicate that they will agree to change their behaviors, it is important during this step not to allow students to develop an unrealistic list. For example, a student may indicate that he will start coming to all his classes, do all of his work, and stop acting out in class. At this point it is important to remind the student that a more realistic list might include a willingness to accept the teacher's expectations and meet with the teacher to work out a plan for the two of them to work together to meet these goals.

Step Nine

Once the counselor has met with the student and examined his needs and responses to the teacher's expectations, it is helpful to schedule another conference with the teacher. This conference provides an opportunity for allowing the teacher to examine and respond to the student's needs and any expectations that the student has described as excessive. When I first began using this model, I met with the parents or teacher and the adolescent without first discussing the student's lists with the adults involved. While this procedure worked in some instances, it was quite destructive in several cases. I discovered the hard way that some adults find it difficult to accept candid, specific information from adolescents. On several occasions teachers and parents initially responded quite negatively to the students' deletion of certain expectations or inclusion of specific needs. Unfortunately, adolescents took this negative response personally, and this created an additional barrier to solving the problem.

Based on these experiences, I began to first meet with the adult(s) to discuss the adolescent's input. While these sessions are sometimes characterized by considerable emotion, these emotions always subside and can be followed by calmer discussions concerning possible compromises that may be needed. This step is therefore an important component of this model and helps to set the stage for a productive three-way conference.

Step Ten

If the previous steps have been successfully completed, the primary focus of step ten is facilitating a positive, goal-oriented discussion. In addition to establishing a workable agreement, an important goal of this conference is to create an improved teacher-student relationship that includes positive expectations from both parties. Since both parties have previously outlined their expectations and needs, the facilitator's role simply involves summarizing these goals and making sure that both the teacher and student believe that the new behaviors agreed upon by both parties are sufficient to create a positive, workable relationship.

It is desirable to provide a written statement that includes the specific behaviors that both the adult and adolescent have agreed to employ. A written statement not only clarifies the decision, but also tends to intensify the commitment. In addition, a written statement eliminates the possibility that one party will at a later date interpret the agreement differently than during the initial conference.

As discussed in Chapter 12, a written agreement may be arranged in the form of a contract that provides the adolescent with designated reinforcers if certain behaviors are maintained. While this type of intervention may prove to be necessary at a future time, it should not be included as part of the initial agreement. In many cases the process outlined in this section provides adequate reinforcement to support the adolescent's new behaviors. These reinforcements include: (1) the clarification of expectations with the accompanying increase in the adolescents' sense of competence and power, (2) improvement of the adult-adolescent relationship, and (3) an indication of respect for the student's competence and potency. While these reinforcers are perhaps less obvious than several minutes of free time or a trip to the school store, they appear to be much more meaningful and to indicate greater respect for the adolescent. Therefore, they have greater potential not only for enhancing immediate behavior change but also for generalizing behavior changes. My experience has indicated that in most instances where tangible reinforcers are seen as a "necessary" component in this form of agreement, this belief is more indicative of the failure to develop a meaningful agreement than a response to the student's "need" for such reinforcers.

Step Eleven

An important but often ignored step in employing this type of behavior-change program is the establishment of a safety net. The term *safety net* refers to a procedure for responding to difficulties that occur in implementing the agreement established during step ten. When working with extremely disruptive students, the agreement developed in step ten will require that the student (and often the teacher) make rather drastic changes in their behavior. Therefore, occasions will arise when students will revert to some form of unproductive behavior. The old behaviors would not have been maintained if they had not provided students with a considerable amount of reinforcement. Consequently, when the new behaviors are difficult or are not being adequately reinforced, students will revert to old behaviors. Cigarette smokers who have quit or attempted to quit smoking acknowledge that it is extremely difficult to make a drastic or complete reduction in their smoking behavior. Similarly, adolescents often find it difficult to make a drastic reduction in behaviors that were previously reinforced. Thus, it is important that counselors develop procedures for dealing with situations in which either the adult or adolescent believes that the other party has failed to behave in accordance with the terms of the agreement.

The simplest and most common approach to developing a safety net is to ask each party to agree to meet at the other's request to discuss any problems that may arise. When establishing this agreement, it is vital to point out that each party should feel free to request such a conference at the first sign of difficulty. As discussed in Chapter 4, problems frequently become intensified because individuals fail to deal with issues when they first arise.

In addition to creating a situation in which both parties agree to discuss any problems that should arise, it is also important to discuss exactly how each person will respond to a situation in which the agreement is being violated. For example, in a situation where a student agrees not to talk out in class, it is important to discuss what the teacher will do if the student talks out in class. Similarly, if a teacher agrees not to criticize a student in front of his classmates, it is necessary to discuss what the student will do if he feels he has been criticized. In many situations it is possible for each party to agree to simply ignore the behavior until they have an opportunity to talk to the other person privately and request that they discuss the problem. Obviously, however, there are some behaviors that cannot be ignored. In such cases it is important for the adult and adolescent to agree upon a signal that indicates to the other party that a behavior is in violation of their agreement. This signal may involve politely saying the individual's name or making a polite request. In settings where other adolescents are involved in working with problems, it is often acceptable to simply make a statement such as, "John, we have agreed that you won't do that" or "That behavior violates our agreement, do we need to talk?" Regardless of the type of cue employed, the important point is that both parties agree that they will cease any behavior that violates the agreement until they have an opportunity to discuss the problem.

It is unrealistic to expect adolescents who have displayed extreme acting-out behavior to eliminate this behavior immediately. Therefore, counselors must continually be prepared to apply their safety net. In addition, they must be willing to discuss situations, provide encouragement, reinforce changes in a positive direction, and where necessary, renegotiate agreements.

Step Twelve

The final step in this model involves collecting some form of data to assist in evaluating the program's effectiveness. There are a variety of methods for obtaining this data. First, the adult and adolescent can agree that each party will collect data and that they will meet at designated intervals to discuss their findings. In addition to providing an opportunity for examining the data, such meetings indicate the teacher's concern and may provide the student with a much needed feeling of significance.

Another common method for collecting data is to have students carry a daily travel card similar to that shown in Figure 11.6. This method is particularly effective when a student has developed an agreement with more than one teacher. This card has the advantage of providing the student with a constant reminder of the behaviors being considered. In addition, by requiring that each teacher initial the card following each period, this data collection procedure provides the student with immediate reinforcement. One difficulty with this form of data collection is that it has a tendency to become rather mechanical and therefore reduce the likelihood that students will experience a feeling of significance when interacting with their teachers. This problem

Figure 11.6   Daily Travel Card

Student_____ Grade_____ Week of_____

Subject	Teacher	Goals	M	T	W	TH	F	Initials
		1						
		2						
		3						
		4						
		5						
		1						
		2						
		3						
		4						
		5						
		1						
		2						
		3						
		4						
		5						

can be eliminated simply by asking teachers to accompany their initialing with several positive statements about the student's behavior. In addition, it is desirable to schedule periodic conferences in which the teacher and student can discuss the progress being made. While these conferences do require more time and energy than initialing a card, they are vital components in creating an intervention program that will have meaningful long-term results.

GIVING STUDENTS THE RIGHT TO FAIL

One of the most important lessons to learn when working with behavior-problem adolescents is that the decision to succeed or fail is ultimately theirs. Everyone has the inalienable right to fail. No matter what teaching or counseling approach adults employ, how much they care, or how skilled they become, they cannot guarantee that their students or clients will be successful. This is not meant to imply that counselors and teachers should not provide behavior-problem adolescents with assistance in understanding and controlling their behavior. It means that as adults develop programs for assisting adolescents in changing their behaviors, they must be aware of the limitations of their interventions. In addition, adults must carefully weigh the advantages and disadvantages associated with their attempts to establish varying amounts of adult control.

There are several definite costs associated with programs that attempt to deny this reality by implicitly or explicitly assuming too much responsibility for adolescents' behavior. First, such programs have the obvious disadvantage of reducing the adolescents' sense of competence and power. Second, when adolescents are aware that adults will take responsibility for their behavior by doing almost anything to assure their success, adolescents often become increasingly manipulative. In essence what they are saying is, "If my success is so important to you and you want it so badly, then let's go about achieving it on my terms." This situation is analogous to one that often occurs with young teachers whose need to be liked by adolescents is so strong that they cannot establish reasonable rules or give candid feedback for fear that they will not be liked. In this situation, adolescents frequently abuse privileges and show a considerable amount of disdain for the teacher. If counselors and teachers begin to believe that their competence is based on how well their clients or students change their behavior, they set themselves up to be manipulated. A third cost associated with taking too much responsibility for adolescents' behavior is that by doing so, adults foster a dependency that is the antithesis of the self-direction that they should support. While behavior-problem adolescents should be able to depend on adults to assist them in understanding their feelings and behaviors and developing new skills; they should not depend on adults to create an unreal world in which they are protected from examining and dealing with the consequences of their behavior.

A counselor once told me about a situation in which he was confronted by a student who stated unequivocally that he did not want to be in school. The student had been involved in a wide variety of acting-out behaviors and had on several occasions been suspended from school. The counselor had implemented numerous behavior-change programs in an attempt to alter the student's behavior. However, none of the interventions seemed to have any lasting effect on the student's behavior. Finally, frustrated by the student's apparent desire to behave unproductively, the counselor informed the student that if he really did not want to be in school all he had to do was walk into the main office and set fire to the wastebasket. The counselor handed the student some matches and informed him that it was time that he made up his mind. The counselor then informed the student that if he decided he wanted to stay in school, the counselor would be glad to assist him in reaching his goal. With this statement the counselor left the student. The counselor reported that the student came to see him the next day and that from that point on the student's behavior showed a rapid and marked improvement.

While the counselor's behavior was certainly both unusual and risky, it does illustrate the fact that adolescents do possess the power to fail, and that behavior-change programs must therefore include a commitment on their part. The following two case studies indicate how giving students the right to fail can function as a valuable intervention with a wide range of problem youngsters.

Example Number One

An excellent example of the positive results that can be obtained by placing responsibility clearly upon the adolescent involved a sixteen-year-old boy who was enrolled in a reading laboratory in an urban high school. The boy's teacher was a concerned, bright, intense woman who worked extremely well with students who were experiencing difficulties within the school environment. In this particular case, however, the teacher was becoming increasingly concerned and frustrated by the student's unwillingness to do a minimal amount of the required work. While the student always came to class and his behavior was not particularly disruptive, he would not become involved in the learning activities the teacher had outlined.

In describing her problem, the teacher indicated that she had employed a variety of tactics in order to motivate the student. She noted that she had confronted the student with his empty folder and his test results. She had asked him if he had any ideas concerning how he might want to work to improve his reading. When neither of these approaches appeared to have an impact, she had developed a series of behavior contracts that enabled the student to receive various privileges for completing designated amounts of work. The privileges available to the student had included assisting the teacher in grading tests, free time, and even a pass to leave the campus and go to a nearby store. Unfortunately, these contracts had been ineffective. Since the teacher had been working with the student for nearly three semesters, she decided that something had to be done.

Since the teacher had developed an excellent relationship with the student and had employed several well-conceptualized interventions, it was decided that it was time to place the responsibility on the student's shoulders. The teacher decided to again share her frustration and concern with the student and inform the student that he would be allowed to remain in the reading laboratory only upon the condition that he complete a designated amount of work each day. If he chose not to work, he would be asked to leave and would be allowed to return only when he had completed the work. The teacher checked her decision with the appropriate administrator; and it was decided that if the student decided not to work, he would be given a pass to a study hall. The decision was made not to closely monitor the student's attendance in study hall. It seemed possible that applying too much pressure at a time when the student might feel rejected might cause him to drop out of school. Since the program's goal was to increase his reading skill, it seemed inappropriate to employ an intervention that would have a high probability of removing him from the very environment in which he could obtain the assistance he needed.

The student appeared puzzled when confronted with the teacher's decision. The teacher effectively separated her feelings about the student from her response to his behavior. She indicated that while she liked him, she was not able to spend more time with him during class unless he decided that he wanted to improve his reading. She strongly encouraged him to stay in class and work. She wisely reduced some of the pressure by informing him that he would have a day to think about her statement.

The next day the student did not come to class. He was also absent the following two days. However, on the fourth day following their conference the student came early to class and informed the teacher that he would like to remain in the class. The teacher again discussed her expectations with the student and he agreed to her conditions. During the next semester the student was in class every day. Test results indicated that his reading skills had improved nearly two grade levels between January and June.

Example Number Two

This example involves a fifteen-year-old ninth grade boy who was referred for counseling because of his frequent violent outbursts that often resulted in fights with his peers. Despite the fact that teachers, counselors, and administrators had worked extensively with this boy, his behavior had shown little improvement during his first two years in junior high school. Initial intervention programs had consisted of assisting teachers in developing individualized academic programs that met the student's needs and providing the student with extensive positive social reinforcement when he behaved appropriately. This program was later supplemented with several behavior contracts that provided concrete reinforcement for appropriate behavior. In addition, the student's parents were asked to provide the student with positive interactions. More specifically, the parents were asked to provide the student with positive verbal reinforcement when they received notification that he behaved appropriately at school.

While these interventions did have a mild impact upon the student's behavior he nevertheless continued to be involved in numerous behaviors that were simply not acceptable within a school setting. For example, when he became upset at someone or something at school, he occasionally ran away from school or became involved in fights with other students. Based on the severity of these behaviors, the student's age, and the fact that a variety of positive interventions had failed to bring about the necessary changes, it was decided that the student would be informed that leaving the school grounds, verbally assaulting a teacher, or fighting with a peer would necessitate his parents picking him up and taking him home.

The program was presented to the student in a conference attended by the student, his parents, his school counselor, his homeroom teacher, and the school principal. The school personnel began the conference by expressing their positive reactions to the improvements the student had made. They then clearly described the behaviors that would necessitate a suspension. The student and his parents acknowledged that these behaviors could not be tolerated within a school environment. All parties then signed an agreement that outlined the procedures that would be followed. The parents were informed that their son's readmittance would occur only after a two-day suspension, and would require a conference attended by the student, his parents, the counselor, and the teacher involved. This intervention—frequently labeled "systematic school exclusion"—is an effective and realistic approach to placing the responsibility on the student. Since students can behave in a manner that requires that they be excluded from school, it is important that adults acknowledge their power while simultaneously dealing with the fact that school attendance is a privilege that can be revoked.

The systematic school exclusion program was associated with a rapid reduction in the student's extreme acting-out behavior. While the suspension was employed twice during the first month following the initial conference, it was not needed during the subsequent four months of school. In addition, results indicated that the student's behavior showed a significant reduction in intense acting-out behavior.

In both of the cases presented in this section, the school provided a good learning environment and employed a wide range of strategies aimed at assisting the student. However, in each case, the student failed to respond to these interventions. When this occurs, it is sometimes necessary for educators to accept their limitations and realize that they can assist adolescents only if they want to be assisted. Ultimately, the decision to change belongs to the individual.

ROLE PLAYING

Within the context of behavioral counseling, role playing usually involves assisting students or clients in practicing the behaviors they wish to develop. Role playing can also be used to introduce adolescents to alternative ways to cope with conflict situations. Finally role playing can be employed to assist adolescents in becoming more aware of their emotions and their own personal style of interaction. When accompanied by constructive interpretation and suggestions, role playing can be extremely effective in increasing self-awareness and instigating behavior change (Gittelman, 1965; Gray et al., 1974; Hosford, 1969; Varenhorst, 1969; Wagner, 1968).

In order for role playing to be effective, it must take place in a safe environment where individuals are reinforced for their attempts and are not ridiculed or punished when their new behaviors are less than perfect. Role playing is also most effective when it takes place in a setting similar to the setting in which the individual will apply the new behavior.

Before examining role playing more carefully, it may be helpful to briefly examine the reasons why role playing is such an effective behavioral counseling strategy when employed with adolescents. First, since role playing focuses on learning specific behaviors, it responds directly to adolescents' needs to experience a sense of competence and to establish a positive self-identity. A student who becomes extremely anxious whenever he attempts to talk to a teacher will feel more competent and positive about himself as he develops skills in approaching teachers. A second reason why role playing is effective is that it provides a concrete response to adolescents' concerns. Rather than providing an abstract understanding of a situation, role playing provides actual practice in skill development. Third, role playing provides adolescents with immediate reinforcement for their efforts. As indicated earlier in this chapter, adolescents frequently focus on the short-term payoffs associated with their behavior. Role playing responds to this limited time perspective and need for immediate payoffs by offering opportunities for adolescents to be immediately reinforced for their efforts. Fourth, role playing combines the kinesthetic, cognitive, and affective components of learning. Individuals not only make a cognitive decision concerning which new behavior to practice, but also experience the movement and the emotions that accompany the new behavior. This combination significantly enhances learning and increases the likelihood that the new behavior can be generalized to other settings.

Role Playing as a Desensitization Strategy

An incident reported to me a number of years ago provides an excellent example of role playing and the procedures that maximize its effectiveness. The situation took place in a graduate school that required a rigorous oral examination in conjunction with an extensive written examination. While a large percentage of the doctoral candidates passed their written examinations, a significant number of students subsequently failed their oral examination. After observing this pattern for several years, a concerned professor decided to develop a program to assist students who had difficulty performing effectively during oral examinations. Since students were provided a second opportunity to pass their oral examination, the professor worked both with students who were concerned about their initial examination and students who had already experienced failure.

Since the professor's field was behavior modification, he decided to assist the students by gradually desensitizing them to the examination setting. This was accomplished through a series of well-designed role playing situations. First, the professor scheduled the room in which all oral examinations were given. He then arranged to have the student meet in this room with a variety of his colleagues. During this first session, the student's colleagues were seated just as the professors would be seated during the oral examination. Furthermore, the topic of this first meeting was the problem the student faced in preparing for his oral examination.

The second session was more formal in that the student's colleagues were dressed quite formally and the topic centered around examination questions that might be included in the oral examination. During the third session, the students were joined by several sympathetic faculty members, and the student was asked to answer questions similar to those that would be included in the examination. This session was structured very much like the oral examination except that the professor who organized the program would occasionally stop the proceedings to provide the student with tips on how a certain response could have been handled more effectively. The fourth session was a dress rehearsal. Every aspect of the setting was as identical as possible to the one the student would confront during the examination. The mock oral committee was composed entirely of faculty members, and the professor who had organized the program was an inactive observer. Following this session the student and the professor had a conference in which they discussed the final simulation activity and made any final preparations for the real oral examination.

The results of this program were outstanding. Following the instigation of this program every student who passed the written examination and became involved in the desensitization program was able to pass his or her oral examination. As this example would suggest, role playing can be employed to assist students in improving such skills as test taking, answering questions within a class setting, responding appropriately to adult and peer criticism, as well as a variety of other emotionally laden situations.

Role Playing in a Group Setting: A Method for Teaching Social Skills

Behavior-problem adolescents often lack the prerequisite social skills for becoming involved in positive interactions with peers and adults. Since they frequently believe they cannot have positive interactions, behavior-problem adolescents often resort to negative responses. While these responses often elicit conflict and anger, they do provide some form of interaction. Furthermore, behavior-problem youngsters are often adept at manipulating this type of interaction. Thus negative responses provide adolescents with a very real sense of control over their environment since these responses bring predictable results; and these predictable results place the interaction within a context in which the adolescent is often quite skilled.

If adults are to assist behavior-problem adolescents in functioning effectively in society, it is imperative that adults provide them with opportunities to learn the skills necessary for developing positive relationships with adults and peers. Role playing within a group context is one method for assisting adolescents in developing these skills.

As outlined in Figure 11.7, there are eight important steps to follow when using role playing within a group setting. First, it is important that the participants perceive the environment as relatively safe and comfortable. Therefore, prior to employing role playing with a group of adolescents, the participants should have an opportunity to become acquainted and to discuss their mutual concerns. Second, it is important to discuss the goals connected with the role playing activities. If the students do not agree with the goals, it is unlikely that they will be willing to employ the skills that the role playing sessions are designed to develop. Third, counselors must carefully set the scene in which the role playing is to occur. For example, if the goal is to assist adolescents in developing ways to cope with student put-downs, they must discuss the types of put-downs, determine in which settings these most frequently occur, and discuss which students are involved. Once counselors have acquired this information they can develop a more realistic role play. For example, they might set the scene by saying: "Okay, let's assume that John is walking down the corridor by the main office, and Jim walks by him, looks at him in disgust, and says, 'fag'."

Once the adolescents have determined the behavior(s) to be practiced and the setting in which they occur, the next step is to discuss the importance of peers' not criticizing the participants. It is also helpful to note that those who actually practice the behavior will be the first to develop a new skill that will enable them to control their environment more effectively. Another extremely helpful strategy is *shadowing*. Prior to beginning the role playing activity, the participants are informed that should they become "stuck" and need some assistance, they can simply raise their hand and another student will take their place. For example, if a student is role playing a situation in which he is being criticized by a teacher, it is possible that the student will

Figure 11.7   Steps in Effective Group Role Playing

1. Create a safe, comfortable environment
2. Obtain consensus concerning the topics to be explored and the goals of the role playing
3. Set the scene
4. Discuss the importance of a supportive audience
5. Introduce the concept of shadowing
6. Ask for volunteers to play the various roles
7. Analyze the interchange
8. Establish a method for having participants practice the new behaviors outside of the group setting

become frustrated with his responses. Rather than becoming angry and increasingly frustrated, the student would be allowed to simply raise his hand and ask for assistance. At this point another student or the group leader could sit in for the student and continue the interaction. By providing the type of support and alternatives outlined above, the leader increases the clarity and safety associated with the role of the participant. This in turn increases students' willingness to participate and to take risks once they are involved in the role playing.

The final step in role playing involves analyzing the interchange. The least threatening and most effective approach is to begin by allowing the student involved to discuss how he felt and what he liked about his responses. This analysis can be followed by asking him to discuss what he might change about his responses. When the student has completed his analysis, the next step is to ask the other individuals involved in the role playing to tell the student which of his responses they found most productive. For example, if another student had played the role of a parent or teacher, they can provide the student with feedback concerning which responses they thought were most helpful in resolving the conflict. Next, the individuals involved in the role playing can be asked to tell the student which statements appeared to increase the tension or in some other way prevent a smooth problem resolution. Following this discussion, those who observed the role play should be asked to comment on what they thought were positive factors and which student responses they thought might need changing. Finally, it is valuable to have the adult facilitator summarize the learning that occurred or assist the group in developing such a summary. In addition, the facilitator should ask the individuals involved how they are feeling. This step is important in order to assure that the role play does not leave anyone feeling frustrated or hurt. If a role playing situation is associated with too many negative feelings, it is unlikely that the behaviors under consideration will be used in other settings.

There are several additional strategies that provide valuable support and reinforcement for role playing. One strategy involves giving students assignments that involve practicing the skills they have developed during role playing. Since role playing focuses on specific skill development, it seems only logical that students should be asked to practice these new skills in the "real world." If role playing has been based upon real situations in which adolescents are experiencing problems, it is important that the role playing be seen as a means whereby the adolescents can begin to cope more effectively in these situations. This connection with real situations can be facilitated by asking adolescents to try out new behaviors and report to the group. If the new behaviors enabled an individual to function more effectively, reporting to the group provides an opportunity to further reinforce the individual's efforts. In addition, it is quite possible that a positive report might provide the impetus needed for another student to employ the same behavior in a similar situation. If, on the other hand, the student's new response was not well received, reporting this to the group provides a format for examining the situation and perhaps developing an alternative approach.

A second strategy that can be effectively combined with role playing involves the use of video tapes. Video tapes provide the participants with an opportunity to review their responses and to examine possible alternatives to these responses. After a role playing activity has been completed, an effective technique is to view the video tape of the role playing and stop the tape immediately prior to a crucial response. The adolescent can then be asked what he thinks would be the best response and why he believes this. After he has answered this question, the tape can be advanced and he can view his initial response. He can then be asked to analyze this response and decide whether he would use it in the future.

Video tapes also provide adolescents with an opportunity to examine their nonverbal behavior. Since adolescents have few opportunities to observe themselves, they are usually unaware of how they look to other people. Behavior-problem adolescents are often surprised when they observe themselves on video tape. When viewing themselves on tape for the first time, I have heard students make comments about their clothing, their menacing facial expressions, a wide variety of mannerisms, and their body image. Since adults and peers are strongly influenced by such nonverbal cues, it is extremely valuable for adolescents themselves to become aware of these behaviors.

Role Playing with Individual Clients

In addition to its effectiveness in small group settings, role playing also provides an excellent counseling tool for working with individual adolescents. The high degree of safety that exists within an effective client-counselor relationship facilitates the risk taking often necessary for role playing highly personal interactions. In addition, this safety enhances the client's willingness to accept critical feedback.

Role playing is most effective as a therapeutic intervention when the client's problems revolve around difficulties in interpersonal interactions. For example, consider the case discussed earlier in this chapter in which a girl was unable to confront her boyfriend with her desire to reduce the intensity and frequency of their interactions. You may recall that the first step in therapy was to ask the girl to consider the short- and long-range payoffs and costs associated with this decision. When the girl had completed this task and analyzed the results, she decided that she did indeed want to change the relationship. However, as is often the case, the girl also stated that she did not know how to accomplish this. In order to assist the girl in developing specific skills for coping with her boyfriend, the therapist asked the girl to practice facing the conflict by having the therapist play the part of the boyfriend. Since clients can almost always vividly describe the responses they have difficulty coping with, it is usually easy for the counselor to obtain adequate information to accurately assume the role of protagonist.

As the role playing unfolded, the client became frustrated with her inability to remain firm in her decision. Therefore, the counselor employed a role reversal—a technique analogous to the shadowing approach discussed earlier. The counselor asked the girl if she could play the role of her boyfriend. Since she had experienced numerous frustrating interactions with him, she was obviously quite capable of assuming this role. The counselor then assumed the girl's role and modeled an effective approach for coping with the boyfriend's manipulative behavior. Following the role playing, the counselor asked the girl whether the approach she had just seen was one which she would feel comfortable using. When the girl responded affirmatively, the roles were again reversed and the girl practiced employing the new approach for confronting her boyfriend.

While it is frequently easy for clients to mimic the counselor's responses, it is obviously more difficult for the client to cope with the real situation. The ability to transfer learning can be enhanced considerably by the counselor's asking the client to consider every possible ploy the other party might use. In this context, it is often useful to ask the client, "What is the worst thing the other person could say or do?" or "What are you most afraid they might say?" The counselor can then help the client to develop strategies for dealing with the concerns that emerge from these questions.

Role playing can be used to assist adolescents in dealing with potentially conflictive situations such as informing their parents that they are pregnant, asking a teacher about a grade, asking for a date, asking a mother for permission to visit their real father, asking to borrow the family car, or informing peers that they do not want to use drugs or be involved in a delinquent act. It is important to realize that role playing is seldom sufficient when used as the sole intervention. Nevertheless, role playing provides a valuable tool for assisting adolescents in working through immediate problems that must be confronted before other issues can be explored.

SYSTEMATIC DESENSITIZATION

A chapter on behavioral counseling would be incomplete without a discussion of systematic desensitization. This behavioral counseling method is based on the assumption that fears or phobias are learned and can therefore be unlearned. The methodology associated with systematic desensitization was developed by Wolpe (1958, 1961, 1962, 1964) and expanded by Wolpe and Lazarus (1966). The technique is based on a three-step procedure. First, the client is taught how to relax using a relaxation method such as that developed by Jacobson (1938). Second, the client is asked to develop a hierarchical listing of related events that cause the anxiety being examined. Third, the client is asked to imagine these events while in a relaxed state. Since the anxiety normally associated with these images is in opposition to the relaxed state, the anxiety will be reduced.

Systematic desensitization has been used to reduce anxieties associated with such behaviors as test taking (Emery and Krumboltz, 1967), class participation (Word and Rozynko, 1974), and handling snakes (Ritter, 1968). When working with emotionally handicapped adolescents, this procedure can be helpful in assisting students in attending classes, speaking in class, taking tests, or making contacts with peers. The case study discussed next provides an example of a teacher using systematic desensitization to assist a high school student in approaching peers.

A Case Study

The client in this case was a sixteen-year-old boy who was enrolled in a school-based program for emotionally handicapped students. The student exhibited a high level of anxiety during any form of peer social interaction. Baseline data indicated that the student averaged only nine and one-half minutes of social contact with peers during a seven-hour school day.

Since several behaviorally based interventions had failed to significantly alter the student's behavior, the teacher decided to ask the student if he would be willing to become involved in a systematic desensitization program aimed at increasing time spent with peers. The student was very receptive to the idea. Therefore, it was determined that the teacher and student would meet for three thirty-minute sessions each week.

The first session focused on defining the dependent variable (social interaction) and clarifying the procedures that would be employed. Social interaction was defined as including four basic components: (1) talking to peers, (2) standing or sitting within three feet of peers, (3) having eye contact with peers, and (4) listening to peers during a class discussion or social interchange.

During the second session the student was asked to develop an anxiety hierarchy (Figure 11.8). The third session centered around examining the hierarchy and introducing the student to the Jacobson (1938) relaxation method. The procedure followed throughout the subsequent sessions was to induce a relaxed state employing the Jacobson method and to have the student visualize each step on the hierarchy while in this relaxed state. Whenever the student experienced any anxiety whatsoever, he was asked to signal the teacher and the teacher would revert to a lower item on the hierarchy. The teacher ended each session on the last item that the student had been able to visualize without experiencing anxiety.

The results presented by the teacher (Figure 11.9) indicate that this procedure was effective in increasing the amount of time the student was involved in peer interaction. While the results suggest that the amount of peer contact varied considerably from day to day, a portion of this variation can be explained by the fact that the student was dismissed from school early every Wednesday. While the student's level of peer interaction remained below the class average of nearly four hours, the improvement was significant. From an average of 9.3 minutes per day during baseline, the student's peer interactions increased to 28.5 minutes during the first week of intervention, 71.0 minutes a day during the second week, and 118.0 minutes a day during the third week. When reporting the data, the teacher indicated that the student began leaving the security of his desk and on several occasions even voluntarily answered the door.

These results suggest that systematic desensitization can be an effective strategy for

Figure 11.8   Anxiety Hierarchy

Most Comfortable
1. In room at house, listening to rock and roll
2. Leaving my room
3. Leaving my house
4. Talking back to a person I know
5. Talking back and looking at a person I know
6. Asking questions to person I know
7. Going downtown
8. Going to new place
9. Exploring new place
10. Taking the bus
11. Looking at new person
12. Being near new person
13. Looking and being near new person
14. Looking, listening to and being near new person
15. Talking back to new person
16. Talking back and looking at new person
17. Asking questions of a new person
18. Talking first to a new person

Least Comfortable

assisting adolescents in coping with a problem as complex as peer interactions. Consequently, this therapeutic intervention appears to have real potential for assisting adolescents in coping more effectively with a wide range of situations in which anxiety inhibits their responding productively.

RELAXATION TRAINING AS AN INTERVENTION STRATEGY

As indicated by the case just presented, systematic desensitization is a complex and rather time-consuming intervention. Furthermore, while the methodology can be employed by professionals without extensive training in these procedures, many professionals are hesitant to employ this therapeutic technique. Therefore, it is important to note that teachers and counselors can employ several interventions that, while less complex, use several of the basic concepts associated with systematic desensitization. One relatively simple intervention that often brings excellent results is to simply train adolescents in the use of deep muscle relaxation.

Behavior-problem adolescents often experience considerable anxiety and frequently have difficulty with impulse control. Since many of these youngsters have experienced

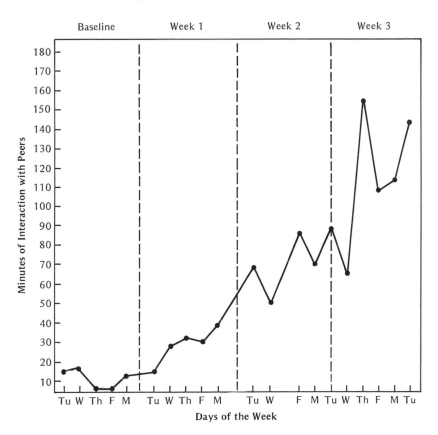

Figure 11.9 Results of a Systematic Desensitization Program with a Seventeen-Year-Old High School Student

frequent failure in a wide variety of settings, they often become anxious or hostile when confronted by what appear to others as minor difficulties or setbacks. For example, consider the student who has experienced considerable school failure. When confronted with a test situation, this student is likely to experience different feelings from the student who has a history of successful experiences. While the successful student may find a test situation positive and stimulating, a student with a history of school failure will very likely experience a sense of anxiety and may respond with anger or withdrawal.

Relaxation training can be employed to assist anxious students in controlling their anxiety and thereby becoming more able to cope with the demands placed upon them. Most students enjoy learning the Jacobson method of relaxation—learning to relax by alternately tensing and relaxing various muscle groups while focusing on the difference between feeling tense and relaxed. Once the students have learned how to obtain a relaxed state using this method, it is relatively easy to phase out the Jacobson method and replace it with less obvious and time-consuming techniques. For example, students can learn to focus on their breathing and to simply let go of their bodies. Another common substitute that creates a sense of relaxation is to envision a warm, soft flow of energy gradually moving through the body. As students develop skills in relaxing themselves, they can be encouraged to employ these techniques when confronted with anxiety-provoking stimuli. This process can be enhanced by offering the students relatively safe situations in which to practice this new skill. For example, if students spend a portion of their school day in a resource room or reading laboratory, they can be given tests in this situation and encouraged to use their skills in relaxation to reduce any anxieties which they may be experiencing. Similarly, relaxation can be coordinated with role playing by encouraging the students to focus on being relaxed as they work through a difficult encounter. When accompanied by specific skill development, relaxation training can significantly increase adolescents' ability to cope with academic tasks as well as with tasks involving interpersonal conflict situations.

CONTACT DESENSITIZATION

Contact desensitization refers to a therapeutic intervention in which the counselor accompanies the client as the client attempts new behaviors.

> While systematic desensitization procedures appear effective in greatly decreasing or eliminating anxiety reactions to imagined situations, the anxiety may appear when the individual is confronted with the phobic situation in real life. However, as Sherman (1973) has suggested, transfer may be accomplished if the individual is exposed to the real-life situation during treatment. (Blackham and Silberman, 1975, pp. 80-81)

As Ritter describes contact desensitization it consists of three major steps:

> 1. Modeling or demonstrating behaviors by the counselor which the counselee and counselor have mutually decided are relevant to the problem.
> 2. Assisting the client in repeating the behavior which has been modeled by using behavioral prompts such as placing the client's hands on the counselor's while the counselor touches a feared object or holding the client's arm while walking in a crowded area.
> 3. Gradual fading out of counselor prompts with a concomitant fading in of independent behavioral rehearsal by the client. (Krumboltz and Thoresen, 1969, pp. 168-169)

This definition can be expanded to include situations in which the counselor desensitizes the client by providing gradual, increased amounts of contact with the anxiety-provoking stimuli. While the counselor is initially present in these situations, it is not necessary that the counselor model the desired behavior or that the counselor have contact with the client.

An example of contact desensitization used with behavior-problem adolescents may help to clarify this intervention. During a recent visit to a school-based program for emotionally handicapped junior high school students, the program's director informed me that he quite often used a form of systematic contact desensitization as a method for reintegrating students into classrooms from which they had been withdrawn or introducing students into classes that they would be entering for the first time. As an example, he described the case of a seventh grade student who had been in a special education classroom during much of the school day, but whom the staff believed was ready to function effectively in a regular social studies class. Since one reason for the student's special placement had been the extreme anxiety he experienced in a regular classroom situation, it was understandable that the student was somewhat anxious about leaving the security of the special education classroom.

Employing a form of systematic contact desensitization, the director first asked the regular classroom teacher to visit the special classroom and work individually with students. Next, the teacher was asked to present a brief lesson in the special classroom. Following this, the special education teacher and the student visited the regular classroom during a period in which the class was empty. After this, the student and special education teacher met with the regular classroom teacher in the empty room and discussed such topics as the class structure, the types of assignments the student might be expected to complete, and whether the student would like to be called on in class. The next step was to have the new student meet with several of his future classmates to discuss the class. Next, the student observed several class sessions and discussed these observations with the program director. Finally, the student began attending the class. The director indicated that this approach had been quite successful in assisting his students in making the transition from an out-of-school or special education setting to a regular classroom situation. This approach can be employed when assisting adolescents in moving into any environment that they initially perceive as unknown and anxiety producing.

SUMMARY

Behavioral counseling can be a highly effective intervention when employed with behavior-problem adolescents. This counseling approach succeeds because behavioral counseling techniques respond effectively to a wide range of adolescent needs and developmental tasks. Through its focus on immediate situations and on specific behaviors, behavioral counseling provides adolescents with much needed structure. In addition, the specificity inherent in behavioral counseling meets the needs of adolescents who respond best to issues that are presented in concrete terms. The focus on problem solving found within most behavioral counseling models provides adolescents with a much needed sense of competence, power, and responsibility. This in turn creates a situation in which adolescents are much less likely to view adults' interventions as battles in which they must protect their integrity and defend their new sense of independence. Finally, by actively involving the adolescent in problem solving and skill development, behavioral counseling significantly increases the likelihood that the new behaviors will become a part of the adolescent's behavioral repertoire and will thereby be available for use in a variety of settings.

The behavioral counseling methods presented in this chapter have been successfully employed in a variety of settings and with adolescents experiencing a wide range of behavior problems. Nevertheless, each method will be most effective when molded to fit the individual needs and style of the professional involved.

Because the behavior contract . . . is definitive, inter-action among the parties is highly predictable, and each person is therefore encouraged to assume his responsibilities. The specificity of the terms makes people face up to "the games they play" and prevents the conscious use of defensive posturing, such as readily invoked excuses. Since the interaction among parties is clearly structured, a sense of security and safety appears to be an important by-product of the stratagem.

Garth Blackham and Adolph Silberman

Modification of Child and Adolescent Behavior

CHAPTER
12

The Use of Contracts with Adolescents

A behavior contract is an agreement between two or more parties that indicates the manner in which one or more of the parties will behave in a given situation. The primary difference between behavioral counseling and a behavior contract is that the latter is a specific, usually written agreement designating the exact behavior(s) that an individual will emit. Furthermore, as outlined later in this chapter, behavior contracts frequently indicate the specific reinforcement or punishment associated with perform-ing or failing to perform the behaviors listed within the contract. Therefore, behavior contracting is a more structured intervention than behavioral counseling. Behavioral counseling is used to assist adolescents in carefully examining their behavior and the consequences associated with this behavior. In addition, behavioral counseling focuses on developing new skills that can enable adolescents to perform new behaviors that they have decided will assist them in reaching desired ends. Behavior contracting, on the other hand, focuses on providing adolescents with a structure that will provide reinforcement for emitting behaviors that the adolescent is unable to emit without some external, concrete payoff or control.

While behavior contracting differs significantly from behavioral counseling, the two share many basic assumptions and are often combined to develop an effective intervention plan. Indeed, some form of behavior contract is often the result of an effective behavioral counseling intervention. For example, a student may decide that his plan for reaching a specific short-term goal is to work out a contract in which he receives a designated reward for maintaining his behavior at a certain level for a specified period of time. Similarly, once an adolescent has determined that the advantages associated with attempting a behavior outweigh the costs, he may develop a specific contract to reinforce the behavior. This contract may provide the structure necessary in order for the adolescent to function appropriately within what is at least initially a somewhat anxiety-provoking environment.

Contracting is also similar to behavioral counseling in that its effectiveness is dependent upon the degree to which it incorporates the basic concepts outlined in Chapter 9. Like behavioral counseling, a behavior contract will be most successful when it focuses on positive behavior, deals with specific behaviors, includes a sound data collection component, and involves the client in the behavior change process.

BASIC COMPONENTS OF A BEHAVIOR CONTRACT

Before moving to a discussion of when and how to employ behavior contracts, it seems appropriate to briefly discuss the major components that should be included in a behavior contract. An effective behavior contract includes an explicit statement concerning the following variables:

1. What is the contract's goal? Why has the contract been developed?
2. What specific behaviors must the adolescent perform in order to receive the rewards or incur the punishment?
3. What reinforcers or punishers will be employed?
4. What are the time dimensions?
5. Who will monitor the behavior and how will it be monitored?
6. How often and with whom will the contract be evaluated?

Behavior contracts may be written in a wide variety of shapes and forms. The form the contract takes is relatively unimportant as long as it includes the six components listed above and the adolescent can easily understand it. Figures 12.1 and 12.2 provide examples of two very different ways of writing a behavior contract. In order to facilitate a comparison, the same case is used in both examples.

It is not always necessary to develop a written contract. Verbal contracts are often appropriate when the contract is based on social and self-reinforcement. Since verbal agreements are a more common occurrence in everyday life, it is desirable to use such agreements whenever possible. However, written contracts are often both helpful and necessary when working with adolescents who are manipulative or have difficulty controlling their behavior.

While younger adolescents often enjoy and prefer a written contract, older adolescents frequently view written contracts as childish and unnecessary. When an adolescent balks at using a formal, written contract, it is best to accept the individual's evaluation and concur that indeed he probably can carry out his plan without the use of a written contract. A simple and inoffensive method for assuring that the contract is

Figure 12.1   Contract

This contract has been made in order to help Bill improve his classroom behavior. Bill has indicated that he finds it difficult to behave appropriately in his regular classes. Despite the fact that Bill understands the problem and realizes the costs associated with his behavior, he continues to have difficulty controlling his own behavior. Therefore, Bill has decided to use a contract for a short period of time in order to help him improve his behavior.

Bill has decided to try this contract for two weeks. During the first week Bill and Miss Carlson (his counselor) will meet each day at the end of sixth period to discuss the contract and Bill's behavior. During the second week Bill and Miss Carlson will meet at the end of sixth period on Monday, Wednesday, and Friday. At the end of this two-week period, Bill will decide if he needs to continue this contract, if he wishes to create a new contract, or if he can work effectively in class without a contract.

Appropriate Behaviors

Bill and his teachers have decided that Bill will:
1. Bring paper and pencil
2. Bring his book or other necessary material
3. Follow teachers' directions calmly
4. Respect other students by not disturbing them during class (Disturbing = talking to them, hitting them, making noise)

Data Collection

Bill and his teachers have decided that at the beginning of each class Bill will give his teachers a card which includes a space for checking whether Bill demonstrated each appropriate behavior. At the end of each class the teacher will place a check in the space beside those behaviors Bill has demonstrated and will return the card to Bill. Bill will bring the card to each conference with Miss Carlson.

Reinforcement

If Bill receives 75 percent of the possible checks during the first week, he will be given free reading time in the library during his reading class on Monday and Wednesday the following week. If Bill receives 90 percent of the possible checks during the second week, he will be given free reading time in the library during his reading class the following Monday. Finally, if Bill reaches his goal each week Miss Carlson will call his mother on Friday and inform her of Bill's success.

clearly understood and can be referred to at a later date is to inform the adolescent that it is necessary to make a note concerning the agreement so that neither party will forget the plan. This note can be shown to the adolescent before it is placed in his file.

TYPES OF BEHAVIOR CONTRACTS

Behavior contracts vary considerably and range from verbal agreements that are based on self-reinforcement and social reinforcement to written contracts that stress immediate, tangible reinforcement. While behavior contracts can be categorized in numerous ways, Figure 12.3 provides a list that summarizes the options available when

Figure 12.2   Intervention Plan

NAME:___Bill Smith_____ Age ___14___ Grade ___8___

DESIGNED BY: _Bill Smith & Miss Carlson_____ Date Started ___·_____

PROBLEM: _Bill has had difficulty behaving appropriately in his regular____

_class._____

BEHAVIORAL DEFINITION: _Bill has frequently arrived at class without the_

necessary materials. He has had some difficulty obeying teacher requests

without arguing. Finally, Bill and his teachers have indicated that Bill has

a tendency to talk to or hit other students during times when Bill should

_be listening or studying._____

BASELINE: _(Baseline period was ten school days) Percentage of classes___

_attended with paper, pencil, and other materials = 38%. Percentages of___

classes in which teachers indicated that Bill had failed to obey at least one

_request without arguing = 37%. Percentage of classes in which Bill's_____

_teachers indicated that he had disrupted class by talking to or hitting_____

_another student = 45%._____

GOAL: _During the first week Bill will attempt to receive a positive_____

response 75% of the time for each of the three problem areas. The second

week Bill will attempt to receive a positive rating 90% of the time in each

_of the three problem areas._____

INTERVENTION PLAN: _Bill and his teachers have decided that at the_____

_beginning of each class Bill will give his teachers a card which includes a__

_space for checking whether Bill demonstrated each appropriate behavior.__

_At the end of each class the teacher will place a check in the space beside__

those behaviors Bill has demonstrated and will return the card to Bill. Bill

_will bring the card to his conferences with Miss Carlson._____

writing a behavior contract. The list is based on the type of reinforcement or punishment employed. The list is arranged in hierarchical order beginning with the type of contract that provides adolescents with the greatest amount of self-control and employs the most natural reinforcement and ending with the type of contract that provides the maximum amount of external control and employs reinforcers that are not part of adolescents' normal daily interactions.

It is possible to argue for a different hierarchical arrangement of this list.

Figure 12.3 Behavior Contracts Listed According to the Degree of External Control

1. Social reinforcement + self reinforcement
2. Activity reinforcement + social reinforcement + self reinforcement
3. Token reinforcement + activity reinforcement + social reinforcement + self reinforcement
4. Activity restriction + social reinforcement + self reinforcement
5. Tangible reinforcement + social reinforcement + self reinforcement.
6. Token reinforcement + tangible reinforcement + social reinforcement + self reinforcement
7. Token reinforcement + activity or tangible reinforcement + response cost + social reinforcement + self reinforcement

Specifically, in light of earlier statements concerning the desirability of focusing on positive behaviors, it can be argued that activity curtailment (number 4 on the list) should be moved much further down the hierarchy—perhaps even to the bottom. The reason for placing this item in the fourth position is that it is a more natural, realistic, and less contrived consequence than tangible reinforcement. All people suffer this kind of consequence in their daily lives. For example, if people fail to clean the house in the morning before their guests arrive in the evening, they may well find themselves cleaning house in the afternoon when they had planned on watching the football game, taking a walk, or taking their family to the park.

Another item in Figure 12.3 that may require a brief explanation is the inclusion of self reinforcement in each category. It has been included because the eventual goal of any behavior-change program is to create a situation in which the individual will display the productive, desired behavior in a wide range of settings—including settings in which other individuals may not reinforce the productive behavior and may even reinforce competing behavior. While this is indeed an idealistic goal that not every adolescent will be able to reach, an effective intervention program must continually direct itself toward this goal. Perhaps the easiest method for continually working toward this goal (regardless of the level of reinforcement and type of structure currently needed) is to simply always ask adolescents to discuss their feelings about positive changes in their behavior. This discussion can be enhanced by asking them to examine the costs and payoffs associated with employing the new behaviors. Finally, counselors can ask them whether they would employ the new behaviors if they were not being reinforced by the terms of the contract or even by the reinforcement counselors provide during counseling sessions. These are extremely important questions that, if processed effectively, can significantly increase the extent to which behavior changes made during therapy will generalize across settings and will continue after the therapy has been terminated.

Before discussing the various types of behavior contracts, it is important to realize that, whenever possible, it is desirable to employ contracts found nearer the top of the list. There are several major reasons why it is best to use contracts that employ consequences directed toward self-management and lesser amounts of external control.

First, as emphasized throughout this book, it is important to maximize the degree to which adults' interactions provide adolescents with a sense of respect and responsibility. Adolescents have a strong need to be viewed as competent and able to control themselves. Therefore, counselors will often meet resistance when their initial attempts to develop behavior contracts are based on the assumption that adolescents require external controls in order to alter their behavior.

Second, whenever counselors write behavior contracts, their ultimate goal should be to assist adolescents in gaining control over their own behavior. No one writes a behavior contract with the assumption that the adolescent will need a contract for the rest of his life. The counselor's goal should always be to gradually reduce the amount of external control while increasing the degree to which adolescents can satisfactorily monitor their own behavior. Unfortunately, this fading process is often quite difficult. Anyone who has worked extensively with behavior-problem children or adolescents has seen numerous instances in which a youngster's behavior was positively altered through the use of behavior management, but returned to pretreatment levels when the behavior management program was terminated. Since it is often difficult to fade out a behavior contract that is based on extensive external reinforcement, it is desirable to, whenever possible, employ a contract that incorporates the most natural consequences.

A third and closely related rationale for employing the most natural consequences is that when counselors use contrived reinforcers such as special activities or tangible reinforcement, they may be creating a situation in which adolescents resent the process, but alter their behavior merely to obtain the desirable reinforcer. Adolescents' combination of abstract thinking skills and their concern for perceiving themselves as competent and respected individuals causes them to respond differently than elementary-age children. Since they are often more concerned about the process than the product, adolescents may alter their behavior in order to receive a reward while all the time resenting their position and reveling in the fact that they are simply taking advantage of the situation. This passive-aggressive behavior is neither healthy for the adolescent, nor does it bring about any real, long-term behavior changes.

During the second year that I directed a program for behavior-problem junior high school students, our program placed a heavy emphasis on individual behavior contracts. While the contracts were quite effective in reducing inappropriate behavior, we often experienced difficulty in weaning the students from their contracts. Fortunately, our students provided us with some very useful insight into the problem. One day during a group meeting several students informed us that they often resented the contracts and that the contracts did not change their attitudes about school. They stated that they "bought into" the contracts only because it was a good way to obtain reinforcers and manipulate the system. They further informed us that they found role playing and problem solving activities more helpful than contracts. Somewhat taken aback by this information, we defended ourselves by asking whether the contracts did not in fact help them in controlling behaviors when other methods had failed. While several students acknowledged that this was indeed true, they noted that contracts should perhaps be presented in this light rather than being presented as a means to a different end. As we examined the manner in which we had presented contracts to students, we became aware of the fact that we had seldom seriously discussed the contract's role in the long-term process of assisting students in reaching goals that they had developed. This incident was a major factor in my gradually beginning to emphasize self-awareness and behavioral counseling while viewing behavior contracts as a sometimes necessary outgrowth of behavioral counseling. Similarly, this discovery reinforced my belief that it is always desirable to begin an intervention by employing contracts that are least dependent upon artificial external controls.

Contracts that Employ Social Reinforcement and Self-Reinforcement

This form of behavior contract is often the natural outgrowth of behavioral counseling. After adolescents have examined their behavior and the consequences associated with this behavior, it is usually necessary to focus on developing some specific approaches that can assist them in changing certain behaviors. Informal behavior contracts can facilitate this process by providing adolescents with assignments that stipulate that they attempt specific tasks that will help to bring about the desired behavior change. When employing this type of contract, the adolescent agrees to employ a new behavior or involve himself in a new situation and to report the results of this attempt at the next meeting with the counselor. Glasser's counseling model described in Chapter 11 is an excellent example of a model that employs a contract of this type.

This type of behavior contract is employed most frequently with mildly acting-out youngsters who possess fairly good impulse control. An informal contract is also useful within a counseling relationship in which the counselor sees the client on a weekly or semi-weekly basis. Within this type of therapeutic relationship, informal behavior contracts are particularly useful with adolescents who have difficulty with reality testing or who manipulate the therapeutic interchange by constantly attempting to engage the therapist in irrelevant banter. This type of client often avoids threatening topics and interactions by utilizing inappropriate, off-task verbalizations to avoid productive therapeutic interchanges. Behavior contracts provide a concrete focus that can assist the client and therapist in staying on task.

One way to incorporate behavior contracts into a traditional fifty-minute counseling session is to simply divide the time into three equal segments. During the first segment the adolescent can be asked to focus on the results of the assignments from the previous session. The second segment is available for interpreting the results and assisting the adolescent in reinforcing himself and developing insights into his actions. The last segment is directed toward developing a new behavior contract, the results of which will begin the next session.

Contracts that Employ Activity Reinforcements

While it would be wonderful if all adolescents would respond positively to social reinforcement, behavior-problem adolescents are frequently unresponsive to social reinforcement either from adults or peers. Therefore, it is often necessary to employ activity reinforcers in order to assist adolescents in altering their behavior. This type of contract is frequently found in schools, residential treatment centers, and homes. Activity reinforcement is also the basis for most contracts with older adolescents who, as a rule, are less receptive to the use of tokens and tangible rewards.

This form of contract is most often established by informing adolescents that the privileges they receive will be contingent upon their following certain predetermined rules. In the case of school-based programs, this process usually involves developing a contract that indicates the behaviors a student must demonstrate in order to earn a desired activity. For example, the student and counselor may agree that the student will earn one period of free time whenever he attends every class on time for two days.

Within residential treatment centers this form of contract is often implemented by creating a series of levels, with each level including more privileges than the previous level. Adolescents are informed that if they obey the institution's rules for a designated period of time (frequently two weeks) they will be moved to the next highest level. Privileges associated with each level frequently include increased freedom to move about the grounds or leave the campus and opportunities to participate in field trips or special events.

Since adolescents are very sensitive about being treated fairly, it is important that this type of contract clearly specify how behavior will be monitored as well as when and how activity reinforcement will be dispensed. It is also helpful to include within the contract a statement indicating the type of behavior that must be displayed while the student is participating in the reinforcing activity.

Contracts that Combine Token and Activity Reinforcement

Despite the fact that they may want to earn the privilege of taking part in a particular activity, some behavior-problem adolescents find it impossible to alter their behavior in order to obtain a delayed reward. For adolescents who require immediate reinforcement, a token system can be incorporated into an activity reinforcement contract. This combination of token and activity reinforcement is often highly effective with behavior-problem adolescents (Borden, Hall, Dunlap, and Clark, 1970; Clark, Boyd, and Macrae, 1975; Liberman, Ferris, Salgado, and Salgado, 1975; Phillips, Phillips, Fixsen, and Wolf, 1971).

This type of contract is most often found as part of a school-based program for junior high or middle school students. The contract is often developed by asking a student's teachers to list the specific behaviors that the youngster needs to demonstrate if he is to function effectively in their classes. These behaviors are then discussed with the student and an agreement arrived at whereby the student receives certain privileges if his teachers indicate that he has demonstrated a prescribed percentage of the behaviors. In order to provide the student with immediate feedback and reinforcement, the student is asked to carry a "travel card" that lists the specific desired behaviors and provides a space for each teacher to check whether the student has satisfactorily performed each behavior (Figure 12.4). The teacher's checkmarks or signature provide the token reinforcement that is later traded in on preferred activities. This type of behavior contract is effective with young adolescents. It can be used as a

Figure 12.4   Travel Card

Student_____ Grade_____ Date_____

		Desired Behaviors				
Period	On Time to Class	Brought Necessary Materials	Handed in Assignment	Obeyed Class Rules	Participated in Class	Teacher's Signature
1						
2						
3						
4						
5						
6						
7						

method for integrating students into regular classes and is a useful tool for adolescents who live at a residential treatment facility but attend a public school. In the latter situation the results from the "travel card" may be connected with privileges or levels that students obtain in the residential setting.

Contracts that Employ Activity Curtailment

When working with behavior-problem adolescents, there are occasions when an adolescent simply will not or cannot alter his behavior in order to obtain a reinforcement offered by a behavior contract. There are two alternatives available for dealing with this situation. First, counselors can allow the adolescent to fail and receive the consquences associated with that failure. However, there are cases in which counselors may believe that the consequences would be harmful to the adolescent and they would prefer to do everything possible to prevent these consequences from occurring. For example, when counselors have worked to create a positive, supportive, learning environment for the adolescent, they would want to do everything possible to assist the adolescent in making a productive school adjustment, unless they believed that the adolescent would definitely benefit from being expelled from school.

The second option available to counselors is to provide an effective deterrent to the adolescent's actions. In order to do this they might present the adolescent with a behavior contract indicating that his freedom will be severely limited if he chooses to emit designated behaviors. For example, the contract might state that he will not be allowed to go out during the weekend if he continues to behave in specific inappropriate ways at school.

There are obviously several disadvantages to using this type of contract. First, since this type of contract suggests that adolescents cannot control their own behavior, it is almost always met with considerable resistance. Second, it is difficult to meaningfully involve the adolescent in developing this type of contract. Third, unless the contract is developed at a secure treatment facility, it is difficult to follow through on restrictions placed upon older adolescents. Even with younger adolescents, this type of contract includes a built-in power struggle. However, despite its limitations, this type of contract is sometimes necessary and effective, especially when employed with young adolescents. For adolescents who live in homes characterized by permissive or nonexistent parenting, such a contract may provide necessary limits. Furthermore, if the contract involves the parents in setting limits, it has potential for serving as an important step in altering the parent-adolescent relationship.

Contracts that Employ Tangible Reinforcement

There are instances in which adolescents will alter their behavior in order to obtain a tangible reinforcement, but will not do so in order to obtain some activity. While many parents and teachers dislike the idea of "bribing" children and adolescents with tangible rewards, this practice is certainly not unique. Indeed, many (if not most) adults would not go to work in the morning if it were not for the paycheck they anticipated receiving at the end of the month. While some adults find their job so rewarding that they would do it for free (if the money was not necessary for survival), these adults are perhaps analogous to the star pupils or athletes who enjoy school because it affords them numerous tangible as well as intangible reinforcements. However, learning disabled or behavior-problem students seldom view these reinforcements as attainable. Perhaps it is only right that educators provide these disenfranchised youngsters with tangible reinforcements at least until they begin to develop attitudes and skills that will enable them to receive some other form of short- and long-term payoffs for their efforts.

Despite the fact that there are justifications for employing tangible reinforcers, their use must be considered in light of the negative side effects that are sometimes associated with tangible reinforcers. Perhaps the most troublesome side effect is that it is often difficult to wean adolescents from programs based on tangible reinforcers. When counselors employ activity reinforcers, it is relatively easy to gradually fade these reinforcers into reinforcements that the school or other setting provides adolescents who behave appropriately. Tangible reinforcers are another matter. Adolescents view the transition from tangible to more natural activity reinforcers as a major step, and it is sometimes difficult to convince them to make this step. Anyone who has employed tangible reinforcers with adolescents has undoubtedly heard a statement such as "Why should I do all this work just for that when I've been getting more for doing less (or the same amount of) work?"

A second problem connected with tangible reinforcers is that they tend to set behavior-problem adolescents apart from their peers. Peers and adults tend to view tangible reinforcement as "bribery" and indicate that this method is not necessary for "normal" adolescents. School-based programs that employ strict token economy systems and tangible reinforcements often become viewed by students as "weird" and by staff as "coddling to childish needs." Associated with this phenomenon is the fact that adolescents themselves seem to internalize a negative self-evaluation when they become involved in programs that emphasize tangible reinforcers. This is particularly true of adolescents who are mildly behavior disordered and whose values are in many ways similar to their better behaved peers.

Given the problems connected with offering tangible reinforcements, this method should be employed only after more "natural" types of interventions have failed. Nevertheless, there will be occasions when a tangible reinforcement is needed in order to motivate an adolescent to become involved in an activity, enter an environment, or change a specific behavior.

Contracts that Combine Token and Tangible Reinforcement

This type of behavior contract is similar to those described earlier that combined token and activity reinforcement. The major difference is that this type of contract is most often found in programs for young adolescents who are operating at a developmental level considerably lower than their peers and with youngsters who have real difficulty with impulse control. The combination of immediate feedback and a tangible reward tends to meet these youngsters' needs for structure and a concrete world.

Contracts that Combine a Response Cost
and Activity or Tangible Reinforcements

One problem that frequently arises when employing any form of behavior contract with adolescents is that adolescents become skilled at manipulating contracts. Adolescents learn how to behave appropriately just often enough to obtain the desired reinforcements while at the same time maintaining the right to misbehave without being adversely affected by the terms of the contract. When this type of manipulative behavior becomes common, it is frequently effective to develop a behavior contract that employs a response cost. A response cost simply creates a situation in which the student not only earns privileges for behaving appropriately, but is also penalized for emitting designated inappropriate behaviors. For example, the adolescent may be allowed to earn two periods of free time by behaving appropriately for two days, but may lose these if he skips a class or talks back to a teacher.

The use of response cost has proved effective in working with adolescents displaying a wide range of behavior problems (Burchard and Barrera, 1972; Kaufman and O'Leary, 1972; Phillips, 1968). Since the use of response cost involves withdrawing something desirable, it obviously has possible negative side effects. Like anyone else, adolescents respond negatively and sometimes aggressively to the loss of a desired item or activity. Therefore, when using response cost procedures, it is important to keep in mind several concepts that will help to reduce the possible negative side effects. First, response cost procedures are most effective when associated with some form of token reinforcement. It is much less traumatic to lose points than to lose valued items or activities. Second, a response cost program should be organized so that adolescents cannot "go in the hole." If the adolescent is placed in a position of having to earn points in order to reach the starting point, the program becomes excessively negative and the adolescent will understandably withdraw or become aggressive. Third, it is best to provide some delay between the emission of the inappropriate behavior and assessment of the penalty. While this cooling-down period should not be so extensive as to make the behavior an historical event, a slight delay allows for a reduction in the emotional level. Fourth, as in any therapeutic intervention, the quality of the intervention is significantly influenced by the quality of the interpersonal relationships. Therefore, response costs will be more productive and more easily accepted by the adolescent when the adult-adolescent relationship is characterized by mutual trust and respect.

WHEN TO USE A CONTRACT

Having described what a behavior contract is and what factors should be considered in creating an effective contract, it is time to discuss the important issue of when to employ this therapeutic intervention.

It is important not to jump too quickly at the opportunity to develop a behavior contract. A behavior contract should be employed only after carefully examining several important factors and alternatives. Before developing a behavior contract, counselors should examine the environment in which they wish to change the adolescent's behavior in order to determine whether this environment can be altered so as to better meet the adolescent's needs. Perhaps even more important, counselors should ascertain whether the adolescent's needs will be met if he alters his behavior in the desired direction. It seems inappropriate and perhaps even unprofessional to employ behavior contracts to convince adolescents to attempt to function in environments that do not support their basic psychological and developmental needs. Furthermore, unless a classroom provides adolescents with a relatively safe environment, a reasonable chance to succeed, and an opportunity to be meaningfully involved in the learning process, it will not be long before feelings of failure overcome any behavior changes counselors have helped to bring about.

Prior to developing behavior contracts, counselors should also employ a wide range of counseling interventions that actively involve adolescents in taking responsibility for their own behavior. Initial attempts at assisting adolescents should incorporate behavioral counseling strategies that assist youngsters in understanding their behavior and developing alternative approaches for interacting with their environment. Frequently, the increased understanding of their environment and behavior and the self-initiated structure provided through behavioral counseling will provide the necessary assistance in helping adolescents to make significant changes in their behavior.

Behavior contracts place an emphasis on external structure and consequently run counter to adolescents' need to develop a sense of independence and an internal locus of control. Counselors should provide adolescents with every possible option that enables them to control their own behavior with the least amount of external control. By doing so adults communicate high expectations and indicate their respect for the adolescent, and, in addition assist adolescents in developing skills that are more readily generalized to other settings. Adults will not always be available to assist the adolescent in writing a behavior contract. Therefore, counselors should assist adolescents in developing behavior contracts only after all other approaches for assisting them in altering their behavior have been exhausted.

As suggested earlier, behavior contracts are often useful and necessary therapeutic tools when working with impulsive, manipulative adolescents who lack an internal locus of control. By providing a structured, externally based form of behavior control, behavior contracting meets these adolescents' need for structuring an often confusing and uncontrollable environment. In addition, behavior contracting is an effective intervention with adolescents who are functioning at lower levels of moral and cognitive development. Since behavior contracting provides concrete, immediate rewards and punishment and fosters dependency, it is understandably most effective with younger adolescents and adolescents who are functioning at lower levels of development.

Regardless of the type of adolescent with whom counselors are involved, situations do arise in which the use of effective communication, environmental changes, and behavioral counseling do not bring about the necessary behavior changes. There appear to be four general types of situations in which behavior contracting is an effective final step.

1. When counselors wish to convince an individual to become involved in a setting that is conducive to his academic and/or emotional growth.
2. When counselors wish to assist an individual in responding more appropriately and effectively within an environment that is conducive to his academic and/or emotional growth.
3. When an individual wishes to make a productive behavior change, but seems unable to do so without the assistance of the structure provided by a contractual agreement.
4. When an individual needs definite limits in order to prevent him from continuing behaviors that are destructive to himself as well as others.

The remainder of this section will present specific examples of how behavior contracts can be employed to deal effectively with these four types of situations.

Encouraging Productive, High-Risk Behavior

Behavior contracts are sometimes necessary in order to entice an adolescent into what counselors believe to be a supportive, productive setting. For example, an adolescent who is extremely anxious about attending school may be encouraged to attend by receiving designated reinforcements for going to school and remaining in school for extended periods of time. Similarly, a contract might be employed to assist an adolescent in attending several meetings of a group that could potentially provide the adolescent with much needed peer modeling or support.

A Case Illustration   An example of how a behavior contract can be employed for this purpose can be seen by examining the case of Mark, a seventh grade boy, who was referred for counseling because of the extreme anxiety he experienced when attending school. Mark's school record showed a history of excessive, but not extreme, absenteeism. Test results indicated that Mark had slightly above average intelligence and scored only slightly below grade level in math and reading skills. However, Mark's family had experienced an extremely tumultuous period the summer before he entered seventh grade. Mark's parents had been divorced and Mark had witnessed a shooting in which his biological father wounded several family members. This incident, coupled with continual family upheaval and the normal anxiety associated with moving into a junior high school, had left Mark anxious and intimidated by the school experience. This anxiety was intensified by the fact that a combination of Mark's fear and a legitimate illness had caused him to miss a large portion of the first three months of school. As a result, Mark became rather isolated from his peers, and school therefore became an even more frightening place.

Prior to working directly with Mark, conferences were held with his teachers to determine whether their academic programs were organized so that appropriate work was available for Mark when he attended class. In addition, conferences and observations were employed to determine whether the classroom environments were positive and supportive. After working with teachers to assure that the environment was conducive to Mark's feeling safe and successful, Mark and his parents were contacted. Conferences with the parents indicated that they would not be resources in helping to improve their son's school attendance. Finally, counseling sessions with Mark indicated that his anxiety level, combined with the availability of his home and television set during school hours, made it unlikely that he would initiate any major change in his behavior.

Given this situation, it was decided that a behavior contract would be a necessary intervention tool. Since Mark would not list any activity as more reinforcing than being at home, it was decided that a tangible reinforcement would be used. The contract in Figure 12.5 was developed by Mark and his counselor. As the results in Figure 12.6 indicate, the contract was successful in enticing Mark to attend school. Furthermore, follow-up data indicated that Mark had begun to find the school environment reinforcing and safe enough to continue his improved attendance without the need for additional contracts.

Directing Adolescents toward More Appropriate Behaviors within a Positive Environment

A behavior contract is sometimes necessary in order to assist adolescents in responding appropriately in a positive environment. This situation often occurs within a school setting where a student is behaving inappropriately despite the fact that the academic material is specifically designed to meet the student's needs and the teachers and peers are providing the student with a supportive atmosphere. In such cases, it is possible that the student has experienced school failure for so long that it is difficult to respond positively within the school environment. A behavior contract can sometimes

Figure 12.5   Contract Developed with Mark

Overview/Goal

Mark has found it difficult to attend his classes. Although Mark says that he would like to do well in school, he often finds it easier and more comfortable to be at home watching television. This contract has been developed to help Mark attend all of his classes so that he can pass the seventh grade.

Conditions

If Mark arrives at school on time and does not cut a class for ten consecutive days (January 16-26), he will receive an official NBA basketball.

Data Collection

Mark will stop by the counseling office before leaving school each day. If Mark has not been listed on the day's absentee list for any class, he will mark this result on his chart.

Signed _____

Mark

_____

Counselor

Revision

Since Mark missed P.E. on the 26th because he could not get a bathing cap, he can earn the basketball if he does not miss a class through January 31.

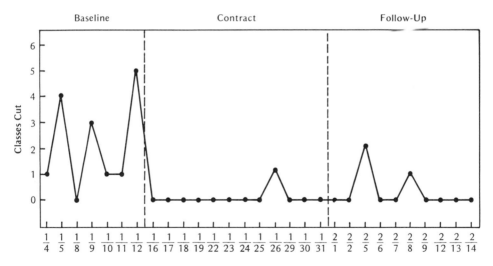

Figure 12.6   Results of Contract Shown in Figure 12.5

provide the impetus necessary for enabling the student to give the school setting a fair chance.

The most effective and common types of behavior contracts used for this purpose are those involving activity reinforcement or token and activity reinforcement. With younger adolescents a "travel card" is often used in order to provide immediate reinforcement. This can be gradually faded out by discontinuing the travel card and asking the teacher to record daily information (Figure 12.7) that is not shared with the student until the end of the week.

Another procedure, which is occasionally necessary and effective when working with younger adolescents, is the use of activity restriction. While other types of behavior contracts should be tried before employing this method, it can be very effective with younger adolescents whose behavior can be restricted. The effectiveness of this type of contract can be illustrated by the following case involving an acting-out seventh grade boy.

A Case Illustration   Jack was referred for counseling because he was in danger of being expelled from school. While Jack scored well above average in intelligence and at grade level in reading and math, his behavior was characterized by almost total defiance. Jack was frequently involved in fights with his peers, ignored or disobeyed teachers' requests, and was verbally disruptive in class. Jack responded poorly to behavior contracts that employed tangible or activity reinforcers. He consistently refused to carry a travel card; and on those occasions when he was convinced to carry a card, he destroyed it as soon as he received a poor mark.

Since Jack had already lost most privileges at school and appeared uninterested in obtaining any school-based activities, it was decided that his home privileges would become the focus of an activity restriction contract. Despite the fact that his parents' extremely lax discipline was perhaps a major cause of Jack's problems, his parents agreed to cooperate with the school. It is quite possible their cooperation was at least partially based upon their belief that the task of restricting Jack on weekends if he

Figure 12.7   Weekly Student Evaluation Form

NAME: DATE:

Day of the Week	On Time To Class	Have Materials	Hand in Assignments	On Task	Cooperative	Teacher's Initials
Monday	Yes No	Yes No	Yes No	Yes No	Yes No	
Tuesday	Yes No	Yes No	Yes No	Yes No	Yes No	
Wednesday	Yes No	Yes No	Yes No	Yes No	Yes No	
Thursday	Yes No	Yes No	Yes No	Yes No	Yes No	
Friday	Yes No	Yes No	Yes No	Yes No	Yes No	

Comments:

misbehaved in school did not appear as formidable as having him at home for an extended period following a school expulsion. When the parents indicated that they were willing to restrict Jack's weekend activities, a behavior contract was instigated. As seen in Figure 12.8, the contract centered around Jack's losing valued privileges at home whenever he emitted designated inappropriate behaviors at school.

As indicated in Figure 12.9, the contract was successful in significantly reducing

Figure 12.8 Activity Restriction Contract[1]

Overview/Goal

Jack is having serious problems in school. His behavior is so disruptive that the school staff and administration are unwilling to allow him to remain in school unless he can change his behavior. Jack has refused to carry a travel card and will not change his behavior on his own or in order to receive privileges or a reward. Therefore, the following contract has been developed in order to keep Jack in school so that he will not have to repeat the seventh grade.

Conditions

If Jack has a discipline problem in school, his teachers will contact his counselor and his counselor will call his parents. A discipline problem includes:

1. refusing to obey a teacher
2. talking out in class
3. fighting
4. skipping class
5. swearing

The first call home each week regarding a discipline problem will mean that Jack will be grounded for that Friday night. This means that his mother will pick him up from school and he will go directly home and not leave the house until 8 o'clock Saturday morning.

If Jack has a second discipline problem during the week, he will be grounded all day Saturday except for attending his hockey game.

If Jack has a third discipline problem in one week, he will be grounded on Sunday.

If Jack has a fourth discipline problem in one week, he will not be allowed to take part in his Saturday hockey game.

If Jack has a fifth discipline problem during any week, he will not be allowed to watch television all weekend.

If Jack has a sixth discipline problem during any week, he will be suspended for two days and will be grounded until he returns to school.

Signed		
Jack		School Psychologist
Mr. R.		School Counselor
Mrs. R.		School Administrator

Revision (12/11)

Jack has made excellent progress in changing his behavior. In order to reinforce this progress, it has been agreed that after Jack goes two consecutive weeks with one or no discipline problems, the contract will be changed so that the first call home causes a Sunday grounding rather than a Friday night grounding.

[1] Figures 12.8, 12.9, 12.12, and 12.13 are reprinted from Jones, V. Junior High School Program for Emotionally Disturbed Children. In J. McDonnel, H. Fredericks, V. Baldwin, W. Moore (Eds.), *Impact 7 of the Title VI Programs in Oregon, September, 1972-August 1973*. Monmouth, Oregon: Teaching Research, 1973.

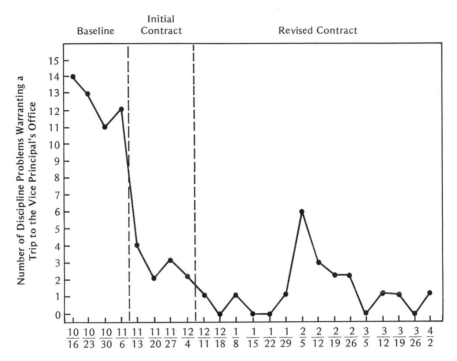

Figure 12.9 Results of Contract Shown in Figure 12.8

Jack's disruptive behavior. The only major problem arose when Jack's parents failed to follow through by grounding him on Sunday following a discipline call during the week of February 5. The following week Jack had six discipline problems by Wednesday and was suspended for the remainder of the week. Fortunately, Jack's behavior convinced his parents of the importance of following through on the restrictions and they restricted him for four consecutive days. This helped to bring about a noticeable improvement in Jack's behavior; and after three weeks, his behavior improved to the level it had reached prior to the parents' neglect.

Helping Adolescents in Meeting Their Stated Goals

A third situation in which behavior contracts are sometimes necessary and effective occurs when adolescents want to change a behavior, but seem unable to do so. While adolescents experience a strong desire to control their own behavior, they sometimes find that the importance of peer pressure and their response to immediate payoffs at the expense of long-term gains creates a situation in which they require an external structure in order to assist them in reaching a desired goal.

A Case Illustration   An example of such a situation occurred several years ago when I was working with an eighth grade student who desperately wanted to remain at a particular junior high school despite the fact that his home was located within the school boundaries of another school within the district. The student had several good reasons for wanting to remain at his school. He had previously experienced difficulty making friends and felt that he had made some good friends at the school he was presently attending. Perhaps even more important, however, was the fact that both he and his older brother had made numerous enemies at the school to which he would be transferred. Furthermore, the new school was located very close to the high school that his older brother attended. Since his older brother had a knack for making enemies, the boy was justifiably concerned that he might be physically harrassed if he transferred to the new school.

The problem arose because the student was frequently late to his classes and was also involved in a rather large number of discipline problems that were serious enough to warrant a trip to the vice principal's office. Due to the consistency and severity of his behavior, the student's teachers were unwilling to allow him to remain at the school unless he showed a rapid and marked reduction in his disruptive behaviors. Unfortunately, the student seemed unable to alter his behavior despite the fact that he was clearly aware of the school's intentions and had articulately outlined the payoffs and costs associated with his behavior.

In an attempt to solve this problem, the student was assisted in developing the contract shown in Figure 12.10. This contract provided the student with much needed

Figure 12.10 Contract

Pat has indicated that he wishes to remain in attendance at L _____ Junior High School despite the fact that his family lives outside of the school boundaries. Since Pat has been frequently late to class and has been involved in a large number of discipline problems, the school staff has indicated that Pat must change his behavior if he is to remain at L _____ Junior High School. Despite being aware of this situation, Pat has not been able to improve his behavior enough so that he will be allowed to remain at L _____ Junior High School. Therefore, this contract has been developed as a final attempt to help Pat reach his goal of staying at L _____ Junior High School.

Conditions

In order to remain at L _____ Junior High School, Pat must meet the following conditions.

1. Pat will be allowed one excused absence per month without a doctor's excuse. This is not cumulative. If Pat is absent without a doctor's excuse more than once during any month, he will be transferred to B _____ Junior High School. An absence is defined as a teacher indicating that Pat was not in class for an entire period.

2. Pat will be allowed one tardiness per month without a teacher's signed excuse. If Pat is tardy without an excuse signed by a teacher more than once during any month, he will be transferred to B _____ Junior High School. A tardiness is defined as any time that Pat's name appears on a teacher's tardy list sent to the office.

3. Pat will be allowed one disciplinary action per month. A disciplinary action is defined as any time a teacher refers Pat to the Vice Principal for a discipline problem. If Pat has more than one discipline problem during any month, he will be transferred to B _____ Junior High School.

Signed _____   _____
            Pat   Counselor

_____   _____
            Mrs. S.   Administrator

assistance in altering a behavior that he was strongly committed to changing. At the same time, the contract satisfied the teachers' and administrations' need for a definitive statement concerning the conditions under which the student would be allowed to remain at the school. While not all behavior contracts that employ a punishment are as effective as the one described here, the results shown in Figure 12.11 indicate that this contract enabled the student to meet his goal.

A Second Case Illustration   Another common situation in which adolescents want to control their behavior, but find it difficult to do so concerns the completion of school assignments. Even when the work is appropriate for their skill level, behavior-problem students often experience difficulty controlling their own behavior in the area of completing assigned work. While behavioral counseling may prove effective for students with a fairly high level of impulse control, students frequently find that a behavior contract is necessary in order to assist them in developing study habits.

An example of such a situation occurred with an eighth grade girl. The girl was receiving very poor grades and was constantly involved in conflict with her teachers and parents over the fact that she completed almost no assigned work. In addition, the girl's classroom behavior was characterized by her frequent off-task conversations with friends. During counseling sessions, the girl expressed what appeared to be a sincere interest in improving her classroom behavior and increasing the number of assignments that she completed. She was able to clearly delineate the causes of her behavior, the costs and payoffs accompanying her behavior, and even several creative alternative approaches. In fact, the girl attempted to carry out a behavioral counseling program in which she reinforced herself with a half hour television program each time she completed an assignment at home during the evening. Unfortunately, the girl was unable to make any significant changes in her behavior. Therefore, it was decided to employ a behavior contract as a last ditch effort at increasing her grades and improving her classroom behavior.

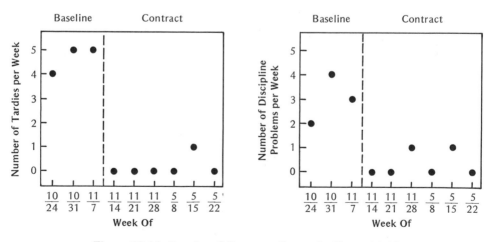

Figure 12.11 Results of Contract Shown in Figure 12.10

Figure 12.12 shows the contract that the student developed with adult assistance. The contract was restrictive in that a poor performance on her part was associated with a major, if not total, reduction of her Friday night free time. While the contract did not bring about a complete reduction in the number of assignments that remained uncompleted on Friday evening, the data in Figure 12.13 indicates that it did help to bring about noticable change. Furthermore, teachers' comments indicated that they noticed anywhere from a slight to a dramatic improvement in the student's classroom behavior.

An examination of Figure 12.13 suggests that the student apparently left unfinished an amount of work that she could complete by the time she wished to leave the house on Friday night. It is possible that the student continually left assignments unfinished in order to continue the contract and receive the attention connected with the contract. Unfortunately, the school year was over only five weeks after the contract began so it was not possible to develop a research design to determine whether the attention was a necessary reinforcer.

Terminating Behavior that Is Destructive to Self and Others

As previously mentioned, behavior contracts are frequently employed as a therapeutic intervention with adolescents who have limited impulse control. These adolescents are often involved in self-destructive behaviors that they are unable to alter in response to cognitive, relationship, or even behavioral counseling interventions. Severely delinquent adolescents frequently fall into this category. A significant number of these youngsters experience difficulty in establishing meaningful personal relationships with others and appear to have never resolved the basic issue of trusting others that Erikson (1968) states is the foundation of personality development. Consequently, these

Figure 12.12.   Contract for Increasing Assignments Completed Contract

Rationale/Goal

Sally has been having difficulty keeping up with her schoolwork. She is frequently behind in her assignments and often talks in class rather than using class time to complete assignments. Sally has tried several plans to improve this situation, but does not seem able to do so without somewhat more structure. Consequently, Sally met with her counselor, teachers, and parents and developed this contract. The goal of the contract is to eventually help Sally to turn in all of her assignments on time.

Conditions

1. After Sally's class on Friday each teacher will make a complete list of all assignments which are overdue. This list will include all worksheets and the names of books which will be needed to complete the assignments. The list and materials will be turned in to Miss M. no later than 3:00 p.m. every Friday.

2. Sally will meet with Miss M. at 3:00 p.m. on Friday to look over the assignments, ask for clarifications if needed, and discuss her behavior during the week.

3. Sally's father will pick up Sally's work and materials at 4:00 p.m. every Friday.

4. Sally will be home by 4:15 p.m. on Friday. She will stay in the house and will not be allowed to watch television until all of her assignments are completed and checked by her parents.

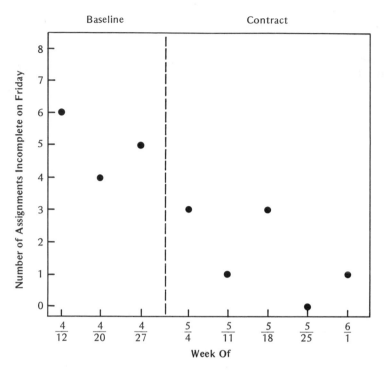

Figure 12.13 Results of Contract Shown in Figure 12.12

adolescents tend to function at a low level of moral development. To a large degree, their actions tend to be based upon the immediate, concrete payoffs and costs that are associated with their behavior.

When developing therapeutic interventions with such adolescents, it is often necessary to develop a contractual agreement that is firmly based on rewarding appropriate behavior and punishing inappropriate behavior. Unless counselors are able to develop a program that channels delinquent adolescents' behaviors in more acceptable directions, it is likely that these adolescents will behave in ways that are destructive to others while simultaneously increasing their own sense of self-depreciation and requiring that further limitations be placed upon their behavior. The remainder of this section describes a specific structured intervention that is highly effective within a school setting. This is followed by a brief note of caution concerning the use of behavior contracts as a method for altering adolescents' destructive behaviors.

Systematic School Exclusion While behavior contracts such as those presented elsewhere in this chapter will often prove effective in controlling disruptive behavior, systematic school exclusion is a logical and highly effective approach to reducing extremely disruptive behavior within a school setting. As described by Keirsey (1969) systematic school exclusion is based on the logical tenet that an abuse of freedom or privileges ultimately leads to a restriction of freedom or a removal of privileges.

Simply, this procedure involves removing the student from the school situation whenever he emits certain predetermined, unacceptable behaviors.

More specifically, the procedure involves a coordinated effort involving the student, his counselor, teacher(s), and parents, and a school administrator. In developing an effective systematic school exclusion program, each party is actively involved in reviewing the problem, acknowledging that previous interventions have failed, and agreeing to accept the fact that the student cannot remain in school when he is emitting certain specified behaviors. The final step involves all parties signing a written contract that clearly outlines the behaviors that will result in school exclusion as well as the role each party will play in responding to a situation in which the behavior is emitted.

There are several reasons why systematic school exclusion is a highly effective form of behavior contract. By clearly outlining the behaviors and consequences ahead of time, this procedure allows students to understand their environment. Consequently, students are much less likely to experience the anger, frustration, and unproductive projection that so often accompanies after-the-fact punishment and restrictions. Similarly, by describing the unacceptable behaviors in observable terms, students are able to clearly ascertain the rules of the game and are therefore given almost total responsibility for controlling their own behavior. A related advantage to this type of program is that it is inherently both logical and nonpunitive. While adolescents are highly critical of arbitrary adult authority, they seem to need and respect logical rules and limitations. If educators have provided the students with a sound and positive school experience, it is totally logical to temporarily exclude those who disrupt this experience. Finally, systematic school exclusion works because it indicates adults' concern for a student, his peers, and his teachers. The program is based on respect for individuals' rights. At the same time, the program provides the student with a sense of significance in that it actively involves a wide range of significant and powerful others in attempting to aid the student.

A Word of Caution   While therapeutic interventions with severely acting-out adolescents frequently require rigid structures, it is also extremely important to keep in mind that these young people almost uniformly suffer from serious personal/psychological deprivation. The fact that these youngsters have difficulty establishing meaningful personal relationships suggests that in order to have significant long-term effects, a treatment program must include a viable treatment component aimed at assisting these youngsters in developing personal skills and sensitivity that will enable them to interact with others in ways that will allow them to meet their personal needs.

Treatment or custodial programs that fail to provide skill development in the areas of personal awareness and interpersonal communication tend to have an extremely high recidivism rate. Because such programs focus almost exclusively on preventing destructive behaviors, they deal effectively with symptoms while almost totally ignoring causes. Consequently, when adolescents from these programs are returned to less restrictive environments they often remain unable to meet their psychological needs through socially acceptable channels. Thus it is not surprising when these youngsters quickly revert to unacceptable behaviors.

For example, while visiting a juvenile prison, I had a conversation with a young man who was nearing the end of his fourth sentence at the institution. When asked if he thought he could "make it on the outside" this time, the boy enthusiastically responded that this time would be different because he had learned a salable skill during his most recent incarceration. He continued by emphatically stating that the reason that he had previously failed in adjusting to society was that he had nothing to do and no way to make an honest living.

In listening to this seventeen-year-old boy, I was impressed with the importance of combining behavior control programs with program components aimed at developing useful skills. However, as I left the young man, I could not help wondering whether his treatment program had failed him in a very important way. While he had developed a skill that might enable him to earn a living, his counselor had indicated that he had serious problems relating to others. Since his treatment program had almost totally neglected this important issue, it seemed likely that although the youngster could meet some of his needs while at work, he would experience considerable loneliness and frustration when he was off work. When confronted with these feelings, it seemed quite possible that the young man would revert to the thrill-seeking or aggressive behaviors that had necessitated his previous imprisonments. The young man's treatment program could certainly not be evaluated as successful if it provided him with the skills needed to earn money and thereby terminate his need to steal cars, but he was readmitted on a rape charge because he could not cope with his personal/sexual needs.

When developing treatment programs for seriously disruptive adolescents, counselors must do more than control adolescents' inappropriate behaviors in hopes that they will subsequently choose to act in more socially acceptable ways. Instead, counselors must develop sound treatment components that attempt to develop skills and attitudes that allow adolescents to meet needs whose deprivation is a major cause of their destructive behavior.

GROUP CONTRACTS

While the majority of behavior contracts employed by teachers, counselors, and psychologists are individual contracts, there are occasions when a group contract can serve as a valuable behavior change tool.

Group contracts have several advantages that make them worth considering for application in schools or residential treatment facilities. First, since group contracts involve all members of a group, they do not single out individual group members. Most of the intervention techniques counselors employ, including academic individualization, individual behavior contracting, individual counseling, and placement in resource programs single students out in one way or another. Unfortunately, to a greater or lesser degree, this singling out process increases the extent to which students with behavior and/or academic problems are viewed by themselves and their peers as being different. By employing a group contract, counselors include everyone within a specific environment, thus indicating that everyone involved may benefit from some added structure.

Another obvious advantage to group contracts is that they can involve a much larger number of students. Most secondary teachers can think of classes in which, while one or two students stand out as extreme problems, many more students are experiencing varying degrees of academic or behavioral difficulty. A group contract allows the teacher to provide structure and assistance to students with less severe problems while at the same time assisting those who are having major problems.

A third advantage of employing group contracts is that this procedure takes advantage of peer group pressure. When employed in a generally positive and supportive environment, group contracts can provide an impetus for students to encourage and constructively criticize their colleagues. While it is obviously possible for the criticism to become destructive, this will almost never occur if the teacher or group leader is respected and has employed activities that have enabled the students to get to know one another.

Finally, group contracts have the potential for teaching teamwork and for establishing a positive group feeling. As Sherif (1958) demonstrated, working toward a goal can serve to enhance group cohesiveness and increase positive feelings toward group members. Group contracts provide adolescents with an opportunity to move away from their self-consciousness and focus on the behavior and rewards available to the group.

While there are a variety of benefits to employing group contracts, there are also several potential pitfalls associated with this intervention strategy. First, and perhaps most obvious is the fact that instead of encouraging peers who are having difficulty, group members may ridicule or berate a member who is preventing the group from achieving its goal. Second, group contracts often require identical behavior from all group members. It is likely that some group members will find it difficult to reach a behavioral or academic goal that other members find relatively easy to obtain. This may create a situation in which one or several members are consistently placed in a position of preventing the group from receiving its reward. This situation can be prevented by arranging group contracts so that the receipt of a group reward is contingent upon each member satisfactorily completing an individualized contract. A third problem sometimes encountered when employing group contracts is that one or more members can decide to subvert the groups' chances of earning a reward. This situation is most likely to occur in groups whose membership changes frequently and in groups composed of angry, sociopathic youngsters.

Based on the fact that group contracts do have some limitations, it is useful to briefly examine the conditions under which this type of intervention will be most successful. First, group contracts are most effective when working with groups in which the membership will remain relatively consistent. When this situation exists, it is much more likely that group members will become interested in working toward a group goal and attempting to support peers in altering their behavior in the desired direction. As discussed in detail in Chapter 5, this process can be facilitated by involving adolescents in activities that assist them in becoming better acquainted with their peers and teach and reinforce skills in positive, supportive group dynamics. As already suggested, group contracts are also more easily employed when group members possess similar abilities in the target behaviors. This situation supports the use of either a single group contract or at least the creation of individual contracts that are not so diverse as to cause confusion or resentment. Finally, group contracts are most effective within groups that do not include one or more members whose behavior problems center around aggression toward or subversion of others' needs, wants, or values. For these individuals a group contract often provides a convenient forum for them to act out their pathology. Nevertheless, a group contract can potentially be extremely therapeutic for this type of individual if the remainder of the group is tolerant and supportive.

Contracts that Require All Members to Perform Satisfactorily in Order to Obtain a Group Reward

This type of group contract is often employed on an informal basis such as when a teacher informs a class that they will be given five minutes of free time at the end of class if everyone behaves appropriately during the class period. A more structured version of this type of contract was presented in Chapter Ten. In this situation the class decided to collect data on their own behavior in order to bring about a reduction in the amount of time it took the class to settle down at the beginning of each period.

A more formal procedure for reinforcing on-task behavior involves providing a group reinforcement contingent upon the entire group's being on-task for a designated percentage of the class period. A method for implementing such a procedure has been developed by Greenwood, Hops, Pelquadri, and Walker (1974). The program, entitled PASS (Program for Academic Survival Skills) is aimed at assisting students in learning and demonstrating specific skills that are necessary for academic success.

In its simplest form, the PASS Program involves the following components: (1) a list of class rules (survival skills); (2) a daily charting of the percentage of time these rules are being followed by all class members; (3) a group reward for improvement; and (4) gradual removal of the major program components such as the visible timing device.

While the PASS Program was initially designed for use with elementary school children, it has been successfully employed with young adolescents. The program provides structure by involving the class in developing class rules stated in terms of observable, measurable behaviors. The class is then informed that they will receive a group activity reinforcement if they can improve the percentage of time during which all members of the class are obeying all of the rules. The students receive feedback concerning their on-task behavior by means of a clock operated by the teacher that shows a green light whenever the entire class is on-task and the clock is recording. A red light indicates that the clock has stopped because at least one student is violating one of the rules. As the class begins to consistently follow the rules more than 80 percent of the time, the frequency of reinforcement is systematically reduced and the clock light is replaced by a stopwatch. Eventually the reinforcement becomes entirely verbal with the exception of periodic maintenance checks and occasional activity reinforcers associated with a particularly positive check. Figures 12.14 and 12.15 present the results obtained from employing this group contract procedure in two different seventh grade language arts and social studies classes. As the data indicate, the instigation of the program caused immediate and dramatic behavior change in one class, while the other class showed much more gradual improvement.

In addition to providing students with a structured behavior contract, this program has the additional advantages of assisting teachers in clarifying their classroom rules and increasing their positive verbal statements. Since the pairing of verbal praise with on-task behavior is an important program component, teachers find that their positive/negative verbal ratio is significantly increased and that the classroom atmosphere becomes much more positive. This type of group contract also has the advantage of pointing out the need for all students to improve their on-task behavior. Therefore, the behavior-problem student is not singled out and merely becomes part of a cooperative effort to improve the group's behavior.

Contracts that Provide Uniform Criteria
for Reinforcing Individual Behavior

Contingency management programs developed on a group-wide basis are another form of group contract. This type of contract is established by either the teacher or the group determining specific behaviors that will be reinforced by providing students with designated activity reinforcers. In most cases the procedure involves assigning a designated number of points to a variety of desired behaviors. Students earn points by emitting the desired behaviors and points can be traded in for activity reinforcers. While this type of behavior contract does emphasize reinforcing individual performance, it can be categorized under group contracts because all group members operate under the same contract and the contract's content is often developed by the group.

This type of behavior contract has been used successfully in school settings with disadvantaged adolescents (Sapp, 1971) and with suburban high school students (Arwood, Williams, and Long, 1974). Arwood et al. (1974) compared the use of contracts developed by the teacher (proclamation) with those developed by the group. Their results indicated that group designed contracts were not only more effective in increasing student on-task behavior, but were also associated with significantly greater academic gains than were found with proclamations.

SUMMARY

Although contracts should not be employed unless other forms of behavioral counseling have proved unsuccessful, they can prove to be valuable tools in assisting adolescents in altering their behavior. Since behavior contracts provide considerable structure, they are generally more effective with younger or less mature adolescents, adolescents who have not developed an internal locus of control, and adolescents who do not respond to social reinforcement.

Behavior contracts may vary considerably in the type of reinforcement provided for

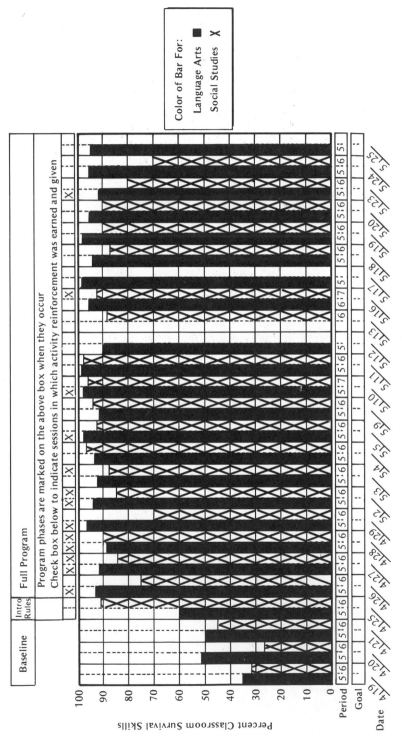

Figure 12.14 Results of Implementing the PASS Program in a Seventh Grade Language Arts/Social Studies Class
Used by permission of Hill M. Walker.

256

Figure 12.14 *Continued*

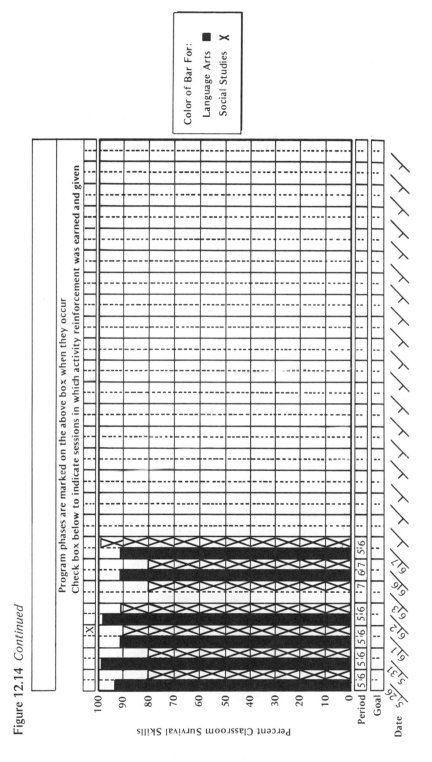

Teacher's Bar Graph for Classroom Survival Skills

257

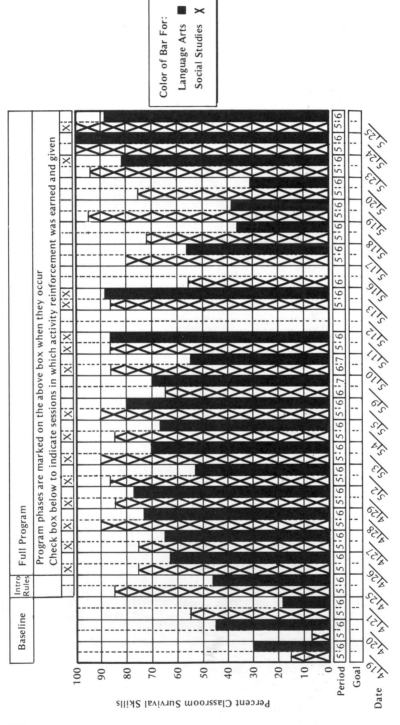

Figure 12.15 Results of Implementing the PASS Program in a Seventh Grade Language Arts/Social Studies Class

Teacher's Bar Graph for Classroom Survival Skills.

Used by permission of Hill M. Walker.

258

Figure 12.15 *Continued*

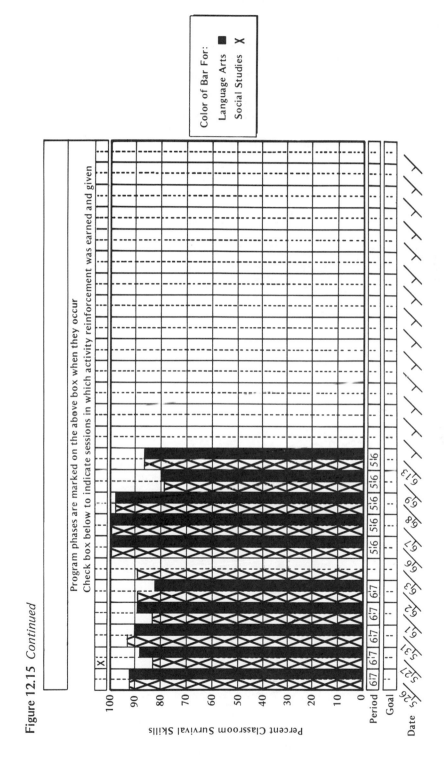

Teacher's Bar Graph for Classroom Survival Skills

259

appropriate behavior. When developing a behavior contract, it is important to begin by employing a contract that does not place unnecessary emphasis on contrived external reinforcers. Finally, while they may serve a variety of purposes, behavior contracts are most often employed as a method for motivating individuals to attempt new behaviors that have a high potential for creating a positive experience.

Working with Parents of Behavior-Problem Adolescents

Regardless of the theoretical perspective used in describing the process of human growth and development, it is impossible to deny the important role the family plays in this process. While this fact is uniformly accepted when examining the behavior of young children, it is important to keep in mind that parents remain a major factor in the lives of adolescents.

> Nevertheless, an increasing body of empirical data indicates that the single most important external influence in aiding or hindering the average adolescent (particularly the younger one) in the accomplishment of the developmental tasks of adolescence—at least in today's relatively isolated nuclear family—is his or her parents . . . (Conger, 1977, p.221. Reprinted by permission of Harper & Row, Publishers, Inc.).

When examining parent-adolescent interactions, it is helpful to distinguish between the parent's role in dealing with younger as compared to older adolescents. During early adolescence a major parental role is that of providing a safe, warm, structured environment that provides the adolescent with opportunities to begin to explore new cognitive, social/sexual, and physical potentials. During early adolescence most parents see themselves as responsible for their child and still able to place necessary limits on their child's behaviors. Consequently, therapeutic interventions with families during this stage often focus on assisting parents in establishing and implementing reasonable rules and limitations and gradually increasing the adolescent's freedom to explore a wider range of behaviors.

As adolescents become older, the central theme of the parent-child relationship should move away from control and towards the issue of how to handle the impending emancipation. While providing behavior guidelines may remain an important concern, this should gradually become secondary to developing a pattern of interaction that will facilitate a smooth emancipation. At this stage it is important that both parents and adolescents begin to clarify their own needs and expectations and that these be clearly and nonpunitively communicated. Since authoritarian, power-oriented means of resolving conflicts become increasingly ineffective and tumultuous as adolescents become older, it becomes vital that parents learn to involve themselves in open, honest, polite two-way dialogue with their children.

In order to assist parents in coping with their difficult and changing role, it is necessary to understand the factors influencing their behavior. In addition, it is necessary that educators and counselors develop skills both in interacting with these parents and developing programs that assist them in improving their parenting skills. Chapter 13 focuses on the first issue by examining the concerns and feelings experienced by many parents of behavior-problem adolescents. Chapter 14 examines a variety of strategies that will assist teachers and counselors in interacting effectively with parents and working with parents to develop productive collaborative behavior change programs. Chapter 15 presents a model for developing an effective parent group for parents of young adolescents. Chapter 16 focuses on providing parents with skills that will assist them in interacting effectively with their adolescent during the often difficult transition from late adolescence to early adulthood.

A day comes in any parent's life when there is a sudden realization: "My child is a child no longer." This is a unique moment of elation and fear. . . . There is also conflict. As parents, our need is to be needed; as teenagers their need is not to need us.

Haim Ginott

Between Parent and Teenager

CHAPTER
13

Understanding the Parents' Perspective

When working with parents of behavior-problem adolescents, it is important to understand the factors that influence them as they attempt to cope with their child's behavior. This chapter will provide an overview of the major factors that influence these parents.

PARENTAL DEFENSIVENESS

It is important to realize that, with few exceptions, parents do care about their children and are concerned about their welfare. Children are an extension of their parents. Therefore, while they may often find themselves angry at, fearful of, or frustrated by their children's behavior, almost all parents believe that their children are basically good and should be treated fairly.

Because they care about their child, parents often have difficulty accepting the fact that their child is having serious behavior problems. This situation is intensified by the fact that parents realize that their child is, at least to some degree, a product of their parenting. Therefore, accepting that their child is having serious problems and is not like other children in some important ways, means considering the possibility that they have been somewhat ineffective as parents. In order to defend against the guilt and anxiety that may accompany this consideration, parents frequently either deny that their child has problems or place the blame on outside factors such as the school.

Rather than being defensive about attacks stemming from this projection, educators' early contacts with parents should take into account the importance of dispensing with the idea that anyone is to blame. This can be done by acknowledging that both the school and the parents have undoubtedly done things that were not maximally effective. Parents often express relief upon hearing that the school staff is aware that their current program may not be providing their child with the necessary assistance. By accepting some responsibility, school personnel can reduce the parents' defensiveness while at the same time opening the door to discussions concerning necessary academic and behavior interventions.

In working with parents of behavior-problem adolescents, it is helpful to realize that these parents have themselves often had unsuccessful and negative school experiences. In addition these parents have often had previous negative experiences with school personnel regarding their child's behavior. It is therefore understandable that their initial reaction to educators may be both defensive and critical. Educators can reduce this defensiveness by indicating their sincere concern for the child and demonstrating competence through a well-conceptualized program for the child. Most parents respond well to a blend of warmth and competence.

PARENTAL CONFUSION ABOUT ADOLESCENT NEEDS AND BEHAVIORS

Parents frequently express that they do not understand their adolescent son or daughter and that they are confused by their adolescent's behavior and demands. There are several factors that explain this lack of understanding. First, most parents have not studied human development. They are often almost totally unaware of the normal conflicts that arise during adolescence. Similarly, most parents have not studied how to parent and consequently are generally uninformed concerning the ways in which they can support their son or daughter in working through the normal developmental tasks of adolescence.

In addition to their lack of formal training, parents' confusion is often influenced by the exaggerated concept of the "generation gap." While adolescents' values and styles do differ from their parents' in various ways, the extent of these differences has been greatly exaggerated (Harris, 1971; Offer, Marcus, and Offer, 1970; Sorensen, 1973; Yankelovich, 1974). Unfortunately, because of these exaggerations, parents assume that a gap will exist between themselves and their adolescent children. The anxiety and confusion associated with this expectation often accentuates problems between parents and their adolescents. This self-fulfilling prophecy is an unfortunate result of the myth in western society that defines adolescence as a time of necessary conflict and upheaval in which conflict will necessarily be experienced as turmoil between adolescents and adults.

A final social factor that inhibits adults from understanding their adolescents is the degree of age segregation that exists. As the White House Conference on Children stated,

... Occupational mobility, child labor laws, the abolishment of the apprentice system, consolidated schools, television, separate patterns of social life for different age groups, the working mother, the delegation of child care to specialists—all these manifestations of progress operate to decrease opportunity and incentive for meaningful contact between children and persons older, or younger, than themselves (White House Conference on Children, 1971).

When combined with the concept of a generation gap, the paucity of cross-age contact has tended to create a situation in which parents expect adolescents to want to be left alone. Consequently, parents tend to have much less contact with their children after they reach puberty. The unfortunate result of this situation is a decrease in available adult models, dialogue, and understanding at the very time when these are most needed in order to provide the support and facilitate the problem solving so important to the healthy resolution of adolescent developmental tasks. Indeed, as suggested in an earlier chapter, adolescents' dependency on the peer group appears to be more a reaction to the lack of meaningful contact with adults than to the desirability of the peer group.

It is also important to recognize that when the peer group assumes an unusually dominant role in the lives of adolescents, often it is due as much, or more, to the lack of attention and concern at home as to the inherent attractiveness of the peer group.

Adolescents who were strongly peer-oriented were found to be more likely than those who were adult-oriented to hold negative views of themselves and the peer group (Conger, 1977, p. 331. Reprinted by permission of Harper & Row, Publishers, Inc.).

ADOLESCENTS' PARENTS ARE THEMSELVES EXPERIENCING A DIFFICULT STAGE OF LIFE

It has been suggested that one major cause of adolescent depression is that adolescents must give up a significant part of their childhood identity at a time when they have not yet developed a new identity (Josselyn, 1971). Interestingly, adolescents' parents find themselves in a somewhat similar dilemma. As adolescents begin to challenge their parents' authority and seek to develop a unique sense of self, parents find themselves faced with the loss of a major portion of their identity. As their children reach late adolescence, the parent's role as childrearing agent, dispenser of information and rules, and primary support system for their child begins to change rapidly. For many parents this suggests not only that they are less valuable, but also that they are less potent and are getting older. It is understandable that this loss of identity will often be associated with varying degrees of confusion, anxiety, depression, and an attempt to hang onto this identity by refusing to give up a parenting role that was more appropriate when their child was much younger.

In addition to their struggle over a changing parent role, parents with adolescent children are often coping with difficult career and marriage decisions. The average parent with adolescent children is slightly over forty years old. This is an age when many men and women begin to reevaluate their career decisions. Men and women begin to question the value of their work and women who have stayed home to raise a family are confronted with the decision concerning what they will do as their children leave home. These concerns are often further intensified by parents' awareness that they are, at least physically, on the downhill side of life. By age forty, people are certainly aware that the body does not respond or recover as rapidly or effectively as it did ten years earlier. This realization is further compounded by the youth-oriented nature of our Western society. These multiple concerns faced by many adults between the ages of forty and fifty are undoubtedly a major reason why marital unhappiness is high during these years.

Given the fact that many parents of adolescents are experiencing a number of difficult life issues, it is understandable that these parents sometimes find it difficult to respond calmly and therapeutically to a son or daughter who is also experiencing difficulty in coping with his/her environment. When working with families, educators must realize that parents also need support and understanding.

PARENTS FACE THE DIFFICULT TASK OF
ALTERING THEIR PARENTING STYLE

Parents are confronted with the difficulty of adjusting their parenting skills as their children grow older. Parent-child interactions must undergo constant change if parents are to respond sensitively to their children's changing developmental needs. Methods that seemed simple and effective with a ten-year-old are suddenly met with resistance and emotionality when applied to a fourteen-year-old. Regardless of whether parents employ a basically authoritarian, democratic, or permissive parenting style, they generally employ greater amounts of control when children are younger. However, while adolescents certainly need guidelines and limitations, they also need gradually increased amounts of responsibility. Therefore, as children grow older, parents must adjust to meet the child's increasing need and ability to experience greater self-control and responsibility. Perhaps even more confusing for parents is the fact that adolescents need to question adult authority and become involved in productive debate with adults. In many families, these new demands create major conflicts and require a major alteration in the way the parents interact with their children. Unfortunately, parents often respond to these new challenges by becoming increasingly authoritarian, and this response is often met with increased confrontation or withdrawal by the adolescent.

This situation is made even more difficult by the fact that in addition to employing new skills, parents must make major attitude changes. It is not easy to realize that the little girl who just four years ago was anxious about leaving home to attend outdoor school now wants permission to bicycle sixty miles to the coast with a group of friends.

In considering the difficulty and complexity of the task faced by parents, it is interesting to consider how effectively teachers or counselors would handle a comparable change in their roles. For example, how many teachers would find it comfortable to move from elementary school to high school or vice versa. Like teachers and therapists, parents develop a style with which they become comfortable and that becomes part of their self-definition. However, in order to effectively meet their children's developmental needs, parents must alter this style in significant ways as their children grow older. This task is further compounded by the amount of emotional investment between parents and their children. Therefore, it is not surprising that parents often have difficulty adjusting to the new demands associated with effectively parenting an adolescent.

LACK OF SUPPORT FOR NUCLEAR FAMILIES

The decline of the extended family and the movement away from small rural communities with their relatively greater sense of community involvement and support has compounded the difficulties associated with parenting.

> In short, it is not surprising that many of today's nuclear families are showing signs of stress. Frequently geographically transient and socially mobile; isolated from the extended family, lifelong acquaintances, and stable cultural traditions; living in urban "honeycombs" or almost equally impersonal and ephemeral suburban "bedroom communities"; often cut off from effective involvement in, and influence on, the social institutions that are playing an ever more dominant role in their lives and those of their children; many traditional functions emasculated, but legal and moral responsibilities undiminished: All these circumstances have clearly increased the difficulties of the adolescent period, both for parents and their adolescent children (Conger, 1977, p. 210. Reprinted by permission of Harper & Row, Publishers, Inc.).

Unfortunately, at the time that adolescents need support and guidance in coping with the stress of growing up in a fast-paced, changing society, parents too often feel unprepared for and alone in their attempt to provide this guidance.

Whenever I consider the difficulties facing the nuclear family, I am reminded of a story a friend once told me. We were discussing the advantages of a supportive community and my friend recalled an incident that occurred when he was a teenager growing up in a town of about 600 people. He reported having walked into the town's general store one Saturday morning and having the owner ask him if he would mind sitting down for a brief man-to-man chat. The owner reported that he had been driving home late the previous night and had noticed the young man's car parked alongside a small country road. He noted that he had not seen anyone in the car. However, since there was nothing but cornfields for several miles in all directions, he suspected that the young man and his girlfriend were in the car but were not sitting up. He proceeded to state that he was not trying to be nosey, but that he hoped the young man was aware of the possible outcomes of this behavior and the effect it could have on both youngsters' plans to attend college. My friend related that while he was initially somewhat upset at the shopkeeper for intruding, he also realized that the conversation was an indication of the man's concern. He went on to note that one advantage to living in a small town was that he always knew that people cared about him and his future and that this concern caused him to consider his behavior more carefully.

As I listened to his story, I could not help thinking that his parents must have been glad (and perhaps rather relieved) that someone else was willing to provide meaningful assistance in raising their son. People often fail to realize that, even without the responsibility of raising a family, adults face a variety of challenges in living in today's rapidly changing world. Therefore, perhaps more than ever before, it is important that society be structured in such a way as to provide parents with support in assisting their children to cope with the changes and decisions that accompany adolescence.

The question then becomes, which institutions should take responsibility for providing this support? Certainly most people would agree that the church should offer programs to assist adolescents in examining and responding productively to major concerns and decisions. However, at least at this point in time, the church reaches only a small percentage of young people and often fails to attract those youngsters who are most in need of assistance.

Given the importance of providing adolescents with support and assistance in the process of "coming of age" in a complex society, it seems logical that the schools should play a major role in this task. This seems especially true given the fact that community support for the family has declined while at the same time the church has diminished as a major factor monitoring social values and decisions. Unfortunately, the school's role has too often been viewed as that of providing basic factual, nonsocial/-emotional information. Perhaps it is time to acknowledge the fact that in order to function effectively in today's and tomorrow's world, adolescents will need skills in clarifying values, making decisions, and communicating with friends, colleagues, and employers. When faced with this argument, school personnel consistently note that the school is already confronted with an increasingly complex curriculum. While this is certainly a valid concern, it is quite likely that schools might find that students' motivation, readiness, and energy for more "academic" subjects would be significantly increased if they were provided with opportunities to deal with and develop skills in coping with their more emotional/personal tasks. Given the amount of time that adolescents spend in schools, it seems reasonable to assume that the school should, at least to a greater degree, attempt to provide the sense of "community" support that has been lost with the demise of the shopowner in the general store. Indeed, perhaps as young people are taught skills in effective communication and the utilization of available resources, they might begin to seek out community resources and thereby gradually rekindle the sense of community support that existed in small, intimate communities. Perhaps rather than attempt to solve adolescents' problems educators should assist them in developing tools they can use to create their own solutions.

SUMMARY

It is interesting to draw an analogy between parents of behavior-problem adolescents and teachers faced with the expectation that they integrate handicapped children into the regular classroom. Parents of behavior-problem adolescents can be compared to a teacher who has no formal training in working with these children, has few if any colleagues with whom she can discuss the problem, and yet has a strong emotional attachment to these children. If this were the first time that the teacher had worked with this type of child and if she defined teaching as a major role in her life, she would be dealing with issues and facing concerns similar to those faced by a large number of parents whose children are experiencing serious behavior problems.

Like the teacher just described, parents often experience a sense of isolation and find themselves not receiving help from the institutions that are attempting to assist their child. It is therefore not surprising that they strike out angrily both at their adolescent son or daughter and at social institutions. Educators must relate to parents in a manner that is not only sensitive to their needs, but also provides them with assistance in dealing with difficult situations during difficult times.

On the one hand, there is the need to expose parents and other family members to new or different ways of dealing with their children. On the other hand, this must be done in such a way as to enhance, rather than lower, the power and prestige of these persons. . . .

Urie Bronfenbrenner

Two Worlds of Childhood:
U.S. and U.S.S.R.

CHAPTER
14

Parent–School Contacts and Collaborative Problem Solving

The material presented in this chapter is aimed at providing school personnel with several ideas that when professionally implemented, can increase the likelihood that a parent-school contact will be positive and mutually beneficial. While the term "teacher" is used throughout this section, it is recognized that in many instances a counselor, special education consultant, or administrator will play a major role in parent contacts. The ideas presented in this section apply to all school personnel involved in conferencing with parents of behavior-problem adolescents.

BASIC FACTORS IN ESTABLISHING POSITIVE CONTACTS WITH PARENTS

The Initial Contact

Teachers should expect some degree of discomfort and defensiveness on the part of the parents whose children are experiencing problems at school. It is extremely important not to personalize parents' critical remarks. Since these remarks are an understandable response to the position in which the parents find themselves, the best policy is to acknowledge critical comments while at the same time redirecting them toward the goals for the conference.

For example, consider a situation in which a parent opens a conference or responds to a request for a conference by stating that coming to school is an inconvenience and they cannot understand why the school cannot handle its own problems. An effective response to this statement would be, "I appreciate your being upset and I will try to be as brief as possible. However, I do think it is important that you know how your son is doing and what we are doing at school to assist him." In a similar vein, it is important that teachers indicate their appreciation of parents' visits. Parents respond positively to hearing that teachers respect the fact that they care enough about their child to take the time to attend a conference.

Initial parent conferences should be primarily informative in nature. This conference should focus on providing parents with information concerning the nature of the problem and the efforts the school has made to create a more appropriate and effective learning environment for their child. If these efforts have included interventions aimed at assisting the adolescent in controlling his behavior, the focus should again be on the interventions rather than on the student's "bad" behavior. It is important not to overemphasize the student's inappropriate behavior. The data and the fact that interventions have been necessary will speak for themselves.

If a major goal of a conference is to obtain parental approval for some form of special service, the emphasis should be on the fact that this service will do a better job of meeting the student's needs. Rather than suggesting that the school has not met the student's needs or focusing on the student's problems, it is best to approach the issue by indicating that the adolescent has special needs in some areas and that the school would like an opportunity to provide the student with a program that can meet those needs.

Since the concept of local school control creates a situation in which teachers are directly accountable to parents, it is understandable that many teachers view parent conferences, and especially initial contacts, as anxiety-producing events. While assisting parents in understanding their child's problems and examining alternative approaches will perhaps always be a difficult task, it can be made easier by providing teachers with opportunities to practice the skills necessary for implementing a positive parent conference.

One effective strategy for improving teachers' skills in handling parent conferences is to combine instruction in the communication skills discussed in Chapter 4 with opportunities to role play difficult parent-teacher interactions. Role playing has the advantage of allowing the teacher to try out the new skills in a situation that involves at least a small amount of anxiety. In addition, role playing in a group setting provides the teacher with an opportunity to receive helpful feedback from colleagues who have experienced similar interactions. This type of sharing and mutual support is a vital ingredient in providing opportunities for professional development.

The Value of Presenting Data

Parents are impressed with data. Data indicates that teachers have invested time and energy in preparing for a conference. Data also speaks directly to teachers' professional competence. The presence of data indicates that they have done their work and that the purpose of the conference is to discuss their findings and not to ask the parent to solve the problem. By focusing on specific data, school personnel quickly move themselves out of the parents' category of professional babysitter and into the category of skilled professional educator. Data also has the obvious advantage of objectifying a discussion. The presence of data greatly diminishes the likelihood that a conference will turn into a debate over whether the adolescent's behavior really warrants concern. Data provides a specific focus for a conference and establishes a basis for future discussions.

In addition to expediting the conference, data has the additional advantage of providing protection for the educator. Data provides a record both of the student's behavior and the teachers' attempts to make thoughtful interventions aimed at improving that behavior. The availability of data prevents teachers from being accused of exaggerating the problem, picking on a student, or not having attempted to solve the problem themselves. Regardless of how competent a teacher may be, the lack of specific information significantly undermines his/her position when working with parents. Consequently, well-organized data is a necessary component of any parent conference that focuses on dealing with inappropriate student behavior or poor student achievement.

At this point it is important to insert a brief warning regarding the possible misuse of data. While data can prove invaluable in clarifying problems and demonstrating a teacher's competence and concern, it is also possible to hide behind data. It is extremely important that teachers do not become so involved in presenting data that they fail to attend to the parents' feelings and needs and the quality of their relationship with the parents. The collection and presentation of data is merely a strategy that provides clarity and direction in obtaining a goal. If data becomes viewed as an end in itself, it loses its effectiveness as a valuable means to achieving an important goal.

If teachers accept the value of bringing specific data to a parent conference, it is necessary to consider the type of data that is most useful. There are four major types of data that are useful in a parent conference: (1) data concerning student behavior and the results of attempts to improve the behavior, (2) data concerning the student's academic work, (3) data regarding conferences held with the student in an attempt to solve the problem, and (4) data concerning conferences with colleagues and specialists aimed at developing a solution to the problem.

The first type of data can be collected in several ways. The data may result from frequency counts taken by the teacher, a colleague, or the student himself. Data concerning the student's behavior can also be obtained through the use of video or audio tapes or by inviting teachers, counselors, or administrators to observe the student and make comments about his behavior. This type of data should be displayed in a manner that makes it easily understood. In most cases this means that the data should be displayed in a well-organized table that shows both baseline data and data associated with the various intervention programs that have been employed (Figure 14.1).

Data concerning a student's academic performance is an integral part of any parent-teacher conference. Since the school's major official function is the transmission of information and the teaching of information processing skills, data concerning

Figure 14.1. Format for Presenting Intervention Data to Parents

	Baseline	Intervention #1	Intervention #2	Intervention #3
Description of Problem Behavior				
			Time	

academic achievement is the most valid index of a student's performance. Indeed, if a behavior-problem student is satisfactorily completing all of his work, teachers may need to focus on providing him with more academic stimulation and concentrate somewhat less directly on controlling his behavior.

If, as is often the case, the academic data indicates that the student is not completing even a minimum amount of work, the teacher should be prepared to provide the parents with examples of ways in which the student's academic program has been adjusted to meet the student's special needs. Before a behavior problem reaches the stage of requiring a parent conference, the teacher should have examined the student's academic skills and determined whether an individualized program is appropriate. The teacher should have data to support such academic interventions and should also have data supporting the fact that conferences have been held with the student to discuss academic problems. As noted earlier, parents are impressed by competence. Very few parents will continue to defend their child and criticize the teacher when they are presented with well-prepared data concerning the teacher's interventions. Such data sets the scene for mutual understanding and, when necessary, shared problem solving and responsibility.

While teachers are responsible for demonstrating that they have responded to a student's individual learning needs, it is also important that teachers accept and communicate to parents the reality that no one can force another person to learn. All that the best teacher can do is provide students with appropriate learning materials within a safe and stimulating environment.

The third type of data provides information concerning when conferences with the student have taken place, what issues were discussed, and what agreements were reached. The collection of this type of data is facilitated by developing a standard form on which the important information can be recorded (Figure 14.2). This type of data has obvious uses aside from providing direction and clarity in parent conferences. This information can be useful when helping a student confront the extent of a problem. It can also provide a reminder to the teacher concerning agreements that have been reached with students. Finally, in this age of accountability, this information can be used during the teacher evaluation process to indicate the extent to which the teacher develops individual academic and behavior programs for students.

The final type of data that can assist teachers in creating a positive parent conference is data concerning the extent to which the teacher has consulted with specialists concerning the student's problem. As is the case in substantiating student conferences, it is helpful to record such conferences on a standard form (Figure 14.3).

There are two primary advantages to presenting this type of data. First, this data indicates that the teacher is not simply running to the parents at the first sign of trouble. Data concerning professional consultation speaks to the teacher's concern and

Figure 14.2.   Record of Student Conferences

Student's Name _____ Date _____

Location of Conference _____ Time _____ to _____

Reason for Holding Conference:

Summary of Conference:

Decision(s) Reached or Agreement(s) Made:

Additional Comments (General Tone of Conference, Feelings about Conference, etc.):

Figure 14.3.   Record of Consultation Conferences

Consultant's Name _____ Date _____

Consultant's Position/Role _____

Reasons for Holding the Conference:

Goals for the Conference:

Information Obtained:

Decision(s) Reached:

Additional Comments:

resourcefulness. Furthermore, it indicates to the parents that their child's problem is not simply a personality conflict with a teacher or the result of an incompetent teacher having difficulty teaching their slightly energetic or creative child. A second and less direct advantage to having consulted with specialists is that this process should assist the teacher in presenting the parents with a clearer and more thorough set of data. Especially in the area of academic difficulties, classroom teachers often have limited skills in diagnosing the specific factors that may be causing a student's problems. By consulting with specialists, the teacher not only can provide the parents with more in-depth information, but also can simultaneously acquire information that can assist in developing a more appropriate academic program for the student.

Presenting Parents with a Well-Designed Intervention Program

Regardless of whether the parents are meeting with a single teacher, a counselor, a special educator, or an administrator, it is important that the conference include the presentation of a clearly articulated intervention program. Like the presentation of professionally prepared data, a well-designed intervention plan indicates to the parents that the school is doing its job. By coming to the conference prepared with a plan, the teacher validates her role as a competent concerned professional. Parents often inform school personnel that conferences are an indication of the school's incompetence since the school should be able to do its job without parental assistance. Parents frequently comment that they do not come running to the school for assistance in controlling their adolescent at home. By approaching a conference with a well-articulated intervention program, school personnel can prevent such accusations and can indicate that they are simply attempting to provide the parents with information concerning their adolescent's school progress and program.

When developing an intervention program, it is important to present baseline data to support why the program has been developed and what is likely to happen if the program is not implemented. For example, the data may indicate that the student has turned in less than 10 percent of his work and that his behavior is so disruptive that its continuation at present levels would necessitate an expulsion from school. The parents can then be informed that the type of intervention being suggested has proved successful in helping students who have experienced difficulties similar to those being experienced by their adolescent. Parents should also be told that they will be informed of the program's result; and that if the program fails to bring about the necessary changes, another program will be developed.

Reporting Positive Student Behavior

Parents whose children have experienced considerable difficulties at school under-standably have a tendency to respond negatively to the school. No one likes to receive consistently negative news, and most people defend against the potential self-deprecia-tion and depression generated by negative interactions by placing the blame elsewhere or aggressing against the agent responsible for initiating the negative interactions. Therefore, when working with parents of behavior-problem students, it is important to provide them with positive information concerning their adolescent's behavior. This is particularly important after parents have taken the time to attend a conference and discuss their adolescent's problems.

Positive contacts can take the form of calls home, notes sent home with the student, letters of appreciation for the parents' concern and time, or reports indicating positive behavior changes. Positive contacts not only serve to increase the likelihood that parents will continue to work cooperatively with the school, but also may serve as a foundation for improved parent-child interactions. As parents begin to receive positive information concerning their child's behavior, they may in turn respond more positively to their child. This often creates a cycle in that the adolescent begins to respond more positively to the parents and the parents' responses become increasingly positive.

An additional benefit stemming from positive home contacts is that parents may begin to view the school more positively and may transmit this more positive attitude to their child. Since parents' values on major issues have a strong impact on their adolescent's values (Conger, 1971), developing parental support for the school can often have a major impact on an adolescent's attitude toward school.

An important concern related to the transmission of positive results is that the school should be careful not to build up unrealistic expectations for immediate and spectacular changes. Behavior change programs often show excellent results during the initial "honeymoon" stage when both the student and teachers are excited about the new program. However, it takes time to alter behavior patterns that have existed for a number of years, and most interventions face periods in which the adolescent tests the program by acting out. If parents have been led to believe that all is well, they may become disillusioned and resentful when regression occurs. Therefore, during the initial conference, parents should be informed that they should expect ups and downs in their adolescent's school behavior. This concept can be clarified by showing parents results from previous intervention programs that show an overall improvement, but include periods of regression. Results sent home to parents should reinforce this concept by presenting a realistic picture of the positive changes. While parents' initial responses to this type of information may be somewhat less reinforcing to the teacher, their long-term support for the school's program will be significantly enhanced.

NEGOTIATING A COLLABORATIVE CONTRACT

There are times when it is necessary to work cooperatively with parents in order to develop an intervention program that can be effective in altering an adolescent's behavior. This situation is more likely to occur with younger adolescents since parents generally have more control over younger adolescents and also dispense a greater percentage of the items that these youngsters find reinforcing. The necessity of parental cooperation stems from the fact that the school is limited in the range of punishers and reinforcers that it can dispense. Some behavior-problem adolescents find a positive learning environment, free time, field trips, and purchases at the school store minimally reinforcing. These same students often view exclusion from school as reinforcing rather than punishing. Therefore, if these students do not respond to less structured forms of counseling, the school is limited in its ability to control their behavior. Since behavior contracts are dependent upon the use of viable reinforcers and punishers, the school sometimes finds itself without the means to develop an effective behavior change program for a particularly defiant student. In such cases, school personnel have two options. They can either accept the student's right to fail or they can seek the parents' assistance in developing an intervention program that includes reinforcers and punishers strong enough to maintain the student within the school setting.

As is the case with any behavior contract, collaborative home-school contracts should not be developed unless the school environment is designed to effectively meet the student's academic and psychological needs. If this is not the case, the contract will merely provide a bandaid solution since adolescents will ultimately reject an environment that does not meet their needs.

A second major factor that should be considered prior to developing a home-school contract is whether school personnel have exhausted their repertoire of less structured interventions. Parents are too often asked to play a major role in influencing their adolescent's school behavior at a point when the school has not explored all the possible interventions at their disposal. In order to keep parents' trust and respect, educators should call upon parents for assistance only when it has become obvious that school personnel cannot maintain the student in the school setting without parental assistance.

While collaborative home-school efforts are usually necessary only when students have shown an extreme inability to control their own behavior, it is nevertheless important to inform students of the intention to employ this type of intervention. While it is unlikely that informing them about intentions to work cooperatively with their parents will significantly alter most adolescents' behavior, it is nevertheless important to inform them. In order to treat adolescents with respect and provide them with a sense of understanding and controlling their environment, teachers must inform them of decisions that affect them in significant ways. When students know the rationale for developing a more extensive intervention program, they are less likely to feel manipulated and more likely to accept the program.

Once it has been determined that the school environment is conducive to meeting the student's needs and that parental assistance is necessary, the next step is to present the parents with an effective, well-articulated intervention program.

Steps in Negotiating a Home-School Contract

Figure 14.4 lists the major steps to follow when meeting with parents to negotiate a collaborative home-school behavior contract. The obvious first step is to reinforce the parents for expressing their concern for their son or daughter. This can be accompanied by a statement to the effect that experience indicates that when parents are willing to work with the school, it is almost always possible to develop a program that will help the student.

The second step is to briefly state the goal of the meeting. For example, if the goal

Figure 14.4 Steps to Follow in Developing a Collaborative Home-School
Behavior Intervention Program

Step 1: Reinforce the parents for their willingness to attend the conference

Step 2: Outline the goal of the conference

Step 3: Describe the problem

Step 4: Indicate what the school has done to alleviate the problem

Step 5: Display the data to indicate that an additional type of intervention is needed

Step 6: Present the anticipated consequences should the student's behavior remain un-
changed

Step 7: Indicate that the school has exhausted its available resources and suggest that a
collaborative home-school program appears most likely to help the student

Step 8: Outline the proposed program

Step 9: Negotiate a final agreement

Step 10: Plan for follow-up

is to obtain parental assistance in developing a behavior management program, it is
important to clearly state that the goal of the meeting is to develop a program in
which the parents and the school will work cooperatively to improve the student's
behavior in school. Most parents will accept this goal. However, should parents
question this goal, it is best to simply indicate concern regarding their adolescent's
behavior and note the importance of developing the most effective program for
helping their child. It can then be suggested that although the parents may decide not
to become involved in reaching the goal, the school staff would like them to be
informed about their child's behavior.

The third step in negotiating a home-school contract is to describe the problem.
During this step, it is important to be specific. For example, if the problem centers
around a student's disruptive classroom behavior, it is helpful to have specific data
indicating the extent of this acting out. Similarly, it is helpful to present academic data
to support the fact that the student's acting out is hindering his ability to perform
academic tasks.

Once the problem has been clearly presented, the next step is to describe what the
school has done to help the student. Again, specific data must be presented. For
example, the parents can be shown records indicating the number of times teachers,
counselors, and administrators have counseled their child. The parents can also be
shown data indicating the type and frequency of meetings aimed at developing a
productive program for their child. In addition, the parents should be shown any
contracts that have been written with the student. Finally, the teacher or counselor
should outline any special academic programs that have been developed to assist the
student.

The fifth step is to present data indicating that the interventions previously
described have not been effective in bringing about the necessary behavior changes.
Ideally, the data would be in a form that includes baseline data followed by data
collected during the various interventions (Figure 14.1). If such data is not available,
the parents can be shown baseline data that indicates why the school staff became

concerned about the student's behavior. This can be followed by data regarding the student's current behavior. The parents can be shown that despite all attempts directed at assisting their child in changing his behavior, the behavior has not shown the necessary improvement. The parents can be informed that the data indicates that something more extensive must be done in order to assure that the student can remain in school and have a positive school experience.

The sixth step is to inform the parents of the probable consequences associated with a continuation of their child's current behavior. This information should not be presented in a threatening or intimidating manner. Instead, the parents should be informed that they have been asked to attend the conference because the school staff sincerely wishes to develop a program that will prevent the student from experiencing the consequences that would be associated with a continuation of the present behaviors.

Once the parents are aware of the impending consequences of their child's behavior, they should be informed that the school has exhausted its resources and that the only solution seems to be a collaborative effort between the home and the school. At this point, it is important to assure them that regardless of whether or not they agree to develop a collaborative program, the school will continue to make every effort to assist their child. However, it is important to inform the parents that, based on past records, it appears unlikely that these interventions will be adequate.

The eighth step is to present the parents with a proposed home-school program. When presenting the program, it is important to begin by discussing the school's role. This indicates to the parents that the school is not abdicating its responsibility and that the school staff will be actively involved in the program. After the school's role has been defined, the parents' anticipated role should be clearly outlined. It is important that this role be presented in terms of specific behaviors so that the parents know exactly what will be expected of them. At this point, it is important to specify the time parameters. Parents need to know how long the program will last. In addition, they should be given some information regarding when they can expect to see the desired changes in their child's behavior. Finally, the parents should be shown how the program will be evaluated. This should include a discussion of the data collection system as well as a tentative schedule of future conferences with both the student and the parents.

After the parents have heard the proposed program, they should be encouraged to ask questions or make suggestions regarding the proposal. Like adolescents, parents are more likely to commit themselves to a project if they are actively involved in the planning stage. It is also important to ask parents where they envision problems arising and whether they feel that they can carry out the roles outlined for them.

When the program has been thoroughly discussed and both parties have agreed to the solution, the final step is to determine when the two parties will meet again to discuss how the program is functioning. During the initial stages of a collaborative home-school intervention program, it will usually be necessary to include frequent correspondence through both phone calls and conferences. However, as the parents become comfortable with their role, and provided that the program is effective, these contacts can be gradually diminished.

A Case Study

A brief case study may help to highlight the steps in developing an effective collaborative home-school intervention. The case involved a fourteen-year-old eighth grade boy named Alan (a fictitious name) who had a history of extreme acting out in the classroom and a high rate of cutting classes. Alan was referred for specialized assistance because, despite employing several well-designed behavior contracts, neither his classroom teachers nor the school counselor had been successful in significantly altering his unproductive behavior.

An examination of Alan's classes indicated that, with one exception, the school was providing him with appropriate academic material within a basically supportive and positive environment. The first step in attempting to alter Alan's behavior involved transferring him out of the one class where the work seemed impossibly difficult and moving him into a class with a more individualized program. At the same time, a program was established whereby Alan would attempt to monitor his talking-back to teachers. Unfortunately, while the latter intervention was somewhat successful in reducing the frequency with which Alan "talked back" to teachers, his general behavior continued to include a greater frequency of aggressive and disobedient behaviors than the school could allow.

Since a wide variety of individual contracts had previously failed in an attempt to alter Alan's behavior, it seemed futile to continue this approach. Apparently Alan received a greater sense of competence and power from manipulating and frustrating his teachers and peers than from achieving the rewards offered by a contract. Given Alan's impaired self-concept and difficulties with his classwork, it also appeared likely that his acting-out behavior provided a defense against having to deal with the anxiety associated with attempting to succeed in school.

Based on the extent of Alan's acting out and the history of failure associated with generally well-conceived school-based intervention programs, it was determined that a collaborative home-school intervention was the last alternative for developing a program to keep Alan in school. When this issue was discussed with Alan, he became quite upset and insisted that he was capable of altering his own behavior. It was therefore decided to work with him to develop one last school-based intervention program. This program involved providing Alan with a structured approach to leaving a classroom when he began to experience anxiety or frustration. In addition, appropriate behavior was reinforced by daily notes sent home to his parents as well as the possibility of earning a trip to an ice cream parlor at the end of each week that involved no major discipline problem.

Unfortunately, Alan was unable to control his behavior and four days after the instigation of this final intervention he was suspended for fighting in class. At this point his parents were asked to attend a conference prior to their son's being readmitted to school. The parents responded quite negatively to this request but agreed to attend. When the parents arrived, the staff members provided them with considerable reinforcement for their willingness to assist the staff and the fact that their attendance demonstrated obvious concern for their son. The parents were then informed that the goal of the conference was to work out a program that would allow their son to remain in school and to begin having a more positive school experience. At this point the staff described the specific problems being experienced by their son and displayed data (Figure 14.5) indicating that, despite the instigation of a wide range of interventions, the school had not been able to develop a plan that would assist Alan in altering his behavior. Following a discussion of the various intervention programs, the principal indicated that Alan would have to be expelled unless a rather major and immediate change in behavior occurred. The parents were then informed that since they seemed to have an ability to control their son's behavior, the staff would like to work with them in developing a program to assist him.

Despite showing some displeasure and suggesting rather critically that the school should be able to control their son, the parents agreed to discuss the possibility of developing a collaborative home-school intervention program. At this point, the staff informed the parents of their intention to implement a systematic school exclusion program (see Chapter 12). Since it was anticipated that the parents would balk at a program that required such an extensive investment on their part, the staff had available the results of two similar programs that had been highly effective in almost identical situations. The fact that other parents seemed willing to become involved in this manner appeared to impress and disarm the parents. The staff then noted that

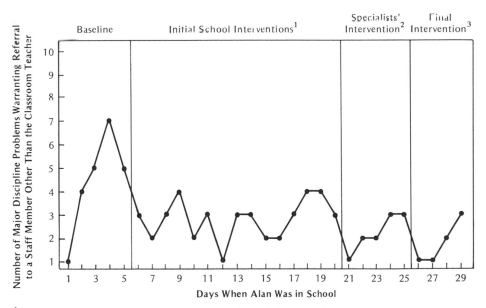

[1] A variety of individual contracts employing activity reinforcers and response cost
[2] Removal from a negative classroom environment and implementation of a self-monitoring program
[3] Discussion of possible parental involvement and contract involving activity reinforcer and positive reports sent home to parents

Figure 14.5   Results of School-Based Behavior Change Programs

while the parents' involvement did seem considerable, it was certainly less than would be required if their son were expelled and would be at home during the remainder of the school year. At this point the parents agreed to attempt the program and a formal agreement was signed (Figure 14.6). Arrangements were then made to meet again one week following Alan's re-entry into school or at the parents' request. The conference ended with the staff again expressing its appreciation and respect for the parents' concern and willingness to assist their son.

As seen in Figure 14.7, the program was successful in assisting Alan to remain in school. Indeed, follow-up data taken two years later showed that while not an honor student, Alan was making a satisfactory adjustment to high school and had maintained a "C" average. While not all collaborative interventions are as successful as this, parents can provide schools with invaluable assistance in working with

Figure 14.6   Agreement for Parental Involvement in a Collaborative Behavior-Change Program

In order to assist Alan in remaining in school and satisfactorily completing the eighth grade, the staff of _____ Junior High School and Mr. and Mrs. _____ have agreed to cooperate in the following manner:

The school staff will continue to do everything possible to assure that Alan is provided with interesting and appropriate work within a positive and supportive environment.

If at any time Alan begins to have problems controlling his behavior, the school staff will attempt to assist him in any way possible. However, whenever Alan begins to: 1) talk back to a teacher, 2) fight with another student, 3) disrupt class by talking out or physically bothering other students, Alan will be informed that unless he stops immediately he will be sent to the office and his parents will pick him up from school.

When either Mr. or Mrs. _____ are called, they will either pick Alan up themselves or arrange to have him picked up by Mrs. _____ within fifteen minutes.

If it is necessary to send Alan home, he will remain home for two complete school days. During this time, Mr. and Mrs. _____ agree not to allow Alan to leave the family's property and to allow no friends to visit. During this time Alan will not be allowed to listen to the stereo or watch television during school hours. When Alan is home on suspension, Mr. and Mrs. _____ will not add additional punishments or "put him down" for having been suspended.

When Alan is on suspension, the school will provide him with all of his homework as well as interesting books for him to read.

Mr. and Mrs. _____ will bring Alan to school at 7:45 a.m. on the third morning following a suspension. At this time they will meet briefly with the principal and counselor.

Mrs. _____ will meet with the school counselor every Friday at 3:30 p.m. to discuss Alan's progress.

If Mr. or Mrs. _____ wish to schedule a conference to discuss the program, they need only give the staff one day's notice and a conference will be held.

Signed _____   _____
                    Principal   Mr. _____

          _____   _____
                    Counselor   Mrs. _____

                                                   _____
                                                   Alan _____

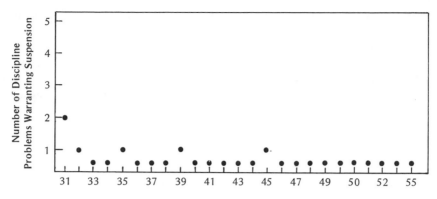

Figure 14.7   Results of Collaborative Behavior-Change Program

youngsters who are experiencing extreme difficulties in coping with a productive school environment. In fact, since parental failure to support school values and personnel is often a major factor influencing students' acting-out behavior, it is vital that schools attempt to involve parents in a manner that supports the school's program. Interestingly enough, it is surprising how often parents will rapidly alter their attitudes and behaviors when school personnel treat them with respect and provide them with support, empathy, and a well-conceptualized collaborative program.

SUMMARY

Although some educators might wish that school personnel would never face situations that required parental assistance, the fact remains that adolescents are capable of rejecting all attempts the school makes at assisting them. Since parents are legally responsible for their children and, especially during early adolescence, often control more important reinforcers and punishers than does the school, it is important that parents become involved when the school's attempts at behavior interventions have failed.

   Since parents may understandably feel anxiety, embarrassment, and resentment when asked to meet with school officials to discuss their child's disruptive behavior or academic failure, it is important to provide parents with support and reinforcement. As is the case when working with adolescents, the success of any parent contact will be greatly influenced by the quality of the interpersonal relationship.

   In addition to employing productive communication skills, professionals who work with parents must be prepared to provide clear explanations concerning the problems facing the youngster as well as specific suggestions for assisting the youngster. Parents are both reassured by and impressed with competence. Consequently, they are much more likely to provide supportive attitudes and actions when they are presented with a well-conceptualized plan of action.

Since the development of collaborative home-school programs can be facilitated by following a thoughtful, step-by-step procedure, the latter section of this chapter has focused on implementing such a procedure. This discussion was followed by a case study in which a systematic school exclusion program was successfully employed with an acting-out eighth grade boy.

Parent guidance might be defined as the offering to parents of information, clarification, advice, support, counsel, directives, supportive psychotherapy, or other interaction with a professional helper, with the intention of indirectly helping the child. It recognizes the profound influence that parents have on their children's development and mental health, an influence far greater than that which any professional could exert even with intensive intervention. It presupposes a cooperative working alliance between the parent and the helping professional, both of whom are interested in the welfare of the child.

Eugene Arnold

Helping Parents Help Their Children

CHAPTER
15

Developing Groups for Parents of Behavior-Problem Junior High-Aged Children

Collaborating in developing intervention programs aimed at improving adolescents' school behavior is one of two major ways in which schools and parents can work together to bring about meaningful behavior changes in adolescents. The second approach, developing parent groups, shifts the major focus and responsibility from the school to the home. When provided in connection with a positive, supportive school environment, this intervention can have a major impact on altering adolescents' behavior.

This chapter will explore the rationale and strategies associated with developing parent training groups for parents of behavior-problem adolescents. While the techniques presented in this chapter can be effectively employed with a wide range of training groups, the specific content suggested is most effective when working with parents of adolescents under age fifteen. The major focus of the model outlined in this chapter is in assisting parents to apply appropriate and consistent—although gradually diminishing—structure in their interactions with their adolescents. While this skill is central to interactions between parents and young adolescents, the focus for parents of older adolescents becomes establishing positive equalitarian parent-adolescent relationships that facilitate mutually satisfying interactions and support productive conflict resolution. While this latter skill will receive some emphasis in this chapter, it provides the central theme for Chapter 16.

There are several advantages associated with working with parents in a group situation. First, individual parent conferences are extremely time consuming. A major benefit derived from group counseling is that it enables the group leader to work with many more parents in a given amount of time. A second advantage to a group situation is that it provides parents with an opportunity to discover that they are not alone in the problems they face. Parents of behavior-problem children frequently feel isolated. This isolation is partially caused by the fact that these parents hesitate to share their problems with other parents because they believe that their adolescent's problems are a reflection of their own inadequacies as parents. A parent group allows these parents to realize that their problems are not unique and are therefore not solely a reflection of their uniquely ineffective parenting. The reduction in anxiety and guilt associated with this discovery can often bring about a significant improvement in parents' relationships with their children.

A third benefit derived from group meetings is that parents can receive ideas from other parents. In addition to providing a valuable addition to the leader(s) ideas, the opportunity to share their ideas and successes with other parents provides parents with a much needed sense of competence. This positive feeling can prove to be a valuable impetus in breaking the negative spiral in which these parents have often become trapped.

A fourth advantage to a group setting is that it provides an opportunity for more reserved parents to initially employ a passive learning style. While family counseling or an individual conference demands an almost immediate confrontation with the problem, a parent group provides an opportunity to test the water before diving in. Although the leader's goal should certainly be to eventually involve all parents in actively dealing with their problems, some people need time and exposure to a situation before they feel comfortable dealing openly with their problems. Parent groups enable these parents to learn without making an immediate commitment.

Finally, a group setting creates a sense of both support and accountability that is often lacking in individual counseling. In addition to providing valuable support and encouragement, the presence of other parents can increase the incentive for parents to follow through on their commitments. Parents report that it is more difficult to break a commitment made to a group than to a teacher or counselor. The fact that others may have tried and succeeded makes it more difficult for a parent to report that they simply did not believe that the idea would work.

Despite the fact that organizing and running a parent group requires considerable time, energy, and personal strength, interventions with parents are often a necessary, key intervention in working with behavior-problem adolescents. While sound therapeutic interventions with young adolescents may provide these youngsters with vital support and skills, a frightening amount of the change brought about through these interventions can be undermined if the youngster continues to live in a family whose interactions are punitive, inconsistent, and pathological. My experience in directing a school-based program for behavior-problem junior high school students clearly demonstrated a high correlation between parent involvement in parent groups and success in maintaining positive changes in student behavior over time. When working with behavior-problem youngsters who will continue to live at home, it is vital that educators assist their parents in developing skills that will enable them to interact productively with their children. Parent groups provide a relatively cost-effective method of providing this assistance.

CHOOSING AMONG SEVERAL FORMATS

Given the numerous advantages that accompany the decision to meet with parents in a group setting, the potential group leader is faced with making a decision regarding the type of group format that is most effective. There are numerous ways to organize a parent group and every group will quite naturally reflect the leader(s)' personal style and skills. Nevertheless, most parent groups tend to follow one of three basic formats: (1) teaching basic principles of behavioral management and asking parents to apply these principles in their homes; (2) teaching parents basic communication skills, and asking parents to apply these principles in their homes; and (3) employing a problem-solving approach in which family problems are discussed and solutions generated. The remainder of this section will briefly examine each of these formats and discuss the advantages and disadvantages associated with their application.

The first approach both originated from and grew with the popularity of behavior modification theory and practice. The most common method employed in applying this model involves providing parents with a relatively simple, often programmed text that provides them with an overview of the basic principles of behavior modification and their application to daily living. Texts developed for this purpose include Patterson's *Living with Children: New Methods for Parents and Teachers* and *Families* and Becker's *Parents Are Teachers: A Child Management Program*. As parents read and discuss this material, they are given homework assignments that reinforce the learning available through reading and discussions. Once parents have learned such basic principles as how to describe and record specific behavioral events, how to reinforce, and how to establish rules, they are asked to design behavior modification programs for use with their own children. These programs are generally shared with the group and results are brought back to the group for discussion.

Parent groups that follow the above format have several advantages. First, they are relatively easy to lead because the leader's role is primarily that of teacher. Good material is readily available and the leader's task is simply to proceed through the material and answer any questions that arise. Even when working with parent-designed programs, the format is generally a straightforward and relatively simple application of behavior management principles. A second advantage associated with this format is that for many parents (especially middle and upper middle class parents) the use of reading material and assignments creates a feeling that they are learning. Parents report satisfaction in completing a homework assignment or succeeding in correctly responding to a programmed text. Finally, this approach has the advantage of focusing on rather simple, straightforward, and safe aspects of parent-child interactions. The focus tends to be on providing appropriate positive reinforcement and punishment. Most parents can accept the need to improve their skills within the basic parameters of an authoritarian model of parenting.

While this approach to developing a parent group offers several real advantages, it simultaneously suffers from several fairly major weaknesses. First, there are several problems associated with placing even a reasonably heavy emphasis upon reading. Reading is often both threatening and unproductive for parents who have low reading skills. These parents will often shy away from groups that are based upon discussions stemming from group reading assignments. Similarly, regardless of their format or reading level, books offer a somewhat abstract approach to a problem. Parents, especially those with limited abstract abilities, are frequently frustrated by an indirect approach to providing much needed assistance. While books often prove threatening or confusing to parents with poor reading skills, parents with good reading and abstract reasoning skills often attempt to hide behind their cognitive skills. These parents frequently find it safe to spend hours discussing ideas presented in reading material while balking at suggestions that they apply this material to their own experience. Therefore, a major problem associated with employing reading materials with parent groups is that the ideas presented in the books often become the focus of attention, while serious family problems are ignored or discussed only as abstract issues.

A second disadvantage associated with this approach is that it tends to focus almost exclusively on providing parents with skills for modifying their children's behavior. This emphasis frequently fails to acknowledge and provide skills for focusing upon shared decision making. Therefore, while this approach is often quite effective when working with parents with young children, it fails to acknowledge and respond to a central theme and major conflict in adult-adolescent relationships.

The second approach to developing a parent group places a major emphasis on the adult-adolescent relationship. By focusing on communication as the most important issue within the family structure, this approach has the distinct advantage of dealing directly with adolescents' need to experience a sense of responsibility, independence, competence, and power. Parent groups based upon this format tend to incorporate a combination of instruction, reading, and homework assignments.

Perhaps the most popular and widely employed text associated with this group format is Gordon's *Parent Effectiveness Training* (PET). While this text can be used effectively by almost any counselor or special educator, special training is available in incorporating the text into a well-planned parent training group. Another useful resource for developing a productive communications-oriented parent group is Brownstone and Dye's *Communication Workshop for Parents of Adolescents*. In the introduction to their Leader's Guide, the authors state that:

> This handbook describes in detail the tasks, materials, rationale, and procedures for conducting a five-session Communication Workshop for Parents of Adolescents. It is designed for a variety of professionals . . . whose work with families has alerted them to the acute need for more effective communication between parents and their children (Brownstone and Dye, 1973, p. 1).

These authors provide a detailed and thoughtful description that includes procedures for beginning a parent group as well as useful activities and assignments.

Another excellent program that focuses on communication skills, but also incorporates a sound discussion of children's behavior as well as a presentation of logical and natural consequences is Dinkmeyer and McKay's *Systematic Training for Effective Parenting*. This program includes an excellent leader's manual that provides assignments, discussion topics, and handouts.

While parent groups that focus on teaching effective communication skills do respond to a major area of conflict in many parent-adolescent relationships, the leader must be careful lest the communication skills become an end in themselves rather than a means to an end. As is frequently the case with reading assignments, activities designed to teach communication skills often become the focus of the group, and parents unconsciously find themselves enjoying the group and the interesting activities, but failing to involve themselves in the sometimes difficult task of employing the new skills with their children. Similarly, it is not uncommon for a leader to become caught up in the excitement and positive responses from parents that often accompany interesting communication activities. It is therefore important that any leader who employs a communications format maintains a commitment to emphasizing practical application of the material presented during group sessions.

The third major approach to developing a parent training group incorporates a problem-solving format. This approach involves asking parents to present specific problems that occur in their daily interactions with their adolescents and examine possible approaches for alleviating these problems. A major advantage associated with this type of intervention is that it places an emphasis on specific, concrete problems and uses an inductive method for teaching basic concepts. Therefore, concepts are taught by asking parents to examine why a particular solution to a problem proved successful or unsuccessful. As parents use their own labels to list such key factors as failing to reinforce appropriate behavior, inconsistency in applying negative consequences, failing to clearly define behavior, failing to involve their child in the decision, the leader can reinforce these observations and suggest a new plan that incorporates the learning. The parents can be asked to try the new plan and report the results to the group. If the new approach is successful, the leader can ask the group to discuss why they believe this intervention was effective. The leader can use this opportunity to once again reinforce the important teaching points. This type of concrete, applied analysis of concepts is almost always more effective than introducing concepts through reading assignments.

A second advantage associated with a problem-solving approach is that most parents of behavior-problem adolescents are anxious to see immediate results. By focusing on practical solutions to specific situations, a problem-solving approach provides parents with skills they can employ immediately. A benefit derived from providing parents with immediate and practical ideas is that in the absence of this type of assistance many parents soon terminate their involvement in a parent training program. Most parents perceive their participation in a parent group as involving a considerable investment of time as well as a sizable risk. In fact, there is a high correlation between the difficulties being experienced at home and the risk taken by the parents. Therefore, if a leader wants to assure the continued involvement of those most in need of assistance, it is necessary to provide them with practical, immediately applicable ideas and skills.

A final advantage to employing a problem-solving format is that, at least initially, it provides an opportunity for parents who do not wish to become actively involved to learn by listening to others. Some parents balk at being required to do assignments, present homework in front of the group, or in any way become actively involved before they are ready. Since these parents are often those who need the most assistance, it is important to employ a format that allows them to become involved at their own pace.

While a problem-solving approach has several major advantages that support its use with parents of behavior-problem adolescents, this approach is somewhat more difficult to employ than more structured formats. Rather than teaching or leading activities, the leader of a problem-solving group must become actively involved in presenting and examining alternative strategies for coping with difficult situations. In addition, the leader must attempt to facilitate an analysis of each solution that highlights the basic teaching points that will eventually assist the parents in generalizing their learning. This task is obviously demanding and requires that the leader be confident, creative, and comfortable interacting with a group of parents. Since it is difficult for anyone to possess these qualities at all times, it is both more comfortable and more productive to include two leaders when developing a parent group based upon a problem-solving model.

While each of the three basic models described above provides parents with assistance in developing more effective parenting skills, I have found the problem-solving approach to be most effective in working with parents representing a wide range of socioeconomic backgrounds, level of motivation and confidence, and type of handicapping condition experienced by their child. Therefore, the remainder of this chapter will present the basic approach to developing a productive parent group using a problem-solving format. The reader who is interested in delving more deeply into one of the other approaches is encouraged to refer to the appropriate materials and references.

PROBLEM-SOLVING MODELS

There are two basic approaches to leading a problem-solving group, and the leaders' first decision is to determine which approach to take. One approach, which is highlighted by Satir's (1967) tenets of conjoint family therapy and Dreikur's (1964) concept of the family council, views unproductive communication as the major source of family problems. If a decision is made to develop a problem-solving approach around this central tenet, the leader's role becomes that of a teacher, facilitator and model who assists parents (and perhaps their children) in learning and employing communication skills that facilitate productive conflict resolution. This approach can be carried out either by actively involving adolescents and their parents in the group setting or by including only parents and employing role playing activities to similate the conflicts described by the parents. A third option is to involve parents and adolescents in separate groups that nevertheless focus on the learning and application of similar skills.

The second approach to employing a problem-solving model initially involves examining parents' methods of reinforcement and punishment and the types of rules they have developed. This behaviorally oriented approach places a major emphasis on changes in the adolescents' behaviors. While parents are provided with strategies for bringing about such changes (strategies that obviously involve changes in the parents' behavior), the focus is on bringing about changes in the adolescent. When employing a behaviorally oriented approach, communication patterns receive a secondary emphasis; they are examined only insofar as they relate to parents' methods of reinforcement, punishment, and developing reasonable rules and expectations.

While the first approach may initially sound as if it is more humanistic and thorough, there are several problems associated with employing this model with parents of behavior-problem adolescents. First, if the adolescents are involved, it soon becomes obvious that many young, disturbed adolescents find it extremely difficult both to listen to and develop appropriate generalizations from the problems being experienced by other families. Second, both parents and adolescents often find it difficult to openly discuss their problems in front of a group of people. Finally, when added to the demands inherent in family therapy, these two factors place extremely high demands upon the leaders. My experience strongly suggests that with the exception of a few individuals who are exceptionally talented, most leaders will find problem-solving groups with families a difficult and far-from-ideal approach to parent training.

It is much easier and more productive to employ a communications-oriented problem-solving approach with a group consisting only of parents. While this approach is certainly valuable, my experience suggests that when working with parents of young adolescents, a behaviorally based approach is more effective. Nevertheless, especially when working with parents of older adolescents, it is extremely important to place a heavy emphasis on communication. In this situation it is usually best to begin the group with a series of classes like those described by Brownstone and Dye (1971). Once parents have been introduced to the basic concepts through a relatively structured approach, the leaders can move toward a problem-solving approach.

While a communications approach can be effective, a behaviorally oriented approach to problem solving is generally more appropriate when working with parents of young, behavior-problem adolescents. There are several factors that underlie this statement. First, parents are initially less threatened by an approach that focuses on altering the adolescent's behavior. While the major emphasis in a parent group is on exploring ways parents can change, a behavioral approach suggests that the ultimate goal is to bring about a change in the adolescent's behavior. Most parents find this approach less anxiety producing than an approach that focuses directly on family dynamics. Consequently, they are more willing to become involved in discussing their problems and attempting to employ strategies to alleviate these problems.

It is important to keep in mind that a behavioral approach may have a significant impact upon family dynamics. For example, as parents begin to develop and employ consistent rules and provide their children with greater amounts of positive reinforcement, major changes are likely to occur in the family. Similarly, as they begin to deal more effectively with their children, parents often find that their interactions with each other become more positive and supportive.

In addition to being less threatening, a behavioral approach focuses on basic, relatively easy-to-change behaviors that nevertheless have a major impact upon children's behaviors as well as the quality of the parent-child relationship. In a significant majority of cases, a major problem at home centers around the parents' inconsistencies in making requests, setting rules, and handling discipline. Since a behavioral approach focuses on establishing specific rules and consequences, it deals directly with a major source of difficulty. Junior high aged adolescents need and want some degree of structure. While they do not want the structure to be punitive or arbitrarily imposed, they usually respond well to clearly defined expectations and limits.

A final advantage to employing a behavioral model is that it can be utilized to deal with a variety of communication issues ranging from the ratio of positive to negative statements to developing clear contractual agreements that alleviate significant amounts of arguing. Indeed, when parents agree to ignore a child's refusal to get out of bed in the morning rather than continually nagging the child, they have made a major change in their style of communicating with their child. In addition to the fact that behavior interventions often positively affect communication, it is relatively easy, and in fact desirable, to incorporate training in communication skills into behaviorally oriented problem solving. As parents work at developing contractual agreements or reducing the use of certain statements and behaviors, they must of necessity examine communication skills that facilitate these changes.

The remainder of the chapter will discuss specific strategies that are necessary in order to develop an effective parent group using a behaviorally based problem-solving model. While an emphasis is placed upon a particular type of parent group, many of the methods apply equally well to the other types of groups discussed earlier in the chapter.

IMPLEMENTING A BEHAVIORAL PROBLEM-SOLVING MODEL

Creating a Positive, Safe Environment

Most parents experience some discomfort when asked to discuss problems they are having with their children. However, this self-disclosure is necessary if a parent group is to have immediate and demonstrable results. In order to decrease parents' anxiety and thereby increase their willingness to become actively involved in the learning experience, it is necessary to create a positive, safe environment. As discussed in Chapter 5, one method for increasing the level of safety within an environment is to insure that individuals know each other. Therefore, the first step in leading a problem-solving group is to assist parents in becoming better acquainted.

A variety of acquaintance activities can be used to help parents become familiar with their colleagues. A name chain (see Chapter 5) is perhaps the best initial activity since it enables parents to learn the names of everyone present. Following the name chain, parents can be asked to talk to another parent for five minutes and at the end of that time to introduce that parent to the group. Parents may also be asked to form groups of four to six and take several minutes introducing themselves to this group.

It is important to continually facilitate a casual, relaxed atmosphere. This can be done by meeting in a relatively comfortable room such as the faculty lounge. It is also thoughtful to have coffee and cookies available. Furthermore, while parents may have become acquainted during the first meeting, it is important to continually reinforce their positive interactions by beginning each meeting with a brief social period as well as some method of acknowledging each person's presence.

One strategy for creating a positive environment is to begin each meeting by briefly discussing or displaying evidence of positive academic achievement or behavior by each student whose parent is present. Parents consistently indicate that this activity provides a positive set for the group meetings and is something they look forward to each week. In addition to showing students' work or data regarding students' improved behavior, parents enjoy seeing video tapes of their children productively involved in the learning process. Most parents of behavior-problem adolescents have had innumerable negative contacts with school personnel. It is exciting to see how positively they respond to positive contacts, and how effective these can be in improving the parents' attitudes toward the school and their children.

Creating Clear and Realistic Expectations

Once parents have become acquainted, the next step is for the leaders to inform the parents that the leaders do not have a magic wand which will allow them immediately to solve all the parents' problems. Parents should be informed that although the leaders can offer them valuable ideas and skills, there is no easy way to change their adolescents' behavior. Parents should also be informed that what they take from the group will be significantly influenced by their willingness to become actively involved in trying out new ideas.

The next step in introducing the group format is to ask the parents to describe what they wish to accomplish by attending the group. This procedure reinforces the beliefs that the parents are the most important component of the group and that they are responsible for the learning that will take place. This task also forces the parents to begin to take an active role and prevents the first session from becoming too leader oriented. Finally, this task enables the leaders to develop a clearer understanding of the parents' needs and interests.

After writing the parents' goals on butcher paper or a blackboard, the leaders should discuss which goals can be realistically met through active participation in the group. This process is vital in creating realistic expectations concerning the group. For example, if a parent lists learning about adolescent psychology as a major goal, the leaders may need to indicate that, while the group will assist parents in better understanding their adolescents, the major focus will be on providing them with skills for changing their adolescents' behavior and improving their relationship with their adolescents rather than on analyzing adolescent behavior.

After discussing what parents can realistically expect from the group, the next step is to briefly outline the procedures that will be followed. At this point the leaders may ask the group members to simply indicate whether they have had any difficulties with their adolescent at home during the past month. In almost every case a significant percentage of parents will indicate that they have experienced some problem. The parents should then be informed that the group's format will be primarily problem solving. Parents will be asked to present a problem and the group will develop a workable solution. The parents involved will then be asked to employ the solution and report the results at the next meeting.

It is quite likely that parents will initially express both surprise and discomfort when they are informed that the group will employ a problem-solving format. If this occurs, it is important to carefully explain why this method has been chosen. This explanation may include the fact that individuals often find it difficult to actually employ ideas they read or are presented to them. Therefore, since the goal for meeting is to assist the parents in developing usable skills, it seems only logical that the group format should stress active involvement in examining specific problems and developing ways to cope with these problems.

Facilitating Problem Solving

Once parents have become acquainted and realistic expectations have been developed, the next step is to involve parents in discussing problems they are experiencing in their interactions with their adolescents. Since acquaintance and goal-setting activities can usually be accomplished in the first session, parents can be asked to jot down any major problems that occur during the following week and bring them to the second session. It is inappropriate to involve parents in problem solving during the first session. Parents need time to assimilate the fact that they will be actively involved in the sessions. Furthermore, by closing the first session with a brief discussion on the value of specificity, the leaders can increase the likelihood that parents will focus on reasonably specific situations when problem solving begins.

Since a significant number of parents will inevitably experience some discomfort at the idea of working on their problems in a group format, it is advisable to call the parents the evening before or the day of the second (and even the third and fourth) session to remind parents about the group and seek a reaffirmation of their commitment to attending. One method for assuring a high rate of attendance is to create a situation in which, although the course is free, parents are required to submit a deposit equal to $5 or $10 per session. As parents attend each session, they receive a designated amount of deposit back until, if they have attended each session, they will have received their entire deposit by the end of the last session. Another method that often enhances enrollment and attendance is to provide a small amount of college credit for the sessions. Many parents find the acquisition of a credit to be highly motivating. Attending a "class" seems to have a greater sense of immediacy and prestige than attending a parent group.

The second session should begin with a brief activity designed to reinforce the acquaintance activities employed the previous week. If the leaders have decided to include a brief statement or display regarding each adolescents' productive accomplishments during the intervening week, this material should be presented next. No more than half an hour should be devoted to these activities. Having created a positive atmosphere through these activities, the leaders should briefly summarize the decisions made concerning the group's goals and format. The leaders should then ask if any parents experienced a problem that they would like to discuss with a goal of developing a useful solution. While there is occasionally some hesitation, I have never experienced a situation in which the group waited longer than one or two minutes for a parent to volunteer a problem. Parents of behavior-problem adolescents are experiencing a difficult time and almost uniformly want help in working with their children. In addition, most parents are somewhat anxious and find it difficult to sit in silence.

When a parent presents a problem, the first task is usually to assist the parent in clarifying the problem and focusing on a specific behavior. Parents frequently describe problems in such general terms as the adolescent never obeying, being totally disrespectful, or being out of control. The leaders can ask the parents to describe the problem in terms of specific, observable behaviors. In addition, the leaders can ask the parents to focus on one behavior or one situation. For example, rather than dealing with the problem of an adolescent who never obeys, the parents can be helped to describe the problem that occurred when the adolescent failed to obey a recent request. As the leaders assist the parents in clarifying their concerns, they should simultaneously point out such major concepts as the importance of clearly defining behavior and the necessity of dealing with one behavior at a time.

Although the leaders may initially be responsible for focusing and clarifying the problem, other parents should be encouraged to suggest possible solutions. By commenting upon parents' suggestions and asking parents to consider the advantages and disadvantages of various solutions, the leaders can insert a variety of teaching points concerning behavior management.

The result of dealing with a specific problem should be that the parents are presented with a clear, effective approach for dealing with the problem. Furthermore, if the solution requires that the parents discuss the intervention program with their adolescent, the parents should be provided with suggestions concerning how to present the issue. If the parents express concern about presenting the new program to their child, it may be helpful to role play the situation with the parents playing their child's role. The leaders or other parents can then model methods for effectively handling any resistance that might arise. Following this, the parents can be asked to take the role of parents while someone else responds in the way the parents indicated their child would react. One obvious advantage associated with coleader parent groups is that if one leader has difficulty conceiving a satisfactory plan or role playing a situation, it is quite likely that the other leader can provide some assistance. In this situation each leader can be more relaxed, creative, and supportive.

Prior to asking the parents to carry out an intervention program at home, the parents should be asked to summarize the program, and a decision should be made concerning the type of data that will be collected in order to ascertain whether the program is effective. My experience suggests that while some form of data collection is valuable in order to encourage parental involvement and objectivity, too much emphasis on data discourages parents and detracts from the real issue of attempting new behaviors. Therefore, data collection should focus upon simple tallies of designated adolescent behavior. For example, if parents are attempting to reduce the frequency with which their child fails to respond to polite requests, they should receive assistance in developing a simple system for recording instances in which their youngster responds or fails to respond to such requests. Similarly, parents will often need assistance in developing a simple chart on which to record the results of a parent-child contract. Charts such as those presented in Figure 15.1 and 15.2 can provide parents with assistance in recording behavior. Charts like these can also encourage parents to continue their intervention by making them more aware of the impact the program is having on their child's behavior.

Once data collection procedures have been established, the parents should then be reminded that they will be asked to discuss the results at the next meeting. Especially during the early stages of the group, it is helpful to establish a designated time during the week when the parents will call the leader to discuss how the program is progressing. This provides the parents with added support as well as an incentive for beginning the program.

Because a behavioral approach to teaching parenting skills requires that parents actually practice the skills being presented, it is necessary that group meetings be scheduled weekly. Parents need support and reinforcement for their efforts. If sessions are scheduled more than a week apart, parents are not provided with adequate opportunities for examining problems that arise as they begin implementing programs.

As parents implement and report on behavior change programs, it becomes increasingly possible for the leaders to take a less dominating role during group

Figure 15.1. Parent Data Collection Form

Day	Time	Parent's Request	Adolescent's Response

Figure 15.2.   Parent Data Collection Form

| Day | Task | Completed on Time | | Amount of | Amount |
		Yes	No	Allowance	Earned
Wednesday	Take out garbage			10¢	
	Feed the dog			10¢	
	Clear the table			10¢	
Thursday	Feed the dog			10¢	
	Clear the table			10¢	
Friday	Take out garbage			10¢	
	Feed the dog			10¢	
	Clear the table			10¢	
Saturday	Mow the lawn			1.20	
	Feed the dog			10¢	
	Clear the table			10¢	
Sunday	Take out garbage			10¢	
	Feed the dog			10¢	
	Clear the table			10¢	
	Clean own room			10¢	
Monday	Feed the dog			10¢	
	Clear the table			10¢	
Tuesday	Feed the dog			10¢	
	Clear the table			10¢	
				$3.50	

meetings. While maintaining the responsibility for assuring that parents are provided with productive intervention programs, the leaders can begin to shed the role of instructor and take on the role of facilitator. This gradual increase in the amount of responsibility given to the parents helps them to develop more confidence while at the same time increasing the likelihood that they will be able to employ the concepts when the group is through. While the number of weeks a group runs will depend on a variety of factors including parents' interest and the leaders' availability, my experience suggests that a twelve week session is ideal for a group of between twelve and twenty parents. Twelve weeks allows adequate time for this number of parents to deal with their major concerns, learn the basic concepts, and become comfortable applying these concepts in their interactions with their children.

A Sample Problem

The description of how a fairly typical parental problem was handled may help to clarify the format employed in a behaviorally oriented problem-solving group. The problem was presented during the fifth session of a group consisting of fourteen parents representing nine families. The parents who presented the problem had been quite reserved during the first four sessions. Their son was a fourteen-year-old eighth grader whose school difficulties centered around his frequent refusal to obey teacher requests and his tendency to fight with peers.

The parents indicated that they were having difficulty getting their son out of bed in the morning. They continued by stating that their son frequently missed the school bus; and that because she had to drive him to school, the mother had been late to work on a number of occasions. In addition to their annoyance at the numerous scoldings and pleadings that took place every morning, the parents expressed their concern over the fact that the mother's employer was becoming impatient with her increasingly frequent tardiness.

The leaders began the discussion by asking the parents if they could pinpoint the number of times their son had missed the bus during the past two weeks. The parents were in agreement that this situation had occurred five times during this period. With the baseline clearly established, the parents were asked to describe the typical series of events that occurred every morning. The mother noted that she first called her son forty-five minutes before the bus was to leave. This call was usually followed by several increasingly loud and aggravated calls until the son finally responded. The mother continued by stating that when her son finally got out of bed he inevitably complained that he did not have some item of clothing. Since the boy's clothes were in a dresser in the hall outside his bedroom, the mother reported that she usually brought his clothes and even made a second trip to exchange an item of clothing that her son refused to wear. In addition to preventing her from having time for the rest of the family or even finishing her own breakfast, this attention did not seem to help her son get ready in time to catch the bus.

After thanking the mother for providing such a clear picture, the leaders asked the boy's parents if they had any idea why the problem existed. When the parents stated that their only thought was that their son simply had trouble getting started in the morning, the leaders asked the other parents if they could pinpoint anything about the way the situation was being handled that might be contributing to the problem. Since the topic of reinforcing appropriate and inappropriate behavior had been discussed on several previous occasions, it was not surprising that several parents immediately commented that the boy appeared to be receiving a great deal of attention for his inappropriate behavior. The boy's parents responded somewhat defensively to these statements and noted that if they did not nag their son, the mother would be forced to drive him to school every day. At this point the leaders intervened. They noted that the parents were in a difficult situation and that they obviously cared about their son. The leaders also summarized the comments made by the other group members and asked the parents if they would be willing to explore an alternative to the pattern they were following. By making a positive statement about the parents' behavior and summarizing the discussion in a positive manner, the leaders provided the parents with important support and increased the likelihood that the parents would be willing to continue their involvement. A major role and responsibility associated with group leadership involves providing a positive, supportive atmosphere within the framework of a critical analysis of behavior.

When the parents expressed their interest in developing an alternative approach to dealing with the problem, the leaders' next task became that of assisting the group in providing a useful solution without making the parents feel embarrassed or inferior. Since the parents had responded somewhat defensively to earlier comments from other group members, the leaders prefaced their request for group assistance by noting that the parents were facing a difficult situation. The leaders might also have approached this situation by asking the boy's parents if they would like to hear any suggestions that other parents might offer. Although this intervention has the advantage of providing the parents with a choice, it has the disadvantage of allowing the parents to refuse and to request that the leaders provide a solution. While this is never a good situation, it is particularly unproductive when the group has been meeting for over a month and parents should be gradually taking increasing responsibility in order that they will eventually be able to generalize their learning. By noting the difficult nature of the problem and treating the situation seriously, the leaders provided support for the parents while maximizing the likelihood that the other group members would approach the problem seriously.

As almost always happens, the other parents offered thoughtful suggestions that provided the basic components for a good intervention program. As each suggestion was offered, the leaders asked the individual to describe the advantages associated with the suggestion. For example, one father suggested that the parents buy their son an alarm clock. The leaders reinforced the father's contribution and asked him why he felt that this would help. The father responded by noting that this would prevent the boy's mother from having to start the morning off on a negative tone and that it would place greater responsibility on the son. When the parents responded that their son would probably turn the alarm off and go back to bed, another parent suggested that the boy be informed that if he failed to catch the bus he would be required to walk to school. This parent continued by stating that since the family lived approximately a mile from school, the boy could reach school on time even if he left soon after the bus. Before the leaders could comment upon this suggestion, the parents noted that this would only get their son in trouble at school. This statement was met by another parent's comment that perhaps that should be the boy's problem and not the parents. This parent stated that the school was responsible for dealing with the boy if he was consistently late.

At this point the leaders stepped in and attempted to summarize the suggestions. They noted that the boy seemed to be manipulating the situation and receiving a great deal of attention for rather unproductive behavior. They continued by pointing out that this situation might be alleviated by providing the young man with an alarm clock, making sure that clean clothes were available, and informing him that he was responsible for deciding whether to catch the bus or walk to school. Since one of the leaders worked at the school, he suggested that the school would very likely support the idea that the boy's tardiness could be dealt with as a matter between the boy and the school. The leaders noted that since the young man lived quite near the school, it seemed feasible to arrange a situation in which the young man would be required to make up after school the amount of time he missed by being tardy.

After summarizing the suggestions and placing them into the context of a workable program, the leaders asked the parents for their response to the proposed solution. When the parents responded enthusiastically, the leaders asked the parents whether they believed they would have any problems presenting this program to their son. The parents responded that they foresaw no difficulties and in fact they intended to purchase an alarm clock as soon as they left the group and start the program the next morning. Since the group lasted until 9:00 P.M., the leaders discussed the advantages of waiting until the following evening to talk to their son. The leaders informed the parents that the school counselor would talk to the youngster the morning after the parents presented the program to him and that the program should begin the day after the boy spoke with his counselor.

The next step involved developing a simple method for collecting data. The parents agreed to report the results of their discussion at the next group meeting and to record the time when their son left the house each morning beginning the following morning. It was also decided that the school staff would keep a record of any tardinesses and report this to the group.

Before concluding the evening, the parents were asked to summarize the program and describe how they would respond in the morning once the program had been instigated. The leaders took this opportunity to encourage the parents not to resort to nagging their son and to provide him with praise when he succeeded in getting up on time. The entire problem-solving process took slightly over forty-five minutes. As seen in Figure 15.3, the intervention was highly successful in altering the young man's behavior. Perhaps more importantly, the parents reported that their mornings as a family became much more pleasant and their interactions with their son became much more positive.

While not every problem is so amenable to a rather simplistic and straightforward solution, I have found the process outlined in this example extremely productive in assisting parents to develop solutions to problems that occur in their interactions with their young adolescents. As noted earlier, it is often necessary to supplement this straightforward problem solving with role playing aimed at assisting the parents in

Figure 15.3   Results of a Parent Group Designed Program

Day	Time left home	Bus Caught	Minutes tardy and held after school (to be filled in by school staff)
Friday	8:05	No	10
Monday	8:10	No	12
Tuesday	7:47	Yes	--
Wednesday	7:45	Yes	--
Thursday	7:52	No	15
Friday	7:45	Yes	--
Monday	7:55	No	7
Tuesday	7:42	Yes	--
Wednesday	7:40	Yes	--
Thursday	7:46	Yes	--
Friday	7:39	Yes	--
Monday	7:53	No	--
Tuesday	7:42	Yes	--
Wednesday	7:40	Yes	--
Thursday	7:41	Yes	--
Friday	7:43	Yes	--

acquiring skills for presenting a solution to their adolescent. Indeed, in some cases the solution may be primarily based on altering the parents' method of interacting with their adolescent. In such cases, the initial method of problem solving outlined here would not change. However, the development of the final solution would incorporate considerable role playing and would place a much smaller emphasis upon designing a structured behavior-change program.

Options for Advanced Sessions

While the format described provides a flexible and productive model for working with parents, there will obviously be occasions when it is desirable to develop training activities that differ from those outlined in the preceding sections. One instance in which additional options may be desired is when parents have attended a problem-solving group for twelve weeks or more. At this point parents may feel that they are interested in and ready to move on to a new approach. As noted earlier, a somewhat different approach may also be equally or more effective in providing parents with specific skills that will enable them to successfully cope with their adolescents' impending emancipation.

While numerous directions can be taken in developing advanced parent training groups, my experience indicates that the best received and most effective are those that focus on parent-adolescent interaction. A primary reason for focusing on skills that can improve parent-adolescent relationships is that as adolescents grow older, parents' ability to influence their adolescents becomes increasingly dependent upon the quality of the relationship. Therefore, especially for parents who have employed a relatively authoritarian parenting style, it becomes necessary to develop skills that enable them to involve their adolescent in family decisions and shared conflict resolution.

There are a variety of approaches a leader can take in organizing a group aimed at providing parents with communication skills that will support the creation of positive, egalitarian adult-adolescent relationships. As mentioned earlier in this chapter, programs based upon Gordon's *Parent Effectiveness Training* (1970) or Brownstone and Dye's *Communication Workshop for Parents of Adolescents* (1971) can provide a good introduction to basic issues in parent-adolescent relationships. Leaders who wish to create their own program or develop activities that expand upon a more structured program can turn to an ever increasing number of good books that outline basic communication skills and present activities designed to develop these skills. Books I have found particularly useful include Castillo's *Left-Handed Teaching: Lessons in Affective Education* (1974), Johnson's *Reaching Out* (1972), Johnson and Johnson's *Joining Together: Group Theory and Group Skills* (1975a), and Simon et al.'s *Values Clarification*. The material available in the area of assertive training offers yet another approach to assisting parents in developing skills that will enable them to cope more effectively with the stress and challenges frequently associated with parent-adolescent interactions. As discussed in Chapter 16, this model provides skills that are particularly helpful in assisting parents in dealing with their adolescents' new sense of independence and power. Finally, another approach to improving interpersonal relationships involves teaching Transactional Analysis to parents of behavior-problem adolescents. When employing this model, parents can be introduced to the basic concepts of TA through books such as Harris's *I'm Ok, You're Ok* (1969) and James and Jongeward's *Born to Win: Transactional Analysis with Gestalt Experiments* (1971). Once parents have learned the basic concepts, they can be asked to analyze and discuss specific unproductive interchanges that have taken place between themselves and their adolescents. This analysis is aimed at increasing parental awareness of the dynamics of the interaction as well as providing parents with alternative approaches for interacting with their children.

While this chapter has focused on assisting parents in developing more effective approaches to dealing with their children, it is important to keep in mind that as professionals help parents to improve their skills in interacting with their children, it is also desirable to, whenever possible, provide similar skill building for the youngsters. Since both parties are involved in the existing style of interaction, problems can arise when one party learns new skills that begin to change the interaction pattern. Simultaneously providing both parties with new skills, increases the chances of creating a smoother transition into a more productive style of interaction. Once both parties have become familiar with the basic concepts involved in applying the new skills and have practiced these skills through role playing and assignments, the ambitious leader may wish to bring the two parties together to practice their new skills.

SUMMARY

Parents of behavior-problem adolescents frequently find themselves frustrated by and concerned about their apparent inability to control or effectively relate to their children. When run effectively, parent groups can provide a supportive atmosphere in which parents can express these concerns and can begin to develop new and more effective methods for dealing with their children.

There are many ways to organize and lead a parent group. Nevertheless, it is possible to categorize groups into those that place a major emphasis on (1) teaching basic principles of behavior management, (2) teaching communication skills, and (3) solving immediate problems. While each of these formats has certain advantages and disadvantages, the problem-solving approach seems most effective in working with parents of junior high aged behavior-problem adolescents.

After the leader of a parent group has determined the format to be employed for that group, the key components to creating a productive group include creating a positive and supportive atmosphere, assisting the parents in developing clear and realistic expectations, and effectively processing the group. This chapter has provided a discussion regarding how to accomplish each of these goals within the context of a behaviorally oriented problem-solving approach. In addition, a case study was presented in order to demonstrate the synthesis of these three components. Finally, several suggestions are presented for those leaders who wish to employ alternatives to or extensions of the types of groups discussed in this chapter.

Whenever an educator organizes and facilitates a parent group, it is important to realize that while a group setting possesses the potential for providing parents with assistance in altering pathological family interactions, group leaders should be sensitive to cases in which parents should be referred for more intensive individual or family therapy. The final chapter examines one approach to working with individual parents and discusses several key concepts in assisting parents in coping with disturbed parent-adolescent interactions.

*. . . the goal of assertion is communication and "mutu-
ality"; that is, to get and give respect, to ask for fair
play, and to leave room for compromise when the
needs and rights of two people conflict. In such
compromises neither person sacrifices basic integrity
and both get some of their needs satisfied.*

Arthur Lange and Patricia Jakubowski

*Responsible Assertive Behavior:
Cognitive/Behavioral Procedures for Trainers*

CHAPTER
16

Teaching Assertive Behavior
to Parents of Behavior-
Problem Adolescents

Since older adolescents are nearing legal emancipation, the issue of parental control is
less paramount than is the case with younger adolescents. When working with parents
whose adolescents are older, a much greater emphasis must be placed upon assisting
them in clarifying their rapidly changing role in relation to their adolescent children
and providing them with skills for coping with their new role. These skills and
understandings are necessary because the central theme of the parent-adolescent
relationship has moved from one of control to one of facilitating a relatively smooth
emancipation. The concepts included under the label of assertive training provide a
basis for assisting parents in interacting effectively with their children during the stage
of late adolescence. This chapter will examine these basic concepts and discuss their
implications for clarifying and improving parent-adolescent relationships.

It is obvious that a single chapter cannot begin to cover the theories or dynamics of
family therapy. In writing this chapter, I have of necessity confined the content to a
presentation of several basic concepts and skills that I have found to be particularly
valuable tools in assisting parents in adjusting and responding productively to their
adolescent's increased independence. The reader who is interested in exploring the area
of family therapy is referred to a variety of excellent books on this topic. In the area
of understanding and responding to the family system and family dynamics, two

excellent works are Satir's *Conjoint Family Therapy: A Guide to Theory and Technique* (1967) and Dodson and Kurpius' *Family Counseling: A Systems Approach* (1977). The field of behavioristic interventions is creatively explored and presented in Mash, Handy, and Hamerlynck's two works *Behavior Modification Approaches to Parenting* (1976) and *Behavior Modification and Families* (1976). While these books offer a well-written presentation of a particular orientation to family therapy, Arnold's *Helping Parents Help Their Children* (1978) and Guerin's *Family Therapy: Theory and Practice* (1976) are well-edited works that offer a wide range of well-written articles on working with parents and families.

DEFINING ASSERTIVE TRAINING?

The word "assertive" causes many people to view assertive training as some form of martial art. Assertive training is more than instruction in the art of being assertive. As defined by writers and trainers in the field, assertiveness involves a wide range of interpersonal skills. In their book, *Your Perfect Right: A Guide to Assertive Behavior*, Alberti and Emmons describe assertiveness as follows:

> Behavior which enables a person to act in his own best interests, to stand up for himself without undue anxiety, to express his honest feelings comfortably, or to exercise his own rights without denying the rights of others we call assertive behavior (Alberti and Emmons, 1974, p. 2).

In a later work, Alberti reinforces this concept when he writes that:

> One may exhibit assertiveness by behaving, within the parameters of a given social situation, in an effective fashion, honestly expressive of one's feelings, while respecting the rights and feelings of others involved (Alberti, 1977, p. 22).

Assertive training includes an emphasis on the honest expression of positive feelings and clearly differentiates between being assertive and being aggressive. Indeed, various writers in the field of assertive training have coined such terms as "responsible assertion," "empathic assertion," and "nonabrasive assertion" to emphasize the fact that while being assertive means honestly expressing beliefs and feelings, it does not mean "bowling over" an opponent or attempting to win a game of "one-upmanship."

Since assertive training places an emphasis on openly and honestly expressing personal feelings, it is helpful to distinguish assertive training from training in communication skills. Effective communication skills are the building blocks to effective assertiveness. It would be difficult to be empathically assertive without using such effective communication skills as sending "I messages", paraphrasing, perception checking, and speaking directly to the other person. However, assertive training goes a step further (a step that has been taken for many years by competent, pragmatic individuals) and more clearly places these skills within the context of conflict resolution and personal need fulfillment.

The procedures for teaching assertiveness have been thoroughly outlined in such books as *Your Perfect Right: A Guide to Assertive Behavior* (Alberti and Emmons, 1974), *Responsible Assertive Behavior: Cognitive/Behavioral Procedures for Trainers* (Lange and Jakubowski, 1976), and *Assertiveness: Innovations, Applications, Issues* (Alberti, 1977). While methods vary according to the needs of the individual receiving the training, the basic procedures include:

1. teaching people the differences between assertion and aggression, nonassertion and politeness
2. helping people identify and accept their own personal rights as well as the rights of others
3. reducing existing cognitive and affective obstacles to acting assertively
4. developing assertive skills through active practice methods

The major difference between teaching assertive training and teaching the parenting skills outlined in the previous chapter is that, for many parents, assertive training requires the parents to make a major change not only in their behavior, but also in the way they define the parent-adolescent relationship. Therefore, it is often necessary to begin a parent group or series of counseling sessions by discussing these changes and why they are important. This task can be carried out by involving parents in discussions and activities that assist them in better understanding their adolescents' needs and wants while simultaneously assisting them in clarifying their changing role as parents. This process can be facilitated both by creating increased parent-adolescent dialogue and by assisting parents in examining the costs and payoffs associated with various methods of relating to their adolescents.

Once parents have decided that they are willing to attempt a more open, egalitarian interaction pattern with their adolescents, they can be introduced to specific concepts of assertive training. Following this, parents can be encouraged to participate in role playing sessions that provide actual practice in employing assertiveness. Finally, parents can be given homework assignments and asked to report the results of their efforts to the group or the therapist.

The remainder of the chapter describes the basic concepts and skills that provide the foundation for assisting parents in employing assertive behavior as a means for improving their relationships with their adolescent children. Since these concepts and skills are important components of any good adult-adolescent relationship, they are as applicable to teachers, counselors, and administrators as they are to parents.

CONCEPTS THAT SERVE AS A FOUNDATION FOR IMPROVING PARENT-ADOLESCENT INTERACTIONS

Figure 16.1 provides a list of the concepts I have found most helpful in assisting parents in developing a more empathically assertive style of dealing with their adolescents. This section will briefly describe and discuss the importance of each concept listed in Figure 16.1.

Figure 16.1 Concepts which Serve as a Foundation for Improving
Parent-Adolescent Interactions

1. Much adolescent behavior which parents find frustrating is a reflection of normal adolescent development.
2. Firmness and directness will be effective only within the context of a relationship characterized by unconditional concern and affection.
3. Indulging and acquiescing does not equate with caring.
4. Parents should be aware of ways in which they aggress against their children.
5. Parents and adolescents have an equal right to be heard and treated with respect.
6. When people have serious things to talk about, they need to set aside adequate time to talk.
7. It is important to be clear about your goals and alternatives before entering into a negotiation.

Much Adolescent Behavior that Parents Find Frustrating Is a Reflection of Normal Adolescent Development

Parents are often confused by their children's behavior and are unable to place this behavior in a realistic perspective. Parents become hurt and frustrated by their adolescent's tendency to disagree with important parental values, challenge parental authority, and spend increasing amounts of time with peers. It is understandable that parents often respond to this hurt and frustration by increasing their demands for respect and obedience.

Because even normal adolescent behavior frequently becomes confusing and hurtful to parents, it is important to begin any intervention with parents by providing them with information concerning the extent to which their adolescent's behavior is merely a response to natural developmental tasks. Parents are often relieved to discover that other parents are experiencing similar conflicts and anxieties. The relief and increase in feelings of competence and power, which often accompany this new understanding, frequently proves to be a powerful impetus for increasing parents' willingness to explore alternative approaches to interacting with their adolescents.

Firmness and Directness Will Be Effective Only within the Context of a Relationship Characterized by Unconditional Concern and Affection

Regardless of whether parents are being taught assertiveness, behavior modification, or other parenting skills, it is important to emphasize that these skills will have a limited impact if they are not employed within the context of a warm, caring relationship. As mentioned throughout this book, adolescents need to experience a sense of significance. They need to know that they are an important part of someone's life and that someone cares about them even when their behavior is annoying and inappropriate. Unless adolescents receive this sense of significance and belonging, they will not expend the energy nor take the risks necessary to work through conflict situations.

This concept can be highlighted by asking parents to provide examples of ways in which they can communicate their concern and affection to their adolescents. Parents can also be asked to record the frequency with which they provide their children with indications of their positive feelings and concern. Parents often require assistance in developing ways of expressing their concern. Open expressions of affection are neither modeled nor viewed as necessary by a surprisingly large portion of our population. Consequently, when assisting parents to develop ways in which they can comfortably express their positive feelings to their children, a therapist must be sensitive to the parents' values and feelings.

Indulging and Acquiescing Does Not Equate with Caring

While this appears to be an extremely simply concept, it is one which many parents have difficulty accepting and translating into action. Parents often "give in" to the adolescent's demands not because they do not care, but because they are confused by their adolescent's feelings and behaviors, do not know how to respond, are concerned about intensifying already existing conflicts or are afraid of losing their adolescent's affection or having their child leave home.

There are several methods that can be employed to assist parents in assimilating this concept. First, when working with an individual family, the therapist can assist the adolescent in providing the parents with a clear and nonpunitive statement regarding the type of structure she wishes and the manner in which she would like these structures to be determined. Parents are often surprised to discover that their children are not so much opposed to rules as to the arbitrary manner in which rules are established and the inconsistency with which they are applied.

Another approach to providing parents with insights into adolescents' responses to rules and structures is to ask parents to examine which rules they perceived as fair and productive when they were adolescents, and how they responded to family rules. Parents often discover that they are treating their adolescent children in ways that they did not want to be treated when they were adolescents. This discovery often serves as an effective stimulus for involving parents in examining and changing their interactions with their children. As parents begin to understand the reasons for their adolescent's rebellion against their rules, they become more able to cope with this situation and are thus less likely to consistently avoid conflict by acquiescing to their adolescent's every demand.

A second method for increasing parents' understanding of the effects and dynamics of indulgence is to ask parents to list the short- and long-term costs and payoffs associated with specific situations in which they "gave in" to their adolescent's request despite the fact that they were strongly opposed to the request. This activity is usually effective in demonstrating to parents that the act of acquiescing was less an act of caring than an attempt to create a more comfortable situation for themselves. In order to prevent this awareness from becoming punitive, parents can be informed that their behavior is a logical response if viable options do not exist. Parents can be told that one goal of their learning assertive skills is to provide them with options for dealing with situations in which their adolescent child pressures them with what seem to be unreasonable demands.

Parents Should Be Aware of Ways in which They Aggress against Their Children

While parents can often articulately describe adolescent behaviors that they would define as aggressive or abrasive, many parents are relatively unaware of the ways in which they behave inappropriately or aggressively toward their adolescent. Since a major goal of assertive training is assisting individuals in becoming aware of the rights of others, it is important that parents explore ways in which their behavior may infringe upon the rights of their children.

There are several common ways in which parents aggress either overtly or covertly against adolescents. First, parents often fail to listen to their children. This may take the form of refusing to discuss matters, dismissing their adolescent's requests or feelings without attempting to find out more about what they need or want, or simply not giving them full attention by continuing to watch television or completing a task while listening to them. Second, parents too often discount their adolescent's concerns by responding with cliches rather than by assisting them to better understand the situation and their feelings. Third, parents aggress against adolescents when they dictate arbitrary rules and punishments and fail to provide adolescents with reasonable input into decisions and reasonable explanations concerning parental decisions. Fourth, parents aggress against adolescents whenever they use sarcasm or employ generalized critical accusations such as lazy or stupid. Finally, parents aggress against adolescents when they scream at them, hit them, or become sexually involved with them.

Although it is obviously somewhat uncomfortable for parents to critically analyze their behavior, awareness is a major factor in stimulating change. One method of approaching awareness more positively is to first ask parents to list ways in which they communicate their positive feelings and show respect for their children. This can be followed by asking parents to build a list of the behaviors they employ that might possibly communicate aggression or lack of concern. Once these lists have been created and discussed, parents can be asked to record both positive and negative responses and report this data at the next parent meeting or counseling session. As noted in previous chapters, the very act of tallying these behaviors will almost always serve to increase the positive behaviors while decreasing the frequency of the negative behaviors.

Parents and Adolescents Have an Equal Right to Be Heard and Treated with Respect

Parents often become confused by and annoyed with the concept that adolescents should have the same basic rights as parents. It is therefore necessary to assist parents in clarifying this concept. The fact is that parents and adolescents are not equal. Parents support their children and have an historically superior position in that they were part of the family unit before the children came and will remain the core unit after the children leave. When adolescents live at home they are to some extent guests in their parents' home. Certainly they are exceedingly special guests who should be treated with special courtesy and should receive special considerations and privileges. Nevertheless, the fact remains that parents support their children and therefore are in the logical position to monitor family decisions. At the same time, however, it is extremely important that parents are aware of the importance of increasingly providing adolescents with opportunities for making their own decisions.

While parents may legitimately have somewhat more power and authority than their adolescent children this should not in any way discount the fact that parents and adolescents have equal rights when it comes to being treated with concern, respect, and dignity. Therefore, the fact that parents are older and pay the bills does not mean that parents can show less respect for their adolescent than they expect for themselves. An understanding of this concept can be aided by asking parents to list their rights and discuss which of these they would withhold from their adolescent. Similarly, adolescents can be asked to list what they perceive as their reasonable rights, and parents can be asked to compare this list to their own and discuss whether they believe that the adolescents' lists include any unreasonable rights.

When People Have Serious Things to Talk About, They Need to Set Aside Adequate Time to Talk

A significant factor contributing to the poor quality of many interpersonal interactions is that people too seldom take the time necessary to assure a relaxed and thorough interaction. For example, consider the situation in which a daughter rushes into the house and immediately informs her mother that she must have a costume for a play within three days. If the mother must have dinner on the table in ten minutes so that her husband and son can leave on time for a scout meeting, it is likely that the mother will be only partially attentive to her daughter. However, if the mother is aware of the intensity of her daughter's concern, she will probably attempt to listen to her daughter's demand while simultaneously preparing the dinner. Unfortunately, the daughter may feel that the mother is not really listening and this might well lead to the daughter becoming angry or hurt.

Situations such as this can be dealt with more effectively if both parties agree to wait and discuss the situation at a later time. Unfortunately, parents' busy schedules and habit of dealing with problems in a rapid, superficial manner cause them to seldom set aside adequate time to solve problems. Parents' awareness of this issue can again be increased through a combination of role playing and home assignments. Parents can be encouraged to schedule specific appointment times to deal with problems that arise between themselves and their adolescents.

It Is Important to Be Clear about Your Goals and
Alternatives before Entering into a Negotiation

Like anyone involved in a helping relationship, parents can be more effective if they understand their role and goals and can therefore develop a certain degree of objectivity in interacting with their child. The simplest and most productive method for creating this objectivity is to assist parents in clarifying their wants, needs, expectations, and areas for compromise that are associated with specific conflict situations that occur between themselves and their adolescent son or daughter. Figure 16.2 summarizes a format for assisting parents in this process.

In order to examine this process in more detail, consider the father who reports that his fifteen-year-old son refuses to follow family rules and, when at home, simply mopes around the house complaining about how bored he is. Since the father very likely has considerable emotional investment in both his ability to control his son's behavior and in his son's future, it is understandable that he would be upset by his son's behavior. However, the frustration, anger, and concern he feels may, if not clarified, hinder his ability to interact productively with his son. Therefore, it is helpful to assist the father in clarifying his needs and expectations concerning his son's behavior.

First, the father should be asked to clearly describe his expectations. This objectivity moves the discussion away from a catharsis about a disobedient son and toward an issue that can be discussed in terms of behaviorally defined goals and outcomes. Suppose that the father indicates that he expects his son to return home on time in the evening, to stop constantly complaining about how bored he is, and to become involved in at least one "productive" organized activity. Once these expecta-

Figure 16.2. Steps to Assisting Parents in Clarifying Their
Expectations and Negotiating These with Their Children

1. Define expectations in behavioral terms
2. Explore these expectations to determine whether they are realistic and appropriate
3. Examine the costs and payoffs associated with demanding that the adolescent meet the expectations
4. Determine areas in which compromise would be acceptable
5. Discuss methods for confronting the adolescent with the demands
6. Explore the options which are available should the adolescent refuse to agree to the demands
7. Present the demand to the adolescent in a productive manner
8. Be willing to consider reasonable compromises which may arise
9. Be prepared to explore the alternatives which face the adolescent should he decide not to meet the parent's expectations
10. Be consistent. If the expectations are not met, begin implementing an alternative

tions have been defined, the father can be asked to explore these rules to determine whether they are appropriate for an adolescent his son's age. For example, if the father insists that his son be home by eight o'clock on week nights and nine o'clock on weekends, the father may be asked to examine his rules in light of those being applied to his son's peers.

Once the father has examined the rules in order to determine their appropriateness, the next step is to ask the father to consider the payoffs and costs that might accompany the decision he has reached regarding appropriate expectations and demands. In this case the father might include such payoffs as not having to worry about his son when he fails to return home on time, a feeling of once again being in charge at home, and the possibility that the new structure might improve his son's grades at school. On the negative side of the ledger, the father could include the possibility that the son might reject his decision and leave home, the time and energy needed to discuss the issue with his son, and the problem of how he would respond if his son tested the limits that were established. This step is important because it focuses the parents' attention on the likely consequences of their placing specific demands upon their adolescent.

Even if the rules seem appropriate, the father can be asked to consider whether there are ways in which the rules could be altered so as to better meet his son's needs while continuing to meet his own needs. The father's motivation to develop a compromise can be increased by reminding him that his son has already rejected the existing rules. Therefore, in order to provide a new basis for discussion and thereby reduce the likelihood of direct and unproductive confrontation, it is important that some degree of compromise be developed.

The next step is to provide the father with assistance in effectively communicating his wants and demands to his son. This step may include providing the father with training in communication skills as well as the assertiveness skills discussed later in this chapter. Since skills in conflict resolution will be an important factor in developing a productive and self-supportive family interaction system, this step should be carefully considered, and may well become a major focus in any long-term intervention.

After the father has explored how he will present his demands to his son, the next step is for him to consider the options that are available if his son decides not to accept the rules. In the case being discussed, the father might be given a homework assignment involving contacting the juvenile court and determining what his rights are and what type of assistance he would receive from the juvenile justice department. This step is important because it allows the parent to deal objectively and straight-forwardly with the adolescent's question, "What are you going to do if I don't obey?" If parents have carefully examined their roles and expectations, developed reasonable rules, considered compromises, examined the consequences of their decisions, and decided that they have made the right decision, it is important that they be prepared to follow through if their adolescent decides not to accept their rules or offer an acceptable compromise.

Once the father has thoughtfully completed the six steps outlined above, it is time to present his expectations to his son. This is a crucial step, and it is often desirable to have the counselor present as a third party facilitator. This is particularly true when there are serious consequences associated with the adolescent's refusal to accept the parent's demands.

During the negotiating process, it is important that the father remain open to considering compromise solutions presented by his son. People are all more willing to agree to rules that they have had a voice in developing. Adolescents need to feel that they are not being treated as children. Indeed, they may desperately want to avoid the consequences associated with refusal to obey, but may need some small compromise to allow them to "save face" by asserting their independence. Consequently, it is important that parents remain flexible during the negotiating process. A great deal can often be gained by a relatively small compromise.

After having carried the process to this point, it is crucial that the father not be intimidated if his son informs him that he will not compromise and will not obey what the father has determined are reasonable rules. If this occurs, it is important that the father begin to assist his son in exploring the options which are available. Fortunately, most situations do not reach this stage. Most adolescents are willing to accept (and are even relieved to be provided with) reasonable rules which have been productively negotiated.

While these general concepts form the foundation for establishing productive adult-adolescent relations, parents also need assistance in developing specific assertiveness skills. The following section provides a brief overview of several of the most important skills.

BASIC SKILLS THAT CAN BE TAUGHT TO PARENTS IN ORDER TO IMPROVE PARENT-ADOLESCENT RELATIONSHIPS

Basic Sending and Receiving Skills

Before introducing parents to the skills more commonly associated with assertive training, it is useful to spend several sessions teaching parents how to employ the basic communication skills presented in Chapter 4.

Whether a therapist is working with parents in individual therapy or within a group setting, these skills can be taught using a combination of interventions. Parents can be introduced to the basic concepts and skills through a book such as Gordon's *Parent Effectiveness Training* (1970). While they do not place a primary focus on what are usually termed basic communication skills, books such as Satir's *Peoplemaking* (1972) and Ginott's *Between Parent and Teenager* (1969) can provide valuable insight into the dynamics of the parent-adolescent relationship. Readings can be supplemented by a series of assignments in which parents are asked to monitor their interactions with their children or practice skills with which they have become acquainted either through readings or discussions. The therapist may need to supplement this learning or provide support by asking parents to role play situations that they find difficult to handle. Finally, the therapist can both model and teach effective communication skills by serving as a third party facilitator in assisting a family in developing a satisfactory solution to a conflict situation.

Making Simple, Direct Requests, Statements of Opinion or Preference, and Statements of Feeling

Perhaps because parents often become concerned that their adolescents are drifting towards new values and norms, parents' statements of requests have a tendency to become demands, and their statements of opinion or preference become either orders or lectures. Unfortunately, this mild escalation by the parents is compounded by the fact that adolescents are particularly sensitive about being treated in a respectful, adultlike manner. Consequently, what begins as parents' attempt to share an opinion or express a concern often becomes a major parent-adolescent debate. This situation can be improved by assisting parents in making requests and statements of opinion or preference that are neither demanding, sarcastic, nor judgmental. Parents are often surprised at the significant impact this simple skill can have on preventing arguments and reducing the tension within their family interactions.

Parents frequently find making simple, direct statements of feeling to be one of the most difficult skills to acquire. Many parents have been taught that sharing their feelings is a sign of weakness. Therefore, in order to maintain their parental authority and to avoid the anxiety associated with self-disclosure, parents often place the blame on the adolescent by sending a "you statement" rather than acknowledging their response to the situation. The "you statement" is frequently accompanied by a demand or mandate, and the adolescent is left feeling hurt and frustrated by the one-way exchange. For example, consider the situation in which a boy is late for a special dinner. Rather than directly and nonpunitively expressing their feelings of hurt and anger, the parents are likely to inform the boy that he is inconsiderate and must come directly home from school for the next two weeks. The boy may respond by angrily defying his parents or by sulking around the house and expressing his anger in passive, subversive ways during the next two weeks. Situations such as this can be handled much more productively if parents can simply make a direct statement of their feelings.

Parents frequently indicate that as their children grow older they find it increasingly difficult to openly and directly share their positive feelings. Unfortunately, this hesitancy comes at a time when children desperately need to have their parents' approval. Adolescents' conflict and anxiety over their increasing need for independence can be greatly reduced by consistent expressions of parental acceptance and support. Role playing, data collection, and home assignments can be employed to assist parents in increasing their skills in sharing their positive feelings with their children. This single skill can have a powerful effect on improving parent-adolescent relations.

Saying "No" with Concern

There will be occasions when a parent must say "no" to an adolescent's request. The manner in which the parent presents this limitation can have a significant impact upon how the adolescent feels about and responds to the limit setting. It is important for parents to realize that limit setting will almost always be accompanied by some degree of conflict. However, the extent of the conflict can be significantly affected by the manner in which the parents set the limitation.

For example, consider a situation in which an adolescent daughter asks her parents to allow her to stay at a party until 12 o'clock—an hour later than the 11 o'clock limit previously agreed upon. The girl's argument might center around the fact that all of her peers can stay until midnight and that she will be teased if she has to leave early. Assuming that the parents have carefully considered the curfew and believe that it is appropriate, they have several alternatives available to them. First, they can prevent a conflict by yielding to their daughter's request. However, if they believe that their rule is fair and in their daughter's best interests, this decision may leave them feeling uncomfortable. In addition to creating a temporary discomfort, it is quite possible that the parents' future interactions with their daughter will be less positive and less clear as a result of their underlying resentment at having given in to her.

Second, they can firmly remind their daughter of the rule and perhaps inform her that if they hear any more complaining she can stay home from the party. The daughter's response to this type of statement is likely to be one of hurt, anger, or resentment. One-way, authoritarian communication almost always breeds resentment and psychological distance when employed with older adolescents.

Finally, the parents can remain consistent with their rule while at the same time letting their daughter know that they appreciate her problem and care about her feelings. For example, the parents might say, "We understand that it is frustrating to you when we tell you to be in by 11 o'clock when your friends get to stay out until midnight. However, we've discussed this between ourselves and have shared our reasons with you, and we are going to stick with the rule because we believe that it is in your best interest." While the daughter may leave this exchange feeling frustrated, it is quite likely that her feelings will be less intense and more positive than had her parents presented an arbitrary statement which included no explanation or response to her feelings.

Since parents find saying "no" with concern to be a difficult task, this skill can best be taught by employing considerable discussion and role playing prior to asking parents to try the skill at home. However, as is the case with all of the skills discussed in this section, practicing this skill at home and sharing the results with a group or the therapist is a key component in incorporating this skill into the parents' behavior repertoire.

Taking Criticism Constructively

While parents may realize that constructive criticism should be received in a positive vein, most of them feel at least some degree of discomfort when being criticized by their children. However, since adolescents possess the cognitive skills that enable them to recognize their parents' mistakes and tend to experiment with their growing sense of independence by pointing these out, it is important that parents learn how to effectively respond to adolescents' criticism.

There are several key steps involved in responding productively to criticism. First, parents should learn to paraphrase the statements and attempt to develop a clear understanding regarding the specific behavior that the adolescent is criticizing. Second, parents should ask the adolescent to present a clear statement concerning what he would like the parent to do differently. This should be stated in terms of observable behaviors and should include a statement concerning the situations in which the behavior should occur. Third, the parent should indicate that they will consider the request and report to the adolescent at a designated time. Finally, the parent and adolescent may need to negotiate concerning the extent to which the parent will make the requested change in behavior.

Prior to teaching parents the steps in handling criticism, it is usually necessary to spend time discussing why adolescents should be allowed to constructively criticize their parents. This discussion can be facilitated by asking parents to list the short- and long-term payoffs and costs associated with allowing criticism. Finally, since many parents find it quite difficult to respond to criticism from their children, it is important that parents be provided with several opportunities to role play this behavior prior to first employing it with their children.

Productively Managing Anger

Regardless of how well parents relate to their adolescent, there will be occasions when they become angry at their adolescent's behavior. Since angry interchanges can become destructive and are often taken personally by adolescents, it is important that parents develop skills in dealing productively with their anger. After parents have discussed the negative effects of angry interchanges, it is often productive to ask them to share behaviors that they have found helpful in dealing with their anger. Since most parents of behavior-problem adolescents frequently experience situations that might elicit anger, it is likely that they have developed several, at least relatively productive, strategies for dealing with their anger.

While parents will vary in the type of response that they find most helpful in preventing or diffusing angry responses, there are several general responses that can be presented for their consideration. First, parents can be asked to consider the advantages of either asking for time out or suggesting to their adolescent that a time-out period might be desirable. While direct, open statements of feeling are helpful in solving conflicts, angry interchanges are usually destructive. Therefore, when one or both parties becomes angry, it is often best to postpone the discussion until a later time. A second method for dealing with topics that consistently elicit angry responses is to agree to have a third party mediator present to facilitate a discussion of the topic. A third approach that parents often find helpful is to exchange letters or notes with their adolescent. The process of writing down one's ideas seems to demand clarity and reduces the emotional tone of the remarks. Notes can be used to exchange ideas prior to meeting to discuss an issue.

Since angry interactions have such destructive potential, it is important that parents receive assistance in developing an individualized approach to dealing productively with their anger. In addition to directly affecting parents' relationships with their adolescents, skills in dealing effectively with anger often have an indirect benefit of improving parents' relationship with each other.

Negotiating Effectively

As with all of the skills presented in this section, parents cannot be expected to employ a new skill until they have decided for themselves that the skill is necessary or useful. Parents who have employed an authoritarian parenting style for a dozen years or more may initially balk at the idea of negotiating with their adolescent. Once again, it is helpful to ask parents to compare the short- and long-term payoffs and costs connected with negotiating rather than dictating rules. Negotiating as a means of conflict resolution will ultimately fail unless the parents accept the basic tenet that adolescents should have meaningful input into decisions that affect their behavior.

As mentioned earlier in this chapter, before negotiating with their adolescent, parents should clearly outline their goals and expectations concerning the negotiation. Once this outlining has been accomplished, parents can be taught procedures for negotiating effectively. When negotiating with their children, parents should be taught to clearly outline the problem, focus on one behavior at a time, specify each party's responsibilities in terms of observable behaviors, and set aside designated times at which the parties will meet to discuss and evaluate the outcome. Before negotiating with their son or daughter, parents should be asked to role play a negotiation and should be encouraged to consider their responses to the various problems that might arise during a parent-adolescent negotiation.

SUMMARY

Regardless of an adolescent's age, the quality of the parent-adolescent relationship plays a major role in influencing an adolescent's behavior and self-concept. Therefore, teaching the parents of behavior-problem adolescents the concepts and skills necessary for responding in a nonabrasively assertive manner can have a major impact both on the quality of the parent-adolescent relationship and on the adolescent's behavior in a wide variety of settings. This chapter has presented a basic description of assertive training and has outlined the major concepts and skills that can be taught to parents in order to assist them in developing mutually satisfying relationships with their adolescent children.

References

Adams, R., and Biddle, B. *Realities of Teaching: Explorations with Videotape.* New York: Holt, Rinehart, and Winston, 1970.

Ahlstrom, W., and Havighurst, R. *400 Losers.* San Francisco: Jossey-Bass, 1971.

Alberti, R. *Assertiveness: Innovations, Applications, Issues.* San Luis Obispo, Calif.: Impact Publishers, 1977.

Alberti, R., and Emmons, M. *Your Perfect Right: A Guide to Assertive Behavior.* San Luis Obispo, Calif.: Impact Publishers, 1974.

Alschular, A. "The Effects of Classroom Structure on Achievement Motivation and Academic Performance." *Educational Technology* 9 (1969):19-24.

Arnold, E. *Helping Parents Help Their Children.* New York: Brunner/Mazel, 1978.

Arwood, B.; Williams, R.; and Long, J. "The Effects of Behavior Contracts and Behavior Proclamations on Social Conduct and Academic Achievement in a Ninth Grade English Class." *Adolescence* 9 (1974):425-436.

Aspy, D. "The Effect of Teacher-Offered Conditions of Empathy, Congruence, and Positive Regard upon Student Achievement." *Florida Journal of Educational Research* 11 (1969):39-48.

Axline, V. *Play Therapy.* Boston: Houghton Mifflin, 1947.

Baird, L. "Teaching Styles: An Exploratory Study of Dimensions and Effects." *Journal of Educational Psychology* 64 (1973):15-21.

Bandura, A., and Huston, A. "Identification as a Process of Incidental Learning." *Journal of Abnormal and Social Psychology* 63 (1961):311-318.

Bandura, A., and Walters, R. *Adolescent Aggression.* New York: Ronald Press, 1959.

Baumrind, D. "Authoritarian vs. Authoritative Control." *Adolescence* 3 (1968):225-272.

Becker, W. *Parents Are Teachers: A Child Management Program.* Champaign, Ill.: Research Press, 1971.

Bellack, A.; Kliebard, H.; Hyman, R.; and Smith, F. *The Language of the Classroom.* New York: Teachers College Press, 1965.

Benedict, R. "Continuities and Discontinuities in Cultural Conditioning." In *Readings in Child Development,* edited by W. Martin and C. Stendler. New York: Harcourt, Brace, 1954.

Blackham, G., and Silberman, A. *Modification of Child and Adolescent Behavior.* Belmont, Calif.: Wadsworth, 1975.

Borden, N.; Hall, R.; Dunlap, A.; and Clark, R. "Effects of Teacher Attention and Token Reinforcement System in a Junior High School Special Education Class." *Exceptional Children* 36 (1970):341-349.

Braun, C. "Teacher Expectations: Sociopsychological Dynamics." *Review of Educational Research* 46 (1976):185-213.

Braun, C.; Neilsen, A.; and Dykstra, R. "Teacher's Expectations: Prime Mover or Inhibitor?" *The Elementary School Journal* 76 (1975):181-187.

Brigham Young University. *Cipher in the Snow*. Provo, Utah: Brigham Young University, (1973) Film.

Broden, M.; Hall, R.; and Mitts, B. "The Effect of Self-Recording on the Classroom Behavior of Two Eighth Grade Students." *Journal of Applied Behavior Analysis* 4 (1971):191-199.

Bronfenbrenner, U. *Two Worlds of Childhood: U.S. and U.S.S.R.* New York: Russell Sage Foundation, 1970.

Brookover, W. "The Relation of Social Factors to Teaching Ability." *Journal of Experimental Education* 13 (1945):191-205.

Brophy, J., and Good, T. "Brophy-Good System (Teacher-Child Dyadic Interaction)." In *Mirrors for Behavior: An Anthology of Observation Instruments Continued*, 1970 Supplement, Volume A, edited by A. Simon and E. Boyer. Philadelphia: Research for Better Schools, 1970a.

———. "Teachers Communication of Differential Expectations for Children's Classroom Performance: Some Behavioral Data." *Journal of Educational Psychology* 61 (1970b):365-374.

———. *Teacher-Student Relationships: Causes and Consequences*. New York: Holt, Rinehart & Winston, 1974.

Brown, G. "The Training of Teachers for Affective Roles." In *The Seventy-Fourth Yearbook of the National Society for the Study of Education*, edited by K. Ryan. Chicago: University of Chicago Press, 1975.

Brownstone, J., and Dye, C. *Communication Workshop for Parents of Adolescents*. Champaign, Ill.: Research Press, 1971.

Buber, M. *I and Thou*. Translated by R. E. Smith. New York: Scribner's, 1958.

Burchard, J., and Barrera, F. "An Analysis of Time Out and Response Cost in a Program Environment." *Journal of Applied Behavior Analysis* 5 (1972):271-282.

Burnstein, E.; Stotland, E.; and Zander, A. "Similarity to a Model and Self-Evaluation." *Journal of Abnormal and Social Psychology* 52 (1961):257-264.

Bush, R. *The Teacher-Pupil Relationship*. New York: Prentice-Hall, 1954.

Canfield, J., and Wells, H. *100 Ways to Enhance Self-Concept in the Classroom: A Handbook for Teachers and Parents*. Englewood Cliffs: Prentice-Hall, 1976.

Castillo, G. *Left-Handed Teaching: Lessons in Affective Education*. New York: Praeger, 1974.

Cervantes, L. *The Dropout: Causes and Cures*. Ann Arbor: University of Michigan Press, 1965a.

———. "Family Background, Primary Relationships, and the High School Dropout." *Journal of Marriage and the Family* 5 (1965b):218-223.

Clark, H.; Boyd, S.; and Macrae, J. "A Classroom Program Teaching Disadvantaged Youths to Write Biographic Information." *Journal of Applied Behavior Analysis* 8 (1975):67-75.

Cohen, H.; Goldiamond, I.; and Filipczak, J. "Maintaining Increased Education for Teen-agers in a Controlled Environment." In *Readings in Prison Education*, edited by A. Roberts. Springfield, Ill.: Thomas, 1973.

Conger, J. "A World They Never Knew: The Family and Social Change." *Daedalus* (Fall 1971):1105-1138.

———. *Adolescence and Youth: Psychological Development in a Changing World*. New York: Harper & Row, 1977.

Conger, J., and Miller, W. *Personality, Social Class, and Delinquency*. New York: Wiley, 1966.

Coopersmith, S. *The Antecedents of Self-Esteem*. San Francisco: W. H. Freeman, 1967.

Cormany, R. *Guidance and Counseling in Pennsylvania: Status and Needs*. Lemoyne, Pa.: ESEA Title III Project, West Shore School District, 1975.

Costin, F., and Grush, J. "Personality Correlates of Teacher-Student Behavior in the College Classroom." *Journal of Educational Psychology* 65 (1973):35-44.

Covington, M., and Beery, R. *Self-Worth and School Learning*. New York: Holt, Rinehart & Winston, 1976.

Cressey, D., and Ward, D. *Delinquency, Crime, and Social Process*. New York: Harper & Row, 1969.

Crombag, H. "Cooperation and Competition in Means—Interdependent Triads." *Journal of Personality and Social Psychology* 4 (1966):692-695.

Daum, J. "Proxemics in the Classroom: Speaker-Subject Distance and Educational Performance." Paper presented at the annual meeting of the Southeastern Psychological Association, 1972.

Davidson, H., and Lang, G. "Children's Perceptions of Their Teachers' Feelings Toward Them." *Journal of Experimental Education* 29 (1960):109-118.

DeCecco, J., and Richards, A. "Civil War in the High Schools." *Psychology Today*, November 1975, pp. 51-56, 120.

Delefes, P., and Jackson, B. "Teacher-Pupil Interaction as a Function of Location in the Classroom." *Psychology in the Schools* 9 (1972):119-123.

Dinkmeyer, D., and McKay, G. *Systematic Training for Effective Parenting*. Circle Pines, Minn.: American Guidance Service, 1976.

Divoky, D., *How Old Will You Be in 1984?* New York: Discus Books, 1969.

Dixon, R., and Morse, W. "The Prediction of Teaching Performance: Empathic Potential." *Journal of Teacher Education* 12 (1961):322-329.

Dodson, L., and Kurpius, D. *Family Counseling: A Systems Approach*. Muncie, Ind.: Accelerated Development, 1977.

Dollard, J., and Miller, N. *Personality and Psychotherapy: An Analysis in Terms of Learning, Thinking, and Culture*. New York: McGraw-Hill, 1950.

Dreikurs, R. *Children: The Challenge*. New York: Hawthorn, 1964.

Dulit, E. "Adolescent Thinking à la Piaget: The Formal Stage." *Journal of Youth and Adolescence* 1 (1972):281-301.

Duncun, P. "Parental Attitudes and Interactions in Delinquency." *Child Development* 42 (1971):1751-1765.

Dunn, R., and Goldman, M. "Competition and Noncompetition in Relationship to Satisfaction and Feelings Toward Own Group and Nongroup Members." *Journal of Social Psychology* 68 (1966):299-311.

Elder, G. "Structural Variations in the Child-Rearing Relationship." *Sociometry* 25 (1962):241-262.

———. "Parental Power Legitimation and Its Effect on the Adolescent." *Sociometry* 26 (1963):50-65.

Elmore, P., and LaPointe, K. "Effect of Teacher Sex, Student Sex, and Teacher Warmth on the Evaluation of College Instructors," *Journal of Educational Psychology* 67 (1975):368-374.

Emery, J., and Krumboltz, J. "Standard Versus Individualized Hierarchies in Desensitization to Reduce Test Anxiety." *Journal of Counseling Psychology* 14 (1967):204-209.

Erikson, E. *Identity: Youth and Crisis*. New York: W. W. Norton, 1968.

Festinger, L. *Theory of Cognitive Dissonance*. Evanston, Ill.: Row, Peterson, 1957.

Flanders, N. "Intent, Action and Feedback: A Preparation for Teaching." *The Journal of Teacher Education* 14 (1963):251-260.

Flanders, N., and Amidon, E. *The Role of the Teacher in the Classroom*. Minneapolis: Minneapolis Association for Productive Teaching, 1967.

Fox, R.; Luszki, M.; and Schmuck, R. *Diagnosing Classroom Learning Environments*. Chicago: Science Research Associates, 1966.

Freud, A. *The Ego and The Mechanisms of Defense*. New York: International University Press, 1946.

Gallagher, J. *Expressive Thought by Gifted Children in the Classroom: Language and the Higher Thought Processes*, Champaign, Ill.: National Council of Teachers of English, 1965.

Gardner, W. *Learning and Behavior Characteristics of Exceptional Children and Youth: A Humanistic Behavioral Approach*. Boston: Allyn and Bacon, 1977.

Gergen, K. *The Concept of Self*. New York: Holt, Rinehart & Winston, 1971.

Ginott, H. *Between Parent and Teenager*. New York: Avon, 1969.

Gittelman, M. "Behavioral Rehearsal as a Technique in Child Treatment." *Journal of Child Psychology and Psychiatry* 6 (1965):251-255.

Glasser, W. *Schools Without Failure*. New York: Harper & Row, 1969.

Glueck, S., and Glueck, E. *Unraveling Juvenile Delinquency*. New York: Commonwealth Fund, 1950.

Gold, M., and Mann, D. "Delinquency as Defense." *American Journal of Orthopsychiatry* 42 (1972):463-479.

Good, T. and Brophy, J. *Educational Psychology: A Realistic Approach*. New York: Holt, Rinehart & Winston, 1977.

Gordon, T. *Parent Effectiveness Training*. New York: Wyden, 1970.

———. *Teacher Effectiveness Training*. New York: Wyden, 1974.

Gray, R.; Graubard, P.; and Rosenberg, H. "Little Brother Is Changing You." *Psychology Today*, March 1974, pp. 42-46.

Greenwood, C.; Hops, H.; Delquadri, J.; and Walker, H. *PASS: Program for Academic Survival Skills*. Eugene, Ore.: Center at Oregon for Research in the Behavioral Education of the Handicapped, 1974.

Guerin, P. *Family Therapy: Theory and Practice*. New York: Gardner Press, 1976.

Gump, P. *Big Schools, Small Schools*. Moravia, N. Y.: Chronicle Guidance Publications, 1966.

Haines, D., and McKeachie, W. "Cooperative Versus Competitive Discussion Methods in Teaching Introductory Psychology." *Journal of Educational Psychology* 58 (1967):386-390.

Hamachek, D. *Encounters With the Self*. New York: Holt, Rinehart & Winston, 1971.

Harmin, M.; Kirschenbaum, H.; and Simon, S. *Clarifying Values Through Subject Matter*. Minneapolis, Minn.: Winston Press, 1973.

Harris, L. "Change, Yes—Upheaval, No." *Life*, January 8, 1971, pp. 22-27.

Harris, T. *I'm Ok, You're Ok*. New York: Avon, 1969.

Havighurst, R. *Developmental Tasks and Education*. New York: Longmans, Green, 1952.

Hawes, G., and Egbert, R. "Personal Values and the Empathic Response: Their Interrelationships." *Journal of Educational Psychology* 45 (1954):469-476.

Hearn, A. "Case Studies of Successful Teachers." *Educational Administration and Supervision* 38 (1952):376-379.

Hefele, T. "The Effects of Systematic Human Relations Training Upon Student Achievement." *Journal of Research and Development in Education* 4 (1971):52-69.

Homme, L. *How to Use Contingency Contracting in the Classroom*. Champaign, Ill.: Research Press, 1970.

Hosford, R. "Overcoming Fear of Speaking in a Group." In *Behavioral Counseling: Case Studies and Techniques*, edited by J. Krumboltz and C. Thoresen. New York: Holt, Rinehart & Winston, 1969.

Hutzell, R.; Platzek, D.; and Logue, P. "Control of Symptoms of Gilles de la Tourette's Syndrome by Self-Monitoring." *Journal of Behavior Therapy and Experimental Psychiatry* 5 (1974):71-76.

Inhelder, B., and Piaget, J. *The Growth of Logical Thinking*. New York: Basic Books, 1958.

Jacobson, E. *Progressive Relaxation*. Chicago: University of Chicago Press, 1938.

James, M., and Jongeward, D. *Born to Win: Transactional Analysis with Gestalt Experiments*. Reading, Mass.: Addison-Wesley, 1971.

Jesness, C.; DeRisi, W.; McCormick, P.; and Wedge, R. *The Youth Center Research Project*. Sacramento: California Youth Authority, 1972.

Johnson, D. *Reaching Out*. Englewood Cliffs, N.J.: Prentice-Hall, 1972.

Johnson, D., and Johnson, F. *Joining Together: Group Theory and Group Skills*. Englewood Cliffs, N.J.: Prentice-Hall, 1975a.

Johnson, D., and Johnson, R. *Learning Together and Alone: Cooperation, Competition, and Individualization*. Englewood Cliffs, N.J.: Prentice-Hall, 1975b.

Johnson, L., and Backman, J. *Monitoring the Future: A Continuing Study of the Life Styles and Values of Youth*. Ann Arbor, Mich.: Institute for Social Research, 1975.

Josselyn, I. *Adolescence*. New York: Harper & Row, 1971.

Jourard, S. *The Transparent Self*. New York: D Van Nostrand, 1971.

Karacki, L., and Levinson, R. "A Token Economy in a Correctional Institution for Youthful Offenders." *Howard Journal of Penology and Crime Prevention*, 13 (1970):20-30.

Kaufman, K., and O'Leary, K. "Reward, Cost, and Self-Evaluation Procedures for Disruptive Adolescents in a Psychiatric Hospital School." *Journal of Applied Behavior Analysis* 5 (1972):293-309.

Kiersey, D. "Systematic Exclusion: Eliminating Chronic Classroom Disruptions." In *Behavioral Counseling: Cases and Techniques*, edited by J. Krumboltz and C. Thoresen. New York: Holt, Rinehart & Winston, 1969.

Kleinfeld, J. "Instructional Style and the Intellectual Performance of Indian and Eskimo Students." Final Report, Project No. 1-J-027, Office of Education, U.S. Department of Health, Education and Welfare, 1972.

Kohlberg, L. "Moral Development and the Education of Adolescents." In *Adolescents and the American High School,* edited by R. F. Purnell. New York: Holt, Rinehart & Winston, 1970.

Kohlberg, L., and Gilligan, C. "The Adolescent as a Philosopher: The Discovery of the Self in a Postconventional World." *Daedalus,* Fall, 1971, pp. 1051-1086.

Kounin, J. *Discipline and Group Management in Classrooms.* New York: Holt, Rinehart & Winston, 1970.

Krumboltz, J., and Thoresen, C. *Behavioral Counseling: Cases and Techniques.* New York: Holt, Rinehart & Winston, 1969.

LaBenne, W., and Greene, B. *Educational Implications of Self-Concept Theory.* Pacific Palisades, Calif.: Goodyear Publishing Co., 1969.

Lange, A., and Jakubowski, P. *Responsible Assertive Behavior: Cognitive/Behavioral Procedures for Trainers.* Champaign, Ill.: Research Press, 1976.

Lewin, K. *Resolving Social Conflict.* New York: Harper, 1948.

Lewin, K.; Dembo, T.; Festinger, L.; and Sears, P. "Levels of Aspiration." In *Personality and the Behavior Disorders.* Vol. 1, edited by J. McV. Hunt. New York: Ronald, 1944.

Liberman, R.; Ferris, C.; Salgado, P.; and Salgado, J. "Replication of the Achievement Place Model in California." *Journal of Applied Behavior Analysis* 8 (1975):287-299.

Lovitt, T., and Curtis, L. "Academic Response Rate as a Function of Teacher- and Self-Imposed Contingencies." *Journal of Applied Behavior Analysis* 2 (1969):49-53.

Marston, A. "Dealing with Low Self-Confidence." *Educational Research* (Great Britain) 10 (1968):134-138.

Mash, E.; Hamerlynck, L.; and Handy, L. *Behavior Modification and Families.* New York: Brunner/Mazel, 1976.

Mash, E.; Handy, L.; and Hamerlynck, L. *Behavior Modification Approaches to Parenting.* New York: Brunner/Mazel, 1976.

Maslow, A. *Toward a Psychology of Being.* New York: D. Van Nostrand, 1968.

McCord, W.; McCord, J.; and Zola, I. *Origins of Crime.* New York: Columbia University Press, 1959.

McGregor, D. *The Professional Manager.* New York: McGraw-Hill, 1967.

McKeachie, W., and Lin, Y. "Sex Differences in Student Response to College Teachers: Teacher Warmth and Teacher Sex." *American Educational Research Journal* 8 (1971):221-226.

McKenzie, T., and Rushall, B. "Effects of Self-Recording on Attendance and Performance in a Competitive Swimming Training Environment." *Journal of Applied Behavior Analysis* 7 (1974):199-206.

Mead, M. *Culture and Committment: A Study of the Generation Gap.* Garden City, N.Y.: Doubleday, 1970.

Middleton, R., and Snell, P. "Political Expression of Adolescent Rebellion." *American Journal of Sociology* 68 (1963):527-535.

Morrison, A., and McIntyre, D. *Teachers and Teaching.* Balitmore: Penguin Books, 1969.

Morse, W. "Self-Concept in the School Setting." *Childhood Education* 41 (1964):195-198.

Muuss, R. *Theories of Adolescence*. New York: Random House, 1975.

Offer, D.; Marcus, D.; and Offer, J. "A Longitudinal Study of Normal Adolescent Boys." *American Journal of Psychiatry* 126 (1970):917-924.

Page, E. "Teacher Comments and Student Performance." *Journal of Educational Psychology* 49 (1958):173-181.

Patterson, G. *Living With Children: New Methods for Parents and Teachers*. Champaign, Ill.: Research Press, 1971.

―――. *Families*. Champaign, Ill.: Research Press, 1971.

Pepinski, H. "The Growth of Crime in the United States." *Annals of the American Academy of Political and Social Science: Crime and Justice in America: 1776-1976.* 1976, 423, pp. 23-30.

Phillips, E. "Achievement Place: Token Reinforcement Procedures in a Home-Style Rehabilitation Setting for 'Pre-Delinquent Boys' " *Journal of Applied Behavior Analysis* 1 (1968):213-224.

Phillips, E.; Phillips, E.; Fixsen, D.; and Wolf, M. "Achievement Place: Modification of the Behaviors of Pre-Delinquent Boys within a Token Economy." *Journal of Applied Behavior Analysis* 4 (1971):45-49.

Podd, M. "Ego Identity Status and Morality: The Relationship Between Two Constructs." *Developmental Psychology* 6 (1972):497-507.

Postman, N., and Weingartner, C. *Teaching as a Subversive Activity*. New York: Delacorte Press, 1969.

Powers, E., and Witmer, H. *Prevention of Delinquency: The Cambridge-Somerville Youth Study*. New York: Columbia University Press, 1951.

Prather, H. *Notes to Myself*. Moab, Utah: Real People Press, 1970.

Putney, S., and Putney, G. *The Adjusted American: Normal Neurosis in American Society*. New York: Harper & Row, 1964.

Rank, O. *Will Therapy and Truth and Reality*. New York: Knopf, 1945.

Ritter, B. "The Group Desensitization of Children's Snake Phobias using Vicarious and Contact Desensitization Procedures." *Behavior Research and Therapy* 6 (1968):1-6.

―――. "Eliminating Excessive Fears of the Environment Through Contact Desensitization." In *Behavioral Counseling: Cases and Techniques*, edited by J. Krumboltz and C. Thoresen. New York: Holt, Rinehart & Winston, 1969.

Rogers, C. *On Becoming a Person*. Boston: Houghton Mifflin, 1961.

―――. *Freedom to Learn*. Columbus: Merrill, 1969.

Rosekrans, M. "Imitation in Children as a Function of Perceived Similarities to a Social Model of Vicarious Reinforcement." *Journal of Personality and Social Psychology* 7 (1967):307-315.

Rosenthal, R., and Jacobson, L. *Pygmalion in the Classroom: Teacher Expectation and Pupils Intellectual Development*. New York: Holt, Rinehart & Winston, 1968.

Ryan, K., and Cooper, J. *Those Who Can, Teach*. Boston: Houghton Mifflin, 1975.

Sapp, G. "The Application of Contingency Management Systems to the Classroom Behavior of Negro Adolescents." Paper presented at the American Personnel and Guidance Association, Atlantic City, April 1971.

Satir, V. *Conjoint Family Therapy: A Guide to Theory and Technique*. Palo Alto, Calif.: Science and Behavior Books, 1967.

Satir, V. *Peoplemaking*. Palo Alto, California: Science and Behavior Books, Inc., 1972.

Schmuck, R. "Some Relationships of Peer Liking Patterns in the Classroom to Pupil Attitudes and Achievement." *School Review* 71 (1963):337-359.

———. "Some Aspects of Classroom Social Climate." *Psychology in the Schools* 3 (1966):59-65.

Schmuck, R., and Schmuck, P. *A Humanistic Psychology of Education: Making the School Everybody's House.* Palo Alto, Calif.: National Press Books, 1974.

Schwebel, A., and Cherlin, D. "Physical and Social Distancing in Teacher-Pupil Relationships." *Journal of Educational Psychology* 63 (1972):543-550.

Sherif, M. "Superordinate Goals in the Reeducation of Intergroup Tensions." *American Journal of Sociology* 53 (1958):349-356.

Sherman, A. *Behavior Modification: Theory and Practice.* Belmont, Calif.: Wadsworth, 1973.

Silberman, C. *Crisis in the Classroom: The Remaking of American Education.* New York: Random House, 1970.

Simon, S., and Clark, J. *More Values Clarification: Strategies for the Classroom.* San Diego: Pennant Press, 1975.

Simon, S.; Howe, L.; and Kirschenbaum, H. *Values Clarification.* New York: Hart, 1972.

Sorensen, R. *Adolescent Sexuality in Contemporary America.* New York: Harry N. Abrams, 1973.

Stanford, G., and Roark, A. *Human Interactions in Education.* Boston: Allyn and Bacon, 1974.

Stanford, G., and Stanford, B. *Learning Discussion Skills Through Games.* New York: Citation, 1969.

Stevens, J. *Awareness: Exploring, Experimenting, Experiencing.* Moab, Utah: Real People Press, 1971.

Stinchcombe, A. *Rebellion in a High School.* Chicago: Quandrangle Books, 1964.

Stoffer, D. "Investigation of Positive Behavior Change as a Function of Genuineness, Non-possessive Warmth and Empathic Understanding." *Journal of Education Research* 63 (1970):225-228.

Swift, P. "Inner City Teens." *Parade* (September 18, 1977):5.

Tait, C., Jr., and Hodges, E. *Delinquents, Their Families, and the Community.* Springfield, Ill.: Thomas, 1962.

Thomas, E.; Abrams, K.; and Johnson, J. "Self-Monitoring and Reciprocal Inhibition in the Modification of Multiple Tics of Gilles de la Tourette's Syndrome." *Journal of Behavior Therapy and Experimental Psychiatry* 2 (1971):159-171.

Varenhorst, B. "Helping a Client to Speak Up in Class." In *Behavioral Counseling: Cases and Techniques,* edited by J. Krumboltz and C. Thoresen. New York: Holt, Rinehart & Winston, 1969.

Wagner, M. "Reinforcement of the Expression of Anger Through Role Playing." *Behavior Research and Therapy* 6 (1968):91-95.

Wheeler, R., and Ryan, F. "Effects of Cooperative and Competitive Classroom Environments on the Attitudes and Achievement of Elementary School Students Engaged in Social Studies Inquiry Activities." *Journal of Educational Psychology* 65 (1973):402-407.

White House Conference on Children. "Children and Parents: Together in the World." (Report of Forum 15, 1970). Washington, D.C.: Superintendent of Documents, 1971.

Wolpe, J. *Psychotherapy by Reciprocal Inhibition.* Stanford: Stanford University Press, 1958.

———. "The Systematic Desensitization of Neurosis." *Journal of Nervous and Mental Disorders* 112 (1961):189-203.

———. "Isolation of a Conditioning Procedure as the Crucial Psychotherapeutic Factor: A Case Study." *Journal of Nervous and Mental Disorders* 134 (1962): 316-329.

———. "Behavior Therapy in Complex Neurotic States." *British Journal of Psychiatry* 110 (1964):28-34.

Wolpe, J., and Lazarus, A. *Behavior Therapy Techniques*. New York: Pergamon Press, 1966.

Word, P., and Rozynko, V. "Behavior Therapy of an Eleven-Year-Old Girl with Reading Problems." *Journal of Learning Disabilities* 7 (1974):27-30.

Yankelovich, D. *The New Morality: A Profile of American Youth in the 70's*. New York: McGraw-Hill, 1974.

Index